PLEASE RETURN TO:

PERFORMANCE CHIROPRACTIC
DR. DONALD F. PICHE   DR. JULIE BRONS
551 S. Garfield, Suite B
Traverse City, MI 49686

D1432975

THE VIRUS AND
THE VACCINE

THE VIRUS AND
THE VACCINE

The True Story

of a Cancer-Causing Monkey Virus,

Contaminated Polio Vaccine,

and the Millions of Americans Exposed

**Debbie Bookchin and
Jim Schumacher**

St. Martin's Press ⋈ New York

www.stmartins.com

Library of Congress Cataloging-in-Publication Data

Bookchin, Debbie.
    The virus and the vaccine : the true story of a cancer-causing monkey virus, contaminated polio vaccine, and the millions of Americans exposed / Debbie Bookchin and Jim Schumacher.—1st U.S. ed.
        p.   cm.
    ISBN 0-312-27872-1
    EAN 978-0312-27872-4
    1. SV40 (Virus)—History—Popular works.   2. Poliomyelitis vaccine—Contamination—History—Popular works.   I. Schumacher, Jim, 1955–   II. Title.

QR406.2.S56 B66   2004
614.5'999—dc22

                                                                                2003019114

First Edition: April 2004

10   9   8   7   6   5   4   3   2   1

This book is dedicated to our daughter
Katya.
It is also for our fathers:
L. Richard Schumacher, a dedicated physician
who imparted a love of science and devotion to critical thinking to those around
him, and Murray Bookchin, with the hope that his pioneering vision of a truly
rational and free society might yet, one day, come into being.

Contents

The only thing I know about this vaccine is that it starts with a monkey's kidney and it ends up going into a child's arm. Could you explain a little to us the process in between?

—Edward R. Murrow, to Dr. Jonas Salk,
See It Now, CBS Television
February 22, 1955

Introduction

THE FIRST THING you see when you walk in the door of Raphaele and Michael Horwin's modest San Diego apartment are photos of their son Alexander. Arranged neatly on bookcases or hung on beige walls, the photos are everywhere, his image set into a gold frame, a pewter frame with flowers, wooden frames, even plastic desk frames. Here is Alexander as an infant, with huge, round brown eyes and dark curly hair, lips parted in a wide, world-embracing smile with two teeth peeking out on the top and two on the bottom. Here he is at age two, in a denim jacket embroidered with colorful fish, holding a stuffed yellow duck. In photo after photo he gazes happily, intelligently, handsomely into the camera.

But move to the rear bedroom of the apartment, and the mood changes; a strange silence falls over the room. There are photos of young Alexander on the wall, and there is a shelf with five stuffed bears sitting on it, but otherwise this is not a child's room. Rather, the room is filled with computer equipment, whiteboards covered with lists, and scientific books and journals. Instead of a child's clothing, the closet is jammed with plastic file folder boxes. In this bedroom-turned-office other photos are kept, ones that are not on display. In these, Alexander is tranquil, but not happy. In one, he is lying on a hospital bed in the University of California at Los Angeles Medical Center pediatric intensive care unit. From the center of his spine to his armpit, a blistering red wound spreads across the upper part of his back—a second-degree burn from a chemical drip that "accidentally spilled" onto his body during treatment at the hospital. In another, he is bald, with sunken eyes staring quietly from a stroller.

Alexander had been "a strong, happy, intelligent little boy," says his father Michael. As a toddler, he loved visiting the ocean tidal pools near the family's Marina del Rey home and exploring the tiny, mysterious marine creatures. He enjoyed being pushed by his mother on the boardwalk while she roller-bladed behind him. By the time he was two, he could already speak English and French.

Then something went very wrong.

On August 10, 1998, two months after his second birthday, Alexander received a diagnosis of brain cancer. Called medulloblastoma, it was one of the more common pediatric brain cancers, accounting for about one-sixth of all childhood brain tumors diagnosed in the United States.

Alexander had two operations—sixteen hours of surgery in all—that successfully removed the entire tumor. But his parents were told that the tumor would return unless he had further treatment—with chemotherapy. "Even after two brain operations, Alexander was still a vibrant, ruddy, strong, energetic child," Michael Horwin recalls. "That changed as the chemotherapy repeatedly filled his body with toxic chemicals. Alexander began to die inside." First there were relentless stomach pains and horrendous projectile vomiting. Then Alexander's curly hair fell out. Next his dark skin turned ghostly pale. "He got sick with fevers and spent weeks in the hospital," Horwin says. "We felt as if we were actively engaged in the slow torture and destruction of our own child."

On January 31, 1999, following three rounds of chemotherapy, Alexander Horwin died. The fact that the chemotherapy appeared to have harmed rather than helped him made his parents' grief unbearable. They felt compelled to find out what had gone wrong.

The Horwins decided to investigate why their otherwise healthy son should have suddenly developed a brain tumor. They looked at environmental exposures but came up empty-handed. They hadn't been exposed to high levels of pesticides; they didn't live near a nuclear power plant; they ate healthy foods. Alexander had been in the ninety-fifth percentile for height and weight for his age group. There was no cancer history on either side of their families. Both of their paternal grandmothers had lived to almost ninety years of age.

Next, the Horwins reviewed Alexander's medical file in the months prior to his diagnosis. Like most children, he had received numerous vaccinations in the first two years of his life. There was nothing unusual about that. Vaccines are one of modern medicine's most important innovations. Not only do they prevent early childhood disease, they are a critical public health tool, having rid the world of scourges like smallpox, and having reduced the number of deaths from childhood illnesses like measles dramatically. Still, could something about the many vaccines Alexander had received have hurt him? The Horwins dug deeper and began to uncover information about vaccines that their pediatrician had never told them. Sometimes, they learned, vaccines contain trace amounts of toxic chemicals: residue from the manufacturing process, or preservatives designed to extend their shelf life. Sometimes they can be contaminated with living organisms, bacteria and viruses that have escaped from the animal tissues that are used during the manufacture of many vaccines.

One of the vaccines Alexander had received was the polio vaccine—mandatory in every state of the union and typically administered four times during the first sixteen months of a baby's life. When the Horwins researched the polio vaccine, they found, to their amazement, that during the 1950s and early 1960s, the vaccine had been widely contaminated with a virus. Millions upon millions of doses administered in the United States and other countries had been tainted—not just by any virus, but by a monkey virus that had gotten into the vaccine during the manufacturing process. Worse still, this strange virus appeared to cause several different types of cancer, including brain cancer, when injected into laboratory animals.

Supposedly, the polio vaccine had been rid of this virus long ago. But what if it hadn't been? Was it possible, the Horwins wondered, that this same cancer-causing virus somehow had gotten into a dose of polio vaccine that had been given to their son?

The Horwins' quest took them to the research laboratories of Michele Carbone, a molecular pathologist at Loyola University Medical School, just outside Chicago. Carbone was a medical doctor with a Ph.D. in anatomic pathology; he was also a leading expert in the simian virus that had contaminated the polio vaccine. He had detected it in a type of human lung tumor called malignant mesothelioma in 1994 while working at the National Institutes of Health (NIH). He wasn't the first investigator to link the virus to cancers, but he was, without a doubt, the most tenacious. In the years since his discovery, he had dedicated his entire laboratory to investigating how it caused human cells to become cancerous.

When the Horwins contacted him in the fall of 1999, Carbone's initial inclination was to refuse them. Because the tests were expensive and time consuming, normally, he tested only those tumor samples that were part of a larger research effort or that had come to him through the Loyola health system. But Carbone found himself moved by the grief of Alexander's mother, Raphaele. He decided, at his own expense, to run a series of sophisticated molecular tests on Alexander's tumor biopsy and the blood from his umbilical cord at birth.

A few weeks later, he informed the Horwins of the results. Alexander's brain tumor contained the simian virus. His cord blood did not. Somehow, their child had been exposed to the virus after birth. Michael and Raphaele had themselves tested. Neither of them showed any signs of the virus. That meant the virus in their son's tumor hadn't come from either one of them. The evidence seemed unbelievable, but the results were conclusive. Taken together, it seemed to the Horwins, the tests said one thing: a strange virus from another species had caused the death of their otherwise healthy son, and its source was a medical intervention that was supposed to protect him from harm—the polio vaccine.

How does a monkey virus get into the brain of a human being? At first blush, the answer seems bizarre—straight out of the script of a 1950s sci-fi thriller. But it is true. For nine years, from 1954 to 1963, almost every dose of polio vaccine produced in the world was contaminated with a cancer-causing simian virus. In one of the biggest blunders in medical history, nearly half the American population—about one hundred million people— and millions more in Canada and Europe, were administered this widely contaminated vaccine. When scientists discovered the virus in 1960, they named it SV40—an innocent-sounding, almost antiseptic appellation, except that SV stands for simian virus, and 40 designates that it was the fortieth such virus discovered. Like HIV, which causes AIDS, SV40 crossed into humans from monkeys and had its own dramatic consequences. Exactly how HIV leapt from monkeys to human beings is as yet unknown; there is no debate, however, about the primary source of SV40: The virus came from the monkey kidneys on which the polio vaccine was produced. At the time, scientists developing the polio vaccine and other vaccines knew that the monkey kidneys they were using were often contaminated with un- wanted simian viruses, but it was assumed they were inconsequential. SV40 proved them wrong.

After it was discovered in 1960, researchers inoculated laboratory animals with the simian virus in experiments conducted during 1961 and 1962. They were astonished—and scared—when their experiments showed that the polio vaccine contaminant readily caused an array of cancers. For a while, there was panic within public health circles as scientists debated what to do, but almost no one outside of a small coterie of health officials and researchers knew what had happened. Determined not to alarm the public, federal health officials kept the news about the SV40 contamination of the polio vaccine under wraps. They refused to recall millions of contaminated doses that had already been released for use; and when one government researcher dared to speak out about the contamination, they punished her. Then, in 1963, federal scientists surveyed the American population and concluded that they could find no evidence the virus was causing cancer in people who had received contaminated vaccine. Based on this one epidemiological study, most of the scientific world concluded the virus had little effect in humans. Meanwhile, vaccine production methods had changed and procedures had been instituted that supposedly made it impossible for SV40 to ever contaminate the vaccine again. Between the one epidemiological study and the switch to what was assumed to be a clean vaccine, SV40 was quickly forgotten and a false sense of security replaced the previous panic. For the next thirty years, almost everyone ignored SV40. The virus's relationship to human disease was almost totally unexplored.

Ignoring SV40 for so long was a mistake, according to Carbone and other cancer experts. "There is no doubt that SV40 is a human carcinogen," says Carbone, who has studied the virus closely for more than ten years. "SV40 is definitely something you don't want in your body." Yet that is exactly where the virus is showing up. Since the mid-1990s, SV40 has been found not only in the type of brain cancer that afflicted Alexander Horwin, and the mesotheliomas studied by Carbone and other researchers, but also in a variety of other brain tumors and bone cancers, as well as leukemias and lymphomas.

Many of these tumors have increased in incidence dramatically since the 1950s and early 1960s—the period when the polio vaccine was contaminated with SV40. Malignant mesothelioma, for instance, was virtually unheard of prior to 1955; today it afflicts and kills about 2,500 Americans each year and many more people in Europe. Brain and central nervous system tumors increased in incidence by more than 30 percent in just one twenty-year period from the mid-1970s to the mid-1990s. Bone tumors are also on the rise. Non-Hodgkin's lymphoma, the disease that killed Jacqueline Kennedy Onassis and Jordan's King Hussein, has also skyrocketed in incidence, increasing by 3 percent annually since the 1970s. It now strikes 54,000 new victims each year. Another 30,000 Americans are afflicted every year with acute or chronic leukemia.

More disturbing still, scientists are now finding SV40 not just in tumors from adults but in the tumors of children like Alexander Horwin—children too young to have been exposed to contaminated vaccine back in the 1950s and 1960s. These findings raise some disturbing questions: Has the simian virus established a permanent foothold in human beings and begun to spread? Or is it possible, as Alexander's parents assert, that polio vaccine continued at times to be contaminated, even after 1963? One thing is clear: The vast majority of baby boomers—almost all of whom received polio vaccine in the late 1950s and early 1960s—have potentially been exposed to the virus. And if what happened to Alexander Horwin is any indication, some of their children have been exposed as well.

This book tells the story of how SV40 came to contaminate millions upon millions of doses of the polio vaccine forty years ago and cause disease today. It follows a group of determined cancer researchers, who, led by Carbone, have revived interest in the long forgotten virus. In the process, they have made important new discoveries about how the virus works and about how cancer is caused in general. But such groundbreaking research has not been welcomed in all corners. Because SV40 was a contaminant in a government-sponsored vaccine, within federal health circles there has been strenuous opposition to the proposition that the virus is a human carcinogen. At times, as this book recounts, that has included pressure on independent scientists to conform to the government point of view and even efforts to cut off their research funds. How—and why—scientific research can be shaped by such external forces lies at the heart of this story, and this book concerns itself as much with the people who practice science as it does with the science itself. For, as the history of SV40 shows, science is not always the disinterested pursuit of pure knowledge we may imagine it to be. It is a venture that, however noble, still can be influenced by the prejudices and predilections of its practitioners—sometimes for better, sometimes for worse.

Much of this account unfolds within the past ten years, the period during which research by Carbone and others exploded the long-standing assumption that the monkey virus was harmless to humans. But to really understand the story of SV40, one must begin many decades ago during a unique chapter in American history, a time when the entire nation was fixated on polio. Today, it is difficult to imagine the anguish that accompanied epidemics of poliomyelitis, a disease that ravaged the United States and much of the Western world during the first half of the twentieth century. For four decades, beginning with the epidemic of 1916, polio swept through the country every summer, leaving thousands of dead and maimed individuals in its wake, particularly children. Polio haunted America, especially its parents, and defeating it became a national obsession. It was against this backdrop that the story of SV40 begins.

THE VIRUS AND
THE VACCINE

1

The Paralyzed President

IT WAS ALREADY getting warm as dawn broke along the coast of Maine on the morning of August 11, 1921. The sun rising over the great expanse of North Atlantic Ocean promised another balmy day, much like the other warmer-than-usual days that had marked the summer that year. Along the coastline, local residents prepared to take up their posts at shops, farms, and fishing vessels. It looked to be one more in a string of uneventful, lazy summer days.

But a few miles out to sea, on a nearby Canadian island in the Bay of Fundy, the morning was taking a sober turn. Here a middle-aged man awoke to find that his life had changed, literally, overnight. An athletic man who had thought nothing of taking a strenuous run and vigorous swim just the day before, he found he could barely stand on his own two feet. One leg was dragging, and the other was on the verge of giving way. A proud man, accustomed to acting decisively on his own counsel, he was suddenly weak and helpless— his hips and legs all but paralyzed. He retreated to his bed, to no avail. The next day, and the one after, his illness worsened, until he found himself in a feverish agony, burning up; even the pressure of bedclothes against his legs was unbearable. He was paralyzed from the waist down.

The upper part of his body was affected as well. His arms were weak. He lost control of his thumbs. He could not sit without assistance, nor turn from side to side. Though he would eventually make a partial recovery from his illness, he would never regain the use of his legs. From this day on, he would have to crawl, crablike, on his hands or employ a variety of stratagems involving crutches, leg braces, wheelchairs, and the strong arms of porters in order to move any distance, no matter how small. He would require the assistance of his family and a small band of intimates to assist him in almost every aspect of daily living.

The man so suddenly afflicted was Franklin Delano Roosevelt, and the disease that laid him so low was polio. Over the next several decades, polio became identified with Roosevelt. For the rest of his life and beyond, whenever someone wanted to put a human face to the disease they inevitably included a reference to FDR, America's beloved president and most famous polio victim. He, in turn, was transformed by polio. The disease and his response to it defined and shaped him and his political career.

In retrospect, the polio that felled FDR that hot summer day more than eighty years ago was one of those chance events that alter history. Whatever other forces helped Roosevelt secure election first as New York's governor for two terms and then as president in four successive elections, there is little doubt among historians that Roosevelt's status as a polio victim—and the strength, resiliency, and grace he displayed in the face of his affliction— helped him win the support of voters. Arguably, if he had not contracted polio, Roosevelt might not have ascended to the White House. How modern history would have changed without FDR at the helm during the depths of the Great Depression and then during democracy's victory over the global forces of fascism is speculative, but doubtless it would have been different, perhaps profoundly different. While the effect of FDR's polio on American history and politics is impossible to gauge, there is one certain result of his illness. Because Roosevelt caught polio, the course of fighting the disease was forever changed.

Roosevelt was vacationing at the family's fifteen-room summer home on Campobello Island when he contracted polio. He had been coming to Campobello since childhood and had established a strenuous routine of sailing, hiking, fishing, and rock climbing during his sojourns. The 1921 summer vacation was the first extended vacation Roosevelt had taken in five years. He hoped it would be a chance to relax and reconnect with his family; he was looking forward to playing ringleader on jaunts through the woods and taking his five children for refreshing dips in the Bay of Fundy's icy waters.

Roosevelt had arrived at Campobello from Washington, D.C., a few days earlier, after pausing to march in a Boy Scouts parade in New York. (He was president of the Boy Scout Foundation of Greater New York and may have contracted the disease at the crowded children's event.) He quickly settled into his rigorous "vacation" routine. But there were alarming signs that Roosevelt was not well. On August 9, while he was sailing on his yacht, he lost his balance and fell briefly overboard. He complained of the "icy shock" in comparison to the heat of the August sun and that the "water was so cold it seemed paralyzing." He was noticeably weary that evening. The next day's schedule was typical of the activity-filled days on which FDR seemed to thrive. A sail on the family's twenty-four-foot sloop, *Vireo,* with his three eldest children turned into an all-day, harrowing adventure when the party stopped to put out a forest fire on a nearby island as they were heading back to Campobello, smothering it by beating it out with pine branches. After the fire had been extinguished, Roosevelt led his children on a cross-island run of more than two miles, followed by a swim in a freshwater lagoon and then a plunge into the bay.

But Roosevelt didn't get "the usual revitalization, the glow [he'd] expected" from the swim and instead returned home exhausted, "too tired to even dress" for dinner. After reading the mail and the day's newspapers, he climbed upstairs and went straight to bed, complaining that he felt chilled. It was the last time he would ever walk unassisted in his life. When he woke on the morning of August 11, something was clearly amiss. He was unable to support his weight on one leg. By evening his other leg had weakened, and by the following morning he could not stand up at all. By the third day, all the muscles from his chest down were involved. Roosevelt was experiencing full-blown paralytic polio.

Polio has afflicted mankind for millennia. An ancient Egyptian funerary carving from the eighteenth dynasty (1580–1350 B.C.E) portrays a priest with a withered limb. Hippocrates referred to paralytic attacks that occurred mainly in the summer and autumn. The Bible refers to individuals with paralyzed and atrophied limbs. A Bruegel painting from the sixteenth century includes a crippled beggar, and in 1921, an archaeological dig in southern Greenland found twenty-five skeletons from the fifteenth century with bone deformations characteristic of polio. Despite the ancient record of the disease, epidemic polio was unheard of until the industrial revolution. The vast majority of polio victims suffered little permanent damage until the twentieth century.

Polio, or more properly "poliomyelitis," is caused by a virus. The formal name combines two Greek words with a Latin suffix to denote polio's characteristic inflammation (*itis*) of the gray nerve tissue (*polios*) in the spinal cord (*myelos*). It is this nerve damage that can lead to paralysis. Humans contract polio by ingesting the virus through the mouth or inhaling it through the nasal passages. The virus quickly moves down the pharynx and lodges in the gut, where it begins to reproduce. Here it attracts the attention of the body's immune system, which usually defeats the poliovirus and rids the body entirely of it by shedding it through the individual's feces. The shed poliovirus, though, remains alive and can now infect any other individual who comes into contact with the excreta of the first individual, say, through changing a baby's diaper or poor hygiene. This second individual now repeats the entire contagious cycle. In this way, polio can quickly spread from person to person, especially those who live in close proximity. Polio epidemics are notorious for striking multiple members of the same household or same neighborhood.

Polio, however, is not just one discrete virus. It has a multitude of variants, which are called "strains." Most polio strains are relatively harmless. If an individual contracts one of the less virulent strains of polio, he or she suffers either no symptoms at all or only a mild, cold-like illness: a headache, often a chill, perhaps a low-grade fever. When he has recovered, the individual has been conferred lifelong immunity, not only against the infecting strain, but also against all strains from the specific genetic family—or "type," of which there are three—to which the strain belongs. All three poliovirus types contain many harmless strains, but all three also contain some extremely dangerous strains. These virulent strains can escape the gut, enter the blood stream, and travel to the central nervous system. Here the poliovirus attacks the brain and the spinal cord, destroying the ability of the nerve cells that control specific muscles to send and receive messages. The affected muscles become paralyzed. Since motor nerve cells, once destroyed, cannot regenerate themselves, the paralysis is usually permanent. In extreme cases, called bulbar polio, the nerve cells that control the involuntary muscles necessary for breathing are incapacitated, and death can result.

Ironically, advances in public health and sanitation that occurred during the industrial revolution created the perfect conditions for sudden and terrifying outbreaks of paralytic polio. For thousands of years, man and virus had achieved a symbiosis of sorts. In preindustrial societies, personal hygiene was poor, even among the wealthy and educated; basic public health measures we take for granted, such as sewers and indoor plumbing, were largely nonexistent. Contact with relatively benign strains of poliovirus

(from fecal matter) was universal. Children were exposed either during infancy, when maternal antibodies helped protect them, or as toddlers, almost
always contracting mild forms of the disease. Immunity was therefore widespread. But that cycle was interrupted during the nineteenth century. Cleaning up the cities of America and northern Europe created perfect conditions
for polio epidemics. With the introduction of modern sewers and plumbing, entire generations grew up in sanitary surroundings, rarely, if ever,
exposed to poliovirus, even to milder strains, and so had little or no natural
polio immunity. Pernicious strains of polio suddenly had millions of vul-
nerable hosts.

Outbreaks of paralytic polio were first described in detail in the nineteenth century. A British physician named Michael Underwood reported
"four remarkable cases of suddenly induced paralysis, occurring in children"
in one village in 1835. A localized outbreak may have occurred in Louisiana
in 1841; another early epidemic swept through young English children on
the island of St. Helena around the same time. By the middle of the
nineteenth century, a German orthopedist, Jakob Heine, had described polio in detail, distinguishing it as a separate disease from other paralytic
disorders. In the second half of the nineteenth century, as physicians began
to recognize this strange, new syndrome of massive, sudden paralysis, spo-
radic outbreaks were reported in Oslo, Lyon, Manchester, Stockholm, Boston, and rural Vermont, where 132 children contracted polio in the Otter
Creek Valley. Eighteen of them died.

Then in the summer of 1916, as if out of nowhere, came a polio epidemic of such ferocity it seared itself into the American psyche for the next
generation. The first cases appeared in early summer in New York City's
immigrant neighborhoods. Public health officials were baffled; no one knew
exactly how the disease was spread, but it was clear that the contagion was
virulent, spreading from borough to borough like wildfire. The number of
paralyzed victims—most of them children—grew from dozens to hundreds
and then to thousands. Panic ensued. Thousands of families fled the swel-
tering disease-stricken city. As news of the mysterious ailment filtered out,
residents of outlying communities treated New Yorkers as if they were lep-
ers, turning them away and threatening violence. Those who stayed in the
city withdrew behind bolted doors, drawing the blinds and shutting their
windows, even as the city's heat and humidity reached its summer cres-
cendo. Public health officials responded as best they could. Sanitation workers washed the streets and sidewalks—four million gallons of water a day

were used—and seventy-two thousand stray cats were killed in the mistaken belief that they might be carriers of the disease. Quarantines aimed at specific neighborhoods or ethnic groups were debated. But the well-intentioned efforts were futile. From its New York City epicenter, polio spread throughout the entire Northeast.

By the end of 1916, twenty of the forty-eight states were affected by the outbreak; more than 27,000 confirmed cases of paralysis, including 7,000 fatalities, were reported. Tens of thousands of milder, nonparalytic cases went undiagnosed because physicians were unfamiliar with the disease. The toll was heaviest in New York City, with some 2,500 deaths and nearly 9,000 confirmed cases. Most of the victims were young children, their parents utterly helpless in the face of such enormous suffering. In recognition of the disease's propensity to strike so disproportionately among this one age group, doctors began to call it "infantile paralysis." Polio had arrived in America.

For more than forty years after that terrible summer of 1916, there were annual polio epidemics in America. With each summer, polio resurfaced like clockwork. But other than its estival reappearance, precious little was known about the disease. Where polio would occur was unpredictable. Reading the tea leaves of past outbreaks to forecast the locations of future ones proved beyond any scientist's prognisticative abilities. Polio simply struck wherever it pleased. Cities, villages, even America's remotest rural areas—no corner of the nation was spared. Polio had no class consciousness; rich and poor alike were afflicted. It didn't play by the rules; healthy and robust children were no more immune from its ravages than the sickly. Polio was maddeningly random. Like a tornado that levels all the houses in a block, but leaves one miraculously unscathed, polio could devastate one village but not its neighbor. Or epidemics could pop up hundreds of miles apart. As a result, no community felt safe.

One fact about polio soon became apparent: Almost all paralytic polio cases seemed to occur between May and September. And so summer, and the annual start of "polio season," was transformed from a time of the year to be relished and anticipated into a season that parents dreaded—especially because no one knew how the disease was spread. The only strategy that seemed effective was to try, somehow, to avoid epidemic epicenters and minimize contact with others. The wealthy would take their families and escape to the country during the hottest months of the year. For everyone else, summertime became a series of restrictions on normal childhood activities: no ball games, no movies, no camps, no trips to the public pool or to the beach. If there were any reports of polio in the vicinity, anxious parents would quarantine their children, shutting them indoors and away from all possible human contact—anything to keep their children safe from polio.

Polio, of course, was not just a disease of children; adults, like Roosevelt, were also sometimes afflicted. And for many, particularly those of lesser means, the economic impact could be devastating. There was no "safety net" to provide for families whose wage earner became incapacitated. How did one find a job when confined to a wheelchair? And what about the stigma of being a "cripple"? Who would accept such a person in a position of authority? Roosevelt came from one of the nation's most famous political families, had served with distinction in Woodrow Wilson's administration as assistant secretary of the navy, and had been the Democratic Party's vice presidential candidate in 1920, but in keeping with the mores of the day, FDR's mother believed polio had effectively ended her son's political career. Once it was clear he was paralyzed from the waist down, she urged her lawyer son to return home to Hyde Park and live out his life in a wheelchair as a gentleman farmer.

Roosevelt's wife, Eleanor, and his closest political advisor, Louis Howe, shared a different point of view, however. For the next several years they kept FDR's political career alive. While Roosevelt concentrated on rebuilding his shattered body—until he had developed a physique that rivaled a weight lifter's, at least in his upper body—Howe kept in touch with party leaders, and Eleanor made public appearances on her husband's behalf.

Their efforts paid off. In 1924, they persuaded New York's popular governor Al Smith to allow Roosevelt to nominate Smith for president at the Democratic National Convention at Madison Square Garden. It was Roosevelt's first public appearance, and he was determined to get to the podium on his own two feet. For weeks he practiced for the event. On the hot July night he was to nominate Smith, Roosevelt locked his leg braces so his knees would not buckle, and tightly gripping his crutches, made the slow, painful walk to the stage. When he finally reached the podium and was facing the crowd, he threw back his head, affected a jaunty air, and flashed the audience a radiant grin. The audience went wild. Applause and cheers filled the hall before he had even spoken a word. His nomination speech produced an even greater effect. At its conclusion, when he placed Smith's name in nomination, there was a moment of silence. Then an ovation erupted that lasted an hour and fifteen minutes.

The Democratic convention appearance secured Roosevelt's stature as a national leader—not only because of his stunning nomination speech, but also because he made it to the podium on his own, refusing to use a wheelchair. The feat earned him instant admiration, with one newspaper describing him as "the real hero" of the convention. Roosevelt had not been defeated by polio; he had risen above it. At the 1928 convention, Roosevelt repeated the feat—this time abandoning crutches entirely in favor of the support of a cane and the rigid arm of his son Elliot. In full view of all the delegates, Roosevelt appeared to walk to the lectern, the picture of a cured cripple who had staged a miraculous recovery. His nominating speech, again for Smith, was as well received as the one four years before.

After the 1928 convention, polio was no longer a hindrance to Roosevelt's political aspirations. That fall, in a year of Republican landslides throughout the country, he won an upset victory in the New York governor's race. The race had started with an ugly rumor that Roosevelt was too weak to hold office and would resign once elected. Roosevelt responded with a barnstorming tour during which he visited more localities and delivered more speeches than any candidate for statewide office before him. His breakneck campaign pace exhausted his staff and the press pool assigned to accompany him, but it energized the electorate and laid to rest any notion that as a polio victim he lacked the stamina needed to govern. If anything, he was more fit than most able-bodied men.

In 1930, Roosevelt was reelected governor by a wide margin, but he had already set his sights on higher office. Within a year, he was seeking the presidency, and in the summer of 1932 he accepted the Democratic Party's nomination. Once again he defied conventional wisdom, which suggested that he not exert himself and instead run a "front porch" campaign as other successful presidential candidates, including Warren G. Harding only a few years previously, had done. Ignoring party leaders' fears that the rigors of a full campaign schedule would draw unfavorable attention to his disability, Roosevelt campaigned whistle-stop style, covering the entire country from coast to coast.

During the presidential campaign, Roosevelt was the picture of a dynamic, active, and confident leader, defiant in the face of his physical paralysis, just as he was urging the nation to be defiant in the face of economic paralysis. Campaign biographies, far from downplaying his polio, described in detail how Roosevelt contracted the disease and his battle to overcome it. The implication was that any man who had suffered but refused to bow under the weight of polio clearly had the character, strength, and compassion to lead the nation out of the Great Depression. Polio, the disease that had struck him down a decade before, now helped carry Roosevelt to the White House.

One anecdote from his presidency exemplifies how polio became the touchstone in defining Roosevelt as a sympathetic and heroic leader. During his first term, First Lady Eleanor Roosevelt was addressing a gathering in Akron, Ohio, when a question from the audience, meant to be hostile, was handed to her. She carefully and unemotionally read the question aloud and then turned the questioner's intent on its head: "Do you think your husband's illness has affected your husband's mentality?" she read. "I am glad that question was asked. The answer is yes," came her careful reply. "Anyone who has gone through great suffering is bound to have a greater sympathy and understanding of the problems of mankind." The audience responded with a standing ovation.

2

A Nation at War with Polio

ROOSEVELT'S ACCESSION TO the White House profoundly affected the way Americans viewed polio. It raised the profile of the disease and evoked greater sympathy among all Americans for polio victims and their families. But beyond raising public awareness, Roosevelt's stature, even as the nation's most powerful political figure, was by itself ineffective in fighting polio. Defeating a disease requires research. And research costs money. By and large, funding for medical research at the time did not come from the federal government—as so much of it does now—but from private sources, large philanthropic organizations, such as the world-famous Rockefeller Institute. Scientists either sought grants from such charities or, in the case of the Rockefeller Institute, went to work directly for them. It was axiomatic: Promising advances in medical science required powerful support. If polio was going to be beaten, some organization would have to step forward and bankroll the fight. But even after years of polio epidemics there was no concerted effort to fund research for polio prevention or for a cure—that is, until a close friend of FDR's created a fund-raising and medical research machine that is still unrivaled today. This friend, a scrappy Irishman named Basil O'Connor, was one of the advisors Roosevelt brought with him to Washington in the spring of 1933.

Born in Taunton, Massachusetts, Basil "Doc" O'Connor was the second son of second-generation Irish immigrants. His father was a tinsmith, and the family was poor—"one generation removed from servitude" was how

O'Connor liked to refer to his upbringing. But from an early age, O'Connor displayed a knack for making money, starting to deliver newspapers when he was ten and then establishing a monopoly on all the city's newspaper routes. Working his way through Dartmouth College in just three-and-a-half years (where he paid his way by playing fiddle in a dance orchestra and was voted "most likely to succeed"), O'Connor headed to Harvard Law School. Married by 1919, he left the Boston law firm of the man who had helped pay his way through Harvard and set out to establish himself as a Wall Street lawyer. It was on Wall Street that he met Roosevelt.

In the fall of 1924, three years after Roosevelt contracted polio, O'Connor and Roosevelt became law partners, but from the beginning Roosevelt was a rather absent partner. Almost all his time was spent hundreds of miles from New York pursuing his polio rehabilitation efforts, specifically a hydrotherapy regimen that he had begun at Warm Springs, Georgia, a tiny farming community ten miles from the nearest paved road.

Warm Springs was named for the hot mineral springs that flow from 3,800 feet below the earth's surface at a constant temperature of eighty-eight degrees from nearby Pine Mountain. Wealthy society types from Atlanta, eighty miles to the northeast, had been coming to the area for a half century to vacation and restore themselves in the spring's waters, which were supposed to provide relief from a variety of ailments ranging from diarrhea to diabetes. Told by a banker friend that a turn in the Warm Springs waters had benefited another polio victim, Roosevelt decided on an extended visit. He began his "swimming cure" at what had once been one of Warm Springs's leading resorts, a Victorian era white elephant called the Meriwether Inn.

When Roosevelt arrived in 1924, the Meriwether was in such disrepair that it was in danger of falling apart. The outbuildings lacked running water and electricity. "Squirrels ran in and out of holes in the roof" was how O'Connor would later describe the Meriwether's appearance the first time he saw it. "The place was a miserable mess." No matter, FDR somehow saw larger possibilities and announced that he wanted to buy the place—something he did two years later. O'Connor remained opposed to the idea until the very end. "Don't do anything, am taking train," he wired when he heard that FDR was about to close on the property. Nevertheless, Roosevelt bought the dilapidated hotel, spending two-thirds of his personal fortune on it, and O'Connor was forced to settle the financial details of the purchase.

Roosevelt's dream was to turn the Meriwether into the world's first re-habilitation center exclusively devoted to polio victims. In short order he evicted the last of the inn's paying guests, embarked on major renovations without any capital, and started accepting patients for little or no remuneration for the elaborate hydrotherapy routine he had devised. (He was known affectionately as "Dr. Roosevelt" by many of the young polio victims who soon flocked to Warm Springs.) With almost no revenue, Warm Springs began to flounder. In the spring of 1927, O'Connor took control of the books, and on his advice, the Meriwether was transformed into the nonprofit Georgia Warm Springs Foundation, with Roosevelt as president, O'Connor as secretary-treasurer, and Louis Howe as trustee. FDR immediately "sold" the hotel and its facilities for a dollar to the new foundation.

The following year, Roosevelt's election to the New York governorship forced him to give up his day-to-day involvement in Warm Springs. He asked O'Connor to take his place. At first O'Connor resisted. "I thought he was crazy to want that big goddam four-story firetrap," O'Connor later said. "I couldn't have been less interested in the project. But in 1926 he bought it and made a nonprofit foundation of it and in 1928 he ups and becomes Governor of New York and nonchalantly says to me, 'Take over Warm Springs, old fella: you're in.' I tell you, I had no desire to be 'in.' I was never a public do-gooder and had no aspirations of that kind. But I started enjoying it. Like Andrew Jackson at the battle of New Orleans, I found myself up to my rump in blood and liked it."

O'Connor remained in the thick of the battle against polio for the rest of his life, eventually becoming its undisputed general. One of his first acts as Warm Springs's new director was to try and shore up its precarious financial footing. Every war machine, O'Connor realized, needs cold, hard cash, and lots of it. In 1929, he hired professional fund-raisers with a charge to raise $1.25 million to support Warm Springs Foundation's operations. The fund-raising effort included pamphlets and press releases extolling the promise of the Warm Springs hydrotherapy cure. Response to the appeal was disappointing. The nation was slipping into the Great Depression, and competition for scarce charitable dollars was fierce.

Roosevelt's elevation to the White House suddenly changed the equation. In 1933, the professional fund-raisers suggested that the Foundation sponsor a series of balls across the nation to coincide with the new president's birthday. Roosevelt was at the height of his popularity, and linking a festive night out with helping the charity dearest to the president's heart proved to be a stroke of genius. With a slogan of "to dance so that others may walk," a national effort was undertaken to tout the balls. On January 30, 1934, in 4,376 communities across the nation, hundreds of thousands of revelers attended almost 6,000 fund-raising balls, from locales as diverse as the gala event at the Waldorf-Astoria in New York to the party for wheelchair dancers at Warm Springs. After the expenses were deducted, the one-night national party had raised more than $1 million, ten times more than O'Connor had predicted.

Between 1934 and 1937, the annual Birthday Balls successfully moved polio to the forefront of American consciousness, so much so that the events became the subject of political attack by Roosevelt's enemies. There were grumblings that the Roosevelt family was personally benefiting from the balls. Opponents to Roosevelt's economic programs resented any charitable activity directly connected to "that man in the White House." When O'Connor urged the President to separate himself and Warm Springs from the polio movement, he heeded the advice. In September 1937, Roosevelt announced the creation of a new nonpartisan polio organization: the National Foundation for Infantile Paralysis. The new charity officially opened for business in January 1938. Its headquarters were at 120 Broadway in downtown Manhattan, in the law offices of its unpaid president, Basil O'Connor. With his new position, O'Connor had become one of the country's leaders in philanthropy, charged by Roosevelt with coordinating a sustained national campaign against polio.

One of O'Connor's first decisions was to expand the mission of the fledgling charity far beyond FDR's initial mandate to advance polio research and education. The new National Foundation, he decided, would pay for the cost for treatment for any and all polio victims who sought its aid, no matter what the expense: iron lungs, crutches, braces, wheelchairs, round-the-clock nursing care. Whatever was needed for recovery and rehabilitation, the National Foundation would cover in full for as long as a polio victim was alive. And it would do so without means testing. Families would not have to prove that they had exhausted their own resources before the National Foundation would step in. Over the next several decades the National Foundation saved countless polio victims and their families from impoverishment by offering free, comprehensive health care to an entire segment of society. The implications were not lost on O'Connor's enemies: more than one detractor of the National Foundation accused it of foisting "socialized medicine" upon an unsuspecting public.

Fulfilling O'Connor's idealistic plans proved to cost unprecedented amounts of money, much more than the Birthday Balls had ever raised. "This is going to have to be more now than a one-day party," O'Connor said in 1937. "I don't know how much it is going to take, but it's going to take millions." The successor fund-raising campaign to the Birthday Balls was born at a strategy meeting at the Metro-Goldwyn-Mayer movie studio lot. Radio personalities and movie stars were deeply involved in antipolio publicity efforts by this time, and Eddie Cantor, a popular radio and vaudeville entertainer, suggested the idea of soliciting small donations in a pitch delivered by celebrities over the radio. "We could ask people to send their dimes directly to the President at the White House," Cantor suggested. "Think what a thrill people would get." Then, in a play on the words of the title of a popular newsreel—"The March of Time"—he coined a phrase still well known today: "And we would call it 'The March of Dimes!' "

The new effort was timed, once again, to coincide with Roosevelt's birthday at the end of January 1938. There was an intensive publicity blitz about polio. Doctors appeared on the radio to speak about the disease, and newspapers donated advertising and editorial space. During the last week of the month, the Lone Ranger urged boys and girls to send dimes to the White House to fight polio. Cantor made an appeal on newsreel and radio, as did many other Hollywood stars. Still, the initial response was disappointing. "You fellows have ruined the president," complained Roosevelt's press secretary to a National Foundation official two days after the broadcasts. "All we've got is seventeen and a half dollars." It wasn't until the next day that the campaign's success became apparent. The White House was deluged with mail. Thirty thousand pieces, six times the normal volume, arrived. The next day it was 50,000, then 150,000. "The government of the United States darned near stopped functioning because we couldn't clear away enough dimes to find the official White House mail," the White House mail chief later said. Fifty extra postal clerks and a small army of volunteers, including the president's children and WPA artists and writers, were pressed into service to deal with the cascade of mail that filled the White House basement. It took five months to clean up the backlog of unopened letters. In the end, 2,680,000 dimes had been sent directly to the White House. Combined with other donations, the National Foundation had raised $1,823,045 from its first March of Dimes campaign. According to the National Foundation's public relations director, Roosevelt was "just tickled pink" by the results.

The success of the first March of Dimes campaign would be dwarfed by those that followed. In 1941, the appeal raised three million dollars. In 1942, with the nation at war, personal sacrifice on the home front was the order of the day, yet contributions to the March of Dimes went up. The take that year was $5 million; "Give 'Til It Hurts" was the new slogan. Some $6.5 million was raised in 1943; more than $12 million in 1944; and in 1945, almost $19 million was contributed. By the early 1950s, the National Foundation was raising more than $50 million annually, and its battalions of armband-clad volunteers, who fanned out in their hometowns every January toting March of Dimes coin canisters, had become a fixture of the American winter landscape. To support his volunteers, O'Connor used a full-time public relations operation, which every year cranked out an intensive campaign of films, posters, ads, and appearances by celebrities—all urging Americans to join in the crusade against polio.

Between his volunteer army and his PR machine, O'Connor built a fundraising machine of unprecedented proportions. By one estimate, the National Foundation collected more than $630 million in the twenty-five years between 1938 and 1962, a staggering amount by any reckoning—especially since it was received mostly in the form of small donations collected by volunteers. And it was all devoted to fighting one disease.

By the end of World War II, O'Connor commanded one of the world's largest charities and had transformed the way the nation responded to polio. Under his direction, the National Foundation became the equivalent of an independent national public health agency, giving direct aid to hospitals and establishing equipment "depots" where iron lungs, rocking beds, and other lifesaving equipment were stockpiled and then transported to polio outbreak hot zones. Mobile teams of National Foundation–trained doctors and nurses were dispatched directly to epidemic sites. And, as promised at the National Foundation's inception, O'Connor paid the full cost for the treatment and rehabilitation of the nation's growing population of polio victims. Even as late as 1972, almost two decades after the last of the nation's polio epidemics, the National Foundation was still paying rehabilitation expenses for two hundred thousand polio victims.

Early on, however, O'Connor decided that a successful war against polio could not be waged simply by tending to the sick and the wounded. What was needed was a cure, and the National Foundation was prepared to generously underwrite researchers who promised one. Initially, O'Connor was frustrated. There simply wasn't much research to fund, and there seemed to be precious few researchers to back. At the time, the accepted scientific wisdom held that polio was caused by only one type of virus; that it only grew in nerve cells; that it always entered the body through the nose, traveled to the olfactory bulb, and thence made its way to the brain and spinal cord; and that the virus never entered the bloodstream. Every single one of these scientific "facts" would prove to be wrong.

Not surprisingly, with scientists knowing so little of the basic facts about polio, early efforts to prevent the disease were equally misinformed. In 1935, Maurice Brodie, a young research assistant at New York University, claimed that he had successfully developed a vaccine by grinding up the spinal cords of polio-infected monkeys and treating the amalgam with formaldehyde. He injected several dozen monkeys, himself, and a few volunteers with his new vaccine. He announced that he was ready to give the vaccine to three thousand children. Scientists at the Rockefeller Institute grew suspicious of Brodie when they couldn't replicate his experiments. Monkeys injected with the Brodie solution promptly died when exposed to polio; no immunity had been conferred. Fortunately, no one died from the Brodie fraud, although there were allergic reactions among the hundreds of children who were injected before he was stopped. At almost the same time, a far more serious vaccine mistake was perpetrated by John Kolmer of Temple University in Philadelphia. Kolmer was convinced that he, too, had successfully developed a polio vaccine. But the Kolmer vaccine was lethal, killing six children and paralyzing many more. The episode of the two failed vaccines came to be known as the Kolmer-Brodie fiasco, and the fallout it created soured O'Connor and the National Foundation on funding crash programs in vaccine creation. When the National Foundation began operations, O'Connor formed a scientific Advisory Committee, which included the heads of some of the top research facilities in the nation, and asked it to draw up a list of research priorities. Basic inquiries into the nature of polio—what caused it, how was it spread, what it did once it entered the body—topped the list. Next were improved treatment and therapy regimens for victims. At the bottom of the list of eleven research priorities was "production of a good vaccine." Given the state of the science, research into polio prevention had to take a backseat. Tending to victims came first.

Then, in the early 1940s, came a decision with far-reaching implications. The National Institutes of Health first considered, then abandoned, the idea of establishing a separate division to focus on polio research. The lead the National Foundation had in funding and the excellence of its scientific advisory group seemed to make any federal efforts redundant. The war against polio was ceded to O'Connor and his army of volunteers. Soon, National Foundation efforts in the field far outstripped those of the federal government. In 1953, for example, National Foundation research grants for polio totaled $2 million; in the same year the National Institutes of Health spent just $72,000 studying the disease. The prolonged effect of the National Foundation's largesse extended beyond polio. "O'Connor practically invented virology," said a researcher at Rockefeller University years later. "He did it by not concentrating research grants narrowly on polio, but by encouraging the most basic studies of all viruses."

But all the money and all the research it supported didn't seem to produce much tangible progress early on. Aside from improving care for victims, the nation seemed to be losing ground in the fight against polio. Even as the number of research dollars the National Foundation distributed was increasing, polio cases—which had held steady in the 1930s—began to spike. In 1940, there were ten thousand cases. By 1945, the number had doubled to more than twenty thousand, where it remained for the next several years. Every summer there was an epidemic worse than the terrible epidemic of 1916.

In 1952, fifty-eight thousand new cases of polio were diagnosed, one for every three thousand people in the United States. It was the worst polio epidemic on record; the "blackest [summer] in . . . polio history" was how *Newsweek* described it. During that one terrible year, paralytic polio killed more children than any other communicable disease in the United States. Polio was becoming America's bête noire, as dangerous as the Red Menace, and just as insidious—an unseen enemy within, a crippler and killer that seemed unstoppable, viciously cruel, with a penchant for young victims. For the new generation of parents who were busily launching the baby boom, polio was practically an obsession. It was their children who were dying, and their clamor for progress against polio grew louder and louder with each passing summer. In one telling incident, in 1953, Queens, New York, parents invaded and occupied the local public health office, demanding release of supplies of gamma globulin, an antibody fraction, which in a series of small trials had shown a very slight potential as a polio preventative. For desperate parents, a highly experimental treatment that worked only once in a while was better than nothing at all.

As the number of polio cases climbed, O'Connor became increasingly impatient. He wanted to fight polio—create a vaccine to stop it dead in its tracks—not just study it. But the scientists he was supporting were spending too much time and effort debating arcane issues and the niceties of lab technique and making far too little headway on vaccine research. Many of them weren't even sure that a vaccine was feasible. Albert Sabin, for example, was regarded as one of the leaders in polio vaccine research. By the early 1950s, he had already received National Foundation grants that totaled hundreds of thousands of dollars. But, he told O'Connor, it might be decades before there would even be a vaccine to test. It takes time, Sabin and other senior polio researchers would tell O'Connor. You can't rush careful science.

But time was something O'Connor did not have. It was becoming obvious that palliative measures were no longer a sufficient response to polio. With each passing year, there were more polio victims. The cost of caring for them was rising, absorbing more and more of the money the March of Dimes efforts raised. The 1952 epidemic alone had added forty thousand new polio victims to the rolls of the hundreds of thousands the National Foundation was already assisting. Caring for each would cost an estimated $40,000 dollars over the course of his or her life. If victims continued to pour in every year, the National Foundation would simply go broke. To O'Connor, it began to feel like the fight against polio was simply an exercise in watching the losses pile up.

Some of those losses were personal. In 1950, one of O'Connor's two daughters became paralyzed. She was thirty years old, a young mother of five children. "Daddy," she said on the phone when she broke the news, "I've got some of your polio." Then, in 1952, a heart attack forced O'Connor out of the office for three months while he recuperated. It was well known that O'Connor had vowed to beat polio in his lifetime. Perhaps he was simply running out of time. The only way to defeat polio was with an effective vaccine. But at the rate Sabin and the others were proceeding, there could be a million or more new victims before there was even an experimental vaccine. Somehow, somewhere, O'Connor had to find a new scientist to back, one who was less concerned with scientific rigidity and protocols and more concerned with results. Someone who was eager to make a name for himself and ready to take a gamble. Someone who wanted to defeat polio as badly as he did—now.

3

A Young Man from Pittsburgh

AT THE MIDPOINT of the twentieth century, the quest to develop a polio vaccine was stalled at a paradoxical roadblock: In the midst of ever expanding epidemics, researchers couldn't get their hands on enough of the virus they were trying to fight. The cruel irony was that even as poliovirus was running amok in its natural setting, in a laboratory the virus was painfully difficult to grow. Researchers simply did not know how to produce quantities of poliovirus sufficient to support an effective vaccine research program, especially on a timetable that could meet the demands of the increasingly impatient Basil O'Connor.

Even today, the first step for any scientist wishing to launch a vaccine development program is to collect samples of the target virus, take it back to the laboratory, and grow billions of copies of it under controlled conditions. Prior to the 1950s, there was certainly no shortage of opportunities to collect "wild" poliovirus. Any researcher who wanted to get into the vaccine development business could get all the virus-laden baby diapers and stool samples from epidemic hot sites that he or she could ever want. Research labs amassed impressive arrays of different disease-causing strains that they had dubbed with names like Mahoney, for the Ohio family from which it had been isolated, or MEF, standing for the "Middle East Forces," in honor of the unfortunate young soldier who had contracted polio while stationed in North Africa during the Allied campaign against Rommel. But collecting virus samples was easy compared to the next step: growing the strains in a laboratory. Viruses, unlike bacteria, need living cells to reproduce themselves. At the time, most virologists used live laboratory animals, usually hamsters, or small rodents, for their virus work. Hen's eggs were also used. But in the wild, polio is a disease that only afflicts humans; rodents do not contract the disease. Scientists had induced polio in monkeys, but after decades of trying; they had achieved only spotty success in infecting any common laboratory animals. That left monkeys as the only reliable "vector" for growing mass quantities of polio vaccine for research.

Monkeys were a nightmare to work with. They were expensive, hard to procure, filthy—they really do like to throw their fecal matter at their captors—and would bite each other and their keepers. They often would arrive sick and be useless for laboratory research. But monkeys were the only animals available for vaccine work, and every researcher devoted countless days and weeks to the tedious, dirty, and sometimes dangerous task of using live monkeys to grow poliovirus. First they injected the monkey with poliovirus and waited until it showed signs of illness. Then the monkey would be "sacrificed" (killed) and a small amount of virus-containing fluid extracted from its ground-up spinal cord. After repeating this work dozens of times, researchers hoped enough virus had been harvested that serious vaccine work could finally begin. But vaccine testing in the laboratory was just as laborious as the virus growth process. Another series of monkeys was injected (this time with the experimental vaccine), followed by another round of waiting to see what happened. If the monkeys got sick from the experimental vaccine, the vaccine was dangerous, and the previous months of work were wasted. If the monkeys did not get ill, the researcher faced another round of experiments in which the vaccinated monkeys next were "challenged" with some of the viral strains that caused disease. Only now— if a potential vaccine prevented paralysis in the monkeys—was there a first sign that it might be effective.

Assuming a polio researcher was lucky enough to reach the stage of a workable vaccine formulation, there still lay ahead months of verifying that the success was not a fluke by repeating the whole procedure in new batches of monkeys. Now the researcher was finally ready to test the putative vaccine in humans, with an initial trial involving no more than a few hundred people, perhaps only a few dozen. But even a small-scale trial would require hundreds of monkeys to produce enough poliovirus for the experimental vaccine. If the initial field tests were successful, then would come larger tests—again necessitating the use of more hundreds of monkeys to produce vaccine. Finally, if the researcher was lucky, years into the process, he or she might be ready for field trials on the scale needed to prove that the vaccine was not only safe in humans, but actually prevented polio. Mass field trials would involve a daunting number of monkeys—hundreds of thousands. And if the vaccine should be approved for commercial production, the numbers of monkeys became staggering. Tens of millions of monkeys might be needed. There would never be enough monkeys to meet the demand. As long as the only way to produce a potential polio vaccine relied primarily on injecting and killing monkeys, the process would remain maddeningly slow.

At the end of January 1949, there came a largely unnoticed announcement that changed this calculus entirely. John Enders, director of Harvard Medical School's new infectious disease laboratory at Children's Hospital in Boston, reported that it was possible to easily grow poliovirus in a variety of tissue cultures.

Tissue cultures were petri dishes or flasks containing cells from only one kind of animal or human tissue. They offered the promise of eliminating the need for whole animals for virus cultivation; instead, the viruses could be grown in cell cultures of the tissue type(s) they preferred in the wild. There had been some earlier attempts to use tissue culture for polio vaccine research, but these had been abandoned because it was assumed that the only tissue type that would support poliovirus growth was nerve tissue. But vaccine preparations that contained even a few nerve cells could provoke an allergic brain reaction, or even death, in a recipient. The conclusion had been, therefore, that nerve cell tissue cultures were simply too dangerous for polio vaccine work.

Enders and his team were trying to identify what tissue types best supported the growth of various disease-causing viruses. His lab had been growing mumps and chicken pox viruses, first in chick amniotic membranes and then in various human tissue cultures. Although Enders's group was not specifically interested in polio, its work was supported by the National Foundation, which by this time was involved in funding viral research of all kinds. The National Foundation support meant Enders's team had received some samples of poliovirus. On a whim, one day, at the end of March 1948, one of Enders's postdoctoral fellows decided to see what would happen if he infected a human tissue culture with the neglected poliovirus samples. That spring, he and another postdoc in the lab cultivated one of the more virulent strains of poliovirus on human embryonic tissue cultures composed of skin, muscle, intestinal, and connective tissue, all derived from miscarried fetuses. The poliovirus thrived, reversing the decades-old misconception that poliovirus would grow only on nerve cell cultures.

Enders and his group published their results in a brief, understated, two-page report in the January 28, 1949, issue of *Science*. Their paper, "Cultivation of the Lansing Strain of Poliomyelitis Virus in Cultures of Various Human Embryonic Tissues," was buried in the back pages of the magazine. But the paper's low-key tone belied its importance. It was a true breakthrough: Here at last was a method for poliovirus cultivation that eliminated the need to infect live monkeys and avoided the use of dangerous nervous system tissue.

Enders and the two younger scientists who were part of his team would receive the Nobel Prize in medicine for their revelation in 1954, but when it first appeared in 1949, their *Science* paper was ignored by almost every established polio investigator. There was, however, one researcher who seemed to fully appreciate the importance of the new finding. Within a few months of reading Enders's paper, this earnest, young doctor—Jonas Salk— was already planning to retrofit his laboratory at the University of Pittsburgh to take advantage of the Boston scientists' discovery. By the beginning of the following year, Salk's lab had perfected and improved on Enders's technique and started tissue culturing on a mass scale, using ground-up monkey kidneys suspended in a special nutrient broth. The efficiency of the new technique was almost beyond belief. The viral yield from one animal's kidneys was better than what could have been produced from dozens or even a hundred live monkeys—and the process took a fraction of the time. By the time anyone noticed, the obscure University of Pittsburgh scientist was beginning small field trials of his own brand of polio vaccine. He had lapped the competition before his more esteemed peers even knew he had entered the race. The name Jonas Salk would soon become synonymous with the long-sought, miraculous cure for polio.

Salk was born in New York City in 1914, the eldest son of Russian Jewish immigrants. He grew up in a predominantly Jewish neighborhood in the Crotona section of the Bronx. Jonas's family expected him to achieve, and he did not disappoint them. When he was twelve, he gained admission to Townsend Harris High School, an elite competitive public high school, where he was "a perfectionist" who "read everything he could lay his hands on," according to one of his fellow students. At fifteen, he entered City

College of New York and fell in love with science. Putting aside aspirations to become a lawyer, he concentrated on the course work necessary for admission to medical school, graduating near the top of his class. He was rewarded with a scholarship to the Medical School of New York University, where he stood out from his peers, not just because of his continued academic prowess—he was Alpha Omega Alpha, the Phi Beta Kappa of medical education—but because he had decided he did not want to practice medicine. During his first-year studies, Salk became absorbed with research, so much so that at the urging of a professor he took a year off from medical school to study biochemistry. When he returned to classes full-time, he juggled his course load to include a heavy concentration in bacteriology, which had now replaced medicine as his primary interest.

In the senior year, NYU medical students were allowed a two-month elective. Salk chose to work in the laboratory of Dr. Thomas Francis. Francis had recently joined the faculty of the medical school after working for the prestigious Rockefeller Foundation, where he had discovered the Type B influenza virus. The two-month stint in Francis's lab was Salk's first introduction to the world of virology—and he was hooked. When he graduated from medical school in June 1939, he immediately returned to Francis's lab. For the nine months between medical school graduation and the start of his residency at New York's Mount Sinai Hospital, Salk worked in Francis's laboratory learning how to kill influenza viruses with ultraviolet radiation. Salk and Francis stayed in touch during Salk's stay at Mount Sinai even though Francis had left NYU to direct the University of Michigan's new School of Public Health. Francis even arranged for Salk to report at a research symposium on a minor innovation he had made in a laboratory technique that improved the recovery of influenza from cultures.

As the end of his residency was drawing near, Salk began applying for research appointments. But the jobs he coveted in New York were closed to him because of the anti-Semitism that prevailed in so much of the medical research establishment. And Mount Sinai was notorious for never hiring its own interns. Disheartened and disappointed, Salk turned to his mentor for help. Francis did not let him down. He secured extra grant money and offered Salk a job. On April 12, 1942, thirteen years to the day before his polio vaccine would catapult him to international celebrity, Salk began work in Francis's laboratory, assisting him on an army-commissioned project to develop an influenza vaccine.

Virology was still a young science in 1942, not even a half century old.

In 1895, two researchers working independently of each other—one in Holland, the other in Russia—were the first to conclude that there existed a class of mysterious disease-causing agents that were smaller than bacteria. The new class of noxious substance was dubbed a "virus," a Latin word that means "venom" or "poison." Forty years later, in 1935, Wendell Stanley (another eventual Nobel Prize winner) definitively demonstrated that the unseeable stuff was actually a living thing, a new category of organisms that dwelled in the shadow and between life and inert matter—seemingly dead until they invaded living tissues and then somehow revived to inflict disease. Even with a burgeoning interest in the field that the work of Stanley and others effected, the new enemy was still largely unknown at the time of Salk's arrival in Ann Arbor. Nobody could even see one of the microscopic "beasties." The electron microscope had just been invented, and it would be many years before it would make it into even the best-funded virology labs. DNA and RNA had not yet been discovered, and how viruses came alive and replicated inside living cells was a mystery. What was known was that, like the tobacco mosaic disease that Dutch and Russian scientists had studied, there was a series of human diseases that were apparently viral, not bacterial, in origin—smallpox, rabies, measles, influenza, and polio, among others—and that drugs that worked against bacterial diseases were ineffective against them. If drugs were useless against viruses, that left only prevention, specifically, vaccines.

All vaccines rely on tricking the immune system. The vaccinologist manipulates a disease-causing virus so that it is no longer toxic, yet still provocative to the immune system. Millions of copies of the manipulated virus are placed in a solution and then injected into an individual. An individual's immune system reacts to the vaccine injection as if the imposter virus in the vaccine were the real thing, gearing up for a full-scale attack on the invader by manufacturing antibodies. If the vaccine works, an individual who encounters the deadly form of the virus is already prepared to fight back, and the individual is considered "immune."

Louis Pasteur was the founder of modern immunology and the first to perfect the art of making vaccines. Pasteur took rabies virus directly from the spinal cord of a rabid dog and injected it into the brain of a rabbit; when the rabbit became sick, Pasteur took the viral fluid from it and injected it into yet another rabbit. He "passaged" the virus this way twenty-five times through a series of rabbits, weakening the virus until the rabies virus no longer could cause disease, but would, when injected into dogs, render them immune to wild rabies. One fateful July night in 1885, Pasteur was visited by a frantic Alsatian couple whose nine-year-old son had been bitten by a rabid dog. The couple begged Pasteur to inoculate the boy with his experimental vaccine even though Pasteur feared it would not work. After a ten-day course of painful injections directly into the abdomen, the young boy, whose death had seemed inevitable, had miraculously survived. With Pasteur's success, modern vaccinology had begun.

Pasteur's vaccine was an "attenuated" or "live" vaccine. The virus in the vaccine was alive, strong enough to multiply and provoke the necessary response in the immune system, but too weak to cause full-blown illness. Most viral vaccine researchers in the 1940s believed that Pasteur's original approach was the best way to make vaccines. A smaller group, which included Thomas Francis, believed in the superiority of "inactivated" or "dead" vaccines. Instead of engaging in the time-consuming hunt to create less virulent viral strains, these scientists would deliberately isolate dangerous viral strains from sick individuals, destroy the viruses' "infectivity" (the ability to cause disease), with chemicals or ultraviolet radiation, and use the resulting "inactivated" viruses as the basis for a vaccine. As long as the killed viruses had not lost their "antigenicity" (ability to invoke an antibody response from the immune system), Francis and other inactivated vaccine proponents believed that a "killed" vaccine was every bit as good as a live, attenuated one, perhaps even better.

An advantage to a killed vaccine is that the vaccine can be easily loaded with more than one strain of virus. Influenza, the virus that was the focus of Francis's research, was a perfect candidate for a killed virus vaccine. Influenza is usually not particularly lethal, but the virus is highly mutable. Every year, new strains circulate the globe, and every now and then a particularly deadly variety surfaces. During the winter of 1918–1919, one particularly virulent strain of influenza wreaked havoc worldwide. At the height of the Spanish flu pandemic, people who had seemed healthy hours before literally dropped dead in the streets. More American GIs were killed by the Spanish flu than died in the trenches and the battlefields of France. As America entered World War II, it was a top military medical priority to develop an effective vaccine against a broad spectrum of influenza viruses. Francis's ability to devise vaccines that could protect against more than one flu strain gave him a decided advantage.

Under Francis's tutelage, Salk became an expert in killed vaccine development. Within a few months he was Francis's chief collaborator, often running day-to-day lab operations. He and Francis soon perfected an influenza vaccine that was widely used at army bases. Salk had been responsible for discovering and isolating one of the flu strains that was included in the final vaccine. But Salk chafed at his role as the junior scientist of the pair. When he and Francis published papers together, Salk would sometimes squabble about whose name was featured. ("Everyone knows who you are," Francis would later recall him saying. "It doesn't matter whether your name is first or last.") By 1947, an impatient Salk had decided he wanted to strike out on his own. After three institutions turned him down, an offer came from William McEllroy, the dean of the University of Pittsburgh Medical School, which included a promise that he would run his own lab. In the fall of that year, Salk left Ann Arbor and headed for Pennsylvania.

After Salk arrived at Pittsburgh, he found that there wasn't nearly as much substance to McEllroy's optimistic promises as he had naively believed. He had been relegated to cramped, unequipped quarters in the basement of the old Municipal Hospital, and his longed-for independence had evaporated. Salk's appointment placed him administratively under a researcher who specialized in plant viruses and was uninterested in Salk's flu work. When Salk's requests for equipment and furnishings went unnoticed, Salk took matters into his own hands and went back to McEllroy, who secured an independent appointment for Salk to the medical school faculty. With McEllroy's backing, Salk gradually annexed more of the unused Municipal Hospital for lab space and secured a $12,500 grant to begin building a working virology laboratory from one of the numerous foundations supported by Pittsburgh's famous Mellon family. With a virology lab finally starting to take shape, Salk resumed the work on influenza he had interrupted at Michigan.

Then came the break that would put Pittsburgh and Salk at the forefront of the fight against polio. A few months after Salk arrived at Pittsburgh, Harry Weaver, the new director of research at the National Foundation, came to visit Salk and asked if he would like to participate in the National Foundation's poliovirus typing project.

Harry Weaver had been an assistant professor of anatomy at Detroit's Wayne State University and had received grant money from the National Foundation when he was still a practicing researcher. In 1946, Basil O'Connor, impatient with the slow pace of vaccine progress, decided he needed a full-time director of research. Weaver had been recommended to O'Connor as having the self-assurance and take-charge attitude necessary to herd the competing and quarreling group of scientists that the National Foundation was funding toward O'Connor's goal of developing a polio vaccine as quickly as possible.

Weaver convened a series of roundtable meetings with the leading polio experts to acquaint himself with the state of polio knowledge and begin plotting a course toward a vaccine. He quickly realized that one of the fundamental challenges to a successful vaccine was that it would need to cover the full range of disease-causing poliovirus variants. By 1948, it had been proven that contrary to what had been supposed for decades, polio was not one, but three, distinct families of viruses (now known prosaically as Types I, II, and III). This meant that any successful vaccine would have to immunize against all three virus types. There also needed to be an assurance that there were no additional types of polio. Someone needed to go through each of the hundreds of known strains of polio and methodically classify each strain into one of the three known poliovirus types (or others, should they be discovered) before vaccine research could advance much further.

Weaver conceived of a massive virus-typing project involving four laboratories working collaboratively under the direction of the National Foundation. The problem was in recruiting the labs. Established polio researchers were uninterested. Virus typing was scut work, the scientific equivalent of bean counting—dull, boring, and repetitive—a laboratory assignment usually foisted on subordinate researchers. There would be little reward even for a job well done. No great discoveries were going to come from Weaver's project. And because Enders's tissue culture discovery was still to come, typing poliovirus strains required growing the viruses that were to be classified in monkeys, with all their attendant problems. (Weaver estimated fifty thousand would be used during the three years the project was scheduled to run.) Participating laboratories needed to be capable of administering the equivalent of a small zoo.

Weaver's recruitment drive led him to Salk and Pittsburgh. Salk appeared to be an ideal candidate. His lab space was suitable. The many empty wings at the Municipal Hospital meant he had sufficient space for the large numbers of monkeys that needed to be housed on-site. He was a talented, though still relatively unknown, virologist, so he had the requisite skills. The only trick would be persuading him that engaging in the drudgery of virus typing was worth his while. Weaver hinted to Salk that the virus-typing project had the potential to lead to "something very much larger."

The hint of greater things to come, along with the $200,000 annual National Foundation grant that came with the project, sealed the deal for Salk. He had come to Pittsburgh hoping to establish himself and move up in the scientific world—of course, he would be happy to work for the National Foundation on Dr. Weaver's important project.

Salk immediately set out planning a future beyond virus typing. In August 1948, four months before the project was scheduled to begin, he wrote to Weaver to suggest that the next logical step after poliovirus typing would be polio vaccine development—and in this next endeavor the National Foundation should favor laboratories, like his, that were already participating in the typing project. He closed by suggesting that Weaver agree to support him for the next five years. He was anticipating a long-term relationship with the National Foundation.

If Salk was audacious, he was also astute. In January 1949, Enders's article about tissue culturing of poliovirus ran in *Science*. Salk was immediately intrigued and asked Weaver to help him secure some tissue cultures from Enders. Weaver rebuffed him: Salk's job was to pursue virus typing, not to use a National Foundation grant to satisfy his own curiosity about an unproven technique. Weaver suggested that if Salk were so interested in Enders's work, he should correspond with the Boston scientist directly—a suggestion Salk took to heart. After Salk contacted Enders, the Harvard scientist agreed to demonstrate the efficacy of his new technique. Salk sent fourteen strains of poliovirus to Enders that he had already classified by virus type. It had taken Salk weeks to classify the strains using monkeys. But it was only days later that Enders got back to Salk with his own results. Using tissue cultures, Enders had accurately typed each strain in a fraction of the time it was taking Salk and the other virus-typing laboratories.

To Salk, Enders's tissue-culturing technique was virtually magic, and its practical applications enormous. If the virus-typing work could be carried out in tissue cultures instead of live animals, the National Foundation obligation could be fulfilled at a relatively minimal expense in terms of time and resources. Salk and his staff would be free to start working on other, more interesting projects, such as development of a vaccine. With or without Harry Weaver, he was going ahead.

In December 1949, Dean McEllroy helped Salk secure a small grant from a Pittsburgh-based philanthropic foundation. Salk used the funds to purchase some basic equipment. He hired a technician and went into the tissue culture business. When Weaver came by a few months later to check on the progress of the virus typing, he toured Salk's lab and noticed the new equipment and staff. What was going on? When Salk explained that he was switching over to tissue culturing, Weaver arranged for the National Foundation to start funding the tissue culture operation. The truth was that Weaver, in the intervening year, had come to see the benefits of the new technique. He had been trying to get other more senior National Foundation–supported researchers to switch to tissue culturing, but none were willing. When it became obvious that Salk was already far ahead, it simply made sense to back him.

Weaver had also taken a shine to Salk. He began to quietly encourage him to pursue his ideas on immunity and start working on a vaccine if that was what he really wanted to do. Salk needed to finish the virus-typing project, but Weaver would make sure he got the money he needed to pursue a vaccine. Salk now had a powerful mentor at the National Foundation and a secure funding source. With his new-found support, Salk's laboratory at Pittsburgh's Municipal Hospital began to expand rapidly. Over the next three years the staff grew from a core of six people to fifty. The laboratory outgrew its original quarters in the former morgue and expanded to fill the entire basement and then the entire first and second floors. (The fourth and fifth floors of the hospital were the polio wards. Salk and his staff spent enough time there that these floors, too, were practically part of his lab.) A full-scale renovation project was underway. A conference room was converted to a den of laboratories. Salk's office materialized from the former staff lounge. Special separate temperature-controlled rooms were created in the basement for growing and storing poliovirus. New, stainless steel equipment was installed. Centrifuges, benches, microscopes, and test tubes soon filled the remodeled rooms.

And there were monkeys. Scores of primates filled the animal quarters that had been set up on the second floor of the hospital, with a staff of expert animal handlers employed to take care of them. Even with the switch to tissue cultures, monkeys remained at the center of Salk's polio research. Once Salk's team had perfected Enders's tissue-culturing technique, it abandoned the human embryonic tissue the Harvard researchers had favored—it was difficult to procure—and began harvesting organs from the monkeys that were originally intended to have been infected live during the virus typing. At first Salk's laboratory used monkey testes to prepare tissue cultures; but in early 1952, it switched to monkey kidneys exclusively. The monkey organs were used as the raw material of what became a tissue-culturing operation of factory-like scale and precision. Soon Salk's lab was reporting viral yields from monkey tissue that were two hundred times greater than what could have been garnered from live animals.

By 1953, Salk's lab was using fifty monkeys a week for polio research. Shipments of monkeys arrived regularly from the special National Foundation monkey center in Hardeeville, South Carolina. (The demand for monkeys in polio research around the nation was so great that in order to guarantee a steady supply, the National Foundation had begun to import the primates itself directly from India and the Philippines, hiring experts in trapping, handling, and transport.) Inside Salk's lab, the monkeys would be removed from their cages and anesthetized. Their kidneys were quickly removed and then the animals were killed by an overdose of ether. In the basement, technicians would take the fresh kidneys and mince them into tiny pieces with scissors. The mash was then placed in large stoppered flasks in a suspension of carefully formulated nutrient broth. After four to six days, fresh nutrient was added and the kidney tissue was "seeded" with one of the three types of poliovirus. In the warm incubator room—kept at near human-body temperature—the seeded flasks were placed on specially designed stainless steel shelves that resembled a minature ferris wheel. As the shelves revolved, the seeded flasks rotated slowly so that the poliovirus would have maximum contact with the monkey kidney cells. Several days later, the flasks would be removed from the incubators, and enormous quantities of virus would be "harvested" from each flask by a gigantic vacuum pump. Then the virus would be inactivated by soaking it for thirteen days in a vat of warm formaldehyde solution, known as Formalin ("cooking the virus" was how Salk liked to describe the inactivation process to laypersons), before being combined with similar amounts of inactivated virus of the other two types of polio to make the final vaccine.

By this time, all serious polio researchers, not just Salk, had switched to monkey kidney tissue cultures. Even Albert Sabin, who had initially been uninterested in tissue culture, decided—after some National Foundation prodding—to convert his own polio research lab to monkey kidneys. In January 1953, he toured Salk's lab so he could pick up some pointers on the new technique.

Monkey kidneys and polio vaccine. The two were now inseparable. For better or worse, whatever was in the kidneys would almost certainly be in the vaccine.

4

The Vaccine that Opened
Pandora's Box

THE KIDNEYS ARE two bean-shaped organs located in the back of the abdomen, nestled between the twelfth rib and the spine, about one-third of the way up from its base. They have important hormonal roles—helping to metabolize vitamin D and manufacturing erythropoietin, the chemical substance that world-class athletes have occasionally been accused of abusing because of its ability to stimulate red blood cell production. But their main function is to extract waste. The two organs act as the primary sewage treatment plants for the body's circulating blood. Millions of nephrons, the kidney's basic functioning unit, comprise an intricate filtration and absorption system that takes in a river of polluted blood, passes it through a series of cellular sieves, removes the waste and poisons, and returns the blood—now cleansed—to the body's circulatory system. The toxins are sent downstream to the bladder to be excreted in urine.

An association between the kidneys and urine may seem to be obvious, but the bodily fluid that defines the kidney is blood. The organ's reddish-brown hue comes from its high degree of vascularity. It is crammed full of blood vessels, a twisting mass of veins, arteries, and capillaries. The kidney is awash in blood, bathed in a constant inundation. Every time the heart beats, 20 percent of the output is sent directly to the kidney through the renal artery. In an adult human, the two kidneys process 425 gallons of blood daily. Cut open a kidney, and whatever is circulating in the blood will be found there: normal metabolites as well as chemical byproducts from drug and alcohol abuse, infectious agents of various kinds, and potentially toxic metabolites. Monkey kidneys, no less than their human counterparts, contain the same admixture of undesirable refuse. They are notorious reservoirs of pathogens. Remove a kidney from a monkey and you reap with it all of the offal circulating through the monkey's blood—parasites, bacteria, unknown viruses—plus whatever microorganisms are actually living in the kidney itself. Monkey kidneys, as one prominent polio vaccinologist, Hilary Koprowski, put it in 1961, are loaded with "dormant" viruses waiting to "go on a rampage" as soon as they are harvested and used for tissue culture. Said another researcher, Leonard Hayflick, testifying before Congress in 1972: A monkey kidney is "a veritable storehouse for the most dangerous kinds of contaminating viruses. . . . the 'dirtiest' organ known."

Despite their unsavory reputation, monkey kidneys were the organs of choice for Salk and almost all others interested in the production of polio vaccine. Hayflick, formerly a senior researcher at the Wistar Institute in Philadelphia and Stanford University, recalls that he once spoke to Salk about why he and other polio vaccine researchers chose to use monkey kidneys for vaccine research and production. Although Salk testified before Congress in 1955 that the choice of monkey kidneys had been the result of a deliberate search to find the tissue that supported viral growth, Hayflick believes the choice of both animal and organ was made much more by default. "No one sat around the blackboard and listed the options. It was simply common sense," he says. Human tissues such as Enders had used in his 1948 experiments were difficult to procure on a large scale, but every lab working on polio had a large supply of monkeys. In labs like Salk's and others, there were "tons of monkey kidneys downstairs," Hayflick says. Of all the organs one could use for tissue culturing, the kidneys were also the easiest to obtain. Kidneys, as opposed to other large organs (the heart and lungs, for example), were both discrete and readily accessible. According to Hayflick, "a seventh-grader could see it." All one had to do was to anesthetize the monkey, lay it face down and make a deep longitudinal cut up the monkey's spine. After peeling back the monkey's flesh and muscles, the kidneys were easily visible. A few quick snips and the organs were removed.

Because it was easy and because they were already using the animals, Salk and other researchers turned to fresh monkey kidneys for their vaccine work: virus production, antibody measurements, potency testing—almost all aspects of the research were switched to monkey kidney tissue cultures. Demand soared, and thousands upon thousands, almost all of them rhesus monkeys from India, were imported annually into the United States for polio research. Two hundred thousand rhesuses alone were required in 1955, the first year of full-scale commercial polio vaccine production.

Despite its diminutive stature and appealing face, the rhesus monkey is known for its nasty temperament. The animals scratch and bite, behavior that is all the more dangerous because they carry viruses that are dangerous to humans. In 1932, William Brebner, a promising bacteriologist, was bitten by a rhesus monkey at the Rockefeller Institute laboratories in New York City and died seventeen days later from a paralytic disease that immobilized his legs, then the rest of his body until he was finally no longer able to breathe. He choked to death. Albert Sabin, then a young researcher who had just started work at the institute, determined that Brebner's death was caused by an unknown, new virus that had stripped the protective myelin sheathing off his nerve cells. The new virus was dubbed Monkey B, in homage to its first victim, and has remained a threat to laboratory workers ever since. A researcher at the Yerkes Primate Center in Atlanta died of the disease as recently as 1997. She had inadvertently been splashed in the eye with urine from an infected monkey.

In the 1950s, as far as anyone knew, B virus was the only dangerous virus monkeys carried. But as Salk and other polio researchers began monkey kidney tissue culturing in earnest, it soon became apparent that rhesus monkeys harbored many other exotic viruses. Seemingly healthy monkeys were killed, their kidneys removed and minced, and the chopped-up tissue placed into nutrient-filled bottles to initiate tissue cultures. Then the cultures began to visibly degenerate. Whereas healthy tissue cultures could be expected to grow smoothly along the walls of the glass containers, these monkey kidney cultures would often clump together and form irregular clusters. Other times they would form spindly appendages that would waver like feathers if the tissue culture bottle were shaken. Sometimes whole clumps of dead tissue would simply slough off the side of the bottle and float lifelessly in the nutrient medium. Under an ordinary light microscope—the only kind available at the time in their laboratories—researchers could not see the viruses responsible for the bizarre growth and tissue death. But they could see the devastation (called the cytopathic effect, or CPE) that the viruses caused within individual cells: some caused gaping holes, called vacuoles, in the cellular cytoplasm; others caused abnormally enlarged "giant" cells. Infection by others caused the cells to bunch up in grapelike masses of tiny, queerly shaped cells, or cells with obliterated nuclei. There was only one possible source for the viruses—the monkey kidneys used to make the tissue cultures.

Most efforts to screen kidneys for unwanted viruses proved ineffective, and the continuing viral infection of kidney cell cultures became a constant source of frustration for all polio researchers. Infected cultures couldn't be used to support poliovirus growth. Researchers would have to scrap them and begin anew. One researcher estimated that, depending upon the manufacturer, from the late 1950s to the 1970s, at least 25 percent and perhaps as much as 80 percent of the monkey kidneys processed for vaccine manufacturing was tossed out because of viral contamination.

Even with all their problems, monkey kidney tissue cultures were perceived as a boon, not a potential biohazard. By being the first to exploit the Enders tissue culture discovery, Salk leapfrogged all other polio researchers. Enders, who would have had several years' head start on every other polio researcher if he had chosen to put his discovery to work, wanted no part in vaccine development and the entanglements with the National Foundation it entailed. Albert Sabin would not fully utilize the new tissue culture technique for his own vaccine research before the mid-1950s. Another potential rival was a Lederle Laboratories group working full-time on a vaccine, but the team would spin its wheels for several years in an unsuccessful attempt to get chick embryos to support poliovirus growth. Thanks to his monkey kidneys, Salk finished his virus typing responsibilities in mid-1951, several months ahead of schedule. He immediately turned his laboratory to research on a vaccine.

During the winter of 1951–1952, Salk perfected his technique for poliovirus inactivation after studying hundreds of variations. By springtime, he had prepared enough vaccine to begin small-scale field trials. During the summer of 1952, more than 150 children were inoculated with Salk's first experimental polio vaccine. That fall, Salk analyzed the results. The vaccinations were an unqualified success, as far as he could determine. Meanwhile, only Harry Weaver and a few other top National Foundation officials knew what Salk was up to.

In January 1953, Weaver asked Salk to come to an invitation-only meeting of the National Foundation's Immunization Committee in Hershey, Pennsylvania, and report on his vaccine tests. The Immunization Committee consisted of twelve of the country's leading polio virologists and four National Foundation representatives. The committee had been meeting since the spring of 1951 and was charged with steering the National Foundation's course toward a vaccine. Salk would be the "new boy" at the two-day conclave, and the report of his field trials was guaranteed to be a surprise. Weaver, Basil O'Connor, and Tom Rivers, the rather crusty chairman of the National Foundation's Committee on Research, were the only attendees who had any knowledge of how far Salk had progressed since he had finished his virus-typing work a year and a half before. It was after lunch on the first day that Salk announced his field trial results: 161 people had been injected with a Formalin-inactivated poliovirus vaccine. No one had been injured, no one had contracted polio, and antibodies in all subjects had been demonstrably increased. It looked as though the young Pittsburgh doctor had a potentially workable polio vaccine.

When Salk completed his presentation, the room divided into opposing camps. National Foundation administrators and officials from the public health establishment wanted to push ahead and start a much larger series of experimental inoculations. "Why don't you get busy and put on a proper field trial?" demanded Joseph Smadel, the head of the Communicable Disease Division at the U.S. Army's Walter Reed Hospital. On the other side were most of the virologists in attendance, several of whom came to the unpleasant realization that the quiet Dr. Salk, whom they had largely ignored at previous gatherings of polio researchers, had suddenly surpassed them with an alacrity that was as unwelcome as it was unexpected. This group found Albert Sabin—who was just beginning his own work on a live virus vaccine—as its chief spokesperson.

Sabin had been studying polio for almost twenty years. He was regarded as one of the country's senior experts on the disease and was outspoken in his belief that a killed vaccine was unworkable. Sabin had a fearsome reputation; he was a ferocious debater and could take apart the research of others, poking holes in almost every aspect of their theories. (One researcher, Stanley Plotkin, would later say that "debating with Dr. Sabin is very much like getting into a bear pit. One does not come out in exactly the same shape as one went in.") Sabin was also openly hostile to Salk, perhaps accurately guessing that Salk was about to challenge him for ascendancy in the polio world. After Salk had concluded his presentation, Sabin mounted a full-scale offensive, engaging in a piecemeal demolition of his presentation. Salk's studies were inconclusive—the boosts in immunity he had demonstrated among his volunteer children proved nothing, since the children had all been previously exposed to polio. To have validity, tests would have to be performed on subjects with no history of exposure.

Salk's antibody data, derived from monkeys, were equally confusing; fig-uring appropriate levels of vaccine dosages for humans would therefore be a vexing problem. Surveys of representative populations would need to be undertaken, a lengthy process by Sabin's estimation. Then human antibody levels would need to be correlated back to antibody levels in the laboratory. It would take ten or fifteen years' work before a killed-virus vaccine of safe and effective dosage levels could conceivably be ready.

Basil O'Connor sat through the Hershey meeting without saying much while the scientists in the room debated Salk's results. Despite the objec-tions of Sabin and some of the other virologists, O'Connor must have liked what he heard. The National Foundation swiftly put its full weight behind Salk. Here, finally, was a polio researcher who had accomplished something.

But O'Connor still had the virologists on the National Foundation's Immunization Committee to contend with. In theory, the National Foun-dation wasn't supposed to back any vaccine without the committee's bless-ing. And most of the virologists on the committee were not predisposed toward Salk. When news about his putative vaccine leaked out in early 1953, Salk became the subject of intense media interest. Articles about the "Salk vaccine" and its discoverer soon were featured regularly in the nation's newspapers. Most of the articles seemed to suggest that, at long last, thanks to the industrious doctor from Pittsburgh, a vaccine was at hand. To some on the Immunization Committee, this kind of news media attention was unseemly; Salk appeared to be a publicity hound, not a serious researcher. It didn't help matters much that Salk sometimes sounded flippant. (Why had Salk decided to devote his life to research? *Time* asked him. "Why did Mozart compose music?" was Salk's reply.) Moreover, most of the virolo-gists on the committee shared Sabin's preference for a live-virus vaccine; they doubted that a killed vaccine was safe or effective. ("Kitchen science" was the derisive term that Sabin, a member of the committee, used to describe Salk's inactivation procedure.) Salk's public reassurances that he would assume "personal responsibility" for its safety were no substitute for hard scientific evidence, especially since Salk had deliberately chosen the most virulent polio strains he could find to put into his vaccine. (In one famous quote Salk, with more than a touch of hubris, said to *Life* that his vaccine "is safe, and it can't be safer than safe.") And even assuming that the vaccine was safe, there was no reason to believe that it conferred any-thing beyond transient immunity.

Rather than attempting to mollify skeptical members of the Immunization Committee like Enders and Sabin, O'Connor decided to sidestep them. In May of 1953, the National Foundation's Research Committee chair, Tom Rivers, convened the first meeting of a decidedly different panel of experts who had been invited to form the National Foundation's new Vaccine Advisory Committee. This group purposely excluded polio experts. Rivers and Joe Smadel, who had both decided several months earlier that Salk's vaccine was the quickest way to beat the nation's annual polio epidemics, were the only virologists on the committee. The rest of the new committee's members had expertise only in public health. The primary interest of these new members was polio prevention. Unlike the Immunization Committee, they had no interest in debating fine points of virus theory. What they wanted was a vaccine. Not surprisingly, under the forceful leadership of Rivers and Smadel, the new Vaccine Advisory Committee quickly decided that a nationwide test of Salk's vaccine should be undertaken during the next polio season—the spring and summer of 1954.

With the go-ahead from O'Connor and the National Foundation for mass tests, the next task was to find a manufacturer capable of producing sufficient quantities of vaccine. Hundreds of thousands of doses would be required—many times more than Salk could produce himself in Pittsburgh. The National Foundation had an exclusive deal with Parke, Davis and Company in Detroit to produce all of the vaccine needed. But once it started production, the company encountered difficulty following Salk's inactivation formula. That led O'Connor to recruit more manufacturers. Five pharmaceutical companies, representing some of the leading drug manufacturers in America at the time, responded to O'Connor's call: Eli Lilly, Sharpe and Dohme, Cutter Laboratories, Wyeth Laboratories, and Pittman-Moore.

At a meeting in November 1953, O'Connor informed the manufacturers that anyone who agreed to produce vaccine for the field trials had to supply it to the National Foundation at cost. But once the vaccine was licensed, companies would be free to charge their standard markup of 300 percent. How much would it cost the companies in royalties and patent fees, someone wanted to know? Nothing, O'Connor explained. As a nonprofit, philanthropic organization, the National Foundation forbade researchers from patenting or receiving royalties from discoveries made as a result of its research grants. There would be no up-front fees. Now everyone was interested in producing Salk's vaccine. "That was some meeting," O'Connor later said. "I asked one of the company presidents, just for fun, how effective the stuff [Salk's vaccine] would have to be for him to want to sell it to the public. He said, 'Oh, maybe 25 percent.' And someone else said, 'Perhaps 15 percent.' " O'Connor was in his own words "stupefied" by the response to his offhand inquiry. The manufacturers were willing to sell to a desperate public—for a hefty profit—a vaccine that they believed might fail 75 or 85 times out of a hundred. The meeting ended with an agreement that all manufacturers would try their hand at producing Salk's vaccine, some no doubt eagerly anticipating future windfalls should the field trials be successful.

At the same time the National Foundation was recruiting additional manufacturers, it also decided to reach out to the federal government. The Eisenhower administration, which had displayed a laissez-faire attitude toward health care in general, had shown little interest in the battle against polio, hoping instead that the National Foundation would solve the problem. There was some justification for this hands-off attitude. Strictly speaking, the National Foundation's planned field trials were a private affair. Since the vaccine being tested was still an experimental product and was not being offered for sale, there were no federal licensing requirements attached to it. But O'Connor, Rivers, and a few other forward-thinking National Foundation officials realized that there was one obligation related to polio vaccine from which the federal government could not escape. Sooner or later, a vaccine would prove to be effective, and the pharmaceutical houses would want to sell it. But only the National Institutes of Health—not the National Foundation—could license a commercially distributed drug or vaccine.

Responsibility for the regulation of biologic products, including vaccines, had been given to the federal government in 1902 after a contaminated antidiphtheria preparation had left several St. Louis children dead from tetanus. Under the law, which was essentially unchanged five decades later, the Public Health Service was responsible for licensing and prescribing regulations for any biologic product that was bought or sold within the United States. In 1937, responsibility for administering the law had been assigned to the brand-new Laboratory of Biologics Control (LBC), which had been established as a division of the National Microbiological Institute, one of the seven scientific "institutes" that, at the time, made up the National Institutes of Health. In practical terms, the LBC held the power to recommend that the Health, Education, and Welfare secretary approve or reject any new biologic, including Salk's vaccine. And once a new product was approved for the market, the LBC was responsible for safety testing and any other evaluations mandated before individual lots of the product could be released to the public. In effect, the LBC was the only federal watchdog to ensure that the drugs and medicines consumed by the American people met the law's triple imperative of "safety, purity, and potency." Despite this enormous responsibility, the LBC was still a small laboratory in 1954. It had only forty-five employees and an annual budget of roughly $300,000. There were few professional scientists at the LBC; only ten staff members had medical or advanced scientific degrees. Most were lab technicians and clerical employees.

The National Foundation hoped that if the LBC became involved during the field trial stage, licensing the vaccine would proceed more smoothly. Federal scientists and bureaucrats would become familiar with the new vaccine, would have seen it work, and hopefully would be more inclined to approve it swiftly. With that in mind, the field trial design assigned the LBC the lead safety role: Every batch of commercially produced vaccine used during the field trials was to undergo independent safety testing at the LBC labs in Bethesda, Maryland. Salk would also test each batch in his laboratory in Pittsburgh, as would the manufacturers themselves. The problem with this arrangement was that there were few in the LBC with experience or expertise in polio. The NIH decision in the 1940s to cede polio research to the National Foundation had left the Public Health Service unfamiliar with vaccine science and unprepared to independently evaluate the new product. "Nobody in the Public Health Service knew anything about polio," the National Foundation's Rivers would later complain. "We had an awful time teaching them about polio."

The new partnership between the Laboratory of Biologics Control, Salk, and the National Foundation was strained from the start. LBC scientists were leery of Salk's claims that his prescribed inactivation procedure, if followed correctly, would result in neutralization of every single one of the countless millions of viral particles contained in a batch of vaccine. On the National Foundation side, there was a feeling that the federal scientists were nitpickers bent on causing unnecessary delays. Four of the five new vaccine manufacturers who had expressed interest to O'Connor the previous November had come on board by the winter of 1953–1954 and started to produce vaccine along with Parke, Davis. (Sharpe and Dohme had elected not to participate.) But the new manufacturers were suffering from the same production difficulties that Parke, Davis had encountered the previous year. Rivers and Salk would review the affected manufacturer's production records (called "protocols") and sound reassuring. Nothing was wrong with the technique; it was the execution that was flawed, a missed step here or there that could be corrected. The federal scientists were not so sure. They continually pushed for more testing, especially since some laboratories could not seem to inactivate polio with any consistency. Batches of supposedly dead poliovirus were frequently turning out to still be virulent, an alarming sign that at some of the manufacturers all was not well.

In March 1954, the vaccine manufacturing pool was winnowed from five to two. Wyeth, Pittman-Moore, and Cutter Laboratories had completed only a few preliminary batches of vaccine and were judged to have not yet accumulated enough experience to be reliable producers. That left Parke, Davis and Eli Lilly, based in Indianapolis. On Sunday, March 21, 1954, the LBC cleared for release the first-ever commercially produced batch of polio vaccine. Two cartons of vaccine were flown from Pittsburgh and delivered to Salk. Some of the vials were flown to Washington. Basil O'Connor himself received one of the first injections.

Then came near disaster.

Monkeys at the NIH, which had been injected with just completed vaccine from both Lilly and Parke, Davis, had contracted polio. According to the NIH, the vaccines contained live, not dead poliovirus. William Workman, director of the LBC, was outraged and threatened to postpone the field trials indefinitely until Salk's entire inactivation process could be rechecked. Even if the tests did go forward, he insisted on a dramatic increase in safety testing: 350 monkeys—a sevenfold increase—would have to be injected and sacrificed and their tissues microscopically examined before any vaccine lot would be cleared by the LBC.

Now it was National Foundation officials' turn to be angry. Meeting Workman's demands would be onerous and expensive (monkeys cost fifty dollars each) and unnecessarily time-consuming; they would end any prospect of national field trials beginning in 1954. There followed some tense and heated meetings in which the National Foundation officials and the NIH scientists jawed at each other. (At one point, Rivers grew fed up with the NIH's assistant director, James Shannon, lecturing him about statistics on safety testing and yelled at Shannon: "I've been making vaccines all my life. As far as I'm concerned, you can take your pencil and paper and shove them up your ass.")

Then a compromise was reached. Rather than increase the number of monkeys tested, it was decided it was more important for manufacturers to demonstrate consistent reliability. Eleven consecutive batches of demonstrably safe vaccine would have to be produced in order for any one batch within that series to pass. The new rule was "one strike and you're out." The other safety change was that the LBC would subject all production to much greater oversight. Parke, Davis and Eli Lilly would have to report on every single vaccine lot they produced—including the ones they had to discard—not just the ones they believed were successful. Unfortunately, after the field trials were over, the LBC's stringent oversight of polio vaccine manufacturers was abruptly discontinued.

With this last hurdle overcome, Salk's vaccine was finally cleared for national testing. At nine o'clock on Monday morning, April 26, 1954, six-year-old Randy Kerr, from Falls Church in Fairfax County, Virginia, received a shot and became America's first "polio pioneer"—one of almost 2 million grade-schoolers in forty-four states inoculated either with Salk's vaccine or with identically tinted cherry-soda-red placebo during the next three months. The field trials were the biggest medical experiment the nation had ever seen—and in keeping with so many of the National Foundation's endeavors, they were staffed almost entirely by volunteers, proof of the national commitment to the defeat of polio. An entire army went into battle that spring and summer: two hundred thousand lay volunteers were dispatched into 14,000 schools with 50,000 teachers enlisted to assist in the trials. Two hundred and seventeen local public health departments helped collect data. Twenty thousand doctors, supported by 40,000 nurses, administered inoculations. Blood samples were drawn from 40,000 of the participating children so that changes in antibody levels could be measured. Two million test tubes of blood were eventually screened at twenty-seven laboratories.

Thomas Francis, Salk's old mentor, lent his considerable scientific expertise and reputation to the National Foundation and agreed to act as the impartial scientific arbiter of Salk's vaccine. Detailed reports on every participating child were sent to Francis and a troop of evaluators at the special Poliomyelitis Vaccine Evaluation Center in Ann Arbor, which had been established with an $850,000 National Foundation grant. Working out of the former University of Michigan maternity hospital, where two of Salk's sons had been born, Francis and his 120-person staff spent eight months analyzing a mountain of results. Some 140 million separate items of raw data were tabulated on 15 million IBM punch cards so that Francis could render final judgment on the vaccine trials.

Meanwhile, hostilities between Salk and most of the other live vaccine adherents continued unabated. Sabin, in particular, had become Salk's nemesis, a role he would play for the rest of his life. At every opportunity—before the press, at scientific conferences, even in appearances before Congress—Sabin would suggest that Salk's vaccine was not safe and not effective, and that the nation was foolhardy to rush to embrace it. The disagreement between the two simmered openly at an international polio conference held in Rome in September 1954. Sabin was already planning to produce his own experimental vaccine; only his would use live polioviruses, not killed ones. At the conference, his recurring criticisms of Salk were bolstered when a vaccinologist from Sweden, Dr. Sven Gard, announced that he believed that Salk's inactivation theory was "fundamentally wrong" and reported that he had found that if poliovirus were totally inactivated by Formalin, it was no longer antigenic—meaning that if Salk's inactivated vaccine were inducing antibodies, it actually must still contain residual amounts of live poliovirus. Later, at the same conference, Sabin and Salk were asked by Tom Francis if they had concerns about possible allergic reactions to the monkey kidney tissue that might be in each of their vaccines. Salk dismissed the problem outright, while Sabin attacked his rival's vaccine, saying that since Salk's vaccine, unlike his, would require a number of booster shots, it increased the potential exposure to monkey kidney tissue and therefore posed greater risk of allergic reactions.

Allergies aside, there was another potentially significant and almost totally overlooked problem with Salk's vaccine—the very real possibility that viruses other than polio could, at times, contaminate it. Full-scale vaccine production for the field trials had started the previous winter and spring, and right away unwanted simian viruses began cropping up in the monkey kidney tissue cultures used for the production and safety testing of the vaccine. At Eli Lilly, a researcher named Robert Hull begun cataloguing the new monkey viruses that were confounding vaccine manufacturers and private researchers alike. Hull devised a systematic classification system for the new viruses based on the characteristic damage they did to cells. The first one, dubbed SV1 (for its status as the first simian virus characterized) was isolated in early February 1954, after it had destroyed 17 percent of the safety-test tissue cultures that had been set up at Eli Lilly. SV2 was isolated at the end of August, just prior to the start of the 1954 Rome conference. By the spring of 1955, Hull had identified eight new simian viruses from monkey kidney tissue cultures. (Eventually, by 1958, the number would increase to twenty-eight. All of them, Hull reported, had come from mon-key kidney tissue cultures used for polio vaccine production.) The problem was not confined to Eli Lilly. Parke, Davis was reporting contamination problems, as were some of the manufacturers whose vaccine would end up not being used during the field trials, including Cutter and Pittman-Moore. The NIH's testing laboratory in the LBC was finding them; so was the lab at Walter Reed Hospital.

It is doubtful that Hull's work was a secret to the Rome conferees. The world of polio virology was intimate. It lacked rigid barriers separating scientists who worked in the private and public sectors. Virologists, even when they were rivals, would freely share notes with one another. Hull's viruses certainly were no secret to Sabin. Sabin had provided Hull with antiserum—blood from animals that contained antibodies specific to the simian viruses Hull was researching—so that Hull could perform various tests on the viruses. If Sabin was worried about monkey viruses in Salk's vaccine, he didn't say so in Rome, even though Francis's question about the possibility of monkey kidney tissue residues in the final vaccine certainly provided him with an opening to impugn the safety of Salk's vaccine in this regard. Perhaps he felt that attacking his rival's vaccine in public as possibly being contaminated with simian viruses made little sense. After all, in Salk's inactivated vaccine any unwanted viruses were presumably dead, destroyed in the same formaldehyde bath that inactivated the poliovirus. Presumably in his own live, attenuated vaccine, they would still be alive.

On February 22, 1955, five months after the Rome conference and a few weeks before Francis was to announce the results of his evaluation of the field trials, Jonas Salk was the subject of a special edition of Edward R. Murrow's famous CBS television news broadcast, *See It Now*. Murrow traveled to Salk's office in Pittsburgh for the half-hour show, which was billed as an interim report on the polio vaccine. Salk sat behind his desk, which held a huge circular rack of test tubes and a microscope. Behind him was a bookcase full of thick volumes. With his white lab coat and his thick-rimmed black glasses, Salk seemed to embody the 1950s image of the doc-tor. He spoke in a calm, reassuring, yet authoritative voice, as if he were lecturing to the local PTA. His responses to Murrow's questions—which were all friendly—were carefully formulated, deliberate and lengthy, punc-tuated by pauses that suggested careful reflection. Many of his answers were almost soliloquies and had a somewhat rehearsed (or at least oft repeated) quality about them. Throughout the program, Salk seemed to take pains to be modest and self-effacing. He denied feeling any particular exultation or pride at the prospect that his vaccine would work. It had been, he said, two and a half years of drudgery and hard work. At the end of the program, he made a lengthy recitation of thanks to almost everyone, it seemed, who could be linked even tangentially to the vaccine, including John Enders, Louis Pasteur, and the inventor of the hypodermic needle. He finished the interview by insisting his vaccine had been merely "an historical accident, just an occurrence, just in the course of a day's work, so to speak." As was his habit, Murrow listened attentively with his chin propped atop his right hand, from which a cigarette dangled.

Two-thirds of the way through the program Murrow looked up from his cigarette and said: "The only thing I know about this vaccine is that it starts with a monkey's kidney and it ends up going into a child's arm. Could you explain a little to us the process in between?" The question was an occasion for a lengthy explication by Salk of the entire vaccine manufacturing process, beginning with one of several strained metaphors that Salk employed throughout the half-hour. "Just as you know," he told Murrow, "that corn grows best in Iowa, and cotton grows best in the South and rice grows best in the fields of China, so it was found that the poliomyelitis virus grows best in monkey kidney." Without missing a beat, Salk produced a petri dish containing a rhesus monkey kidney, which he said had just been removed from a monkey. Salk spent the next several minutes demonstrating the tissue culture and virus growth processes—complete with a Waring blender, which he used to mince up the kidney on camera.

Then came a surprising assurance from Salk: The monkey kidneys used to produce polio vaccine were free of contamination. "One of the reasons this particular method of growing virus for vaccine is most satisfactory is because it is possible with a microscope—through the glass—to examine the cells to be sure that there are no other agents, either viruses or other harmful influences, present. So that these cells are in a good state of health at the time we shoot the [polio] virus in." Picking up on Salk's earlier farming metaphor, Murrow quipped in response: "That's to be sure there are no cornstalks in the cotton field, is that right?" Not to be outdone Salk replied, "That's right. No boll weevil or anything else like that."

The reality, however, was far different than Salk's reassurances suggested. His monkey kidneys—and everyone else's—were crawling with "boll weevils," monkey viruses that were not visible under the ordinary light microscopes used by Salk and the vaccine manufacturers and whose CPE might not become apparent for weeks. Like every other vaccine researcher at the time, Salk was forced to throw out hundreds of kidney tissue cultures that had spontaneously degenerated because of simian virus contamination. Salk may have believed that all the affected kidneys were discovered this way and that they were discarded rather than used to produce vaccine, but this was not true. As Robert Hull later discovered, the screening techniques and observation periods that Salk and the vaccine manufacturers employed were not capable of always catching the contaminants. It was inevitable, Hull concluded, that virally contaminated monkey kidneys at times were used to grow vaccine and that monkey viruses sometimes were slipping through undetected into the final vaccine.

The truth is that Salk and most other researchers regarded the monkey viruses more as a nuisance than anything else. In their minds, either the monkey kidneys were so grossly infected that they couldn't support polio-virus growth, or they were not, and were therefore perfectly acceptable for vaccine production. If someone proved, after the fact, that some kidneys had been contaminated and that meant a few simian viruses had snuck through into the final vaccine, what of it? Maurice Hilleman, who directed Merck's vaccine research for three decades and was awarded a National Medal of Science in 1988 for developing a variety of vaccines, summarized the prevailing attitude: "You didn't worry about these wild viruses," said Hilleman. "It was good science at the time." According to Julius Youngner, Salk's longtime assistant at Pittsburgh, Salk shared that view. Viral contamination of the kidneys simply wasn't an issue to him, Youngner says. Perhaps Salk assumed the self-evident: If formaldehyde could kill a virus as potent as polio, surely it would wipe out any "passenger" microorganisms that might sneak into the vaccine, whether they were bacterial or viral.

But formaldehyde, as it turned out, was not nearly as effective as Salk and everyone else thought. Several companies had already begun full-scale production of Salk's vaccine. Despite Salk's reassurances to Murrow, none of them had effective procedures to ensure there were no unwanted monkey viruses in the final doses. Tens of millions of those doses would prove to be contaminated.

5

Triumph and Disaster

On the morning of April 12, 1955, on the tenth anniversary of the death of Franklin Delano Roosevelt, Thomas Francis stood before a packed auditorium of scientists, public health officials, and medical dignitaries in the University of Michigan's Rackham Hall and began reading from the lengthy analysis he had conducted of the previous summer's field trials. Salk's vaccine, he had concluded, was an unqualified success. As the official press release that accompanied Francis's report succinctly put it: "The vaccine works. It is safe, effective, and potent." Within minutes of Francis's pronouncement, the news about the field trial results was being carried coast to coast by wire services and radio and television newscasts. Across the nation, there were spontaneous celebrations. Church bells rang, fire whistles whined, and business came to a halt as the news spread. The mayor of New York City interrupted a city council meeting to announce the news, adding, "I think we are all quite proud that Dr. Salk is a graduate of City College." By the next morning, politicians around the country were falling over themselves trying to figure out ways they could congratulate Salk, with several suggesting special medals and honors be awarded to the Pittsburgh researcher. In the Eisenhower White House, plans were already afoot to present Salk a special presidential medal designating him "a benefactor of mankind" in a Rose Garden ceremony.

Around the world, the news prompted an immediate international rush to vaccinate. Israel had committed to the Salk vaccine just days before the

Francis report was released, and now Canada, Sweden, Denmark, Norway, West Germany, the Netherlands, Switzerland, and Belgium all announced plans to either immediately begin polio immunization campaigns using Salk's vaccine or to gear up to quickly do so. Overnight, Salk had become an international hero and a household name. His vaccine was a modern medical miracle.

There remained only the question of a government license for the vaccine. A few days prior to the April 12, 1955, announcement, the National Institutes of Health had asked a distinguished group of physicians, public health officials, and virologists to sit as an ad hoc "Licensing Committee." Despite the intense pressure to immediately license the vaccine, the NIH had to engage in (or at least appear to engage in) its own independent consideration before it told manufacturers they could begin commercial production. The Licensing Committee's unbiased evaluation and imprimatur would ensure that Salk's vaccine had received the scrutiny that any other federally regulated medical product was expected to endure. The fifteen-member committee included Albert Sabin, Salk's chief detractor, along with other notable disparagers of Salk's vaccine. Supporters of Salk, such as Walter Reed's Joseph Smadel, were included as well. Other members predisposed to the new vaccine included a representative from the National Foundation, as well as Francis and his deputy at the Vaccine Evaluation Center. William Workman, chief of the Laboratory of Biologics Control, who had been dubious all along of some of Salk's claims, chaired the committee but did not vote.

As Francis's announcement in the crowded hall concluded, Workman and the committee convened in a nearby hotel room. The conclusion of the Licensing Committee was expected to be swift, and it was expected to be favorable. Standing by in Washington, D.C., on an open phone line was Oveta Culp Hobby, the secretary of Health, Education, and Welfare. The plan was for the Licensing Committee's approval to be relayed from Workman in Ann Arbor to Surgeon General Leonard Scheele in Washington, who, by law, had authority over standards for biologic products. He, in turn, would immediately deliver a recommendation to Hobby to license the vaccine, since only the secretary held the authority to actually license a product. All of this was to be accomplished by 4:00 P.M. so that Mrs. Hobby could sign the manufacturing licenses in front of a cadre of assembled press and photographers who had been alerted to be on standby for the event.

Back in Ann Arbor, however, the committee proved to be less complaisant than originally contemplated. It took the committee more than two hours to grant approval. Sabin, as had been the case for the previous two years, was once again the lead proponent of postponing use of Salk's vaccine until further study. In the end, however, the committee voted unanimously to recommend licensing the Salk vaccine. But the delay meant that Secretary Hobby's press event was canceled. When she finally received the official recommendation from the Licensing Committee, it was 5:15. The press and photographers were gone; only Scheele and a few other staff members of the Public Health Service were present.

The two-hour debate may have ruined the show in Washington, but given the Licensing Committee's mandate to review Francis's entire fifty-page report and the thirty-page production records (manufacturing "protocols") for each of the forty lots of vaccine the manufacturers had presented as ready for release, the committee's consent was astonishingly expeditious. Salk's vaccine probably received the swiftest government endorsement ever granted, before or since, for any medical product.

During its meeting, the Licensing Committee also heard from Workman that there had been a change in LBC regulatory philosophy. Given the expected demand for vaccine, speedy government approval, not rigid government oversight, was now the order of the day. Gone was the procedure used during the field trials—a stringent triple check (tests at the manufacturer, the NIH, and Salk's lab) of every lot. Instead, LBC clearance of lots would be based primarily upon review by two LBC scientists of the written protocols submitted by the manufacturers; occasionally, the agency would conduct some spot tests on its own. Gone also was the requirement that manufacturers prove they had produced eleven consecutive passing batches before any one of those batches could be cleared. Failing batches were no longer reported—if there were problems at vaccine plants, no one outside of those plants was going to know. The effect of these procedural changes was dramatic. During the 1954 field trials, the NIH's deliberately redundant testing had meant that it had taken up to a month for a given lot of vaccine to be cleared; now vaccine was approved in as little as twenty-four hours. Viewed against the backdrop of the live virus problems that had beset almost every manufacturer the previous year, the decision to subject the vaccine to less government oversight now that it was about to be commercially distributed to tens of millions of Americans was both perplexing and shortsighted. It quickly proved to be disastrous.

The first group of Americans scheduled to receive the newly licensed Salk vaccine were schoolchildren. In the fall of 1954, shortly after the field trials were finished, but many months before Francis finished analyzing the results, the National Foundation had announced that it would immunize for free nine million first-, second- and third-graders the following spring and summer. O'Connor had simply assumed (accurately, as it turned out) that Salk's vaccine would work. In November 1954, he contracted with all six vaccine manufacturers to begin work immediately to produce the 27 million vaccine doses that would be required for the next year's free vaccine campaign. One of the companies that was awarded a National Foundation contract was Cutter Laboratories, based in Berkeley, California.

Cutter was a trusted name in biologics. (The company's insect repellent is still a favorite among outdoors enthusiasts.) But producing polio vaccine reliably seemed to present a challenge that the company could not surmount. "The name Salk is a dirty word out here," wrote one of its scientists to a friend. "Every batch of vaccine is a damned research project," said another. For whatever reason, Cutter scientists and technicians were having dreadful difficulties in following Salk's inactivation recipes. It would later be discovered that of the twenty seven lots of vaccine that Cutter initiated between the summer of 1954 and the spring of 1955, one-third, according to the company's own records, contained live poliovirus. But under the new federal guidelines adopted after April 12, 1955, since the failing lots were not submitted for commercial release, the LBC was unaware that the plant was having such problems.

Cutter had been assigned responsibility for providing vaccine for the National Foundation's free immunization program in the Mountain States and the Far West. The day after Francis's announcement and Hobby's signatures on the licensing applications, Cutter vaccine was being administered in elementary schools throughout California. By the next week, mass immunizations with the company's vaccine were underway in Arizona, Idaho, Nevada, New Mexico, and the territory of Hawaii. By the last week of April 1955, almost 310,000 school children had been immunized with the company's vaccine. Meanwhile, the company had sent some free vaccine to its sales force, including a division based in Chicago. And it had shipped an additional 160,000 cc's of vaccine around the country for distribution through commercial channels.

"On April 24, 1955, an infant with paralytic poliomyelitis was admitted to Michael Reese Hospital in Chicago, Illinois. The patient had been inoculated in the buttock with Cutter vaccine in April 16, and developed flaccid paralysis of both legs on April 24." So ran the opening lines of what would become a seminal report by the still fledgling Center for Disease Control. The case of the Chicago infant, which was reported to the Chicago Board of Health the same day as the hospital admission and thence relayed to Washington by April 25, at first attracted little attention at the LBC. Francis's report on the field trials had stated that there had been thirty-four cases of paralytic polio observed among vaccinees, but all of them were attributable to the fact that the victims had already contracted polio prior to inoculation. There was no reason to suspect that the news of this one case of paralysis from Chicago differed in any way. On April 26, an official from the California Health Department called Washington with decidedly more alarming news: six vaccinated children in California had contracted polio within ten days of the first of their scheduled three polio shots. Paralysis was in the arms where they had received the Salk injection. Since classic paralytic polio almost always began in the legs, the site of paralysis seemed to strongly suggest an association with vaccination. All the children had received Cutter vaccine, as had the Chicago infant.

The assistant director of the NIH, Dr. James Shannon, hastily convened a 7:30 P.M. meeting of seven other NIH officials and scientists to discuss what to do, including halting all immunizations with Salk vaccine, regardless of manufacturer. Unable to reach agreement among themselves, at 3:00 A.M. on April 27, the group telephoned Surgeon General Scheele and asked for a decision on what to do about the polio vaccine. Scheele, awakened in the middle of the night, had no immediate answer. Later in the morning, he telegrammed Cutter Laboratories and asked the company to stop distributing vaccine. The company complied with the request immediately; within thirty minutes it had contacted all its distributors. The massive vaccination programs in schools throughout the Far West were abruptly halted. On the morning of April 28, the press reported the news of the withdrawal of Cutter's vaccine.

With the announcement that Cutter was withdrawing its vaccine, there ensued a nationwide panic. The AMA put out a warning to all its members to stop using Cutter vaccine, although regrettably some doctors never received the word. Many states and cities announced immediate cessation of National Foundation mass immunizations, even though their vaccine had come from manufacturers other than Cutter. Local health departments began to track down every single dose of Cutter vaccine, which, it was soon discovered, had traversed the entire country. Throughout May and June, cases of polio caused by Cutter's vaccine spread beyond the Far West and began to appear in every region of the country. The epicenter of the devastation was in California and the rural state of Idaho. Ninety-nine cases of polio would eventually be attributed to Cutter vaccine in California, with the incidence of polio among Cutter vaccinees exceeding the textbook definition of a wild polio epidemic by nearly threefold. In Idaho, with eighty-eight polio cases attributed to Cutter vaccine, the rate was fifteen times greater. Before it was over, the "Cutter incident," as it was euphemistically called in scientific circles, resulted in 260 people contracting polio and almost 200 cases of paralysis. Eleven people died. A devastating epidemic had been caused by two particularly bad batches of vaccine.

After Scheele pressured Cutter into withdrawing its vaccine on April 27, there seemed to be no other official response from Washington to the crisis for some time. Behind the scenes, however, there was a flurry of activity. On Friday, April 29, most of the members of the Licensing Committee, along with several other prominent virologists and medical men, were summoned to Washington. Many of these fifteen scientists had pronounced Salk's vaccine safe seventeen days earlier—now they were expected to decide why it suddenly was not. The "new" committee—now dubbed the "Special Committee to Consider Problems Related to Poliomyelitis Vaccine"—spent two days reviewing data from all six manufacturers. Salk was included on the committee and was thus in the unusual position of being asked to pass judgment on his own vaccine when it was under fire. During the first day of meetings, little happened other than a conclusion by the assembled scientists that the NIH should resume some sort of more regular and stringent safety testing on every batch of vaccine. The Laboratory of Biologics Control's chief, Workman, responded to this suggestion perhaps a little too defensively, emphatically declaring to the committee that the decision to reduce NIH vaccine testing from the field trial levels had been forced upon the LBC because the agency "simply has not had the facilities and personnel and space and equipment or money" to independently test each batch of vaccine. Who was to blame, rather than what should be done, was already becoming a primary concern. It was also during this first day of meetings that both Sabin and Harvard's John Enders suggested suspending all Salk immunizations. No one else was prepared to adopt that position, in part because most of the committee members were unwilling to believe that a link between Cutter vaccine and the reported paralysis cases had been established.

The second day of meetings was attended by representatives from all the vaccine producers. For the first time the manufacturers began to reveal that there were failing lots about which the LBC had no knowledge. The other startling development was a presentation from Eli Lilly's Robert Hull concerning the viral contamination of the monkey kidney tissues that he had begun documenting the previous year. According to Hull, the new viruses were at times compromising the safety tests to detect live polio in the vaccine because they were interfering with interpretation of the tests. "We have almost missed [live] polio [in a final vaccine] because it was tied to one of these wild viruses. It was just caught on the tail end going through," he said. Another Eli Lilly scientist noted that the company had attempted to devise a method to screen out the new viruses but had been unsuccessful. An official from Cutter then speculated that perhaps the phenomenon of poliovirus being "masked" by these new simian agents was the reason his company had failed to detect the live virus in its final vaccine preparations. Two of the remaining vaccine manufacturers stated that they, too, were having trouble with wild viruses during vaccine production. Hull was asked if he thought any simian viruses had made it to the final vaccine. His reply was that he simply did not know—an answer that he acknowledged was far from satisfactory. Every dose of Salk vaccine, it appeared, had become an unregulated and unplanned experiment—perhaps the final vaccine contained simian viral contaminants, perhaps it did not—and no one really knew what would happen if it did.

While the virologists and the NIH officials debated among themselves whether Salk vaccinations should continue at all, there was a concerted effort to persuade the public that there was no reason for concern. On April 28, Scheele was reported as voicing "complete faith" in the Salk vaccine. There was no reason, he said, to believe that the Cutter vaccine or Salk's formulation was "in any way faulty. These children may have already been on the way to having polio." That would be the official line for several weeks, echoed by others within the Eisenhower administration, including Hobby. The president himself weighed in, declaring that he "couldn't be happier" about the fact that his seven-year-old grandson had been inoculated. If Salk's vaccine was safe enough for Ike's grandson, then surely it was safe.

Independent of Washington, similar pronunciations were emanating from the National Foundation. On the day after the Cutter story broke, the National Foundation's medical director, Hart Van Riper, appeared on CBS television and maintained that there was no proof that anything was amiss with Cutter vaccine. "How do we know that these children who have developed paralytic poliomyelitis might not have been incubating the disease before they were vaccinated," he said. "Certainly the vaccine was not in them long enough to protect them." If vaccinated children were contracting polio, it was not the fault of the vaccine; the children were at fault for contracting polio before being vaccinated.

Eventually, the discord between the increasing number of Cutter cases and the bland official reassurances could no longer be harmonized. On May 4, a Public Health Service scientist reported that his own investigations of the Idaho Cutter cases had convinced him the vaccine was responsible. California, by this point, had canceled all vaccinations regardless of manufacturer. Several other states were considering doing likewise. In Sweden, news of the Cutter cases had caused the government to cease its Salk vaccine program. Several West German regions announced they were discontinuing Salk vaccinations; Great Britain responded by waiting an additional year before it began any polio immunizations. Then, at 4:00 A.M. on Saturday, May 7, only hours after stating that "we have to have a lot more evidence before [the federal government] could decide" whether the Cutter vaccine was actually responsible for any paralysis, Scheele abruptly reversed course, issuing the surprising pronouncement that as of May 8, he was ordering a shutdown of the nation's entire polio program until LBC scientists could complete a plant-by-plant inspection of all five manufacturers and ensure that each had adequate safety precautions in place. "The nationwide program of vaccination against polio, so eagerly awaited for so many years, so recently greeted with clarion calls of hope," had, in the words of *Time*, "ground to . . . a sickening halt."

During the next three weeks, amid great publicity, each manufacturing plant was inspected and found to achieve passing marks. Vaccine that had been already manufactured and approved by the LBC was officially rereleased for mass use. In Washington, Scheele and Shannon publicly outlined a proposed new set of safety tests, which, by and large, only involved increasing the amount of vaccine tested at any given stage, along with the addition of more intermediate tests during the inactivation process to ensure that the formaldehyde was actually decreasing the virulence of the polioviruses in the vaccine. The new standards did not include reinstating the procedures of the 1954 field trials, such as the rigorous check by three independent labs of each batch of vaccine and the requirement that there be eleven straight passing batches. Nor did they include any plans by the LBC to repeat lot-by-lot safety tests, and manufacturers would still not be required to disclose when lots had to be discarded because they contained live poliovirus. Despite the Cutter deaths, the lesson—as far as the federal government was concerned—was that there was no need for increased surveillance of the manufacturers.

There followed a lengthy NIH investigation and an official white paper from Surgeon General Scheele to President Eisenhower, but what caused the Cutter deaths was never fully explained. The only clue seemed to be the discovery that some of the manufacturers had neglected to adequately filter the vaccine pools of each type of virus before mixing all three in the final vaccine. The result was that clumps of live poliovirus had been able to escape the supposedly lethal effects of the formaldehyde. While Cutter apparently was the worst offender, several other manufacturers were guilty as well—it had been mostly a matter of luck that they, too, had not released virulent lots of vaccine. Viral "particulates" was as close to an official explanation for the Cutter disaster as any government official, manufacturer, or vaccinologist would ever offer; if there was another, no one seemed particularly eager to find it. Hull's suspicion that the real culprits might have been the unwanted viruses harbored by the monkey kidneys used to make the vaccines was never investigated. (The one outcome of Hull's appearance before the special committee was that whenever manufacturers found new viral contaminants in their tissue cultures, they sent them to him to identify. After April 1955, Hull became the de facto cataloguer of the new simian viruses.)

By June, the NIH had pronounced that all manufacturers (save Cutter, which never produced another vial of polio vaccine) were now turning out safe vaccine. But the nation's polio program was mired in a funk. The Cutter scandal had dragged on for the better part of two months, and during that time Salk and his vaccine were the subject of almost daily page-one newspaper stories, which were no longer laudatory, but alarming. Parents, who had prayed for the day a vaccine would be available, were now anguished. Was the risk of polio greater from the vaccine or from an epidemic? Physicians grumbled that they had been railroaded by O'Connor and the National Foundation into accepting a vaccine about which they knew little. Some of them suggested that parents forgo exposing their children to a medical product that they felt had been incompletely tested. One such doctor was Herbert Ratner, the public health director for Oak Park, Illinois. Ratner decided to impound several of the cases that had been sent to Oak Park for the National Foundation's free immunization program, rather than use it on local children. The vials would remain in his refrigerator for forty years, unused.

Not surprisingly, participation in the National Foundation's immunization campaigns began to fall off. Only 70 percent of eligible schoolchildren in New York City showed up for vaccinations in late May—a sizable drop from the almost 100 percent participation rate in the field trials the year before. According to *Newsweek*, in August—the height of polio season—only one percent of eligible children in New York came for their second polio shot. Around the country the effect was similar. On August 1, *Newsweek* reported that Idaho, Illinois, Maryland, Nevada, Utah, Kansas, Arkansas, and Washington, D.C., had all canceled their free National Foundation immunization programs. Because of the Cutter incident scare, it would take two full years and millions of dollars of National Foundation publicity before parents agreed to vaccinate their children in numbers sufficient to bring epidemic polio under control.

Fallout from the Cutter incident was not limited to a drop-off in vaccinations. Over the next several years, Cutter was sued by dozens of its victims. By 1961 it had paid out $3 million in damages to vaccinees and their families—$1 million more than its insurance coverage. And in Washington, the incident resulted in a wholesale shake-up of the federal health establishment. Oveta Culp Hobby, the HEW secretary, resigned on August 1, 1955. Ostensibly, she left government to return to Houston to spend more time with her ailing husband. But her departure was widely attributed to her agency's poor showing during the fiasco as well as her ineptitude. Surgeon General Scheele was gone by 1956, taking a position as a pharmaceutical company executive. In early July 1955, NIH director William Sebrell resigned, and was replaced by his deputy, William Shannon. Throughout the entire crisis, Shannon had been critical of Salk's vaccine behind the scenes, while at the same time offering public reassurances that NIH testing and procedures ensured that the vaccine was safe. During his tenure as NIH director, Shannon would transform the NIH from a relative scientific backwater to the world's most powerful scientific organization, largely by successfully lobbying Capitol Hill to dramatically increase the

NIH budget. Big science and big government would become increasingly synonymous, with the federal government supplanting the leading role that private nonprofit scientific organizations like the National Foundation and the Rockefeller Institute had played in funding innovative medical research in the first half of the twentieth century.

The bureaucratic makeover occasioned by the Cutter incident extended deep into the NIH. In midsummer, the Laboratory of Biologics Control was dismantled and revamped as the Division of Biologic Standards (or "DBS"); the new agency had nearly triple the number of staff members as the old LBC. To advise the new agency on polio vaccine, the NIH created a permanent, standing "Technical Committee on Poliomyelitis Vaccine." Once again, the six-member panel of scientists included Salk and notably excluded any of the scientists who had doubted the safety and efficacy of his vaccine. Workman, even though he had been persistently skeptical of Salk's vaccine, was not named as head of the DBS. He was, instead, ousted in favor of his former assistant, Roderick Murray.

Murray, a native of South Africa, was a taciturn, inscrutable, and exceedingly cautious leader; under his direction the DBS continued to live under the cloud of Cutter and proved unwilling—some critics would say afraid—to make almost any changes in government policies regarding polio vaccine regulation for his entire decade-and-a-half tenure. As a result, the United States would lag far behind Western Europe in adopting advances in vaccine safety. For day-to-day supervision of the operations of the division's vaccine testing laboratories, Joseph Smadel, the distinguished virologist and Salk booster, was brought in from Walter Reed. One of the scientists he inherited from the old LBC was a veteran government researcher named Bernice Eddy. It wasn't long before the two found themselves on a collision course over the safety and purity of the polio vaccine.

6

Does Anyone Know What's in This Vaccine?

BERNICE EDDY WAS born in 1903 and grew up in rural West Virginia in a town so small it didn't have a high school. Eddy had originally aspired to be a physician like her father and three of his four brothers (the fourth was a veterinarian). But when her father died while she was still in high school, she abandoned dreams of medical school because she believed it was beyond the family's means, deciding instead to pursue a professional research career. In 1927, a few months shy of twenty-four, she received her Ph.D. in bacteriology from nearby University of Cincinnati, which she had attended on a scholarship. Ten years later, after a series of one-year teaching and research fellowships at Cincinnati and three years of work at the world's only research leprosarium, in Carville, Louisiana, Eddy moved to Washington to take a job as a medical bacteriologist for the National Institute of Health in the division that would later become known as the Laboratory of Biologics Control.

Eddy's initial work at the NIH was on pneumonia, which had been the subject of her doctoral thesis ten years earlier, but when influenza vaccines began to be produced in the mid-1940s, she was assigned the task of standardizing tests to measure the potency and antigenicity of the new vaccines, as well as typing flu viruses recovered from various epidemics. By 1944, she was in charge of the LBC's influenza virus vaccine control unit, a position she held for a decade.

In the summer of 1952, Eddy asked LBC chief William Workman if she could expand her duties and work on poliovirus. She believed that it would be only a matter of time before there was a vaccine and that her experience with flu vaccine testing would serve the LBC well. Almost as soon as she began, the National Foundation announced that research it had conducted the previous summer demonstrated that gamma globulin, a naturally occurring antibody in human blood, was effective in providing transient immunity—just long enough for a recipient to be safe during a localized polio epidemic. Since there was still no vaccine, demand for the new treatment was anticipated to be tremendous. Eddy spent four straight months during the winter and spring of 1952–1953, working seven days a week, ten to fourteen hours daily, devising successful potency and safety tests for gamma globulin, in order to ensure that there was a supply available for the polio outbreak expected the next summer. In recognition of her extraordinary efforts she received a Superior Accomplishment Award from NIH Director Sebrell in October 1953.

By the time Eddy was finished with gamma globulin, planning for the Salk vaccine field trials was under way. The LBC and the National Foundation had already agreed on the safety test design, and Eddy was instructed to follow it—a fact that miffed her since she had seventeen years of experience with vaccine safety tests and was accustomed to devising her own procedures. Nevertheless, during the 1954 field trials, she was in charge of all LBC polio vaccine tests. Safety testing every batch of Salk vaccine using the new protocol, she soon became an expert in the procedure. Eddy, however, like so many other LBC employees, was caught up in the aftermath of the Cutter scandal. After 1955, she was no longer in charge of polio vaccine safety and was instead reassigned exclusively to influenza vaccines. Her polio vaccine control position went to a scientist almost thirty years her junior, a young pathologist named Ruth Kirschstein. But the reduction in her responsibilities actually suited Eddy. It allowed her freedom to work with a colleague conducting research on a subject in which she was increasingly interested: the possibility that viruses could cause cancer.

There had been interest in linking viruses to cancer from the infancy of virology. In 1911, a Rockefeller Institute researcher named Peyton Rous had transplanted tumors from one chicken to another by grinding the tumors up and forcing them through a filter so fine that not even bacteria could pass through. Rous injected the resulting extract into healthy birds and watched as they all contracted identical tumors. Rous said the tumors were caused by a virus (which became known as Rous sarcoma virus), but his fellow virologists were slow to embrace his theory. In the 1950s, it still remained well-established scientific dogma that since viruses were cytopathic—that is, they destroyed cells—no virally infected cell could ever be "transformed" from a normal cell into a hyperproliferative cancer cell. In theory, once a cell was invaded by a virus, the cell would be swiftly killed; it could never live long enough to become a tumor cell. No less an authority than Sir McFarlane Burnett, regarded as one of the world's leading microbiologists throughout the 1940s and 1950s, had dismissed the notion that viruses could cause cancer as "nonsense."

One scientist who was not held captive by the accepted dogma was a middle-aged government cancer researcher named Sarah Stewart. Stewart began her career at the NIH in 1936, at a time when the NIH had few female scientists. When Eddy arrived the following year, Stewart sought her out, and the two women became friends.

Stewart's subspecialty was anaerobic bacteria, such as those that cause botulism and tetanus, but she was also interested in viruses. In 1944, Stewart asked for NIH support for research on the possible link between animal tumors and viruses but was told that since she was not a pathologist, she was not qualified. Rather than take no for an answer, Stewart enrolled in Georgetown University Medical School. She graduated in 1949, and, after completing her internship, was appointed to the National Cancer Institute in 1951 as a commissioned officer of the United States Public Health Service.

Now that she had the credentials, Stewart began to pursue viral cancer research in earnest. A Rockefeller Institute scientist, Ludwik Gross, had published experimental results suggesting that some mouse leukemias and parotid (salivary) gland tumors were caused by viruses. Stewart repeated the Gross experiments and by 1953 confirmed that a virus of some sort was responsible for the tumors—a result that her NCI seniors and peers scoffed at. Undaunted, Stewart decided to try injecting tumor extracts from the mice into other laboratory animals, but her own NCI laboratory in Baltimore lacked any efficient way to isolate and grow more of the tumor-inducing virus. Eddy's laboratory in Bethesda, however, was in the business of producing tissue cultures for polio and influenza vaccine safety testing and thus had a ready way to grow all the viruses Stewart could ever want. Stewart turned to her friend for help, and the two women began to collaborate on a series of experiments beginning in 1956.

Stewart brought samples of the mouse tumor fluids to Eddy; Eddy injected them into the rhesus monkey kidney cultures used for vaccine testing, and after a few weeks' time, Eddy would remove the mouse virus fluids from the tissue cultures. At first the pair injected the harvested fluids only into newborn mice and mouse embryos. The results were unprecedented: The mouse virus fluids caused not just the two types of tumors that Gross had described, but twenty distinctly different types of tumors. Then Eddy and Stewart started injecting the mouse tumor fluids into other species of laboratory animals. This time the results were even more spectacular. The mouse virus could cause tumors in many different mammals—hamsters, rabbits, guinea pigs, rats, and several other types of rodents. At Eddy's suggestion, the virus was dubbed polyoma, meaning "many tumors." When the discovery of the mouse SE polyoma virus (SE for Stewart and Eddy) was announced, the pair achieved international recognition. A July 1959 *Time* cover story on the National Cancer Institute played up the newly discovered role of viruses in cancer. "Right now," the NCI's head, Dr. John Heller, was quoted as saying, "the hottest thing in cancer is research on viruses as possible causes." A picture of the two women along with several paragraphs on their research, including an extensive quote from Eddy, followed the Heller quote. The SE polyoma virus was studied by virologists throughout the world, and a whole new field of science—viral oncology—was born.

Stewart's work on the mouse polyoma virus led the NCI to put her in charge of her own oncology laboratory. During the 1960s, she and her team began work on identifying possible viral agents for human tumors, describing some of the first viruses ever linked to human cancers, including Epstein-Barr virus, which is a herpes virus that causes Burkitt's lymphoma, a cancer found mainly in individuals living in sub-Saharan Africa.

For her part, once her collaboration with Stewart ended in 1959, Eddy returned to her lab at the Division of Biologic Standards with nagging doubts. She and Stewart had just proved that a mouse virus could cause cancer in other small mammals. Could a monkey virus do the same thing—cause cancer in other primates, including in humans? Like everyone else who was working with monkey kidney tissue cultures, during her years of vaccine safety testing Eddy had been forced to scrap hundreds of cultures because of viral contamination. Now she began to wonder about the implications of all those viruses. What if there was an undiscovered cancer-causing virus in the monkey kidneys used to produce polio vaccine?

Eddy began to think of a way to test her theory. This was a bold step. No one had ever publicly raised the specter that simian viruses could cause cancer. Eli Lilly's Robert Hull, despite his well-publicized misgivings about monkey virus contamination of vaccine tissue cultures, had never raised such a possibility. In fact, his suggestion that the simian viruses appeared to be neutralized during the poliovirus inactivation process had provided reassurance to most researchers and manufacturers—as well as the DBS—that the viral contaminants could simply be ignored. As one senior vaccine researcher put it, the attitude was: "If there was a virus, it was inactivated by formaldehyde—then the hell with it." The simian viruses were pesky, at times even troubling, but for the most part virologists regarded them chiefly as annoying irritants that delayed vaccine production. The idea that they could cause cancer seemed to have crossed no one's mind—except for Bernice Eddy's.

Acting on her own and with no official support, Eddy began a series of unauthorized experiments with rhesus monkey tissue cultures right around the same time she and Stewart were featured in *Time.* Beginning in June 1959, Eddy took rhesus kidney cell cultures that were being cultivated for vaccine safety testing, froze them, ground them up, passed them through a fine filter, and injected the ground-up extract into newborn hamsters. As a "control" of sorts, she injected another series of hamsters with feline and human tumor extracts.

None of the sixty-five animals injected with the human and cat tumor extracts developed any abnormalities. However, 70 percent of the 154 hamsters she had injected with the rhesus kidney-cell extract eventually developed tumors—109 hamsters in all were stricken. Every rhesus monkey kidney tissue culture Eddy used caused cancers, and every animal that contracted cancer eventually died.

Interestingly, most of the tumors developed relatively late in the hamsters' life spans—seven to nine months after injection—suggesting that whatever was causing the cancers might have a long latency period. The tumors were found mostly at the site of injection, though some hamsters also developed cancerous masses in their lungs and kidneys.

As a second step in her experiment, Eddy extracted three of the induced hamster tumors, ground these up, and injected them into another batch of hamsters. Two of the tumor transplants caused cancer in every single one of the dozens of animals into which they were injected, and every animal injected died within two months as a result of exposure to the concentrated tumor-causing agent; one of the transplants was "passaged" through five different batches of hamsters without losing its ability to induce cancer in every animal into which it was injected. A third tumor transplant caused tumors in ten of twelve hamsters; all ten of these animals then died.

Next, Eddy took the hamster tumor extracts and inoculated them into rhesus monkey kidney tissue cultures in an effort to identify what was causing the hamster tumors. Curiously, when she put the tumor extract fluids back in the rhesus cultures, none of the fluids produced the cytopathic effects that were indicative of the presence of a virus. Eddy's conclusion was that something in her original rhesus monkey kidney cultures—she suspected a virus—had indeed caused the hamster tumors, but she was unable to isolate it from the full-blown tumors. Unable to identify what was causing the hamster cancers, she labeled it with the generic term "substance." Her substance, whatever it was, was both hardy and virulent. The cancer and mortality rates among the inoculated hamsters were staggeringly high. And the tumors could be transplanted from one animal to another with ease, meaning that whatever was causing the cancers, it could survive passage from one animal to another over a long period of time and still be oncogenic.

Eddy was now worried: If her new substance was in the rhesus monkey kidney cells used to make the polio vaccine, why was there any reason to believe it wouldn't be in polio vaccine itself? Every one of her rhesus kidney cultures had yielded this strange cancer-causing substance. If the substance was as ubiquitous and as hardy as her experiments suggested, perhaps it could survive the formaldehyde inactivation procedure.

Alarmed, but also determined to speak out and put her results before a scientific audience wider than just the NIH, Eddy wrote up her results and prepared a manuscript for publication in a scientific journal. On July 6, 1960, she presented her results to her new boss, Joe Smadel, who only a week before had taken over as head of her vaccine safety testing section within the DBS:

> This concerns the induction of tumors in hamsters by the inoculation of specially prepared monkey kidney cells when the animals are newborn. Tumors occurred at the site of inoculation and were not widespread as in polyoma infections. Eventually the animals die.

Smadel, as Eddy was about to find out, was not a boss who welcomed unauthorized initiative among his subordinates, especially if it produced results like Eddy's.

Within the world of virology, Joe Smadel was a force to be reckoned with. He had graduated from Washington University Medical School in 1931 and joined the Rockefeller Institute, and there he had collaborated on experiments with the National Foundation's Tom Rivers, who was considered one the country's top virologists. With the outbreak of World War II, Smadel entered the medical corps and, while stationed at Walter Reed Hospital in Washington, D.C., made the militarily significant discovery that typhus, which was a serious threat to troops in the Pacific, could be treated by antibiotics. Smadel's discovery dramatically reduced the incidence and mortality of the disease. By the time Smadel became Eddy's boss, he had been elected to the prestigious National Academy of Sciences and had moved beyond typhus, perfecting antibiotic treatments for several other diseases, including plague and cholera.

Smadel was a bit of a cowboy—he was not above deliberately exposing himself to a disease and trying out experimental treatments on himself—and he had a reputation for intimidating underlings. Before Maurice Hilleman assumed control of Merck's vaccine development programs, he had worked under Smadel for eight years at Walter Reed. Smadel, Hilleman said in a 1987 interview, was a very tough boss—a hell-raiser who was "dictatorial." Hilleman, who spices his own conversation with profanities, recalled "the only way you got along well with Joe was if you could out cuss him." Smadel was also dismissive of women scientists. "Joe Smadel was not particularly enamored of women scientists in any way," Ruth Kirschstein recalls. "He didn't have much truck with us, to tell you the truth."

Smadel was also a staunch a believer in the polio vaccine. In 1953, he had been one of the first scientists to call for field trials of Salk's experimental vaccine. He had worked closely with O'Connor and the National Foundation to push other virologists to accept it. During the darkest days of the Cutter incident, when there was discussion before a congressional committee about whether Salk's vaccine should be withdrawn from the market, Smadel had been one of its strongest public defenders. The persuasiveness of his testimony and his stature in the world of virology were critical in convincing the panel that it should not cancel the Salk vaccine program outright.

When Smadel read Eddy's report, he was angry. Its implications—that something in the polio vaccine could cause cancer—was an affront to his career. They also were a threat to one of the nation's most important public health programs. By 1960, tens of millions of Americans had been vaccinated against polio, and it was official federal health policy that everyone should be vaccinated and continue to receive periodic Salk booster shots.

About the last thing anyone in the NIH wanted to hear was news emanating from the DBS that once again might scare people away from polio vaccine. It would be a repeat of the Cutter incident, only given the numbers of people who had already taken the vaccine, it would be much, much worse.

Smadel was going to make sure no such news came from his section of the Division of Biologic Standards. He immediately made it plain he would not support any efforts by Eddy to get her results published, and he discouraged her from pursuing the matter further, dismissing the hamster tumors as "lumps." In an October 1960 memo to Eddy, Smadel recalled his reaction when he first reviewed Eddy's manuscript with her during the summer of 1960:

> In August, I reviewed with you some of your experimental data which had to do with lumps in hamsters which had been inoculated with material from monkey kidney tissue cultures. At that time, it was my conclusion, which I stated to you, that you had inadequate data to draw any conclusions whatsoever about the pathological nature of the lumps, the possible viral origin, . . . or the possible relation of the lumps to one or another of the extraneous monkey viruses. . . .

Smadel, in the same memo, wrote that it was his recollection Eddy had stated that her findings "might have something to do with cancer in man." Smadel had berated her for making the suggestion. "It was my recollection that I was not even diplomatic in telling you that you had no basis for [the] statement."

Smadel's outrage in August was a sure sign that Eddy had stepped into dangerous territory. In fact, as Eddy was about to find out, casting doubt on the safety of the polio vaccine was a good way to short-circuit one's career.

Even if Smadel disapproved, Eddy felt she had an obligation to pursue the possible link between the monkey kidneys and cancer—because, as she put it in a 1986 interview with historian Edward Shorter, "children were getting all this [vaccine] and they didn't know what the heck was in this." She began looking for allies but found little support among her peers; few people in the Division of Biologic Standards were prepared to confront the implications of what tumors might mean for the polio vaccine. One of the DBS scientists Eddy approached for help was Ruth Kirschstein. Eddy asked her to examine some of the hamster tumors. After examining the tumors, Kirschstein worried that the tumors had not been caused by the monkey kidney extracts but were actually caused by mouse polyoma virus that had somehow contaminated Eddy's laboratory. Eddy, on the other hand, had already determined that the tumor types caused by the monkey kidney extracts, as well as the microscopic characteristics of the tumors, differed substantially from mouse polyoma tumors. She had also tested the blood of the hamsters that had contracted cancer; none of them had antibodies to mouse polyoma virus. The available evidence, she felt, definitively ruled out mouse polyoma as the probable cause of the tumors. Some other virus was responsible.

Kirschstein, who has since become deputy director of the NIH, apparently had already made up her mind. When Eddy, by then in her mid-fifties, asked the much younger Kirschstein to coauthor a paper on the tumors, Kirschstein refused. In 1999 she candidly acknowledged the rationale for her decision. As a young scientist, "I had to make my reputation," she says. Being associated with Eddy's experiment "was not a very smart thing to do." In fact, shortly after Eddy presented her findings to Smadel, he announced plans to reduce her laboratory space—proof to Kirschstein or any other observant DBS researcher that Eddy's choice of research topics had not been politically astute.

Eddy, however, seemed unconcerned about the career implications of her research. Undaunted by Smadel's reaction to her research, Eddy decided she would simply announce the news about the tumorogenic "substance" to the outside scientific world—and the consequences be damned. Eddy had been invited to speak at an October 11, 1960, meeting of the New York Cancer Society. The subject of her address had been announced in advance as concerning hamsters and tumors. The audience was expecting that the NIH scientist who had achieved prominence for her work on polyoma virus would share some new information about the virus. "I had a pretty good story about polyoma," Eddy recalled. But once she finished it, she added the unexpected punch line: She believed there was something similar to polyoma in monkey kidneys.

The news took the room by surprise and created an immediate stir in virology circles. If there was any truth in what Eddy was saying, then, by implication, the safety of the polio vaccine was at risk—this time not because it was improperly inactivated, but because it might contain some unimaginably dreadful virus.

Eddy suspected that her unauthorized announcement, like her unauthorized experiments, was only going to earn her more enmity in Bethesda. "I knew when I was doing it, I'd be in trouble," she recalled, in the 1986 interview. "I didn't care much if I was, because at that point I didn't care much what they [the DBS] said." Eddy went back to Bethesda, and at first there were no repercussions from her New York speech. But the National Foundation's Tom Rivers had been in the audience that night. Through Rivers, news of what Eddy had said before the Cancer Society made it to Albert Sabin, who then told Division of Biologic Standards director Roderick Murray. Murray was visiting Sabin in Cincinnati and apparently had no idea what Eddy was up to. Murray was not happy and contacted Smadel. Smadel, as Eddy put it, "called me up, and I think if there was anything in the English language, any awful name he could call me, he did. . . . I never saw anybody so mad."

Smadel was, indeed, furious. After screaming at Eddy on the phone, he officially noted his displeasure in a memo to her the same day:

> I have just heard through Dr. T. M. Rivers of the National Foundation, that you are rumored to have said in a New York at a meeting of The Cancer Society, that you had experimental proof that normal kidney tissue cultures contained a cancerous agent capable of inducing tumors in hamsters. Whether you yourself or the audience went the next step to imply that individuals receiving monkey kidney tissue culture material containing either live or dead viruses would develop cancer, I do not know. In any case, you have apparently stirred up a hornet's nest, and there are some who are sufficiently credulous to believe that the use of monkey kidney tissue cultures in man may induce cancer in them. . . .

Determined that Eddy should never again raise the possibility in public that there was anything wrong with polio vaccine or any other vaccine, Smadel immediately placed severe limitations on her research. From October 1960 onward, Eddy was forbidden to speak anywhere without Smadel's permission. Permission, as Eddy soon found out, was rarely forthcoming, and invitations to appear at scholarly conferences were sometimes not even forwarded to her by Smadel. She was not allowed to publish any research without first clearing it through Smadel. Manuscripts were returned unapproved, returned too late for publication, or returned so highly edited that they had been rendered meaningless. Eddy spent six months trying to get Smadel to release her hamster tumor study. Smadel only relented after Eddy appealed to an outside researcher at New York's Sloan Kettering Institute and described how Smadel was squelching her papers.

The final humiliation came in February 1961, when DBS director Murray announced via memo that he and Smadel had decided to strip Eddy of all her vaccine responsibilities. Suggesting that Eddy had expressed her "personal dissatisfaction with the present arrangement under which you are working" and that "[t]his expression of unhappiness on your part has given rise to a great deal of thoughtful consideration," Murray determined that as of July 1, 1961, Eddy would be freed of her "irksome responsibilities" connected with vaccine control work, which Murray suggested were creating "conflicts" with Eddy's tumor virus research. Instead, Eddy would be left free to "pursue your desire for unsupervised, independent research"—even on tumor viruses if she wished—in a newly created DBS Section on Experimental Virology. Eddy was even encouraged to take the next three months off to "visit other centers in the United States carrying on work in your field of independent research." Although Murray's bland bureaucrat-speak sought to sugarcoat it, Eddy's "reassignment" was a deliberate attempt to marginalize her. For a laboratory staff, she was given two assistants—a small fraction of her previous workforce—and for a laboratory space she was assigned a former broom closet in Building 29 on the NIH campus.

The message from Murray was clear. Eddy had gone public with her doubts about the safety of America's premier vaccine and had thus directly threatened the integrity of the Division of Biologic Standards. When she had been engaged in polyoma research, the DBS had regarded her work as a harmless diversion, since it had no implications for vaccines, and the DBS had given her free hand to do as she liked. Her hamster tumor experiments, however, were a "conflict" with her responsibilities since, by impugning the polio vaccine, her research called into question DBS's effectiveness in fulfilling its primary mission of ensuring the vaccine's safety.

Eddy, characteristically, did not go down without a fight. In a blistering memo to Smadel and Murray two days later, she offered a detailed exposition of her shabby treatment at their hands, concluding that "it seems to me that dictators are out of place in a scientific organization where creative work is being done." As to Murray's insistence that she was not capable of simultaneously fulfilling her vaccine control duties and pursuing her interest in tumor virus research, she asserted that there was "no conflict whatsoever" between her official duties and her hamster experiments and that she had been diligent about her official duties. "Any of my assistants can tell you that the control work is always done first—all other work is done as time permits," she wrote. "The guard's logbooks will show that I spend much extra time in the laboratory. In addition, I did writing at home."

There was an even larger issue in Eddy's mind: How could an agency responsible for regulating vaccines not be interested in finding out if the substrate used to produce them might be dangerous? What possibly could be more important than resolving the issue her research had uncovered? As she wrote to Murray:

> The work on the tumor-inducing agent from monkey kidney cell cultures is not unrelated to biologics control since both the adenovirus and poliovirus are propagated in monkey kidney cell cultures in vaccine production.

Her memo went on to request that she be allowed to remain in her current position, "I am intensely interested in biological control work or, I can assure you, I would not have stayed here as long as I have (since 1937)."

There was, however, no dissuading Murray or Smadel. On July 1, 1961, Eddy assumed the "directorship" of the tiny new Section on Experimental Virology. An effort at enlisting the support of the new Kennedy administration surgeon general Luther Terry had been to no avail. As she had done in 1955, Eddy took this second reassignment in stride, deciding she would simply stay on at the DBS no matter what Smadel and Murray did. Although she was never again given adequate laboratory space or staff within the DBS, she continued to pursue research on oncogenic viruses until she retired in 1973 at age seventy. She died sixteen years later in 1989.

If Smadel and Murray thought that by muzzling Eddy they had put an end to rumors about the safety of the polio vaccine, they were wrong. Eddy may have been almost completely isolated within the DBS, but news of her work had been circulating within the scientific community for months. A pair of researchers at one of the nation's largest pharmaceutical houses was already taking a second look at rhesus monkey kidney cultures. It wasn't long before they isolated a simian virus that behaved like none of the dozens of others discovered before it. Almost immediately, everyone in the vaccine world knew about the new virus, and almost immediately, everyone was scared.

7

The Virus Discovered

THE START OF commercial production of Salk's inactivated vaccine in 1955 ended the first lap of the polio vaccine race, but it by no means ended the competition. Live vaccine adherents viewed licensure of Salk's vaccine as a temporary setback and assumed that one of their own vaccines would soon replace his. After 1955, they redoubled their efforts to produce a workable live virus substitute to Salk's vaccine. It was during this second phase of the polio vaccine race that SV40 was inadvertently discovered and Bernice Eddy's mysterious cancer-causing substance was positively identified as a virus.

There were three competitors in this second leg of the vaccine competition. One was a research team from Lederle Laboratories, led by Herald Cox. Another was a team from Philadelphia's Wistar Institute, led by Cox's former protégé, Hilary Koprowski. Albert Sabin, the third contestant, was clearly in the lead. By the end of 1956, Sabin had sifted through hundreds of viral strains and picked some that seemed capable of inducing antibodies, but not disease, in recipients. A small trial on 130 prisoners in Ohio was viewed as so successful that Sabin was ready to move immediately into full-scale field trials. Sabin's research, however, had been funded by the National Foundation (he had received more than $1 million by 1956), and without National Foundation financial support, he could not undertake anything like the 1954 field trials that had led to the national acceptance of Salk's vaccine. The National Foundation, less than two years after the introduction of Salk's vaccine and still struggling to put the Cutter incident behind it, was not in any hurry to push forward a rival vaccine. "The foundation has not given him [Sabin] permission to put on field trials," Tom Rivers told the *New York Times* in October of that year, "but they can't stop him if he wants to finance the tests on his own." Sabin would have to look elsewhere for help. Sabin now put out a call that qualified scientists from anywhere in the world were welcome to test his vaccine.

The country that responded was the Soviet Union. During 1957 and 1958, a preliminary safety trial was completed. Soviet scientists confirmed that Sabin's strains were safe and did indeed confer immunity. In 1959, the Russians began a field trial so massive its dimensions dwarfed anything that had ever been contemplated for Salk's vaccine. In June of that year, they reported that 1.8 million children in Latvia, Byelorussia, and Moldova had been vaccinated with no ill effects. Within a few months, the number of vaccinated Russians had grown to twelve million.

By mid-1960, the Soviets could count sixty million Sabin vaccinees. In the United States, public grumbling arose about the new "front" that had suddenly opened in the cold war. It was the "polio gap," and like the "missile gap," the United States seemed to be on the short end of the tally. There were already public doubts about the efficacy of the Salk vaccination program—polio cases actually increased in the United States during 1958 and 1959, although they were still far below 1954 levels—and it appeared that by embracing the rival live vaccine, the Soviets were once again asserting to the world that, as with economic systems, when it came to matters medical, they had made the better choice. The Soviets had protected one-third of their people against polio in just one year; five years after Salk's vaccine had been introduced, only about half of the American population had been immunized. The Sabin vaccine was more effective than Salk's— 100 percent immunity for life after one inoculation, according to the Soviets. Salk himself admitted that the commercial versions of his vaccine peaked at 87.5 percent effectiveness, and that was after three shots. The Sabin vaccine, which was an oral preparation, was so easy to administer that it could even be given painlessly to babies. The Soviets had already announced a comprehensive program to immunize all infants. There was also the issue of production costs—Sabin's were a fraction of Salk's. And there was the issue of safety—the Soviets reported no side effects among the tens of millions of vaccinees, a safety record that, after Cutter, Salk's vaccine would certainly never equal.

In the viewpoint of some commentators, the American rush to embrace Salk had been rash; the Russians' more considered decision to use Sabin, much wiser. Several producers of Salk vaccine apparently agreed; by 1960, three were poised to begin producing Sabin vaccine the moment it was licensed.

One of the companies that had initially expressed interest in Sabin's vaccine was Merck. Sabin actually produced much of the experimental "seed" stock, used later for his vaccine trials in the Soviet Union, in Merck's laboratories. But the company's alliance with the Sabin vaccine ended in 1958 when Maurice Hilleman, Joe Smadel's top assistant at Walter Reed Army Hospital, assumed control of all of Merck's vaccine development and research. After arriving at Merck, he abandoned the company's involvement with Sabin's vaccine and decided instead to concentrate all polio efforts on production of what he referred to as a "purified" Salk vaccine. By 1960, Hilleman had achieved his goal: an inactivated vaccine of standardized potency that clinical trials showed had 91 percent effectiveness with only two shots, one month apart. Merck was set to unveil the product, which would be marketed under the name Purivax, when Hilleman learned that Ben Sweet, one of the researchers he supervised, had made an unusual discovery.

Sweet had a doctorate degree in immunology from Boston University and had worked as a research associate for Albert Sabin at in Cincinnati for three years before leaving in 1955 to become an assistant professor of medical microbiology at the University of Maryland. Hilleman, who was constantly scouting for talent to add to his team at Merck, offered Sweet a position because of his immunology expertise and the virological training he had received working with Sabin. In 1959, Sweet left Maryland and joined Hilleman's growing research center.

Sweet was assigned to a Merck project to develop a vaccine against adenovirus, a virus that was responsible for the troubling outbreaks of acute respiratory disease and primary atypical pneumonia that were a recurring problem at military installations during the 1950s. Sweet was using monkey kidney tissue cell cultures to grow all the adenovirus he needed to produce a vaccine. Everything was proceeding well until he reached the stage when he began to run tests on his vaccine. The tissue cultures he was using for the tests were degenerating for no apparent reason. When he examined the cells under the microscope, they showed unmistakable signs of viral contamination. Perhaps Sweet had incompletely inactivated the adenovirus in his vaccines and some residual amounts of it remained alive in his final vaccine and were destroying his tissue cultures. But adenovirus produced a grapelike cytopathic effect in infected cells. This virus produced cellular damage of a sort Sweet had never seen before: the cells were enlarged, ballooning in size and filled with holes; in some cases the nuclei of infected cells appeared to have become badly disorganized.

But what was this new virus? It happened that Sweet's adenovirus vaccine had been produced on rhesus kidney tissues. But his tests—ones in which there were unmistakable signs of viral contamination—were being conducted in kidney tissue cultures from a different species of monkey, the African green monkey.

Sweet realized he had stumbled onto a new simian virus that contaminated rhesus monkey kidneys. This one differed dramatically from all the rest. In its natural host—the rhesus monkey—the virus was essentially invisible. It infected the rhesus kidneys but caused no obvious cellular damage. It was not until the mystery virus was transplanted into tissue cultures from another species that it began to grow out—replicate enough to produce a cytopathic effect—and become discernable.

The implications of this discovery disturbed Sweet. It was his chance decision to use another species of monkeys for his vaccine tests that had allowed him to discover the virus, yet it had been contaminating his adenovirus vaccine all along. He realized that if his mystery virus were present in the kidneys of any of the hundreds of thousands of rhesus monkeys used every year during polio vaccine production, it was almost certainly unnoticed. Since manufacturers at the time were using rhesus kidney cells both for vaccine production and for their safety testing, the virus, if present in polio vaccine, never had a chance to grow out and be detected. Very likely that meant that this new virus was slipping through into many batches of final vaccine.

Sweet tested all the adenovirus stock that Merck had on hand. All seven types had been prepared in either rhesus or cynomologus monkey tissues (another species occasionally used for vaccine production). Every one of the seven types he tested was contaminated with the new virus. And in every case the virus could not be seen until Sweet injected the adenovirus stock into the African green monkey kidney cells. Sweet's hunch was correct: Vaccines prepared on rhesus and cynomologus cells were being contaminated with a new "undetectable" virus.

When Hilleman learned of Sweet's unexpected discovery, he was keenly interested. The two began to refer to the virus Sweet had discovered as the "vacuolating agent," in recognition of the characteristic holes (or vacuoles) it created in the cytoplasm of the infected African green monkey cells. Both men realized that it appeared to be exactly the sort of simian contaminant that Hull and others had dreaded—a virus that was present in rhesus monkey kidneys and was essentially invisible, yet able to break through and overwhelm the cells in a new host as soon as it got a chance.

Hilleman decided that Sweet should test polio vaccine seed stock for the presence of the vacuolating agent. The samples Sweet was directed to test were not, as might have been expected, of Salk's vaccine—still the only vaccine licensed in the United States—but the Merck samples of Sabin's experimental live, attenuated vaccine. Hilleman was eager to find some marketing advantage for Purivax. The presence of the vacuolating agent in Sabin's vaccine seed stock would give him that advantage. Because Sabin's vaccine was a live vaccine, any viral contaminants contained in the seed stock—including the vacuolating agent—would almost certainly still be alive and multiplying in his finished vaccine. Presumably, the vacuolating agent would be dead in an inactivated vaccine like Merck's Purivax. Purivax could therefore be called safer than the Sabin vaccine everyone was so eagerly anticipating.

Sweet remembers feeling embarrassed that he had to perform the tests. He knew his discovery was about to be used against his former boss. All of Sabin's poliovirus seed stock—as Hilleman had expected and Sweet feared—proved to be contaminated with this new virus, and at even higher concentrations than had been found in the adenovirus seed stock. Hilleman and Sweet next tested what happened to the vacuolating agent when it was subjected to the same kind of formaldehyde treatment used during the inactivation procedure to produce Salk vaccine. The virus appeared to be totally neutralized. (When they tested actual samples of Salk's vaccine later that year, their initial results were confirmed, or at least it seemed that way; no vacuolating virus appeared to be present in samples of inactivated vaccine.)

Hilleman was in the catbird seat and he knew it. He had stumbled on a very potent scientific fact that might derail some of the enthusiasm for the Sabin vaccine and all other possible live polio vaccines. He decided to unveil the news at the most public setting he could find: the second international conference on live polio vaccine, which was scheduled for Georgetown University in Washington, D.C., at the end of the first week of June 1960. Jointly sponsored by both the Pan American Health Organization

and the World Health Organization, the conference brought together leading researchers and public health officials from around the globe to be
updated on live vaccine progress, including results of field tests conducted
by Sabin, Cox, and Koprowski. Koprowski's field trials had been conducted
in his native Poland and in the Belgian Congo; Cox had tried his vaccine
in Nicaragua, Costa Rica, Florida's Dade County, and Minnesota. But it
was Sabin and the Soviet delegation, headed by the renowned Russian virologists Mikhail Chumakov and Anatoli Smorodinstev, who were expected
to occupy center stage. The trio had appeared at several international scientific conferences during the past year, and at each assembly the news
coming out of the Soviet Union had become better and better—more and
more vaccinees and a still unblemished safety record. The Washington presentation would hopefully bring more good news and provide an American
forum to highlight the reluctance of the Division of Biologic Standards
and the rest of the U.S. public health establishment to embrace what clearly
appeared to be a superior vaccine.

Hilleman had been invited to speak on the first afternoon of the first
day of the five-day event. The fact that the conference was devoted to
promoting a live virus vaccine while he was still championing inactivated
vaccine gave him some extra motivation. It was with some delight that he
coolly outlined the discovery he and Sweet had made. "The question has
often been raised," he said, "concerning hypothetical 'nondetectable' simian
viruses, i.e., those agents which might be present in monkey kidneys but
which cannot be detected by current procedures." To the astonishment of
almost everyone in the room, he announced that Merck had detected such
an agent.

The new simian virus was "repeatedly uncovered," Hilleman said, in
rhesus and cynomolgus kidneys, but because it did not damage its host's
cells, it was unseen until it was put into African green monkey kidney
cultures, at which point, it "cause[s] very marked and distinctive cytopathic
changes." Robert Hull had been apprised of the "vacuolating agent" and
had classified it as the fortieth simian virus, suggesting that, in keeping with
the nomenclature he had established, it be referred to as SV40. (It would
be several years before scientists consistently followed Hull's classification
suggestion instead of using the term "vacuolating agent.") The new virus,
Hilleman concluded, was "essentially ubiquitous" in rhesus monkey kidney
cell cultures, often present in kidney cultures from the cynomolgus, but
almost never present in African green monkeys. Not surprisingly, since all

of Sabin's vaccine had been prepared on rhesus monkey kidney tissue sub-strate, it was present in all three types of Sabin's live polio vaccine seed stock that Merck had tested—the source for all of the final doses of Sabin's vaccine. Hilleman also reported that initial tests that approximately repli-cated the Salk inactivation procedure showed that formaldehyde destroyed the virus's infectivity.

There was no need for Hilleman to state the obvious conclusions: The new virus was alive in possibly every dose of Sabin's (and any other live) vaccine grown on rhesus kidney cultures, whereas it was dead in the Salk vaccine—a variation of which Merck happened to be producing.

In Hilleman's recollection (and in the recollections of others who at-tended), his surprise announcement was the subject of much of the official and off-the-record discussions for the remainder of the conference. As with other controversies that surrounded the polio vaccine, opinion seemed to divide at once into two opposed camps. Hilary Koprowski (whose vaccine Sabin himself had recently attempted to discredit with an insinuation of contamination) voiced the sentiments of one group, suggesting that the importance of viral contaminants in vaccines should not be exaggerated. If one looked hard enough, they could be found in every vaccine preparation of any kind. Undoubtedly, tens of millions of people in the Eastern Bloc by now had been exposed to live viruses in Sabin's experimental vaccines but with no obvious ill effect. The important question, he suggested, was whether such viruses multiplied in human beings. Experience suggested that there was little to worry about, since humans consumed viruses from other species in their food all the time with no apparent ill effect. (Hilleman later rebutted Koprowski in the scientific paper he and Sweet published on the discovery of SV40, noting that Koprowski's argument had little merit "since raw monkey kidney is not ordinarily part of the human diet.") The other side of the argument was advanced by future Nobel Prize–winning virol-ogist, Renato Dulbecco, who had been working with Eddy and Stewart's mouse polyoma virus. He raised the possibility that the vacuolating virus might be akin to polyoma, capable of causing cancer across species lines, and theorized aloud about the possible ill consequences that would develop if vaccines containing the vacuolating virus were administered to newborn humans.

The vacuolating agent remained a hot topic for the remainder of the year among polio workers, yet somehow the news was almost completely ignored by the press—a somewhat surprising development considering the strong journalistic interest in Sabin's new vaccine. *Time,* in early July, noted, "Hilleman . . . has discovered other monkey viruses in oral vaccines prepared by Cincinnati's Dr. Albert B. Sabin. The PHS's Division of Biologic Standards has independently confirmed Hilleman's findings. Whether these viruses are dangerous for man is not yet known. . . ." But other than that brief mention, Hilleman and his discovery seemed to escape public notice.

Behind the scenes, however, the Merck researcher was busy. He visited Washington and briefed Joe Smadel, his former chief, about the vacuolating agent, leaving samples so that the DBS could begin its own tests on the new virus. He also began urging researchers and manufacturers to switch to African green monkeys, the species of monkeys that Hilleman had decided to use for more and more Merck vaccine work because he had grown frustrated with the "dirty" rhesus. ("You cannot develop vaccines with these damn monkeys" was his conclusion about the animals and the plethora of noxious viruses they carried in their kidneys.) Privately, he confronted Albert Sabin with his own suspicions that the virus could indeed be tumorogenic as Dulbecco had suggested at the Washington, D.C., conference in June. Sabin, Hilleman recalled, "was very upset" that anyone would suggest such an idea, but Hilleman assured Sabin that he had already formulated an antiserum to SV40. If Sabin's poliovirus seed stock was treated in an African green monkey tissue culture with the antiserum, all the SV40 would be neutralized and rendered harmless. Sabin's seed would be safe for future vaccine production. All the contaminated lots that had already been produced, needless to say, should be discarded.

In the middle of August 1960, the Division of Biologic Standards convened a conference in Bethesda to discuss its proposed draft regulations for live polio vaccine. Vaccine researchers attended as well as scientists and representatives from leading manufacturers. This was their chance to exercise some influence on the manufacturing and testing procedures to which the DBS would require them to adhere as soon as it granted permission to manufacture live vaccine. Leading polio experts from Britain, which had moved far down the path toward adopting an oral vaccine, also attended. Cox and Koprowski were both invited to the August 1960 DBS meeting but failed to appear. Albert Sabin did. He dominated the meeting, and at times it was difficult to tell who was running the conference, Sabin or DBS chief Roderick Murray. With neither of his rivals present, Sabin was free to hold forth, frequently inveighing against proposed regulations he found too burdensome and interpreting others as he deemed fit. Especially when the issue was the possible presence of extraneous viruses in the final vaccine, Sabin seemed anxious to get in the last word and steer the conference toward a consensus of his design.

The extraneous virus of the day was the vacuolating agent. At this point in 1960, no one had yet connected the vacuolating agent with Bernice Eddy's cancer-causing "substance," though the two were one and the same. (It would be more than a year before Eddy would publish a paper proving this fact.) Yet even without knowing exactly what the vacuolating agent could do, Hilleman's presentation two months earlier on the virus and its implications for live vaccine was on everyone's minds. Within minutes of the opening of the conference, a discussion ensued about the thorny dilemma presented by the new virus: How was one to know whether a vaccine preparation was ever free of viral contaminants if something like the vacuolating agent had been undetected for years by what were considered to be state-of-the-art tests? The manufacturers made it clear they wanted the federal regulatory agencies to tell them what to test for and how to test. Robert Detweiler from Eli Lilly summarized the position:

> [T]he regulatory agency has the responsibility for defining for the manufacturers their thoughts about a particular new agent. . . . We all have degrees of things, and one manufacturer or one scientist may not agree with another as to just what a "microbial agent" means. . . . At what stage do you recognize this is an agent? I believe it is up to the regulatory agency to take some initiative there in establishing the particular point.

Smadel dismissed that position as "passing the buck to the NIH." Federal health officials and manufacturers both had "a responsibility to remain abreast of current knowledge" about how to detect contaminants like the vacuolating agent, he said.

A Pittman-Moore representative countered that the manufacturers needed some certainty: "What we are attempting to do is to give the producers some leg to stand on legally in the event that something goes wrong. . . ." Here was the nub of the problem: If an undetected contaminant, such as SV40, later proved to be dangerous, were the manufacturers liable? They would be in a much stronger position if the federal government were backing them up and if the regulations were crafted so that they were not responsible for anything about which they did not know.

The second day of the conference opened with a special DBS presentation on studies it was conducting on SV40. Smadel, before introducing the studies, summarized his own feelings about the contaminant:

> Now, I would not overdramatize this particular agent. I would merely point out that this is a curved [sic] ball that arrives late in the game and is an example of the sort of thing we can expect to encounter from time to time as we deal with primary monkey kidney cultures. The problem of eliminating extraneous agents from our seed and from our final product will be with us as long as we make live polio virus vaccine by the methods which are proposed.

Having offered his disclaimer about the seriousness of the problem, Smadel introduced J. Anthony Morris. Morris, who had a Ph.D. in bacteriology from Catholic University, had come to the DBS a year before at the behest of Smadel himself. Morris was studying a virus known as respiratory syncytial virus (RS) virus. He and his team had infected a large group of prisoner volunteers with small doses of RS virus and were waiting to see if the volunteers would become ill, when Hilleman delivered his vacuolating agent samples and antisera to DBS. Morris checked his own RS virus cultures—grown on rhesus kidneys—and discovered that, like Sweet's adenovirus cultures, they, too, were contaminated with SV40. His volunteers had all been accidentally exposed to live SV40 in addition to RS virus.

Interrupting his first experiment, Morris decided to undertake a controlled study of SV40's potential infectivity in humans. Isolating the SV40 from the RS virus cultures, he prepared a nebulized spray and squirted it into the nose and mouths of thirty-five of his original group of prisoners. Some received both RS virus and SV40, some just SV40, and some RS virus with neutralized SV40. Throat and rectal swabs were collected for twelve days afterward. None of the prisoners developed obvious illness after the SV40 exposure, but within eleven days, SV40 could be recovered from throat swabs taken from men who had received live SV40. The simian virus was alive and multiplying in their tracheae.

Blood serum analysis showed that, within a month, none of the prisoners who had received neutralized SV40 had developed antibodies, while two-thirds of the subjects exposed to live SV40 had, meaning they had been actively infected by the virus, it had multiplied, and their immune systems had detected it and launched a counterattack.

There were two other brief presentations that morning on initial studies under way at DBS to further characterize the virus, but Morris's was the most significant. His results were directly counter to what Sabin had been reporting throughout the summer of 1960—that his own efforts to find SV40 antibodies in the blood sera of children fed SV40-infected oral vaccine were all negative, and therefore he had concluded that the virus couldn't live in humans. The Morris study said the opposite. His study may still have been in a work in progress, but it was a dizzying development. The assumption for years had been that other than B virus, simian viruses would not cross the so-called "species barrier," infect human beings, and then stick around long enough to replicate in sufficient numbers to provoke an immune response. But this is precisely what had happened in the Morris study. If the vacuolating agent were alive in vaccines, it was quite capable of infecting vaccine recipients.

The ramifications of Morris's presentation weighed heavily on the rest of the conference, which was largely spent debating a proposed regulation that was worded: "Live poliovirus vaccines shall contain no viable microbial agent infectious for man other than attenuated poliovirus vaccine viruses." Sabin pounced on the contradictory results he and Morris had obtained. He suggested that there was no conclusive proof that SV40 was still capable of living and multiplying in humans. Therefore it should not fall under the jurisdiction of the regulation, since the proposed regulation only applied to viruses that were "*infectious* for man." He suggested the standard contained in the proposed regulation should be reversed. Why shouldn't the DBS require proof that the vacuolating agent was infectious *before* demanding its exclusion from vaccines? Murray demurred, saying that he couldn't respond specifically to Sabin's proposal but he certainly regarded SV40 as "potentially infectious for man." Other scientists spoke up, urging caution as the better course: exclude the virus from vaccines for now and study its infectious potential in the meantime.

Sabin then made a statement that he would repeat more than once during the rest of the day. After considering the problem, the conclusion he had reached was this: "If insistence will be made on eliminating the vacuolating agent, then it may not be possible to produce live poliovirus vaccine."

Was Sabin threatening withdrawal of his vaccine, or was he pointing out that it appeared impossible to make vaccines free of SV40? A short while later, Sabin's motivation became clearer. Division of Biologic Standards director Roderick Murray had admitted that "killed polio vaccine must have contained simian agents undetected at the time of preparation and undetected and undetectable after inactivation." Murray's statement raised a fairly obvious question in Sabin's mind: What about his rival's vaccine? Had Salk's vaccine ever been contaminated with SV40? The issue provoked the following colloquy:

> SABIN: . . . [H]ave you altered your requirements for Salk vaccine . . . [to] also require testing for vacuolating agents or are you assuming that the [use of formaldehyde, called] formalinization also removes this?
>
> MURRAY: It does, doesn't it?
>
> SABIN: I don't know.
>
> MURRAY: I believe by the formalinization process this is inactivated.
>
> SABIN: Would it require testing for that assumption?
>
> MURRAY: [*referring to six years' use of Salk's vaccine*]: We have a system that we have here that has been operating for a great many years without apparent difficulty.
>
> SABIN: [*referring to the Soviet Union field trials of his vaccine*]: It may be similarly said that there is also evidence on the basis of use in more than 80 million persons of material prepared from monkey kidneys that has been fed without production of harmful results. . . .

Koprowski's argument from the June international live polio vaccine conference had come to Sabin's rescue. Eighty million Russians couldn't be wrong. If SV40 was in the vaccines being used in the Eastern Bloc and there were no reported problems, why was there so much concern?

A few minutes later, Sabin renewed his objection to DBS policy: Someone should test Salk's vaccine for the presence of SV40. Murray, for one of the few times in the conference, had the final say. Hilleman had already demonstrated that SV40 was neutralized by formaldehyde. That, along with the DBS's "great many years without apparent difficulty," was sufficient reassurance, as far as Murray was concerned, that SV40 presented no threat if present in Salk's vaccine.

The meeting then moved on to a lengthy debate about how long one should hold monkey kidney tissue cultures for controlled observation. During the vaccine manufacturing process, after the initial tissue cultures had formed, some of the tissues were set aside for observation and were not inoculated with poliovirus. The purpose of the observation period for these "control bottles" was to give any simian contaminants that might be present in the monkey kidneys enough time to "grow out," that is, replicate sufficiently to cause cellular damage in tissue culture and thus be noticeable. The expectation was that even if the vaccine had already been made, if there were any sign of contamination in the control bottles, the entire vaccine pool derived from the original tissues should be discarded.

Sabin argued vociferously for, in essence, waiving the observation period. His argument was that his experience indicated that the vacuolating virus was often in "eclipse" in the rhesus kidney cultures—a term that, according to Sabin, meant the SV40 was only in "one out of a million cells," present at such low concentrations that it was not observable, since it was not destroying large numbers of cells and producing visible tissue culture degeneration. At such low concentrations in the kidney cultures, it was, Sabin reasoned, impossible for any SV40 to make it into the final vaccine.

Several scientists at the conference, however, were not sure that Sabin's hypothesis was correct. They expressed their unease about the possibility of such "lurking" viruses. If the vacuolating agent—or any other virus—was present in the monkey kidney cells, even at the low concentrations Sabin was theorizing, it could still be dangerous. They advocated more stringent tests or other, cleaner substrates. In response, Sabin again implied that the proposed regulations were oppressive and that live polio vaccine could not be produced if they were in effect. At this point, Smadel blew up. The presentations of Morris and the other DBS researchers he had introduced that morning had been designed to impress upon the manufacturers that SV40 was potentially a serious problem. Sabin had spent the whole afternoon insisting it was not and that trying to exclude the virus from the vaccine was not worth the effort. Smadel said:

> Whether you make any or not, Albert, whatever reasoning you apply . . . until this matter is settled, for my interpretation of the vacuolating agent, it is capable of multiplying in man. It is not an innocuous agent. So for my money it doesn't belong in the same category [as other viruses]. There will be additional data at a later date, but right now, you can interpret that the way you want to, and I shall interpret it the way I want to.

The two sparred a little longer about the significance of SV40. Smadel pressed Sabin, and Sabin made a surprising admission: he thought any amount of SV40 "massed in the final [vaccine] material that is used in man" was of little consequence. Smadel then stated his own belief that no amount of the virus in a vaccine was necessarily safe.

The DBS meeting concluded without a clear resolution of the issue, and the question of how far manufacturers should go to eliminate SV40 from oral vaccines was left open. The final DBS regulations released in November 1960, however, were modified from the draft discussed during the August conference. The contamination threshold was significantly altered. In the original draft, any "viable" microbial agents were to be excluded from the final vaccine. Now the vaccine only had to be free of agents that were both "demonstrable" and "viable"—meaning that even if there was a "viable" (live) contaminant, such as SV40, if it didn't grow out readily (and therefore was not "demonstrable"), it could safely be ignored. In the end, Sabin had won at least half the battle. If SV40 were in his so-called eclipse phase—alive but not visible—there was no responsibility on the manufacturer's part to detect it and screen it out of the final vaccine.

As soon as she heard about the Hilleman and Sweet discovery, Bernice Eddy suspected the cancer-causing substance she had found in the rhesus cells and the vacuolating agent were one and the same. In July 1960, she suggested to Smadel that she conduct tests to confirm her hunch. Based on what he said the next month at the August 1960 DBS meeting, Smadel was clearly concerned about SV40; however, he continued to give short shrift to Eddy. Smadel was not only uninterested in more experiments, he was determined to prove Eddy wrong.

Anthony Morris, the DBS researcher who first proved SV40's infectious potential in humans, recalls what happened next. Smadel, says Morris, ordered Eddy to bring her hamsters into his office and repeat her experiment: once again inject the animals with the rhesus kidney tissue culture fluids. Eventually, Morris says, the hamsters in Smadel's office developed tumors, just as Eddy had predicted. Smadel, surprised and disturbed by what had happened, called a small meeting in his office. Eddy was not invited to attend. Morris, and at least one other DBS virologist, Lawrence Kilham, were present. According to Morris, Smadel told him and Kilham at the meeting that ". . . we know the Russians are collaborating in the development of . . . [oral] polio vaccine . . . with Dr. Sabin. We cannot let the Russians beat us at this game. Therefore, we cannot release this information at this time." Cold war politics was more important than vaccine safety. Smadel was not going to let the news about the hamster tumors get outside the DBS.

Kilham, according to Morris, was deeply shaken by the idea that Smadel would sit on such an important scientific finding. "I'm leaving this place," Morris says Kilham told him after the meeting. "I will not work under this set of circumstances." Kilham was so upset by Smadel's subversion of fundamental scientific integrity that he told Morris that he not only intended to quit the DBS but that he was also going to abandon medical research for good.

The contemporaneous record supports Morris's recollections. A June 1961 letter from Kilham to an unsympathetic surgeon general's office details the treatment Eddy was receiving at the hands of Smadel and Murray. The letter, written just days before Eddy's ouster from her vaccine control work was to take effect, clearly states that Eddy was, in Kilham's opinion, being muzzled in an effort to keep the outside scientific world in the dark about her discovery:

> It would appear that she [Eddy] is to be handicapped in her present work before this research has a chance to become internationally known, as I feel it will be, in spite of official opposition. You question whether Dr. Eddy's work has been proved. It is clear to me, however, that an official delay has prevented her from giving full exposition of her results to other scientists. . . . Your comment that Dr. Eddy doesn't communicate her findings was amazing to me in this regard. She has tried to do so over and over, only to be turned down. . . . Dr. Eddy's case, to many of us, represents a somewhat Prussian-like attempt to hinder an outstanding scientist. . . .

Kilham left the NIH two days after writing this letter, and, just as Morris states, left medicine for good, switching careers entirely and becoming a respected ornithologist.

As for Smadel, the Eddy affair was a blemish on what was universally regarded as a distinguished career. Smadel died of cancer in 1963 at the age of fifty-six. Morris, who knew Smadel well, insists that at the end of his life he regretted what he had done to Eddy. Perhaps Smadel was incapable of overcoming his prejudice against women scientists; perhaps he could not admit he had been wrong about Eddy's work and that what she had discovered was indeed serious, not trivial. Perhaps motivated by some misguided notion of patriotism, he felt it was his duty to suppress her research since it impugned the reputation of the Salk vaccine, which America had chosen and the Russians had rejected. Or perhaps he believed that so soon after the Cutter incident, news of this new, potentially dangerous, viral contamination of Salk's vaccine would erode public confidence drastically, vaccination rates would fall, and the nightmare of recurring polio epidemics would return. For whatever reason, the scientist who had publicly chastised Albert Sabin's cavalier attitude toward SV40 was unwilling to acknowledge that a dangerous contamination of the polio vaccine had occurred during his watch.

The Eddy affair can justifiably be described as a DBS cover-up—one in which Smadel clearly did not act alone. DBS director Roderick Murray, for example, certainly must have played a part. Even if one were to assume Murray did not know about the specific meeting Morris describes, he certainly was aware of Smadel's general decision to suppress Eddy's research. And if he did not actually direct Smadel to sit on Eddy's research, he was, at the very least, complicit in Smadel's conduct by refusing to contravene it. One other thing is clear: As the Kilham letter demonstrates, discussion of Eddy's tumor findings had progressed as high as the Surgeon General's office. But no senior official in the NIH was listening.

Even with the short tether, Eddy continued her work. Early in 1961, she initiated a yearlong series of experiments that would prove her cancer-causing "substance" was indeed SV40. News of her hamster tumors was finally escaping the NIH and catching the attention of the scientific world. On January 7, 1961, Eddy, in a memo entitled "Tumors in Hamsters Induced by Monkey Kidney Cell Cultures," wrote to Murray and Smadel that at least one manufacturer, Lederle Laboratories, had heard about her experiments and was alarmed about the prospect that something might be amiss with the tissue cultures they were using to make polio vaccine: "This is to let you know that Dr. Herald Cox has learned about this work and he wonders why the manufacturers were not informed about it before this."

There is no record of a reply to Eddy's inquiry. In May 1961, she raised another concern with DBS officials: Shouldn't the division act more forcefully by insisting that SV40 be kept out of all vaccines? She asked: "Since the vacuolating virus is known to be exceedingly stable and its effect on human population is unknown at present, should a requirement be added to the Regulations to the effect that that the vaccine should be free of this vacuolating virus?"

Eddy, of course, had been excluded from the debate that Sabin had initiated the previous summer about whether it was really necessary to screen SV40 from vaccine. Her judgment on the issue was neither sought nor valued by her superiors, but once again her prescience was dead-on: The virus was a threat to all vaccines produced on rhesus and cynomolgus kidneys. Even as she was pressing Murray and Smadel to act, more disturbing facts were emerging about the vacuolating agent. SV40 was far more dangerous to humans than anyone had ever suspected.

8

"We Were Scared of SV40"

FOR MANY MONTHS after Hilleman's surprise June 1960 announcement, SV40 was viewed strictly as a concern for live vaccine and for those who promoted it. In late August 1960, the Public Health Service had chosen Sabin's poliovirus strains as superior to Cox's and Koprowski's, and it was now a given that a Sabin oral vaccine would soon be licensed in the United States. Within the tight-knit world of polio researchers, manufacturers, and health officials—the only people as yet who even knew of the virus—the vacuolating agent was regarded as an unexpected challenge to "Albert's vaccine," a surprise setback that, given Sabin's persuasiveness and inventiveness, would probably prove only temporary. Techniques, such as Hilleman's antiserum, were being perfected to remove it from Sabin's virus seed, and progress toward commercial release of an oral vaccine would continue unabated.

In the meantime, thankfully, there was still Salk's vaccine, in which any simian agent—including SV40—was presumably neutralized by formaldehyde. Formaldehyde was the "old friend"—in the parlance the National Foundation's research director, Tom Rivers—of the working virologist. If it could kill poliovirus, it could kill anything. As long as there was formaldehyde, there was nothing to worry about.

But then, in the spring of 1961, the seemingly infallible safety net of formaldehyde was ripped to shreds. The SV40 in Salk's vaccine had not been reliably killed by formaldehyde. Much of the SV40 in Salk's vaccine was alive, not dead. Countless millions of people had been exposed. In public health circles, the previous year's buzz about SV40 turned into panic.

The events that sparked the panic began with the March 11, 1961, edition of the highly regarded British medical journal, *The Lancet.* In an unsigned editorial, the journal attacked live polio vaccine, stating that the discovery of SV40 "in many seed lots of the vaccine raises doubts about its long-term safety. . . . What little we know about tumor viruses suggests that it is unwise to use a possibly virus-contaminated living vaccine when there is an inactivated alternative"—the Salk vaccine. The following issue of *The Lancet,* March 18, 1961, contained a rebuttal letter signed by a scientist from a government health laboratory and two scientists from Wellcome Research Laboratories, a British pharmaceutical concern actively working on live vaccine. The letter criticized the previous week's editorial because it had failed to mention that no one had actually tested Salk vaccine for the presence of SV40 (Sabin's objection of the previous summer). But at Wellcome, those tests had finally been performed. SV40, according to the letter, was "resistant to formaldehyde," meaning it was not killed during the inactivation process. Moreover, tests of British subjects who had received the Salk vaccine showed they had antibodies to SV40. The SV40 in British Salk vaccine was alive, and British citizens were infected.

The conclusion of the signatories was that since it was possible to eliminate SV40 from the oral vaccine seed stocks using Hilleman's antiserum, an oral vaccine was preferable to a sometimes-contaminated inactivated one, especially since an injection of Salk's vaccine "carries the certainty of introducing directly into the tissue whatever is in the syringe"—including SV40.

As might be expected, the significance of the British finding was not lost on Sabin, who was quickly given a very public forum to announce that his rival's vaccine was contaminated. In mid-March 1961, the House Interstate Commerce Committee held hearings on polio vaccine. The occasion was a hastily drawn request by the new Kennedy administration for a $1 million appropriation to stockpile oral vaccine in case of polio epidemics. Early in March, Kennedy had offered Cuba a gift of Salk vaccine to fight an epidemic raging on the island. Castro had not yet officially embraced Communism, and efforts to woo him were still a political priority in Washington. The Kennedy gift turned out to be an embarrassment when it was noted that inactivated vaccine was useless for fighting an ongoing epidemic, since it could not quickly confer widespread immunity. The Russians, of course, had the real solution to Cuba's plight and that was ample stocks of Sabin vaccine, which they were only too glad to make available, just as they had to their client states throughout Eastern Europe.

Stung by its faux pas, the Kennedy administration rushed the emergency appropriation request to Congress, and it landed at the House Interstate Commerce Committee. Most of the focus during the two-day hearing was the perception that the United States lagged behind the Soviets with regard to Sabin's vaccine. A number of congressmen questioned the government's delay in approving it for commercial distribution.

On the first day, officials of the National Institutes of Health defended the health bureaucracy's deliberate pace toward licensure of Sabin's vaccine, citing in part the danger of rushing to market an oral vaccine that might contain live simian viruses. The DBS's Murray observed that dozens of viruses had been found in the monkey kidneys used to make the polio vaccine. There was little to worry about in the case of the Salk vaccine, Murray explained, "because all of the simian viruses were . . . inactivated by the formaldehyde" used to prepare the vaccine. But there was a very serious problem, according to Murray, with Sabin's attenuated vaccine. "When we come to live virus vaccine," Murray testified, "we have another problem." Since "the inactivation step" used in the Salk process "cannot be applied," the only way of producing a contaminant-free live vaccine was through "an elaborate system of testing," which rendered the entire live vaccine manufacturing process "complex."

One of the most troubling of these viruses, Murray explained, was the vacuolating agent. He related to the committee a brief history of its recent discovery and the fact that it was a frequent but unseen contaminant of the rhesus and cynomolgus kidneys used for vaccine production. However, he assured the committee that the DBS would insist on the "absence of any adventitious agents" from Sabin's vaccine, since this was "the only certain course to follow in order to assure a safe vaccine."

The clear implication of Murray's testimony was that Salk's vaccine already was contaminant free, whereas Sabin's might never be. The next day, Sabin refuted Murray, and in the process, as he had done in other appearances before Congress, challenged the safety of Salk's vaccine. Referring to the newly published British data he told the committee:

> The vacuolating virus . . . has been administered now by mouth to millions of children, and we know from studies that we have carried

out, also from studies that have been carried out in England, that when it is taken by mouth, it doesn't multiply, and it doesn't have any demonstrable effect in the children. On the other hand children receiving injections of Salk vaccine have been found to produce the reaction in the blood which indicates that it was either present in the Salk vaccine in unmodified living form or in very large amounts in the killed form. So the Salk vaccine is not necessarily free from this same agent.

Sabin had publicly played his trump card on the issue. SV40 taken orally was, he asserted boldly, harmless; but in Salk's vaccine it was dangerous. Sabin pointedly did not tell the committee about the Anthony Morris research on prisoner volunteers that had been presented the previous August at the DBS conference on oral vaccine regulations. That research found SV40 did multiply in the trachea of those who inhaled the virus, belying Sabin's assertions that SV40 "when taken by mouth . . . doesn't multiply." Moreover, Murray's testimony from the day before directly contradicted what Sabin was now saying. Both points were lost on the committee.

Within the DBS, some effort was finally underway to look for SV40 in Salk's vaccine. Paul Gerber, a DBS researcher, had been assigned the task of testing samples of Salk's vaccine since the previous fall, but by March 1961 he had tested only four samples in five months. All had been negative. This preliminary work by Gerber had bolstered the DBS's self-assurance that Salk's vaccine was not contaminated with live SV40. Then came the surprise British announcement in The Lancet that SV40 was alive, not dead, in Salk's vaccine—news that caught the DBS completely off-guard, slamming into Bethesda with the impact of an angry spring storm. Suddenly, Gerber was directed to pick up the pace. Beginning in March 1961, ten Salk vaccine samples were tested in the space of five weeks. All shortly proved positive for live SV40, some right around the time Murray was testifying on Capitol Hill.

By early April, Murray knew he had a problem on his hands. On April 10, 1961, he sent a memo to all polio vaccine and adenovirus vaccine manufacturers "proposing" a change in test procedures. African green monkey tissue cultures, the ones Sweet had used to discover SV40, should now be used as part of the viral screening tests. Still, Murray was not actually promulgating any official change in vaccine regulations. For now, manufacturers were free to decide for themselves whether they would look for SV40 in Salk vaccine.

In early May 1961, Gerber completed his experiments. Two things had become apparent from his work. The first was that it took longer than anyone had ever suspected—eleven to fourteen days—before SV40 "grew out" and destroyed enough cells to become visible in tissue cultures. This explained why Sweet and Hilleman's original search for SV40 in 1960 in Salk's vaccine had proved negative. The Merck researchers had stopped their tissue culture observations after only ten days. The second finding was that if the initial concentration of SV40 was high enough in the virus pools prior to inactivation, some residual fraction of it invariably remained alive in the final vaccine. In fact, a theoretical abstraction of Gerber's SV40 inactivation curve suggested that the Salk process might never kill all of it even if inactivation extended beyond the fourteen-day observation period in use. (Hull actually found that SV40 could survive thirty days of formaldehyde treatment.) "In retrospect," Gerber wrote in his published paper, "one can assume that large groups of the population in this country and abroad must have been injected with varying amounts of SV40 during the course of immunization with formalinized poliomyelitis and adenovirus vaccines."

Murray's problem had now become a crisis. Gerber's results meant that the DBS was almost certainly allowing distribution of a vaccine tainted with live SV40. This was a reprise of the Cutter incident—unwanted live viruses in Salk's vaccine, with a potentially dangerous health effect. The situation clearly called for action, not more proposals. The NIH response to this latest challenge to Salk's vaccine, however, was not to act; instead, it summoned a select group of scientists, the Public Health Service's standing Technical Committee on Poliomyelitis Vaccine, to Bethesda for consultations.

The Technical Committee had been appointed by Surgeon General Scheele in 1955, after the Cutter incident. The Committee's mission was to advise the federal government on improving federal oversight of Salk's vaccine. During 1955 and 1956, the six-member panel had been active in redrafting the safety and testing standards for Salk's vaccine, but had been given few responsibilities since. In 1961, it numbered eight scientists. Two of these had no obvious association with Salk's vaccine, but the other six all had close personal connections to the vaccine whose fate they were about to decide. These included Thomas Francis, Salk's mentor, who had declared

Salk's vaccine "safe, effective and potent" in his analysis of the 1954 field trials. Another member was Joe Smadel. Given his role in shepherding Salk's vaccine through the federal health bureaucracy in the 1950s and his decision to cover up Eddy's damaging discoveries about SV40 the previous summer, he was hardly a disinterested observer. Murray and his boss, James Shannon, the director of the NIH, were also on the panel. Both men had a significant career stake in the vaccine that they had been responsible for regulating for the past five years. Another committee member with a tie to Salk's vaccine was David Bodian, an expert on polio pathology. In the spring of 1954, he had played a crucial role in convincing the NIH that Salk's vaccine was safe after the NIH had threatened to call off the field trials.

The final member was the vaccine's inventor, Jonas Salk. Aside from the obvious conflict of interest in allowing Salk to pass judgment on his own vaccine, Salk's indifference to viral contamination of vaccines was also noteworthy. He had followed Sabin before the House Interstate Commerce Committee at its mid-March hearing and had made a lengthy presentation, complete with slides, to support his contention that statistics showed his vaccine remained superior to Sabin's. During his testimony, he never once raised the assumed absence of simian agents in his vaccine as a point in his favor—even though Sabin had just stressed the viral contamination issue during his own appearance before the committee.

It was the opinion of at least one contemporary that Salk was simply oblivious to the issue of viral contaminants. "Salk was off in a cloud," when it came to the issue of monkey viruses, this scientist said. However, another contemporary, Salk's longtime research assistant, Julius Youngner, believes the source of Salk's lack of concern was a fundamental blind spot that he shared with Sabin. "He would never admit there was anything wrong with his vaccine. Just like Albert Sabin," Youngner says. Both men's cavalier attitude toward any potential dangers associated with their inventions was based on their overweening egos, according to Youngner: "They believed their press notices and they acted that way," he says. As far as SV40 was concerned, Youngner says that he believes Salk "didn't think it made any difference. And he also doubted that it was ever in his vaccine."

The Technical Committee met on May 17, 1961, at NIH headquarters in Bethesda. There is no record of deliberations or testimony from witnesses as there is for the similar meetings that occurred during the Cutter incident. The question of whether the members truly engaged in a dispassionate scientific debate about the wisdom of continued use of Salk's vaccine, therefore, can only remain conjecture. Given its membership, however, one may reasonably assume that, at a minimum, the committee was not predisposed against Salk's vaccine. A close reading of the only record of the Committee's work—a five-paragraph report signed by Shannon as committee chair and dated May 18, 1961—supports such a conclusion:

Presence of Vacuolating Agent in Poliomyelitis Vaccine

Studies undertaken at the National Institutes of Health and elsewhere during the past few months indicate that certain lots of inactivated poliomyelitis vaccine, like many lots of experimentally produced live polio vaccine, contain a recently recognized monkey virus called "vacuolating agent" or simian virus No. 40. . . . Indirect evidence suggests that many of the lots of inactivated poliomyelitis vaccine prepared and used in previous years must have contained live vacuolating virus as well as inactivated vacuolating virus. The careful clinical observations made over the years on selected groups of persons who have received inactivated poliomyelitis vaccine and the careful surveillance of the general population receiving polio vaccine indicate no untoward effects can be attributed to this agent . . . At the present time, there is no evidence that small amounts of this agent introduced subcutaneously or intramuscularly in formalinized vaccines are capable of producing disease in man.

What "careful clinical observations" and which "careful surveillance of the general population" the committee was referring to, it did not specify. Most likely this was because the only thing the Technical Committee or anyone else "knew" at the time about SV40 and the Salk vaccine was that so far nothing seemed dramatically wrong with the millions of vaccinees. But there were no published studies, nor were any under way at the time, that objectively and scientifically examined overall health status of the vaccinated versus the unvaccinated population. In fact, there had been no systematic scientific inquiry of any sort on SV40's effects on humans—other than Morris's preliminary study on his prisoner volunteers who had ingested or inhaled the virus. Yet, without any such scientific support, the Technical Committee was willing to take a position that essentially required a leap of faith, asserting there was "no evidence" that SV40 administered in Salk's vaccine was "capable of producing disease in man." The virus was simply assumed to be harmless. In effect, the Technical Committee had created a new health standard for vaccine contaminants: All are presumed benign until proven otherwise.

On the strength of this unsupported conclusion that SV40-contaminated vaccine was safe, and "since steps have been taken to insure that future vaccines will be free of this agent," the committee recommended no change in vaccine policy. Inoculation should continue with present stocks on hand until all the contaminated vaccine was used up:

> The importance of poliomyelitis vaccine in the prevention of paralytic poliomyelitis and the absence of untoward effects from this agent in this vaccine lead the Committee to recommend that the present poliomyelitis vaccination program continue to be pursued with vigor with the materials presently available.

The first official federal health decision about SV40 had been taken. Any new Salk vaccine produced would eliminate the virus, but vaccinations would continue with "materials presently available"—meaning there would be no recall of old vaccine containing SV40. Millions of children would continue to receive live SV40 as part of their Salk injections. As had been the case during the Cutter incident, the official conclusion was that the nation's polio program was simply too important to interrupt, despite a known problem with the vaccine. But, unlike Cutter, this time the federal government would keep the news to itself. There would be no announcement to suppliers and physicians to stop administering SV40-contaminated vaccine. And there would be no warning to consumers that the vaccine they and their children were receiving contained a live monkey virus whose effect on humans was entirely unknown. U.S. citizens were not going to be afforded the chance to decide for themselves whether they were willing to be exposed to SV40; the government had decided that they would.

It looked like the Salk vaccine had dodged another bullet. But before any sense of ease could settle in at the DBS, a new crisis broke. Studies underway at Merck since the previous winter had revealed that SV40—as Eddy's work had demonstrated and Hilleman had originally suspected—definitely caused cancer in laboratory animals.

The cancer discovery was made by a team of researchers headed by

Anthony Girardi. Girardi was another bright young scientist Hilleman had recruited to come to Merck. He had been working as a microbiologist at Children's Hospital in Philadelphia until 1959 and now, like Sweet, directed his own lab under Hilleman's sponsorship. His concern was not vaccines, but cancer, specifically, whether viruses could cause human tumors. His experimental protocol was to look for promising viral candidates and inject them into laboratory animals. When Sweet found SV40 in the adenovirus and Sabin vaccine seeds, Girardi was intrigued. Here was a novel virus to which millions of people had evidently been exposed. Could it be carcinogenic?

In January 1961, Girardi began the first of three experiments with SV40, injecting the virus into newborn hamsters less than twenty-four hours old— just as Eddy had done with her rhesus kidney tissue fluids. The inoculations were either directly under the skin between the shoulder blades or into the brains. By the end of the first week of June 1961, five months after the SV40 injections, one of the surviving hamsters had developed a tumor. By the middle of June, eight of the animals had tumors. Clearly something was amiss. As was the case with Eddy's experiments, many of the tumors were at or near the site of injection, and they were taking a long time to become apparent. Some of the tumors were in the brains, and one was a lung tumor, but most were "fibrosarcomas," small malignant nodules of cancerous connective tissue just under the animals' skins. These appeared to be identical to the tumors that Smadel had dismissed as "lumps" when Eddy had discovered them a year before in her hamsters. Eddy, of course, had been unable to determine the "substance" that was causing her tumors. Girardi could. Tests in African green money kidney cultures showed the tumors contained SV40 and ruled out other potential viral causes. (The reason Eddy had not been able to isolate SV40 from her tumors was that all she had had to work with were rhesus cell cultures which were unaffected by the virus. Presumably, if African green monkey cultures had been available to her, she would have identified the virus a year before Sweet and Hilleman.)

As with Sweet's discovery of SV40, Hilleman was by now monitoring Girardi's progress closely. Girardi's experiment was only half completed; eventually 80 percent of his first group of hamsters would develop tumors. Two additional sets of hamsters would also develop cancer at high rates after SV40 inoculations. Yet, in June 1961, even with only partial results, the implications were unmistakable. The vacuolating agent acted like Eddy and Stewart's polyoma virus: It was apparently harmless to its host, but when it crossed species, it could cause cancer. However, there were crucial differences between the two viruses—differences which implied SV40 was far more dangerous than polyoma. Polyoma's natural host was a mouse. SV40's was a primate, suggesting it might have a much stronger affinity for humans than polyoma. Polyoma appeared to be somewhat of a scientific novelty, having no real public health consequences because there had never been any large-scale human exposure. But nearly half of the American population had been exposed to SV40-contaminated Salk vaccine. And now that it was clear SV40 caused cancer when injected under the skin of hamsters, what would the virus do to humans who had been injected with it? Would millions of Americans contract cancer as the hamsters had?

Sweet recalls the fear that suddenly filled the Merck researchers: "I'll tell you, we were scared of SV40," he recalls. "If it produced tumors in hamsters, it could produce tumors in man." Girardi remembers thinking that his children had just been vaccinated with Merck's new Purivax. Now, he realized, the vaccine was full of SV40—his children had all been exposed—and since he had been handling the virus, he, too, had probably been exposed. What would happen to him and to his family?

Girardi, Hilleman, and Sweet realized they were sitting on a potential public health disaster of enormous proportions. In the space of one year, SV40 had gone from just "one more of the troublesome simian agents"—Hilleman's phrase at the June 1960 Pan American Health Organization conference, where he had first discussed the virus—to something almost too monstrous to contemplate. Something had to be done. Hilleman again assumed the role of Cassandra, only this time the warnings were not about Sabin's vaccine, but about Merck's and every other Salk-type inactivated vaccine on the market. He traveled to Bethesda to tell his DBS contacts about Girardi's hamsters. Smadel, he later recalled, was floored by the news.

The Public Health Service Technical Committee hastily reconvened on June 20, 1961, to consider the latest developments. Hilleman was invited to present the Merck SV40 hamster research to the committee. Admittedly, he had only preliminary results, but it was sufficient evidence in his mind to cause concern. Some hamsters were clearly developing tumors months after exposure to SV40, and the virus was being recovered from the tumors. The cause-and-effect relationship seemed irrefutable: SV40 induced cancer in laboratory animals. It was now known to be a live contaminant of millions of doses of inactivated polio vaccine. Given the stakes—possible human cancer—and the number of people potentially at risk, the only prudent course, Hilleman told the Technical Committee, was to withdraw all Salk vaccines, including his own Purivax. Delaying vaccine production for six months while steps were undertaken to correct the SV40 problem was the only sensible course of action.

Hilleman's reasoning proved unpersuasive. The six committee members in attendance did not share his alarm and doubted the significance of SV40's cancer-causing potential. This was perhaps not altogether surprising given the Committee's makeup. Five of the committee members hearing Hilleman that June day (Salk, Francis, Smadel, Murray, and David Bodian) were Salk vaccine boosters. The sixth, Richard Shope, a Rockefeller Institute virologist, had published an editorial the previous fall in which he had revealed his skepticism that viruses could cause cancer. Reading the Technical Committee's brief page-and-a-half report, one wonders how seriously the committee took Hilleman's presentation. Most of the document concerns DBS tests on vaccine stocks, which the DBS said showed that live SV40 contamination was an issue for only two out of the seven vaccine manufacturers. "Fortunately," the report indicated, even if these contaminated lots were held back from the market, there would still be enough vaccine to continue the nation's polio vaccine program—by now, it appears, the Technical Committee's primary concern. The Merck tumor findings were practically a footnote. Only two sentences in the entire report were assigned to the hamster tumor research, and in these the Merck research was lumped together with the research of the discredited Bernice Eddy:

> The Committee reviewed again the work of Dr. Eddy and her colleagues dealing with tumors in hamsters and the more preliminary report of Dr. Hilleman along the same lines. It is of the opinion that it is too early to draw any conclusions concerning the significance of the reported findings.

With that brief notice, the Technical Committee stated it was "reaffirming" its May 18 conclusions, saying that Salk vaccinations should "continue to be pursued with vigor with the materials presently available."

This was to be the last pronouncement from the Technical Committee on the issue of SV40. It had found the virus not guilty. There was still no reason to halt vaccine production or remove tainted vaccine from the market, even if SV40 caused cancer in Girardi's hamsters. Hilleman had failed.

Did he ever have a chance? One Technical Committee member's later recollection indicates the scant regard with which the committee had considered Hilleman's presentation at the time. At a scientific conference in 1967, Salk's mentor, Thomas Francis, remembered that the Technical Committee thought Hilleman had overreacted to SV40. Addressing Hilleman directly at the 1967 conference, Francis said of his June 1961 appearance:

> I would like to remind Dr. Hilleman of another experience. When he had found that SV40 was occurring in the rhesus monkey kidneys and that some of this was likely to be in the polio vaccine, he argued that this was a fearful thing and that we should withdraw all polio vaccine from the market. Fortunately, the Technical Committee did not agree.

Whose good fortune it was, Francis did not say.

On June 30, 1961, Division of Biologic Standards director Murray wrote to the manufacturers to inform them of the Technical Committee's June 20 deliberations. Unlike the memo he had sent out after the May 1961 Technical Committee meeting, he did not include the committee's final report. He also failed to mention that the committee had been briefed on the Eddy and Merck research linking SV40 to cancer. Apparently, the DBS was not eager to communicate the SV40 tumor findings even to the polio vaccine's makers. Instead, Murray's memo only concerned itself with the results of the DBS tests for the presence of SV40 in selected lots of each manufacturer's vaccine. For the first time, Murray now directed the manufacturers to start conducting their own tests for the virus. Effective August 1, 1961, all manufacturers would have to submit, as part of their protocols, test results that indicated that samples from each lot of their final vaccine was free of SV40. The DBS had finally undertaken a decision on its own without the support of an expert committee to bolster it: Four full months after the discovery of live SV40 in Salk vaccines, it would become official federal health policy to exclude the monkey virus from the final vaccine.

But the Murray promulgation only covered live SV40. SV40 that had been inactivated was still permitted in the final vaccine. It was not until nearly two years later, in March 1963, that a more stringent regulation would take effect—a specific requirement that there be no SV40 in the viral harvest pools *prior* to inactivation. Scientifically, the 1963 standard was a far superior safeguard than the one Murray was now pronouncing. Given

SV40's ability to often escape total inactivation, it was much sounder to err on the side of caution and eliminate SV40 from the poliovirus pools rather than rely on formaldehyde to knock it out during the final phase of the manufacturing process. In essence, Murray's August 1961 testing requirement allowed vaccine production to continue as it had before. The assumption was that the manufacturers' tests as specified by the DBS were sensitive enough to detect live SV40 in the final vaccine. But as with many other assumptions about SV40, this one, too, later proved to be false.

The fact was that in August 1961, no manufacturer could have possibly guaranteed that its virus pools were free of SV40. Every manufacturer was still using rhesus and cynomolgus monkeys—natural SV40 carriers—to make polio vaccine. More than a year had passed since Hilleman had urged a switch to African green monkey kidneys, which were SV40-free. In the interim, there had been almost no preparations to make such a change at any of the vaccine houses—not surprising since the DBS, wrongly assuming that SV40 was dead in Salk's vaccine, had not urged any change in manufacturing procedures. Predictably, no manufacturer was going to go to the trouble and expense of procuring a new source of animals, arranging transport for them, and building housing unless they were required to do so.

Perhaps, if anyone—including the NIH—had heeded Hilleman's counsel from the previous summer, there might have been a plentiful supply of African greens available by August 1961. Instead, it would take until 1963 before all manufacturers completed the necessary arrangements and polio vaccine in the United States was finally produced on an SV40-free substrate. This delay, combined with the NIH's refusal to recall contaminated vaccine, thus unnecessarily lengthened the American public's exposure to SV40 by two years. This tendency to delay, rather than to act decisively, would become the hallmark of the federal government's response to SV40.

9

"The Worst Thing in the World"

As June 1961 was drawing to a close, it appeared that the NIH had weathered the brunt of the SV40 storm. The controversy that erupted after the discovery of live SV40 in Salk's vaccine had played out mostly behind closed doors, with only a handful of federal health officials and vaccine researchers privy to the events. The damage had been successfully contained, and there had been no interruption of vaccine supplies. The lay press had missed the SV40 contamination story entirely, and, other than the *Lancet* letter in mid-March, news of SV40 had also escaped the attention of the medical press. As far as the American public and almost all of its doctors were concerned, the only problem with the polio vaccine was that the Russians were using Sabin's superior vaccine, while, for the most part, Americans were still stuck with Salk's. The possibility that there might be a cancer-causing agent in the polio vaccine was about the last thing on almost anyone's mind.

But in late June, just days after the last Public Health Service Technical Committee meeting, Hilary Koprowski abruptly rent this veil of silence. In a speech before the annual convention of the American Medical Association, Koprowski announced that polio vaccine contained a cancer-causing virus. Millions of vaccine recipients, he said, might be at risk.

Only one year before, Koprowski had publicly downplayed the significance of Hilleman's discovery of SV40. At the June 1960 joint World Health and Pan American Health Organization conference in Washington, he had suggested that monkey viruses in a vaccine were of little consequence. After that meeting, however, his thinking about simian viruses had undergone a profound change.

In late October 1960, he and one of his top Wistar assistants, Stanley Plotkin, sent comments to the World Health Organization division that was drafting international standards for oral polio vaccine production. Koprowski and Plotkin wrote that they had concluded it was time to conduct research that would lead to polio vaccine production on something other than "tissue culture explants of fresh removed monkey kidneys." One compelling reason to abandon monkeys, they said, was the ever-present chance that a virus capable of causing cancer across species lines might be hiding in some of the rhesus kidneys.

In March 1961, when Sabin and Salk testified before the House Interstate Commerce Committee about oral vaccine, Koprowski sent a letter to the committee, warning that the continued use of monkey kidneys placed an insurmountable barrier to a safe and cost-effective oral vaccine. This was because monkey kidneys were "host to innumerable simian viruses," with the number detected limited only by "the amount of work expended to find them." Given the almost universal contamination of the kidneys, manufacturers were faced with the prospect of "having to discard most . . . lots of vaccine," Koprowski said, if they were truly serious about screening out unwanted simian viruses. "This will inevitably raise the costs of the vaccine. . . ." The solution, Koprowski said, was to switch to tissue cultures of virus-free human cells for vaccine production, a technique that a young researcher in his own laboratory, Leonard Hayflick, was in the process of perfecting.

Three months later, on June 29, 1961, Koprowski found a very public forum to raise the issue again, the annual meeting of the American Medical Association. Membership in the AMA was standard for almost every practicing American physician in the early 1960s. The organization and its publications were the premier source of new medical information for most of the nation's doctors. Scientific news released at its annual meeting had great impact on the front lines of American health care and a far greater audience than almost any research-oriented publications could ever hope to garner. Whatever was said before the AMA convention was going to be heard by the nation's doctors.

Koprowski's speech was nominally a review of the status of live polio vaccines, but he used almost half of it to talk about simian viruses, singling out SV40 for special attention and noting that it had been found alive in batches of Salk's vaccine. For most of the physicians in attendance, this was the first notice that, along with the polio vaccine they had been administering for the past several years, they were injecting their patients with a live monkey virus. And if that revelation wasn't disquieting enough, Koprowski proceeded to describe SV40 as "cancer-inducing."

To any AMA member who felt bound by the portion of the Hippocratic Oath that entreats a physician to "first, do no harm," Koprowski was presenting a serious challenge:

> The question may be asked, "Should the discovery of [SV40] cause a widespread alarm among advocates of prophylactic [preventative] immunization against poliomyelitis, knowing that they have unwillingly or, what is worse, unwittingly endangered the millions of individuals who received monkey kidney products containing not only dead or living poliovirus but other agents in the course of vaccination campaigns?"

Koprowski told his audience in one breath that "as far as is known, there is no cause for alarm at present" from the massive simian virus exposure, but in the next added that things were only likely to get worse, since "the next batch of killed monkeys may contain more 'virus surprises.' " In closing, he told the doctors, as he had told the House committee, that at Wistar, a safe alternative had been developed, and he hoped that it would only be a matter of time before the "obsolete methods of slaughtering thousands of monkeys" for their tissues would be replaced by use of these new substrates, composed of clean, virus-free, human cell strains.

Four decades later, Koprowski, who still retains a distinct Polish accent (he fled Poland in 1939 after the Nazi invasion), proudly remembers his 1961 AMA appearance because "it put me on a stand for a clean vaccine. It was my position from then on: Make it safe!" He had, in effect, demanded that the nation's medical community react to the use of contaminated polio vaccines, rightly assuming that most of them did not wish to "unwillingly" or "unwittingly" expose their patients to possible carcinogens.

The AMA as a body took no stand on the issue, but news about SV40 began to spread through the medical community and was soon being reported in the popular medical press. "Pediatricians were really exercised about this. It was no minor thing," says Salk colleague Julius Youngner of the reaction of many doctors to the unwelcome development. Vaccine researchers were upset, too. Eddy's paper on the cancer-causing rhesus kidney tissue culture fluids was finally published in a scientific journal in May 1961. When it appeared, Eddy's paper "was disturbing to many people," Robert Hull later wrote. "It caused a great concern in our laboratory [vaccine manufacturer, Eli Lilly] in respect to whether or not our established monkey kidney strains possessed such properties."

Thanks to Eddy's research and Koprowski's AMA appearance a month later, SV40 was no longer just an insiders' secret. It had become a public health and public relations issue that could no longer be ignored. Pressure began to build on Washington for some answers.

On July 7, 1961, eight days after Koprowski's speech before the AMA, the DBS issued its first public statement on the virus:

Statement on Monkey Viruses in Relation to Salk Vaccine

Approximately one year ago a new monkey virus was reported as being present in some Rhesus monkeys. This virus was designated "vacuolating virus" or SV40 and was the fortieth in the line of monkey viruses which had thus far been isolated and studied. . . . Although the initial information had indicated that the formaldehyde inactivation step used in the manufacture of Salk vaccine would inactivate the vacuolating virus as well as poliovirus . . . it became apparent that the vacuolating agent was present in small amounts in some lots of vaccine. This is the only virus which is known to have survived the inactivation process.

Presumably, readers of the DBS statement were to feel a sense of relief that the DBS had discovered only "small amounts" of live SV40 in vaccine and that thus far it had proven to be "the only virus known to have survived the inactivation process." (Exactly why, if one had slipped through, others could not, was never addressed.) The next two paragraphs of the DBS statement offered the same reassurances—word for word—that had been contained in the Technical Committee's May 18, 1961, report: "careful clinical observations made over the years on selected groups of persons" and "careful surveillance of the general population receiving polio vaccine" indicated that "no untoward effects can be attributed to this agent." There was "no evidence" that when present in vaccines SV40 was "capable of producing disease in man."

In the remainder of the press statement, the DBS reported on the work of the Technical Committee, relating that the Committee had met and "reviewed the work of Dr. Eddy . . . as well as that of other investigators performing similar studies" and had found it "too early to draw any conclusions concerning the significance of the reported findings."

The "other investigators" were, of course, Hilleman, Girardi, and Sweet. But specific reference to Hilleman and his team was omitted in the DBS public statement. It is doubtful the reason was that the agency wished to spare him or Merck embarrassment. Rather, the DBS likely feared that linking Hilleman to reports of SV40-induced tumors would have greatly increased the credence lent to any such research. Hilleman was highly regarded in the lay press and frequently quoted as an expert in news articles on vaccines. If his name had been associated with reports of SV40 and cancer, it is reasonable to suppose that more press attention would have been paid to the entire issue than subsequently proved to be the case. The DBS release concluded with the news that, based on the Technical Committee's recommendation, the agency had decided not to halt vaccinations or withdraw vaccine. The final paragraph included a reassuring statement that even with the contamination problem, it appeared there was still more than enough SV40-free vaccine to go around.

The first notice to the general public about SV40 came in a July 25, 1961, Associated Press story announcing the surprise cessation of Salk vaccine production by both Parke, Davis and Merck. The story ran in the *New York Times* on page 26. Its placement in the newspaper and the fact that the *Times* did not assign any of the several science writers on its staff familiar with polio to cover the story suggests that the DBS's effort to downplay SV40 had paid off. The AP article quoted directly from the DBS press release in several places; the *Times* subhead to the story said SV40 was "believed harmless," and the body of the story repeated the NIH reassurance that "there was no evidence that small amounts [of SV40] when introduced through the vaccine produced illness in man." The words "cancer" and "tumor" never appeared in the AP write-up.

The story behind the story was much more interesting. Merck had stopped shipping Purivax as soon as its own tests in May 1961 confirmed that the vaccine was contaminated with live SV40. Its unilateral withdrawal of vaccine from the market had not been well received by the DBS. If Merck recalled vaccine, then everyone else would have to. That would have resulted in public panic and would have run counter to the Technical Committee's May 18 directive that polio vaccinations "continue to be pursued with vigor with the materials presently available." In June, after the Girardi cancer results had come in, Hilleman had tried one more time to get all vaccine production halted. That suggestion, as we have seen, was rebuffed. Merck had already suspended production and was trying to figure out how to screen SV40 out of the vaccine when DBS tests on vaccine samples indicated that Parke, Davis supplies were also badly contaminated. Parke, Davis now also stopped vaccine manufacture. The truth was that by the time the Associated Press reported the "news" in late July, both companies had not produced vaccine for several weeks. Parke, Davis eventually resumed production, but Merck would soon decide that producing a polio vaccine that at times might be contaminated was not worth the risk. In vaccine circles, Purivax was now derisively being called "Impurivax," and Ben Sweet was labeled the "million dollar man" because that was the cost of the vaccine program that had just been killed by his discovery of SV40.

If the mainstream press was inclined to repeat the government's line on SV40, there was one news outlet that was not. The *National Enquirer* was (and still is) not necessarily regarded as a reliable source of hard news, but its August 6–12, 1961, edition carried that year's most thorough public airing of SV40 contamination—albeit with the paper's trademark sensationalism. On the newspaper's cover was a full-page photograph of a hypodermic needle with an enormous headline superimposed on it. "The Great Polio Vaccine Cancer Cover-Up," the headline ran in boldface type an inch and a half high. In smaller type, underneath the headline, the cover proclaimed: "The polio shots you have taken may KILL you! Medical researchers know it. The U.S. government knows it. But the terrifying facts have been hidden from YOU—until now." The inside story ran three pages and included a concise and accurate recounting of the highlights of Eddy's hamster experiments. The *Enquirer* story was the first to stress that although the NIH had termed SV40 harmless, the agency had made a point of forbidding release of any vaccines that contained it.

Despite its tabloid status, the *Enquirer* managed to obtain a series of remarkable quotes about SV40 and polio vaccine. A spokesperson for Merck said of SV40, according to the *Enquirer:* "We'll have this virus licked in several weeks"—an assertion of transparent insincerity, since the company was about to relinquish polio vaccine production entirely. A Scottish virologist, Dr. Norman R. Grist, of Ruchill Hospital in Glasgow, was quoted as saying that it was "reasonable to conjecture that there is some connection between these [simian] viruses and the incidence of leukemia," thus becoming the first health or medical official to take a public position that contaminated vaccine could cause human disease. Arlene Butterfly, information officer for the DBS, was asked by the newspaper whether persons taking the vaccine were facing a choice between avoiding polio or risking cancer. Butterfly's reply, according to the story, was an odd, off-the-cuff rejoinder: "Fiddlesticks! Polio is reality. Cancer is a fantastic guess." Alan Goffe, the British scientist who was one of the three signers of the March 1961 *Lancet* letter that had originally broken the news that Salk vaccine contained live SV40, was also quoted. He expressed doubt that inactivated vaccine would ever be totally safe: "We do not know how long it will be before we can produce absolutely 'dead' vaccine." Koprowski also appeared in the story, once again promoting a switch from monkeys to human cells, saying that "monkey kidneys are subject to violent infection" and that they continued to be used only because they were "favored by manufacturers through fear of change."

But, other than the reports in the Associated Press and the *Enquirer,* there was no more news for the remainder of 1961 about SV40. Hull was in the midst of conducting his own experiments at Eli Lilly on SV40. He had found, just as Eddy and Girardi had, that the simian virus caused cancer in suckling hamsters, but his results were never published as a scientific paper. At Merck, Girardi and Sweet began a different set of SV40 experiments, but these were halted before completion. The pair had discovered that when SV40 was injected into tissue cultures of normal human cells it "transformed" them into cancer-precursor cells. Hilleman decided, however, that this alarming development was not going to emanate from Merck. There was only so much self-inflicted damage ("hanging out dirty laundry" were Hilleman's words according to one of his subordinates) that the company could take about its SV40-contaminated vaccine. Instead, to Sweet's displeasure, Hilleman contacted John Enders at the Harvard Medical School and sent him some SV40 and encouraged Enders to undertake the same experiment.

Girardi had also started another experiment that was never to be completed. From the throngs of monkeys that came through Merck, he had found nine non-rhesus pregnant females. After they had given birth, he injected six of their newborns with SV40, leaving three as controls. The significance of this experimental design was that monkeys are far closer to humans than hamsters. Whatever might happen to them after SV40 exposure would provide a strong signal of what the virus might do after it had been injected into people. Before Girardi could continue much farther with the live monkey experiment, word came down from higher up at Merck to quit the project.

The next big news about SV40 came in mid-April 1962. The American Association for Cancer Research, the organization that still publishes the influential scientific journal *Cancer Research,* was holding its annual meeting in Atlantic City, New Jersey. The association's annual weekend meetings were often the occasion for the announcement of important breaking news on the cancer front, and lay press interest in the conference was considerable. On Sunday, the last day of the scientific gathering, Girardi presented a summary of his Merck experiments that had showed SV40 produced tumors in newborn hamsters. At the very end of his report, he announced that he and Sweet had also found SV40 transformed human cells in vitro (in tissue culture as opposed to in vivo, in a living organism). Earl Ubell, the president of the National Association of Science Writers at the time, wrote up the Girardi presentation for the *Chicago Sun-Times:*

Polio Vaccine Virus Puzzles Scientists

Atlantic City, N.J.—Those strange viruses found floating alive in both live and killed polio vaccines display increasingly disturbing peculiarities. . . .

A year ago, it was reported for the first time that something in the monkey cell cultures broth could cause cancer in hamsters. A few months ago, scientists at Merck & Co., identified that "something" as SV-40. Now, these same Merck researchers have found that SV-40 will grow in human tissue kept alive in a test tube. They will make the cells in those tissues multiply at a greater rate.

Sunday, another report said SV-40 can get into human tissue cells growing in test tubes and change the microscopic chromosomes, destroying one of the 46. . . .

Ubell's article finished with a description of three theories under debate at Atlantic City after Giradi's report. One was that SV40 was a human carcinogen, a prospect Ubell described as "the most frightening idea" since "[m]illions of persons" had received Salk injections and SV40 had been administered alive to them. A second conjecture was that SV40 was totally harmless. The third was the somewhat wishful notion that the massive exposure to SV40 would somehow act as an anticancer vaccination for Americans. (Ubell labeled this "a far-out idea.") *Time* also reported on the conference, noting that SV40 was "the first primate virus shown to cause cancer in any animal." In the article, Bernice Eddy, for one of the few times in her career, was publicly credited for her contributions to the understanding of the relationship between viruses and cancer.

Hilary Koprowski came to Atlantic City and heard Girardi's presentation. Afterward, he invited the Merck scientist out for a cup of coffee. Girardi recalls that Koprowski was fascinated by the idea that SV40 could turn normal human cells into cancerous ones. What was Girardi seeing in his human cells, the Wistar scientist wanted to know? Girardi described the chromosomal damage he had observed. While the two shared notes on SV40, the conversation turned to a possible career change for Girardi. Koprowski had come to Philadelphia's Wistar Institute only a few years earlier with the charge of reshaping the institution into a leading biological research facility. Like Hilleman at Merck, he was always on the lookout for talent for the institution he was in the midst of revitalizing. He made it evident that he hoped Girardi would leave the strictures of private industry and come work for Wistar, free to pursue his SV40 research in any direction he chose.

Girardi joined the staff of the Wistar Institute a year later. One of the many discoveries he made about SV40 during the next several years was that it sometimes took more than a month before the virus grew out and could be detected in tissue culture. The DBS, based on Gerber's experiments, believed that fourteen days was a sufficient observation period to detect SV40 and had drafted its new regulations for oral polio vaccine on that assumption. Manufacturers were required to look for evidence of SV40-induced cell damage for only two weeks in various tissue culture safety tests. Any slower growing SV40, such as the kind Girardi had discovered, would not be uncovered by following these new regulations. Girardi says that his findings about how long it sometimes took SV40 to appear in tissue culture were communicated to the DBS as soon as he discovered them in the early 1960s. The agency, however, never changed this section of the vaccine regulations to lengthen the observation time.

Having secured another promising scientist for Wistar and some crucial knowledge, Koprowski rushed back to Philadelphia and personally oversaw the completion of research already underway at Wistar on SV40 and human cells. Cultures of skin and cheek-lining cells had been infected with SV40 by a team of five Wistar researchers. The SV40-infected cultures multiplied at out-of-control rates and piled up on top of each other—bizarre behavior when compared to healthy human tissue. The SV40 cultures also had readily discernable chromosomal abnormalities, confirming the unpublished Girardi research. (The published Wistar paper included photomicrographs of rearranged and fragmented chromosomes.) All were unmistakable signs that the cells were no longer normal and were well on the way to malignancy. Worse, the Wistar team concluded that the "transformed cells seemed to have a selective advantage over normal cells." Apparently, not only could SV40 turn normal human cells cancerous, it also turned them into bullies—completely overgrowing uninfected cells until they were suffocated to death.

The Wistar human tissue study appeared in midsummer 1962, shortly before the human tissue study that Enders had completed at Hilleman's urging. Enders and his collaborator, another Harvard researcher, Harvey Shein, reached essentially the same conclusions as the Wistar group, with a different kind of tissue, human kidney cells. Koprowski had rushed the Wistar study into press hoping to scoop Enders and gain some publicity for Wistar. But in the end, despite being second, the Enders study attracted a good deal more attention because it was published in the prestigious *Proceedings of the National Academy of Sciences*. A lengthy *New York Times* story on August 10, 1962, reported on the Enders study:

> A cancer-causing virus has for the first time produced cancer-like changes in human cells. . . .
>
> Changes that the virus produced in cultures of human kidney cells included greatly accelerated growth patterns and chromosomal aberrations. . . .

The virus, the *Times* said, was SV40. The *Times* story described Eddy's SV40 discovery, noting that "fortunately" her original findings had come before the use of any commercially licensed oral vaccines. But, the story continued:

> There is no doubt, however, that a large part of the Salk vaccine and of the live-virus Sabin vaccines that were used in clinical trials throughout the world were contaminated with SV-40 virus.

The Koprowski and Enders studies fit the last pieces into the SV40 puzzle. At first there had been a question as to whether SV40 was even a concern, since it was believed that it had not actually made it into the final Salk vaccines. It was now known that it had contaminated most of the polio vaccine ever produced. Next there was debate about whether SV40 was infectious in humans. The Anthony Morris study on prisoners showed that the monkey virus, when ingested or inhaled, multiplied inside humans. A 1962 study by Baylor University's Joseph Melnick, which found that children who had taken contaminated Sabin vaccine excreted the virus in their stools for up to five weeks, reinforced the point. Obviously, when injected—a far more potent transmission route than oral or nasal expo-sure—SV40 would infect and multiply inside humans. Then, there had been doubt whether the virus would produce anything beyond the mild subclinical illness that Morris had observed among his prisoner volunteers. The Eddy and Girardi experiments both demonstrated that the virus had lethal consequences for laboratory animals. Presumably the virus could do something similar to man. Still, skeptics pointed out, tumors in hamsters were not necessarily relevant to human beings. Now that point, too, had been addressed. What SV40 did to hamsters, it could do to human cells in a test tube. Chromosomes had been damaged, and normal cells had been rendered malignant. SV40 was as dangerous as many of attendees at the American Association for Cancer Research had suspected four months earlier.

When Enders and Koprowksi's studies on human cell transformation by SV40 were published in the spring and summer of 1962, it seemed as if everyone's darkest apprehensions about the polio vaccine contaminant had suddenly come to life. By the fall of 1962, as news of the most recent SV40 research spread, the anxiety that had been growing in scientific circles about the simian virus reached its zenith. "It was the worst thing in the world," Hayflick recalls of the news. "Please tell me: What else could we find *worse* in monkey kidney cells?" In Britain, Wellcome Laboratories decided to stop inactivated vaccine production and switch entirely to live polio vaccine production. (As in the United States, however, both the British and Canadian governments decided not to recall old stocks of Salk vaccine. Britain had a surplus of 6 million injections in 1961.) In Sweden, the concern was about Sabin-type vaccine. There were plans to give monkey gamma globulin to four thousand children who had received oral vaccine in the belief that it would contain antibodies against any simian viruses, including SV40, which might have contaminated the oral doses. In the Soviet Union, site of the most extensive use of Sabin's vaccine, tests were conducted to determine the spread of SV40. Many of the technicians and scientists involved in Chumakov's massive vaccination trial proved to have been infected by the virus, and the Soviets were now fearful of SV40's possible long-term effects. Among American researchers and health officials, a joke with gallows-type humor began to make the rounds: The Soviets would lose the 1964 Olympics because their athletes would all have tumors thanks to SV40.

But, in Bethesda, even this jibe at the cold war enemy was of little comfort. The DBS's own research was suggesting that SV40 could no longer be downplayed as a health threat to the American public. The division, to its credit, had become quite busy researching SV40 during the past year. Gerber's study confirming that the virus was not killed in Salk's vaccine had been published in the spring of 1962, and there were a dozen or so other SV40 research projects now under way. None seemed to offer reassurance that the virus was as inconsequential as Murray and Shannon had believed (or hoped) in 1961.

A young DBS researcher named Alan Rabson—future deputy director of the National Cancer Institute—found that SV40 caused ependymomas, a rare brain cancer, in a species of rats. This was the first proof that the virus could cause cancer in a mammalian species other than hamsters. Another DBS experiment led by Rabson determined that when human thyroid tissue was infected with SV40, it became cancerous. When the infected human thyroid cells were, in turn, transplanted into the brains of hamsters, the hamsters developed ependymomas. Ependymomas were also induced in hamsters by Gerber, who inoculated the animals directly with SV40. In a third Rabson experiment, SV40 was found to produce kidney cancers in hamsters. Interestingly, a coauthor on all of these newer DBS tumor studies was Rabson's wife, Ruth Kirschstein, the pathologist who two years earlier had refused to participate in Bernice Eddy's original hamster tumor study.

Gerber, meanwhile, confirmed that SV40 was a DNA virus—making it different from most viruses, which contain only RNA—and that it had a preference for invading the nuclei of infected cells. He also found that SV40 seemed to go into hiding once inside the cell, yet could reemerge much later and still cause cancer in the hamsters he was using for his experiments. This seemed to suggest that the virus could perhaps "go underground" in humans, as the *New York Times* termed the phenomenon, and theoretically do damage long after initial exposure.

Now that the NIH's own research had established the potential carcinogenicity of SV40 virus, the health agency was confronted with a very frightening public health question. Almost half of the American population had received Salk vaccine by 1963. Were the nearly 100 million Americans who had been potentially injected with live SV40 in contaminated Salk vaccines going to contract cancer? Attempting to answer that question became a complex research project that fell to a young physician named Joseph Fraumeni.

Fraumeni came to work at the National Cancer Institute's Epidemiology Branch in the summer of 1962. He was born in Boston in 1933 and graduated from Harvard in 1954. After earning his M.D. from Duke Medical School in 1958, he was chief resident at New York City's Memorial Sloan-Kettering Cancer Center in 1962, where he had been preparing for a career as a clinician before taking the NCI position. The NCI Epidemiology Branch, Fraumeni recalls, was very small when he arrived. It was essentially himself, chief Robert Miller (who had hired him), and a couple of other staff members. Miller had come to the NCI only shortly before Fraumeni. As its name implies, the mission of the office was to research the epidemiological facets of cancer—the occurrence or incidence of cancer among particular populations. Interestingly, for someone hired to be the principal investigator for an office devoted to epidemiological studies, Fraumeni admits that, at the time, "I knew very little about statistics—or epidemiology for that matter." Before he officially assumed his new position, Fraumeni took a six-week summer school crash course in biostatistics at Stanford.

Fraumeni's very first assignment was thrust on him as soon as he arrived at Bethesda—a massive epidemiological study to assess whether SV40 might have harmed any of the nation's Salk vaccinees. Fraumeni knew nothing about the virus, and, just as he had with epidemiology, immediately had to get himself up to speed about the vaccine contaminant. He recalls the meeting where the study's design was discussed. It was in a large room on the NIH campus in a structure called "The Nave" building in reference to its resemblance to the bridge of a battleship. Befitting the battleship motif, the mood of the meeting was somewhat grim, but focused. Scientists from several different branches of the NIH had been summoned; each one was to assume command of a particular aspect of what was hoped to be a decisive judgment on whether SV40 had any measurable health effect. Gerber was there from the DBS because of his expertise on SV40. Alexander Langmuir represented the CDC. During the Cutter incident, Langmuir and his staff had traced all the polio cases back to two specific lots of Cutter vaccine. As a result, he had detailed information on vaccine shipments and vaccinations by all manufacturers. Another scientist attending represented an NIH branch that collected mortality data.

The group decided to focus just on children who had been enrolled in the National Foundation's 1955 spring and summer immunization program. Gerber would test samples of 1955 vaccine and determine which lots were contaminated with SV40. Langmuir would figure out where the contaminated lots had gone. Fraumeni would collect the mortality data from an NIH data repository. He would look at overall cancer mortality in general and for cancer deaths specifically attributable to brain, kidney, and connective tissue cancers—the kinds of cancers that Eddy, Rabson, and other DBS researchers had most frequently induced with SV40.

With the study design set, Fraumeni began his work in the summer of 1962; he completed the epidemiological survey in 1963. The retrospective study examined whether any statistically significant increase in cancer incidence had occurred in the population of children ages six to eight who had been vaccinated during the months of May and June 1955. Fraumeni followed the children for a four-year period ending in 1959.

When it was published in *JAMA* at the end of August 1963, the conclusion of Fraumeni and his boss, Robert Miller, the study's only authors, was that, despite the "questions about [SV40's] oncogenic potential in man," their investigation had found there were "no significant alterations in mortality rates for cancer" for the three cancer types surveyed and that overall cancer mortality rates appeared unaffected. There had been a blip upward in leukemia rates, but as far as the authors could determine, SV40-

exposed and unexposed children alike had higher rates, so contaminated vaccine was not at issue.

The take-home message from the Fraumeni study was obvious: Despite all the fears and worries of the past three years, SV40 had no measurable consequence for human health. Even though Fraumeni was careful to state in the *JAMA* paper that "it would be premature to conclude from this study that SV40 is innocuous to man," that was exactly how his study was interpreted.

Because it seemed to definitively dispel the SV40 anxieties, the NIH was eager to share the Fraumeni study with the public, releasing it to the press even before its *JAMA* publication—a move designed to heighten interest. Just as in July 1961, when news about SV40 first became public, mainstream media coverage ran true to form—an uncritical presentation of the NIH's interpretation of the results. "Public Reassured on Polio Shots; U.S. Finds No Links to Cancers" ran a *New York Times* headline to a story about the Fraumeni study. The body of the story was a recitation of the study's conclusions with little elaboration. The story was filed by a general assignment correspondent. Once again, the *Times* had not assigned one of its own science writers to a critical polio vaccine story.

The Fraumeni study soon became the rationale for concluding that SV40 was a moot issue. By 1964, Sabin's vaccine, which was first licensed in 1961, had largely replaced Salk's as the vaccine of choice. Sabin's vaccine was grown not on rhesus but on African green monkey kidney tissues—presumably free of SV40—and the Sabin virus seed had been presumably freed of SV40 by Hilleman's antiserum. There was therefore a minimal danger of continued SV40 exposure posed by new vaccines now that Salk's vaccines were mostly gone from the market. (Old, contaminated stocks were used up as of 1964.) As for the Salk vaccine, despite the animal studies and the human tissue studies that suggested that SV40 was oncogenic, Fraumeni's epidemiology had found no link between it and cancer. The final word in public health circles was that epidemiology seemed to find the virus harmless—though the laboratory studies had suggested it was extremely dangerous.

Especially with the passage of time, most physicians stopped worrying that they might have harmed their patients with tainted Salk vaccine. Future generations of medical practitioners, if they learned about SV40 at all during their medical training, would find it related to them as a novel bit of medical history—an odd virus that had once contaminated the polio vaccine, but had proved to be inconsequential. Indoctrination within the medical establishment about the putative harmlessness of the virus had begun.

Despite the import attached to it, the 1963 Fraumeni study design was clearly lacking when measured against rigorous epidemiological standards. Fraumeni himself says that "the study had lots of limitations [and] caveats." Some of the limitations were beyond the control of the study's authors and designers; some were at least partially self-induced; most were probably not obvious to readers unless they had some background in epidemiology.

The first limitation was acknowledged by the authors. They had only followed the children for four years, so any cancer that took more than four years to develop, even if SV40 were the culprit, would have gone undetected. Many cancers have more than a four-year latency period—a fact known at the time. In fact, it would be fairly unusual for any carcinogen—unless applied in very high doses, such as radiation after a nuclear explosion—to produce cancers quickly on a large scale. This limitation alone suggests that a much longer follow-up of the children was warranted. This never occurred.

Another limitation was also acknowledged by the authors: The study would have failed to detect "small differences" in cancer rates caused by SV40; it was sensitive enough to notice only "gross variations" in cancer occurrences. In effect, the study's authors were admitting that SV40 could have caused increases in some cancer rates, but the techniques and analysis used were not necessarily statistically sensitive enough to note them.

A third limitation concerned the types of cancers surveyed—just three types—brain, kidney and connective tissue. A number of cancers with which SV40 was later associated were not included in the study. Mesothelioma, which has a two- to four-decade latency period, was not included; nor were lymphomas.

A fourth limitation centered on how "a cancer" was defined. Only cancer deaths—as opposed to cancer diagnoses—were included. This excluded any cancers contracted by children who were ill, but still alive, in 1959, four years after vaccination. Another problem lay in determining who was defined as having contracted cancer. Cancer diagnoses and statistics are considered inherently unreliable the farther back one goes in time. The federal government did not even begin to maintain its own database of cancer cases until 1972. Many clinicians at the time misdiagnosed cancer when confronted with it. The Fraumeni study, therefore, could not have possibly included all cancer cases, even among just the three types he had preset for close examination.

The final limitation was the study's definition of who was exposed to SV40 and who was not. The study assumed, on the basis of Gerber's tests of polio vaccine samples, that the continental United States could neatly be divided into three SV40-exposure "cohorts," or population study groups: high SV40-exposure states, low SV40-exposure states, and no SV40-exposure states. Central to the study's design was Fraumeni's comparison of cancer rates in "high" SV40 exposure states to "low" and "no" SV40 exposure states. All of the study's conclusions on SV40's influence on cancer incidence were predicated on the accuracy of these cohort assignments. The validity of Fraumeni's cohort definitions, in turn, was dependent upon the assumption that the Gerber tests of vaccine lot samples always detected SV40 if it was present—an assumption that Tony Girardi later proved false. At the time, the DBS detection methodology was to observe tissue cultures for only fourteen days. However, as Girardi subsequently discovered, some strains of SV40 take longer to manifest themselves in culture. The DBS detection protocols would have missed any 1955 vaccine lots that contained such slower growing SV40. These lots would have been erroneously defined as SV40 free in the Fraumeni study—thus casting into doubt Fraumeni's entire basis for comparing SV40-exposed states to SV40-unexposed states. (There was also the possibility that in some states defined as "high exposure" states, some of the vaccine used was actually free of the virus at times.)

Even assuming that the paper's state-by-state assignment of SV40 exposure levels were flawless, there were still other problems with how SV40-exposed cohorts were defined for the study. Fraumeni, for example, did not really know the number of children aged six to eight during May and June 1955 for any given state. He instead took census data from 1950 and 1960, state by state, and, using that data, estimated the population of children aged six to eight for each state—extrapolating the 1955 ages six to eight population as the midpoint between 1950 and 1960. Secondly, Fraumeni did not really know who received polio vaccine in this population. He assumed that everyone age six to eight was vaccinated in 1955—or at least that the rate of vaccination for this age group did not vary from state to state. But with the Cutter incident dominating the news at the time, many parents withdrew their children from the National Foundation's free immunization program. Rates of withdrawal (and therefore vaccination) did vary from state to state, thereby making it impossible to assume that the percentage of children vaccinated in state A was the same as state B. The final flaw with the cohort design was that Fraumeni assumed that none of the children moved from one state to another from 1955 to 1959—or if they did, they conveniently always moved from a high SV40-exposure state to another high SV40-exposure state and never to a low SV40-exposure or no-exposure state.

Taken together, the flaws in Fraumeni's cohort selection add up to one important shortcoming: Defining exactly who was exposed to live SV40 in contaminated vaccines is impossible. This same flaw has been present in every subsequent attempt to use epidemiology retrospectively to determine whether or not the virus is causing cancer in human beings. In 1963, Fraumeni had no way of being certain which children actually received live SV40 in their polio shots; no epidemiologist since has been able to clear this technical hurdle. Looking backward in time, it is simply impossible to know for sure which individuals were exposed to SV40 and which were not.

Taken as a whole, the flaws in the 1963 study suggest that its conclusions were open to challenge, if not highly suspect. Yet no effort was made to do a more precise or more thorough subsequent study on Salk vaccinees, despite the fact that one-half of the American population had received potentially SV40-contaminated Salk vaccine. It was, Fraumeni says, the intention that the 1963 study be only "a first cut" and that more efforts be made over time to reassess the Salk vaccine situation and SV40. But during the next twenty-five years, a true epidemiological follow-up on the tens of millions of Salk vaccinees was never conducted by the NIH.

Interestingly, after Fraumeni's 1963 study, there were epidemiological studies that showed cause for concern in connection with Salk vaccines. A 1968 Australian study of several hundred hospitalized children with malignancies showed they were more likely to have received polio vaccine, while two American studies in the 1970s found an increased brain cancer incidence among groups of children born from mothers who had received Salk vaccine during pregnancy. Even though these epidemiological investigations contradicted Fraumeni's findings, the studies by the NIH researcher held sway.

Meanwhile, research within the NIH on the virus's cancer-causing potential essentially ceased as of 1963. There were one or two DBS studies still in progress. Morris found that it was impossible to separate SV40 from adenovirus (since they were both DNA viruses), and this effectively killed any hopes for a commercial adenovirus vaccine. Gerber found that children still had antibodies to SV40 three years after their last Salk vaccinations. But neither of these efforts stimulated further research by the federal government into SV40 and its effect on human health. Based largely on the Fraumeni study of Salk vaccinees, the good news about SV40 had eclipsed the bad news. Over the years, the Fraumeni study would become the linchpin in established scientific dogma about SV40—a virus that causes cancer in laboratory animals but, thankfully, is harmless to humans.

In the private sector, more or less the same phenomenon was occurring. One more startling paper about SV40 was still to come from Wistar. In April 1964, Koprowski reported at the American Association for Cancer Research that a Wistar team had injected SV40-transformed human cells under the skin of terminal cancer patients, and lumps had formed that, while not specifically cancerous, appeared precancerous in nature. But even when reporting this development, the *New York Times* stressed that polio vaccines were now free of SV40 and "that there has been no evidence to date that its former presence has done any harm." This would prove to be the last concerted effort for nearly three decades to determine whether the simian virus could cause human disease. Koprowksi was more interested in vaccines than in cancer, and no other private researchers picked up where and he and his Wistar team had left off. In the minds of most public health officials, doctors, and science writers, the virus reverted to its June 1960 status: an annoyance to vaccine makers, a virological curiosity because of its cancer-inducing properties in animals, and of no consequence to humans.

10

Why Not a Safer Vaccine?

LEONARD HAYFLICK WAS a young researcher at Hilary Koprowski's Wistar Institute in Philadelphia in the early 1960s when the news of SV40's contamination of inactivated polio vaccine first shocked the vaccine world. Hayflick, who received his Ph.D. in medical microbiology and chemistry in 1958 from the University of Pennsylvania, joined Wistar in the midst of the race between Koprowski, Albert Sabin, and Lederle's Herald Cox to produce a live vaccine. Wistar was a beehive of activity, Hayflick recalls, as a result of the competition between the trio of rival vaccinologists. But one thing troubled Hayflick about this second heat of the polio vaccine competition. Once again, almost no thought had been given to the substrate used to produce the vaccine. All three researchers were still using monkey kidney tissues to produce their live vaccines—a primitive, outmoded technique in Hayflick's view, especially when contrasted with the scientific expertise each of the three competing laboratories was devoting to research on poliovirus itself. Injecting monkey cells into humans was inherently dangerous, Hayflick thought, a fact that should have been painfully obvious after the discovery of SV40.

Clearly there was a need for an alternative to monkey kidneys for vaccine production and Hayflick felt he had the answer. In 1962, Hayflick announced that he had perfected WI-38, a human diploid cell substrate. (Diploid means a normal number of chromosomes.) WI-38 had an enormous advantage over monkey kidneys. It was "fully characterized," meaning it was carefully screened and found to be free of extraneous viruses. It was a "standardized" cell strain, meaning that the substrate's daughter cells were all the direct descendants of the carefully screened mother cells, and thus each cell culture was as clean and safe as the original one Hayflick had first created. Unlike tissue cultures derived from chopped-up monkey kidneys, WI-38 would always be virus-free and always be safe. As important, it was suitable for polio vaccine production on a commercial scale. At Wistar, Koprowski quickly embraced Hayflick's discovery and permanently switched all his polio vaccine research to WI-38. Hayflick assumed that all other researchers would soon do the same, either voluntarily or because the federal government would compel them to do so. In his own mind the choice was obvious: After SV40, no rational vaccine regulator would continue to allow the use of monkey kidneys now that WI-38 could be used as an alternative. "If this doesn't force them [the DBS] to use human diploid cells, nothing will," Hayflick thought at the time.

The first sign that the federal health bureaucracy was not going to embrace the solution Hayflick offered came at the end of the summer of 1962. In January of that year, NIH director James Shannon appointed an internal committee of NIH scientists (Joe Smadel was one of them) to examine whether it was feasible to replace monkey kidneys with Hayflick's human cell substrate. On September 4, less than four weeks after the public had learned that SV40 could transform normal human cells into cancerous ones, the review committee—which held no hearings and took no testimony from outside scientists—reported to Shannon that it did not recommend any changes in vaccine production policy. The committee did acknowledge the "serious limitations [that] have been revealed by experience with cultures of monkey kidneys," including the difficulty in procuring monkeys, the discovery of forty previously unknown viruses that infected their kidneys, the SV40 scare, and the possibility of even more dangerous viruses to be discovered in the future. But then, in a truly tortured turn of reasoning, the committee concluded that just because Hayflick's cells so far had proven to be absolutely free of unwanted viruses and other adventitious agents, there was insufficient assurance that they would remain so. "There can be no absolute guarantee," the committee said of WI-38 and other such cell strains, that they "will never yield a previously unknown virus or some nucleic acid or nucleoprotein that is infective and pathogenic for some cells, in vitro [in test tubes] or in vivo [in the body] under some conditions." In effect, Smadel and the other committee members had concluded that it was preferable to stay with a contaminated substrate rather than switch to an obviously safer one. Their reasoning: There always remained the possibility that Hayflick's cells and other cell strains might harbor a hitherto unknown, covert, oncogenic substance of their own—even though there was absolutely no evidence to support this supposition.

The committee's conclusions quickly became official policy at the DBS, the NIH lab responsible for all vaccine licensing. There would be no change in vaccine substrates—not an altogether surprising decision, since DBS director Roderick Murray had a reputation as risk averse, especially when it came to polio vaccine. The scars from the Cutter incident were still fresh (Murray had ascended to his present position when his predecessor had lost his job because of the scandal), and as far as Murray was concerned there was no room to take any more chances. Granted, monkey kidneys were frequently contaminated, but at least the hazards involved in using them were, presumably, known and therefore, presumably, controllable. WI-38 may have appeared to be pure and safe—but, then again, according to the NIH review committee, maybe it wasn't. As Hayflick observed later, Murray and other NIH bureaucrats had concluded "the devil you know is better than the devil you don't know"—even if the latter devil was only a figment of their imaginations.

Hayflick was incredulous that his cell substrate was being maligned on the basis of an entirely theoretical oncogenic contaminant. He decided to fight back. For the next decade, he waged an unrelenting struggle to gain acceptance among vaccine regulators and manufacturers for his new substrate, publishing papers and letters to scientific journals and making frequent appearances at scientific conferences on vaccines. In the process, he gained a reputation in vaccine circles as the proverbial "angry young man" who was not afraid to assail the DBS and accuse it of hypocrisy and poor science. In each case, his basic message was the same: There was an accumulating body of evidence that demonstrated that human diploid cells were safe and were superior to monkey kidneys. All the objections to WI-38 were speculative, while all the risks presented by monkey kidneys had been substantiated—many times over. Moreover, the hoops the DBS insisted WI-38 jump through were hoops that monkey kidneys could not clear. WI-38, for example, had been injected into hamsters with no ill effects. Bernice Eddy and Tony Girardi had demonstrated what happened when hamsters were inoculated with monkey kidney cells—they got SV40-induced cancers. WI-38 had even been injected into the arms of volunteer terminally ill cancer patients. Again, the cells had proved to be totally harmless. Almost no scientist, Hayflick insisted, would ever try the same experiment with monkey kidneys. The results would be too risky (as Koprowski's 1964 experiment had suggested).

Hayflick's efforts to promote WI-38 also included his own version of shuttle diplomacy. Throughout the 1960s, he served as a roving ambassador for WI-38, personally delivering dozens of vials of his substrates to labs all over Europe, including many behind the Iron Curtain. When some of the labs experienced problems in properly constituting a growth medium to support the cultures, Hayflick, with the help of another Wistar scientist, devised a standardized, dry formula that could be easily transported. Hayflick's deliveries soon included not only the cells but also enough powdered medium to sustain them for years.

WI-38 was now gaining adherents among many foreign scientists and manufacturers. More important, foreign vaccine regulatory agencies began to view Hayflick's discovery favorably. In 1967, Yugoslavia became the first country to license polio vaccine produced on WI-38. The Soviet Union followed in 1970, and in 1971, the United Kingdom and France both accepted the cells as a suitable vaccine substrate. The French licensure meant that pharmaceutical giant Pasteur-Merieux began distributing vaccines grown on WI-38 to tens of millions of people throughout the world.

But in the United States, Hayflick made little progress. DBS resistance to WI-38 was stiff and unwavering throughout the 1960s. It was bolstered by no less a figure than Albert Sabin, who became one of the leading nongovernment critics of Hayflick. In one highly visible example, Sabin publicly took the position that the use of human diploid cells for vaccines was unacceptably dangerous. At a three-day NIH scientific conference in Bethesda on rubella vaccines, he asserted that since "there is always a hypothetical something for which you cannot test," WI-38 could never be termed virus-free. In his mind, there might never exist a technology sufficient to declare WI-38 absolutely safe. In fact, according to Sabin, if it was true that there existed a possible human leukemia virus—a widespread theory at the time—then one would have to assume that it came from human tissues. Since Hayflick's substrate was derived from human cells, according to Sabin's reasoning, that meant WI-38 was just as likely as not to contain such a leukemia virus, a "hazard," Sabin said, with which "I think I should prefer not to become involved." As long as the DBS and as prominent a vaccinologist as Sabin were against WI-38, no American vaccine manufacturer was going to waste much effort or money on developing vaccines that used it as a substrate, even if they privately agreed (as some did) with Hayflick's position.

A golden opportunity, or so it seemed to Hayflick, for widespread adoption of WI-38 occurred in 1967. In the late summer of that year, the vaccine world was rocked by an outbreak of hemorrhagic fever at monkey-handling facilities in Belgrade, Yugoslavia, and the German cities of Frankfurt and Marburg. The unknown disease, which had no cure, left seven lab workers dead from complications caused by unchecked internal bleeding. Many of the two-dozen survivors never fully recovered, suffering from permanent liver damage, severe weight loss, and impotence. One survivor became psychotic for the remainder of his life. The Marburg virus, as it became known, was later identified as a filovirus, a family of viruses that include Ebola. The source of the disease was quickly pinpointed as a batch of African green monkeys shipped from Uganda that were to be used for the production of polio vaccine. Like SV40, news of Marburg virus caused panic throughout the vaccine world. The threat was deemed so serious that, for a while, vaccine production using African green monkeys was halted in Europe. In the United States, all measles and polio vaccine production, both of which used the African greens as a substrate, also came to a virtual standstill.

It was against this backdrop that at the beginning of November 1967, close to three hundred virologists, vaccine researchers, and vaccine manufacturers from around the world gathered in Bethesda for a scientific summit to revisit the issue of viral vaccine substrates, including the use of WI-38. Once again, Hayflick was sure that a vaccine disaster would force a change of heart in U.S. vaccine policy and that the conference would finally force Murray and the DBS to act. Once again, he was disappointed.

Hayflick was one of the first presenters at the conference. He reviewed all WI-38 research to date, observing that over one million individuals had received a variety of experimental vaccines produced on his new substrate since 1963. In essence, a massive field trial had been conducted and WI-38 had passed. Directly referring to the recent Marburg disaster, he stated that the time had come for widespread use of his human diploid cells for vaccines.

Over the next three days, most of the European scientists who spoke tended to side with Hayflick, many of them also citing Marburg disease as deadly proof that continued use of monkey kidneys could no longer be justified. Typical of their sentiments was a statement by Frank Perkins, who headed England's equivalent of the Division of Biologic Standards, the Medical Research Council. Marburg, he said, showed that dangerous viruses in monkeys were not just a threat to monkey handlers and lab workers but to vaccine recipients, as well: "How long will it be before a simian virus pathogenic for man will remain undetected in final vaccine, causing a tragic accident? Our present knowledge of virology is such that this possibility is not out of the question when monkey kidneys are used, and we must not let this happen."

The Americans in attendance, particularly the federal regulatory officials and some of the older virologists, held a very different point of view. Marburg virus was not a reason to abandon monkey kidneys. Murray, for instance, offered the following explanation as to why Marburg did not concern him: "From what information we have gathered and what we have heard here thus far, it would appear that the system for production and testing of vaccines which is in force [in the United States] would probably have picked up this agent."

As for WI-38, Murray saw no reason to change his present position: Since it was impossible to regulate against the unknown, it would be impossible to ever know if WI-38 was safe. Therefore, vaccine production would continue on monkey kidneys, devils and all.

Four and a half years passed before there was finally some movement in Bethesda on the issue. In the spring of 1972, the British vaccine manufacturer, Charles Pfizer, announced that it had received a DBS license for a new polio vaccine, Diplovax, which would be produced on WI-38. In a March 8, 1972, *New York Times* article on the announcement, Hayflick touted the fact that his substrate was free of any viral contaminants. "The monkey kidney is a notorious reservoir of unwanted viruses," he told the *Times*. In contrast, "WI-38 . . . is the most thoroughly tested cell population." Promotional brochures prepared by Pfizer for Diplovax attempted to exploit the substrate difference to its full advantage. The cover of one handout featured a full-color photographic display of the face an African green monkey "morphing" into a human one. "The Polio Vaccine Evolution: The Advances Are Important!" the cover exclaimed. Inside, readers (presumably pediatricians) were given an overview of the advantages of WI-38. Safety and freedom from unwanted simian viruses topped the list. Another brochure featured a close-up of an African green monkey, with a headline that proclaimed: "The Beginning of the End of the Simian Era in Vaccine Biology?" Inside, it made similar points as the first one and also made overt references to the fact that "the past" was monkey kidney tissue and "the present and the future" was WI-38.

In 1972, when Pfizer released Diplovax, Lederle Laboratories controlled more than 80 percent of the polio vaccine market in the United States. Pfizer was confident that with its superior substrate, its vaccine would make swift and serious inroads into Lederle's market share. (A handout it prepared for its sales force predicted capturing 50 percent of the market in the first year.)

Lederle, however, was determined to fight off the intruder. In November 1971, Lederle officials first got wind that some Pfizer sales personnel were actively courting an influential committee in the American Academy of Pediatrics. The committee was responsible for annually updating "The Redbook" desk reference that can still be found in American pediatricians' offices. The Pfizer sales reps were predicting that once Pfizer's vaccine was licensed, the committee would recommend that American pediatricians switch from Lederle's vaccine, known as Orimune, to Pfizer's Diplovax. The news demanded an immediate response from Lederle, according to a November 15, 1971, internal company memo: "The commercial importance of seeing that the Academy Committee does not take action to recommend the diploid vaccine cannot be overstated. We need them to at the very least remain neutral."

In addition to meeting personally with the committee to try to dissuade them, Lederle decided it should seek out aid from the DBS—specifically from the official who had been responsible for overseeing safety testing for the polio vaccine for the previous decade: "In preparation for such a confrontation [with the Academy Committee], it would be valuable to have the support of the DBS. Could we count on Dr. Kirschstein . . . ?" Presumably, Dr. Kirschstein, who in 1993 became deputy director of the entire NIH, could be relied upon to proffer only favorable opinions about Lederle's vaccine.

At the end of January 1972, with licensure of Diplovax imminent, Lederle hinted in another memo as to how it intended to counter claims about the superiority of Diplovax over Orimune: "The tissue which was used to develop what is now designated WI-38 was considered to have oncogenic potential in the beginning. Many noted investigators, including Dr. Albert Sabin, have spoken out against its use for vaccine production."

By the spring of 1972, just in time for Pfizer's announcement of Diplovax's licensure, Lederle had fully prepared its counterattack. On April

12, 1972, a month after the release of Diplovax, Lederle launched an anti-Diplovax publicity campaign. First, it released a two-page press back-grounder, entitled "Corrections," which sought to counter the "erroneous impression that vaccine prepared from [WI-38] cells is safer than the presently-available oral polio vaccine." This was followed by a six-page in-formational packet unfavorably comparing Diplovax to Orimune, which was made available to the nation's pediatricians. On the packet's cover were the letters Q and A, in gigantic type. Carefully placed underneath the Q on the right-hand side was the word "Diplovax," a clear signal that there was much to question about the new Pfizer vaccine. "Orimune" appeared on the left-hand side of the cover, strategically—and reassuringly—placed under the A. Lederle still had the answer when it came to polio vaccine. Although there were no overt misstatements of fact in the brochure, there were some broad misrepresentations, including a misleading statement on the first page concerning the reason it had taken a decade for Murray's DBS to approve a human diploid cell-based vaccine:

QUESTION: Is polio vaccine produced in human diploid cells safer than that produced in monkey kidney cells?
ANSWER: No. In fact it has taken more than ten years for the [DBS] to approve a vaccine produced in human diploid cells because of scientific concern that the human cell substrate may contain latent human viruses that could be transferred to the vaccine, and more likely cause disease in children since they would not have to cross the species barrier.

What Lederle neglected to say was that the "scientific concern" it de-scribed was shared by very few scientists outside of the Division of Biologic Standards. Moreover, WI-38 had now been used for five years for com-mercially produced vaccines in Europe, without incident.

Other topics covered in the Lederle brochure included whether another Marburg-type outbreak could occur among the monkeys Lederle used for vaccine production. Impossible, the brochure reassuringly asserted, because of the careful screening checks Lederle conducted on its monkeys. Lederle's own efforts in diploid cell research were also touted. The company was under contract with the NIH to develop a fetal monkey diploid cell line, a simian version of WI-38 that was also free of any extraneous viruses; the project was presumably a response to WI-38.

Two other statements in the packet were particularly provocative. The first asked whether adventitious agents could get into a final vaccine undetected. Lederle claimed that in the case of its own vaccine, this was almost impossible. "The most sensitive tests for extraneous agents," the company claimed, were in "the homologous host," that is, testing in the same species as the one in which the vaccine is produced. "We can do this with monkeys since Lederle produces in a monkey cell substrate. Manufacturers of human cell origin vaccines cannot test in humans, so they must employ a less sensitive host (monkey) and consequently cannot get as conclusive a test."

Aside from the clever attempt to reverse the tables on the safety issue (with Lederle suddenly having an advantage over Pfizer), there was scant, if any, scientific justification for this assertion. Indeed, many of the DBS's required tests for adventitious agents in polio vaccine were in animal species other than monkeys. Moreover, polio vaccine history demonstrated just the opposite of the Lederle claim. The discovery of SV40 had only occurred because Sweet had safety-tested his adenovirus vaccines in cells from a monkey species *different* from the one he had used for vaccine production. There were clear advantages—not disadvantages, as Lederle asserted—to using a different cell substrate for viral screening than the one used during vaccine production.

The other provocative statement was the last one in the brochure:

QUESTION: A fair amount of public and medical press information has been printed about the human diploid cell vaccine. What do other, non-Lederle, researchers have to say about this substrate?
ANSWER: The concerns of a number of conservative researchers are summarized in the viewpoint of Dr. Albert Sabin in a quotation in *Medical World News* of October 8, 1972.

What followed was a restatement of the earlier remarks Sabin had made in the 1960s about WI-38 at the conference on rubella vaccines, including his view that the "potential hazard of human leukemia" from an unknown virus in WI-38 was one in which "I would prefer not to become involved."

Pfizer's vaccine never caught on among U.S. pediatricians, and by the end of 1976, it had stopped manufacturing vaccine for sale in the United States, its attempts at breaking Lederle's monopolistic hold on the polio vaccine market having clearly failed. Lederle's campaign against Diplovax certainly played a role—perhaps a crucial one—in ousting it from the country, but there were other reasons as well. One factor contributing to Diplovax's demise may have been supply problems that plagued Pfizer from the very beginning. Initially, all vaccine had to be shipped from England, and this seems to have led to chronic supply shortfalls in the United States. A Lederle memo in August 1972 notes that "it will be two years before there is abundant supply of Diplovax," a fact, the memo said, that would ensure that the Lederle's own polio vaccine received favorable treatment from the DBS, since the agency "cannot risk Lederle being off the market." (Around this time, Lederle's marketing to physicians began to stress that it, unlike Pfizer, was never out of stock of polio vaccine.)

Another reason for Diplovax's failure may have been the animus that Hayflick seemed to arouse in federal health circles. In April 1972, just as Diplovax was being released, Hayflick made the impolitic decision to appear before a Senate subcommittee that was considering a reorganization of the DBS. (The DBS was subsumed into the Food and Drug Administration after 1972.) Hayflick was one of the star witnesses in support of dismantling the DBS. In his testimony, he excoriated the agency, particularly for its foot-dragging on licensing WI-38 and its failure to acknowledge the dangers presented by monkey kidneys. At the same time, he also published a highly critical article about vaccine policy in a Stanford University journal. The DBS, which never really resolved itself to the use of human diploid cells, decided to strike back, overtly working hand in hand with Lederle to do so. On April 26, 1972, a Lederle memo, authored by one of its PR personnel, noted that that the DBS itself had decided to publicly contest Hayflick's claims concerning the superiority of WI-38 and was counting on help from Lederle to do so:

> Received a call from DBS Information Office informing us that they have finally decided to take strong action in opposing Dr. Hayflick's allegations concerning monkey tissue vaccines. Apparently the CDC is involved in this counter move. . . . The Information Office has asked that we send them copies of the "Correction" backgrounder put out recently.

It had taken more than a decade for Hayflick to gain acceptance for WI-38 as a polio vaccine substrate in the United States, but in just a few weeks organized opposition had been roused against it. The opposition now included not only the largest manufacturer of polio vaccine in the country but also the federal regulatory agency responsible for the vaccine. The result was inevitable. Diplovax was doomed. By 1977, Lederle was the sole supplier of oral polio vaccine in America. American consumers once again had no choice when it came to polio vaccine—either one produced on "filthy" monkey kidneys (as Hayflick termed them) or none at all. Not until the year 2000 would Americans have access to a polio vaccine that was produced on a clean, standardized, virus-free substrate—nearly two decades after Canadians and three decades after Europeans had been given that option.

If Diplovax had failed to gain the recognition it deserved from the scientific community, SV40 was suffering a different fate. After the publication of Joe Fraumeni's 1963 epidemiologic survey that found no correlation between inoculation with the Salk vaccine and increased cancer incidence, SV40 ceased to be a concern for the nation's public health officials. But interest in the virus among bench scientists was growing. The virus's ability to cause cancer in animals and cell cultures so readily made it a subject of immense interest to virologists. Beginning in the 1960s and extending over the next three decades, investigators probed its every aspect, from its architecture to its behavior in animal cells. Scientists examined the virus under the electron microscope and studied its "viral capsid"—the protective coat of proteins that envelops a virus's genetic material. In the process they gained a deeper understanding of how all viruses are structured physically.

They also studied its machinery. Probing SV40's single chromosome, scientists eventually sequenced all of the base pairs in its genome, detailing the exact order of every single nucleotide on its lone, circular, double-stranded DNA. SV40 thus became the first virus—and first living organism of any sort—to be completely sequenced genetically. The insight gained in deciphering SV40's genetic code helped revolutionize the nascent field of molecular biology, allowing investigators to become adept at sequencing and manipulating the DNA of increasingly complex organisms. Efforts to map the individual structure of living things—most strikingly, the human genome project—can, in many ways, be traced back to these early efforts to understand SV40.

SV40 soon migrated from the virologist's bench to cancer research laboratories. Cancer investigators were awed by its ability to transform healthy animal cells into tumor cells in test tubes. Here was a tiny, yet mighty, life form that interacted with cells in such fashion as to completely disrupt them. What were its properties? How did it work? Like other viruses, SV40 needed to invade host cells to reproduce itself. But unlike most viruses, which burst or budded forth from the host cell during that process, SV40 sometimes had a different effect: It caused the cell to lose control of itself and reproduce wildly. Scientists soon discovered that SV40 had two tumor-causing proteins, dubbed the large T-antigen and small t-antigen. By studying them, they began to learn how an oncogenic virus, in the process of simply trying to replicate itself, could cause disruptions in the host cell that could lead to cancer. This understanding led to the discovery of an entire new class of oncogenic proteins and helped uncover the intricacies of the body's cancer-fighting mechanisms at the molecular level. Renato Dulbecco, the researcher who had raised the specter that SV40 might cause cancer back in 1960 when Maurice Hilleman first announced its discovery, began to investigate SV40's tumor-causing proteins more closely, winning a Nobel Prize in 1975 for his studies. In 1979, Arnold J. Levine, then at Princeton University, codiscovered one of the body's most important anticancer heros, the gene p53, as a result of experiments with SV40. Scientists now estimate that more than half of all human cancers are associated with the inhibition or inactivation of p53. Today's understanding of how human cells become cancerous is based in part on these early studies that employed SV40 to infect human cells.

SV40 also became the "reference" carcinogen of choice for research on many other cancer-causing substances. Scientists would use SV40 to create malignant cell lines and then use them as a baseline against which to measure the effect of other carcinogens. For example, a scientist researching how a cell repairs its DNA after exposure to the sun's ultraviolet rays would employ SV40 as an experimental control, contrasting the mutations or changes in the cell's activity following exposure to sunlight with mutations or cellular changes following exposure to the tumor-causing proteins contained in SV40. The contrast between the mutations caused by SV40 and those caused by ultraviolet light allowed the scientist to quantify specifically how sun exposure can damage cells.

Amid this prolonged outburst of SV40 research, there was one glaring omission. For some reason, few scientists thought to examine whether the virus might play an oncogenic role in human beings similar to the one it played in laboratory animals or human and animal cell cultures. Throughout the 1960s, '70s and '80s, SV40's potential consequences for human health were almost completely ignored.

This oversight could be explained in part by the dearth of sophisticated molecular techniques for the detection of viruses. It was not until 1984, for instance, that molecular biologists invented the technique called polymerase chain reaction, in which small fragments of DNA can be amplified millions of times—allowing scientists to search with relative ease for viruses in human tumor biopsies. Prior to the invention of the technique, scientists had to employ much more laborious methods to detect viral DNA. The lack of incentive to link SV40 with human cancers was also a reflection of the widespread dependence on SV40 in research laboratories: Any change in its status would have made SV40 a biohazard and required new precautions in handling the virus, and that would have prohibited scientists from working with it outside an approved facility.

But perhaps the most significant reason for the failure to investigate whether the virus was harmful to humans was hidebound medical dogma: Joe Fraumeni's 1963 study of injected vaccinees had found no evidence of increased cancer incidence. A subsequent study of 925 recipients of SV40-contaminated oral vaccine—the only SV40 epidemiological study ever performed on American recipients of Sabin vaccine—reached the same conclusion. Based largely on those studies it had become established medical "fact" that exposure to contaminated polio vaccine did not result in cancer. The virus, therefore, did not warrant serious investigation as a human health threat. "For thirty years the line has been that SV40 doesn't cause any disease in humans," explains Janet Butel, head of the Department of Molecular Virology and Microbiology at the Baylor University Medical School in Houston and an SV40 expert. "I said it like everybody else. It's in [book] chapters that I've written. It's in every textbook. It's very hard to change a paradigm."

There was one final disincentive to conduct studies that might have linked SV40 to human disease: fear. "One of the reasons SV40 was not studied more diligently was the behavior directed toward Dr. Eddy," said Anthony Morris in a 1997 interview. Eddy's decision to investigate SV40 had incurred the wrath of her superiors. It had cost her her laboratory, her staff, her position, and essentially her career as a serious investigator. "When other scientists saw the behavior directed toward Dr. Eddy, they were not about to touch SV40 and explore its possibilities as a potential agent for infection in man," Morris said. The polio vaccine had achieved legendary status. It was not to be compromised, regardless of the unanswered scientific questions its contamination had posed. In fact, it would be a long time before a researcher emerged with the tenacity Bernice Eddy had displayed—a quarter of a century, all told. It happened, finally, in 1986. That was the year that a twenty-six-year-old medical doctor—born in 1960, the same year that SV40 was discovered—arrived on the NIH campus from Italy. His name was Michele Carbone, and though he did not know it at the time, he was about to rewrite the book on SV40.

11

Everyone Knows SV40 Doesn't Cause Cancer

IN 1986, MICHELE Carbone was a junior scientist, newly arrived at the National Institutes of Health from his native Italy. Although he had not originally set his sights on Betheseda, there was never any doubt he would be a physician. For seven generations every firstborn son on his father's side has been named alternately Carmine or Michele (pronounced Me-KE-lay). And for seven generations each Carbone son has followed in his father's and grandfathers' footsteps, becoming a doctor. Carbone recalls spending hours as a child in the family medical library, poring over its aging medical texts, some of them hundreds of years old, fascinated by their fine calligraphy and mysterious Latin titles. Inside one of the volumes is a liner page that traces the family's lineage back in time and deep into the heart of Calabria, Italy's southernmost province. The family's ancestral home is in Cellara, a thousand-year-old village in the great La Sila mountain range in Calabria's interior. Carbone's father, Carmine, recalls that his own grandfather would set off every morning in a horse-drawn carriage to tend to his poor and sick neighbors, often without remuneration.

Carbone was born in Rome, where his father attended medical school and practiced orthopedic surgery. In 1966, when he was six years old, his family left Rome and returned to the eastern shore of Calabria, to the town of Catanzaro Lido, which sits on the Ionian Sea.

Carbone's father could easily have afforded to send his son to private schools, but he wanted Carbone to attend public schools so he could fraternize with people from "all walks of life." This he did—and more, indulging in teenage escapades like poaching fish while scuba diving, riding his motorbike up and down the high school stairwells during a student strike, and romancing the local girls on long horseback treks in the nearby mountains. But he was also apparently a bright and diligent student, with a taste for science that announced itself in the eleventh grade when his teacher asked him to research and present to the class a lecture on the subject of viruses. Carbone turned to the family medical library and read everything he could find on the subject. At the end of his research, he lectured the class for two hours, describing the different families of viruses, their subclasses, and their varying properties. Carbone's presentation was largely beyond the comprehension of those in attendance, including the teacher and the principal of the school. The mother of one of the students still remembers her daughter coming home that day complaining of "the biggest headache of her life."

Carbone's mother, Italietta, is an accomplished artist whose bronze sculptures and drawings have been exhibited widely in Europe. And, it is from his mother's side of the family that he seems to have derived the self-assurance and intuition that characterize his abilities as a researcher. She was raised in Buenos Aires, where her father, Manfredi Corsani, was the Italian consul under Mussolini. By the time Carbone was born, Corsani had retired and was living in an apartment two stories above Carbone's parents in Rome. Charged with caring for his young grandson while Carbone's parents worked, Corsani spent many hours each day cultivating the boy. The pair developed a daily ritual: they spent the morning at a play group where Carbone could interact with children his own age, and the afternoon among his grandfather's friends. During these social gatherings, Carbone would sit among the weathered former generals of Italy and listen as they reminisced about Mussolini and disparaged the current government. When the old men went out to the local cafe, the five-year-old seated alongside them was expected to confidently order a Coke while they ordered their espressos. Carbone's grandfather taught him chess, and Carbone became one of the youngest players in the Italian championships; he taught him to ride a horse, and Carbone became an expert rider, once winning a rodeo contest in the United States.

Carbone's grandfather died many years ago. And Carbone is an American citizen now. But the influence of his grandfather remains. Carbone is enduringly, almost stereotypically, Italian—and proud of it: generous with his emotions, outspoken, and gregarious. He still insists on opening doors for women. ("My ancestors would kill me if I didn't," he pleads.) He has a thick accent that is replete with Italian mannerisms (whenever he refers to a virus, for example, he calls it "he" in accordance with its masculine gender under the rules of Italian grammar). And he is strikingly handsome, with deep-set eyes, patrician features, and shoulder-length brown hair. With his penchant for fine tailored clothes, he cuts what fashion aficionados might call a *bella figura*, a truly incongruous look for a laboratory researcher.

Today Carbone lives in the Chicago bedroom community of Oak Park, an established, comfortable suburb with a friendly downtown and wide residential streets covered in spring and summer by an umbrella of broad-leaf trees. He is an associate professor of pathology at Loyola University Medical School in Maywood, Illinois, and researcher at Loyola's Cardinal Bernardin Cancer Center. He keeps a busy schedule. Even on days when he has performed an early morning autopsy or taught a seminar, he will often labor into the evening over an experiment in his laboratory, dash across the Loyola campus to teach a karate class, and then return home at nine P.M. to his wife and young daughter. (His grown daughter, whose mother is a physician in Italy, has been studying mathematics and chemical engineering at the University of Wisconsin in Madison.)

He cooks dinner every night, an activity that he says "relaxes" him. On holidays, or when time permits, he'll cook for twenty people or more, throwing multicourse dinner parties that show off his culinary skills and his home, an 1893 Frank Lloyd Wright house, one of many such homes by the famous American architect that are found in Oak Park. At these festivities, Carbone eschews shoptalk, but will discuss the fine points of Calabrian anchovies with the same enthusiasm and attention to detail he bestows upon a delicate molecular experiment. Carbone makes time for less typical passions as well. He rarely misses a chance to play Ping-Pong at the local YMCA on Saturday afternoons. He has earned black belts in three martial arts and obsessively makes room in his schedule for occasional, all-day sparring sessions with fellow black belts at a gym.

"Michele is a very unique person," confirms Paola Rizzo, Carbone's long-time research associate, who is also Italian. "He's not afraid of thinking differently from other people. He's not afraid to have an idea, even if at this moment others don't believe it. He has an independence of judgment—this internal drive, this courage to pursue whatever he thinks is necessary—which is unique. . . . I don't think I've ever met anybody who had this as strong as Michele. Maybe an artist, but not in science."

Carbone studied at the University of Rome's prestigious medical school La Sapienza. It is one of the largest medical schools in the world and the same school his father attended. Michele was a top student, and that, in combination with the fact that his father was president of the Italian Society for Orthopedics and a renowned surgeon, led to his immediate acceptance into a residency for the competitive and lucrative specialty of plastic surgery. He toyed with the idea but found it "incredibly depressing." ("So many stitches," he says, waggishly. "It takes two hours and then you get all done and you still have to do the other breast.") He discovered, instead, an affinity for pathology, the field in which one diagnoses and interprets disease-induced changes to tissue and bodily fluids. His attraction to it was straightforward: "I wanted to find out why things happen," he says, adding, as if by way of explanation: "In America you don't want to be a pathologist because you are the slave of the surgeon. The surgeon screams at the pathologist. But in Italy it's exactly the contrary. The pathologist has the ultimate truth. The surgeon is completely afraid of him."

Carbone earned his M.D. with highest honors and began to specialize in anatomic pathology. As one of the youngest pathologists at La Sapienza, he was given the task of preparing and examining lymph node slides for patients who had developed acquired immune deficiency syndrome, or AIDS. It was 1984, and little was known about the disease. Many doctors were fearful of coming into contact with the virus that caused it. Carbone was not. "I'm not afraid of things in general," he says, impassively, "I was not afraid of it." As a result, he was the pathologist for some of the earliest AIDS patients in Italy, an experience that led him to challenge certain assumptions about where the virus, human immunodeficiency virus (HIV), was located. Contrary to accepted scientific wisdom at the time, which stated that the AIDS virus was located in a type of white blood cell called the lymphocyte, Carbone observed that it was located in the macrophages, a type of cell that engulfs and consumes foreign invaders. Carbone says that when he told this to his professor, the professor was adamant. "Bob Gallo [the NIH researcher cocredited with discovering HIV] says that is in the lymphocytes," he insisted. "How can you be right?" The professor suggested that Carbone stick to making small, solid advances, rather than risk ridicule by making a major assertion, such as he had. Carbone was chagrined. "I thought the whole idea of science was finding something new," he says. A couple of years later, the accepted wisdom changed and HIV's strong predilection for the macrophages was confirmed. But Carbone says he understood his professor's reluctance to believe him and deference to the AIDS experts publishing at the time. "He doesn't know whether to trust you because he's totally detached from what is happening in the laboratory," Carbone explains. Without having seen the evidence himself, the professor is going to assume "most likely his student is wrong, not the experts in the field." The experience taught him a lesson: Never allow your laboratory to grow too big. "If you have a lab of twenty people, you have no idea what the people are doing in it," he says. It also reinforced his intuitive approach to science: Seek out the new; don't embrace the accepted wisdom until you've proved it yourself.

As a young doctor in Italy, Carbone began each morning by performing an autopsy. He spent much of the rest of the day in the pathology lab preparing and analyzing tissue culture slides. It was customary to break for coffee in midmorning and midafternoon. One day, during his ritual 10:30 A.M. visit to the hospital coffee bar for a cappuccino, Carbone found himself in conversation with a poetry professor who was standing next to him at the bar. The professor told Carbone that his son was at the NIH and that if Carbone would provide a résumé, he would forward it to his son, who would find him a fellowship at the NIH.

The NIH, with its twenty individual institutes and seven research centers, is home to hundreds of visiting scientists from around the world. It is a training ground for some of the top minds in medicine. Each year, through its extramural program, the NIH awards billions of dollars in research funds through a competitive grant process to researchers at institutions across the country and in some cases outside the United States. In fiscal 2001, for example, the National Cancer Institute, just one of the NIH's twenty institutes, awarded $2.9 billion in extramural research funds. But the NIH also has an "intramural" program, reserved for scientists employed by the government on-site at the NIH Bethesda campus and its environs. It is designed to provide a collegial setting in which scientists and clinicians can pursue largely self-designed research interests. Researchers ranging from young postdoctoral scientists to tenured senior investigators, many of whom help run the institutes, work in teams or design and lead investigations depending on their experience and status.

If accepted, Carbone would have joined the intramural program. Initially, he was skeptical about applying, unsure of his qualifications for a position at one of the world's largest and most important medical research institutions. At the same time, he was eager to match wits with some of the best minds in science. He decided to take the poetry professor up on his offer. Today Carbone's résumé is impressive—running seventeen pages and listing more than fifty peer-reviewed studies, fifteen book chapters, and forty scientific abstracts. He has served as the personal physician to the Italian ambassador to the United States and holds a knighthood from the Italian government in recognition of his anticancer research efforts. At the time he applied, however, Carbone's résumé was, in his own words, "nothing." He recalls, "I was an M.D. I had no experience except for an abstract for my work on AIDS." The chances of the encounter producing a job offer were diminished when the professor's son was unexpectedly fired from the NIH. On his way out of Washington, however, the professor's son deposited Carbone's résumé on the desk of Giovanna Tosato, the scientist who was chief of laboratories at the Food and Drug Administration. A few weeks later Carbone received two letters, each containing an offer of a fellowship. One was an offer to assist in a biochemistry research project, but the work was in a subspecialty so far out of Carbone's field he could barely comprehend the offer. The other one, from Andrew Lewis at the National Institute of Allergy and Infectious Diseases, was intriguing. It was an offer to work with Lewis on a series of experiments testing how viruses could cause cancer in laboratory animals. One of the viruses Lewis was testing was SV40.

When he arrived at Lewis's lab, Carbone knew little about SV40. Like most other physicians, his acquaintance with the virus during medical school was limited to a brief description of SV40 that can be found in standard medical textbooks: SV40 was a common contaminant of the early polio vaccines; research had found that it caused cancer in laboratory animals, but it had turned out that the simian virus was harmless to humans. Carbone also knew that because of its ability to cause cancer so easily in cell cultures and animals, SV40 was a popular tool among cancer researchers. In particular, Carbone knew that one researcher, Renato Dulbecco, had won a Nobel Prize in medicine for his work delineating SV40's cancer-causing mechanisms, a fact that stuck in his mind because, coincidentally, Dulbecco also hailed from Catanzaro. But other than his geographic connection to a prominent SV40 researcher, Carbone was an SV40 neophyte.

Lewis was trying to determine which viruses, taken outside their normal hosts, caused cancer most efficiently. He was infecting laboratory animals with adenoviruses, the same viruses against which Ben Sweet, thirty years previously, had been trying to develop a vaccine. Although adenoviruses cause respiratory infections, they are otherwise harmless to humans. Some, however, can cause cancer in rodents. Lewis was comparing adenoviruses with SV40 to determine how efficiently each caused cancer; he had determined that SV40 was by far the more carcinogenic virus to the animals. Carbone's job was to help Lewis determine what happened when the animals' immune systems confronted the oncogenic viral proteins.

In addition to his work at the NCI for Lewis, Carbone worked on a side project at a different branch of the NIH, the National Institute of Child Health and Human Development (NICHD). Carbone and another researcher were working with the NICHD's scientific director, Arthur S. Levine (a different scientist from Arnold J. Levine, the codiscoverer of p 53); they were examining SV40 and a mutant version of the SV40 virus, which had been stripped of one of its two tumor-causing proteins, the small t-antigen. They were trying to determine how well the mutant SV40 caused cancer compared to its natural counterpart.

After three years working for Lewis and Levine, Carbone's appointment at the NIH was due to expire. He had completed his fellowship, was well on his way to earning his Ph.D. in human pathology, and had been offered a position at the University of Rome as a researcher. In conformance with the Italian university system, the position required Carbone to work under a full professor. It meant he would have little control over his research subjects. Yet it was a coveted position, in the city he loved. Carbone began to make plans for his return to Italy when, out of the blue, Levine offered him a job running a laboratory unit studying oncogenes—genes that, when mutated, can permit or induce uncontrolled cell growth, or cancer. As scientific director, Levine controlled the funding for all investigators working within his institute. He prided himself on recognizing and mentoring young talent; it was Levine who had hired Richard Klausner, a scientist who became director of the National Cancer Institute during the Clinton administration. In Carbone, he felt he had found another talented researcher. Levine also believed that scientists should largely control their own budgets. The position Levine offered Carbone came with funding for two postdocs—assistants who would perform laboratory experiments for Carbone as part of their postdoctoral training. "It was a dream," Carbone says,

"I never thought I was qualified for it. I never would have asked for it." Given the freedom to design his own research project, Carbone decided to pursue an offshoot of work he had been doing with Levine.

During the previous three years, Carbone had been studying the biology of SV40 in vitro—in a test tube. Because he was trained as a pathologist, these biochemical experiments didn't satisfy his curiosity about the virus. He wanted to see what would happen when he injected the virus missing its small t-antigen into an animal. The common wisdom about SV40 was that it was not associated with any particular cancer in laboratory animals, but rather that it might transform any cell type with which it happened to come into contact. When Bernice Eddy had injected the virus under the skin of hamsters in 1960, she had observed cancers on the skin at the site of SV40 injections—the tumors her boss Joe Smadel had dismissed as lumps. She also had observed tumors far from the injection site—in the lungs, abdomen, and brain and occasionally in other organs of the animal. Eddy described these cancers as sarcomas—a fleshy, malignant growth of the connective tissue of the bone, cartilage, or striated muscle. She had assumed that they were metastases of the original tumors that had formed at the injection site.

Thirty years had passed, and Carbone wanted to repeat Eddy's original experiments—but with a twist. He injected the small t-deleted, mutant virus into the hearts of six hamsters. As an experimental control, he injected another group of hamsters with the complete SV40 virus; he also injected some with a solution containing no virus at all. He was curious to see whether animals would react differently depending on whether they received "whole" or "mutant" SV40.

About three months after he had injected the animals, one of those injected with the complete SV40 virus began to show signs of serious illness. The creature sat scrunched in a corner, gasping for breath, extremely ill. Carbone—who saw that the hamster was near death—euthanized him and performed an autopsy. As he opened the animal's chest, he observed that the lungs were encased with white tumor tissue. When Carbone sliced into the tumor tissue, he noticed that it was confined to the membrane around the lungs, known as the pleura; it was not inside the lungs themselves. In fact, the tumor hardly penetrated into the lung. Rather, it had spread extensively over the chest wall and diaphragm. "It had clearly grown from the outside in, not the inside out like a typical lung tumor," Carbone says. "Then I looked at it under a microscope, and I saw that it was a mesothelial cell," a type of cell that lines the cavities surrounding the organs in the abdomen. The hamster had developed a mesothelioma, a rare tumor of the mesothelial cells lining its lungs.

Malignant mesothelioma is a fatal cancer of the lining that surrounds the lungs, heart, and abdominal cavity. Virtually unheard of prior to 1950, the disease is associated with exposure to asbestos, the dusty mineral fiber used in insulation applications, from roofing to shipbuilding to plumbing. It is considered to be a relatively rare cancer, striking and killing about 2,500 Americans a year and thousands more people in other parts of the world. (An estimated 250,000 people worldwide are expected to die of the disease between 2000 and the year 2030.) It is a highly aggressive cancer and is unresponsive to standard cancer-treatment protocols such as surgery, radiation, or chemotherapy; most people who contract it die within twelve months of diagnosis. It is an agonizing disease. "The misery of this disease comes with the failure of the therapy and the spiral downward," says Harvey Pass, a prominent mesothelioma surgeon. As the cancer chokes the lung cavity, fluid escapes and must be drained repeatedly to keep the lung from collapsing. The sufferer becomes short of breath and susceptible to pneumonia. But many die of what is called cancer cachexia, their bodies so ravaged by disease that they can no longer eat.

Coincidentally, Carbone had seen a mesothelioma the first time he conducted a human autopsy as a medical student in Italy. Even though the cancers were infrequent, his pathology background allowed him to recognize it. As he increased the magnification of his microscope, his diagnosis was confirmed. The cell staring back at him looked like a fried egg, a large cell containing a plump nucleus with a thick cytoplasm surrounding it. There could be no confusing a mesothelial cell with any other cell. A fellow pathologist and former NIH researcher named Antonio Procopio happened to be visiting the NIH from Italy that day. He had dropped by Carbone's laboratory to say hello. "Look at that. It looks like a meso," said Carbone to his friend. "Why the heck has he got a meso? Only asbestos causes meso," Carbone mused aloud. Procopio arched his eyebrows and smiled. "Maybe you've discovered something important," he said.

After he had finished his diagnostic work on his first hamster, Carbone went to see Levine, his boss. Carbone was excited, convinced that the rodent's rare mesothelioma was significant. He wondered if this first hamster's affliction with such an unusual disease might mean some of the other animals would also develop mesothelioma. But Levine, Carbone recalls, cautioned him not to expect to go very far with the notion that SV40 was responsible for the disease, especially since asbestos was a well-known cause. The result might be an anomaly, Levine said.

A few days later, another of the hamsters that had been injected with complete SV40 presented with the same symptoms. Carbone wondered what type of tumor he would find this time. His autopsy revealed another mesothelioma. Within a few days, another hamster was on the brink of death. Once again, it was a mesothelioma. Viewing the tumor cells under an electron microscope and staining them further confirmed the diagnosis. Carbone was stunned. It was highly unusual for so many animals in an experiment to become so sick, so quickly, with such a rare disease, even when injected with a large dose of a known carcinogen. When hamsters are exposed to asbestos, for example, only a fraction develop mesothelioma. Something was making Carbone's animals become sick at a remarkably high rate.

"The first animal got a meso. The second animal got a meso. The third animal got a meso. What's going on here?" he thought to himself. "Why would the virus cause this rare cancer and not cause cancers in all the other tissues that had been exposed to the virus through the blood stream?" Soon, two or three animals were dying a day, more than half of them from mesothelioma. Carbone packed up the mesothelioma slides and sent them to Angelo Festa, a well-regarded pathologist at the University of Rome, and mentor to Carbone from his days at La Sapienza. Festa confirmed his diagnosis.

Nine months after he first injected the animals with SV40, Carbone had concluded his experiment. Except for one case of mesothelioma, the animals that had been injected with the SV40 that was missing the small t-antigen had all contracted lymphomas, although they had taken somewhat longer than the normal SV40 control group to become ill. About half the hamsters that were injected in the heart with the complete SV40 virus developed mesotheliomas. Those that did not came down with other malignancies, including lymphoma and a bone cancer called osteosarcoma. And the control group of hamsters that had been injected with virus-free solution did not develop any disease.

His results, Carbone thought, demanded follow-up experiments. The hamsters had developed mesothelioma with great frequency—more than 50 percent of the time—even without the virus being injected directly into the lung; the other cancers the virus caused were also far from the site where Carbone had introduced the virus into the hamsters. This seemed to suggest that the virus did not cause cancer at the injection site as Eddy and some other early SV40 researchers had concluded. Instead, SV40 seemed "tropic"—or drawn to—certain tissue and cell types in which it thrived. SV40 seemed to be particularly drawn to mesothelial cells, causing the cells to become cancerous at a rate that was extraordinarily high.

Carbone decided to repeat his first hamster experiment, but he altered its design slightly. In the first experiment, he had injected SV40 into the left ventricle of the heart, believing that intracardial delivery would allow the virus to be distributed throughout the hamster and maximize its chance of causing tumors. This time, in addition to injecting some hamsters intracardially, he injected the virus directly into the pleural tissue (lung space) of some animals. He also injected SV40 into the peritoneum, which lines the abdominal cavity and is another site susceptible to mesothelioma. Once again, half of those injected in the heart developed mesothelioma, but every one of the eleven hamsters injected in the pleura developed mesothelioma. Four of the six injected in the peritoneum also developed mesothelioma.

"I began to wonder what this virus was doing on a cellular level to cause such a rare cancer so readily in these poor animals." Carbone recalls. "I hardly knew anything about mesothelioma," Carbone says, "because the medical books at that time did not devote much space to mesothelioma. But I knew it was a tumor that was caused by asbestos. So I started looking into it. And the first thing I found is that asbestos will induce tumors in only a small fraction of the animals injected. And I had 100 percent of my animals developing the tumors—so obviously the virus was much, much more potent."

Now that two different sets of experiments had shown that SV40 induced mesotheliomas in hamsters at high rates, Carbone felt there was ample reason to explore what seemed to him an obvious question: Could there be a connection between human mesothelioma and SV40? The accepted wisdom about the virus had been that it was harmless to human beings. But maybe the accepted wisdom was wrong. Without further studies, how would anyone know that the virus, which produced a rare but fatal lung tumor in hamsters, couldn't cause the same disease in human beings?

Carbone approached Andy Lewis, the scientist who had brought him to the NIH, with the question. Lewis gave him a copy of a review of SV40 that he had authored in 1973—one of the few accounts in the scientific literature that recounted how more than 100,000 experimental doses of the adenovirus vaccine administered to military personnel until 1965, and millions of doses of the polio vaccine administered between 1954 and 1963, were contaminated with the simian virus. In his review, Lewis recounted the early research on the virus, including the work of Bernice Eddy. Carbone asked Lewis if he thought that SV40's oncogenic potential had been adequately investigated. Lewis said he did not feel a conclusive study had been done.

Carbone wanted to know more. He read every study he could find about the virus and human cancer. He researched the history of the virus and the polio vaccine. As he absorbed the limited literature, Carbone concluded that scientists in the 1960s had been premature in asserting that SV40 was harmless to humans. Almost no one had systematically searched for evidence of the virus in human tumors. And in his mind, there simply hadn't been enough data for epidemiologists to conclude that the virus did not cause human disease.

Wanting to get to the source of the studies, he called on Joseph Fraumeni, author of the crucial 1963 epidemiological study that had concluded that exposure to contaminated Salk vaccine had no effect on cancer rates. Fraumeni had followed his 1963 study with his much smaller study of 925 newborns who had been exposed to live SV40 orally in contaminated experimental Sabin vaccines at one Cleveland, Ohio, hospital from 1960 to 1962. Published in 1970, with a follow-up in 1981, Fraumeni's studies determined that, in this one small cohort, exposure to the SV40 in contaminated oral vaccines did not lead to increased risk of cancer. Like a handful of other researchers who were involved with SV40 studies at the time of the initial discovery of the virus, Fraumeni still worked at the NIH. He had risen greatly in stature within the health bureaucracy and was now one of the most powerful men in the NCI, heading the Division of Cancer Epidemiology and Genetics, one of three giant divisions within the National Cancer Institute. Fraumeni showed Carbone a drawer full of notebooks containing data from his original study conducted three decades before. Carbone went through the notebooks. "I thought he was very nice," Carbone recalls thinking. "But when I lookd at his data, I thought: Is that all there is?"

Despite the prominence of their author, the Fraumeni epidemiological studies did not impress Carbone. For one thing, his 1963 epidemiological study had lasted only four years and was thus too short to have detected certain slow-developing cancers—a shortcoming that Fraumeni himself had acknowledged at the time. Mesothelioma can take twenty to forty years to develop after exposure to asbestos. If mesothelioma took as long to develop after SV40 exposure as it did after asbestos exposure, Fraumeni's time frame would have missed increases in mesothelioma related to exposure to the virus from contaminated Salk vaccine. His subsequent studies on oral vaccine exposure had the same weakness. They were too short in duration to detect any rise in mesothelioma rates. And the cohort Fraumeni had surveyed included only a very small number of people—too few to capture increases in relatively rare cancers, such as the ones with which SV40 had been associated in laboratory animals.

Carbone discovered something else in his review of the literature: In some studies, as many as 50 percent of mesothelioma victims reported no history of exposure to asbestos. Moreover, fewer than 5 percent of the people who had been heavily exposed to the fibrous mineral ever contract mesothelioma. Carbone wondered if SV40 might explain these two puzzles, either in the case of individuals with no history of asbestos exposure or as a cofactor—a collaborating factor with asbestos—in some of those who had been exposed.

Meanwhile, Carbone began to talk to other, more experienced scientists at the NIH about SV40. The more he learned, the more uneasy he became. There were rumors floating around the NIH about the virus, including one that a couple of NIH scientists who had worked with it for many years had contracted cancer. When Carbone asked old hands at the NIH about the virus and its relationship to the polio vaccine, they were evasive; they suggested that his curiosity would be better directed elsewhere. They told him that the virus was one of the most studied in history. In more than thirty years no one had established any evidence associating it with rising mesothelioma rates—or any other human cancers. Besides, they said, echoing Levine, everyone knew that asbestos was the cause of mesothelioma.

They also reminded Carbone that the last thing anyone wanted to hear was that the exalted polio vaccine was linked to cancer. Too much was at stake. Linking SV40 to human cancer meant, by implication, linking the polio vaccine to cancer—a proposition that was decidedly unpopular at the NIH. Moreover, implicating a vaccine contaminant in cancer—even if the contamination occurred some thirty years ago—might easily shake public confidence in vaccines in general. "I got the impression that this was something that people did not like to hear—that the polio vaccine could cause this cancer," Carbone says.

Yet the more people tried to dissuade him, the more Carbone felt compelled to press ahead. It was 1992; Carbone was thirty-two years old, still early in his career by research standards, early enough that whatever choice he made could make or break his career. He made a fateful decision. He would investigate the hypothesis that some viewed as a waste of time and that even he doubted but couldn't stop thinking about: Could a monkey virus that inadvertently contaminated polio vaccine three decades before now be causing cancer?

Clearly, the way to find out was to search for SV40 in human mesotheliomas. Using state-of-the-art molecular tools that hadn't been developed when SV40 was discovered in 1960, Carbone wanted to look for signs of the monkey virus in biopsies of human mesothelioma tumors. But there was a problem. He needed approval from his scientific director to conduct the experiment. Carbone had discussed his hamster results with Levine on a number of occasions, and Levine did not share his enthusiasm for the project. Much like Carbone's professor in Rome, who had insisted that HIV was drawn to the lymphocytes, Levine's objections were based on the common wisdom of the day: It's well known, he said, that mesothelioma is caused by asbestos. Extensive data had been gathered implicating asbestos exposure in the cancer. Levine said that since there was conclusive evidence associating asbestos with mesothelioma and no hard evidence associating SV40 with the cancer, there was no reason to fund such an experiment. Levine was not, by far, the only skeptic. Another scientist told Carbone it was such a waste of time looking for SV40 in human tumors, he might as well go to the Caribbean for six months instead. But Levine was the authority who counted. Carbone couldn't perform the experiment without his boss's approval.

Carbone was in a catch-22: without some evidence that SV40 could be involved in human mesotheliomas, he couldn't convince Levine to grant approval for his study. But how could Carbone produce any evidence if no one else had looked? Then Carbone got a lucky break. It came in the form of an accidental discovery by an unlikely research scientist at one of the most respected cancer research institutions in the world.

12

"A Wild-Assed Idea"

THE TWIN PLATE glass and steel towers that house the Dana Farber Cancer Institute rise from a small sea of medical buildings a few miles southwest of historic downtown Boston in an area bordered by museums and Northeastern University. Immediately surrounding the Dana Farber towers are the Beth Israel Deaconess Hospital, Brigham and Women's Hospital, Joslyn Diabetes Center, and the cancer institute's affiliates: Harvard Medical School and Children's Hospital Boston. Each institution individually is renowned as a prestigious center of medicine, research, and teaching; together, they offer perhaps the highest concentration of state-of-the-art patient services to be found in any single location in America. For seriously ill patients in New England, they are the tertiary care facilities of last resort, the centers referred to when the most elite experts are required. Their stature as distinguished institutes of medicine and higher learning are belied by their aging, distinctly urban cast. Unlike the friendly and peaceful green campuses of many newer medical centers, these aged research and clinical buildings are abutted by towering concrete parking garages, not trees. Outside there is a constant din from the clanking and whirring of their air filtration and vent systems. At street level, the area feels positively claustrophobic.

But inside, up high, the feeling is entirely different. The fourteenth-floor research laboratories of Dana Farber, for instance, offer a commanding view of the city of Boston spreading to the horizon. In 1986, as a struggling young scientist, Daniel J. Bergsagel often found refuge in this picture-window tableau. Sitting at his research bench, he could see the Back Bay Fens, part of the extended "emerald necklace" of parks that landscape architect Frederick Law Olmsted designed in Boston before moving on to his more famous urban greenery, Central Park, in New York City. Over the Fens, Bergsagel could see Fenway Park, home of the Boston Red Sox; the Charles River; and, beyond the river, the buildings of the Massachusetts Institute of Technology, in Cambridge. Bergsagel tended to arrive at work late and often worked into the evening. "I would see the lights come on at Fenway Park," says Bergsagel, "and if things weren't going well with an experiment, I would say to myself, I'm just going to the ball game." If Roger Clemens—pitching in those days for the Red Sox—was on the mound, Bergsagel often headed out the door.

Bergsagel, a pediatric oncologist, has a self-deprecating sense of humor and kind eyes that seem particularly suited to working with seriously ill children. His father, Daniel E. Bergsagel, was a pioneering Canadian expert in myeloma, a malignancy that originates in the bone marrow cells and manifests itself in a skeletal lesion type of bone cancer; he was one of North America's very first medical oncologists. When Bergsagel was a child, in the 1960s, his father was employed as doctor and researcher at the M. D. Anderson Medical Center in Houston, a "beautiful—shiny and new" Houston, Bergsagel recalls, whose growth was powered in part by the fledgling NASA space program and by the baby-boom prosperity that was sweeping the country. On Sunday afternoons after church, Bergsagel's father would take one of his four children with him to the laboratory to see how his research mice were holding up under exposure to experimental chemotherapy treatments. As a five-year-old, Bergsagel was fascinated by his father's work, even if he was unsure at the time of its exact purpose. "For a long time," he says, "I thought he was a mouse doctor."

As the elder Bergsagel's experiments continued—eventually producing two chemotherapy agents that remain cornerstones in the treatment of myeloma today—the younger Bergsagel realized that he, too, wanted to be a doctor, not a researcher like his father, but a pediatrician. In 1986, after graduating from medical school, he went to Stanford for a three-year pediatrics residency. He found himself particularly stimulated by the strong pediatric oncology program at the school. He decided to specialize in pediatric oncology and in 1989 headed for Dana Farber. Affiliated with Harvard University and the Children's Hospital Boston, Dana Farber was widely respected for its treatment of children with cancer.

Dana Farber's program called for fellows to spend a year caring for patients, followed by two years devoted primarily to research. In 1987, after months of grueling clinical work, Bergsagel found himself casting about for a research project, unsure of what to do. The number of possibilities in the combined research facilities was overwhelming. One day, on an impulse, Bergsagel decided to approach a Harvard faculty member who happened to see his patients in clinic every Friday, the same day as Bergsagel. Dr. Robert Garcea was quiet and reserved, and Bergsagel knew little about his research interests. But Garcea was a well-respected pediatrics professor who also had extensive expertise in microbiology. Bergsagel slid into a chair across the table in the Dana Farber basement cafeteria where Garcea was sitting down to lunch and came right to the point. "I said, 'I'm confused. I've talked to everybody and I don't know what to do for the next two years of my research. I'm getting all this advice and I don't know who to listen to.' " The senior doctor didn't miss a beat, Bergsagel recalls. "He said, 'You should listen to me. I know what you need to do.' "

What Bergsagel needed to do, according to Garcea, was work for him. Specifically, he was to learn how to use a new technology that had the potential to revolutionize the study of viruses—polymerase chain reaction, known by its acronym as PCR. The molecular technique allows a scientist to detect the presence of even the tiniest amounts of viral DNA in a tissue or other specimen. Instead of searching for the presence of an entire viral genome, researchers use PCR to look for much smaller viral genetic fragments: segments or "regions" of viral DNA unique to the virus they are studying. The technique uses "primers" or chemical agents specifically designed to find these unique viral segments by "annealing" or binding to them. Once even one such viral DNA segment is found, it can be amplified rapidly a millionfold. Used in virology, PCR has become a valuable tool in helping scientists unravel the mystery of what role viruses play in tumor formation. It provides them with a simple method for determining whether viral DNA is present in a tumor. In 1989, when Bergsagel was beginning his research, PCR was still in its infancy.

Garcea, a clinician and researcher, had a long-standing interest in polyoma viruses. The term "polyoma," originally coined by Sarah Stewart and Bernice Eddy, reflected the fact that the mouse virus they had isolated in the mid-1950s could cause multiple tumor types in different species. The next polyoma virus to be discovered was, of course, SV40, a simian version of the mouse polyoma Stewart and Eddy had identified. Other species, as it turned out, also harbor polyoma viruses, including rabbits, hamsters, and baboons. In 1971, scientists discovered humans are host to their own polyoma viruses: JC and BK (named for the individuals in whom they were first isolated). JC and BK are widely transmitted among human beings—an estimated 80 percent of all adults are infected with one or both of them. In healthy individuals, they are usually considered harmless. In immunocompromised individuals, however, both viruses—particularly JC—have been associated with progressive multifocal leukoencephalopathy, a demyelinating disease, in which the nerve cells of the brain lose their protective lipid coating. BK, which was first isolated from the urine of a kidney transplant patient, has also been associated with kidney infections and some rare cancers.

Like their simian and mouse cousins, the two human polyoma viruses proved capable of causing cancer once unleashed from their natural host. In experiments, scientists had successfully used these two human polyoma viruses to induce brain tumors in laboratory animals. Scientists had also, on a few occasions, identified BK or JC in human brain tumors, called ependymomas and choroid plexus tumors, but from these limited observations no one had been able to ascertain whether they were involved in causing the tumors or just happened to be residing in the tumor tissue. Both tumors are rare, often fatal, and often develop within the first two years of life. Choroid plexus tumors account for only 3 percent of all childhood intracranial tumors. Between thirty and sixty cases per year occur in the United States. Ependymomas are more common, accounting for up to 10 percent of all childhood brain and spinal cord tumors, but they are still considered rare. Garcea wondered whether BK and JC might play a role in the onset of the tumors in humans. To investigate his hypothesis, he wanted, as a first step, to see how common they were in human brain tumor tissue. The new PCR technology made it possible to screen a number of tumors for the virus with relative ease.

"He was very well aware that all of the polyoma viruses were potent inducers of tumors" in animal studies, Bergsagel says of Garcea. "And there had been a variety of very suggestive experiments that BK and JC virus could possibly be the cause of tumors in humans. But it's very difficult to prove, because they were extremely small viruses that didn't leave much evidence of their infection. It occurred to him that one of the best ways to look for evidence of infection would be to use this new technology, polymerase chain reaction, which was incredibly sensitive for detecting traces of DNA. What he wanted me to do was become an expert in using

PCR and use that technology to look for evidence of polyoma viruses in human tumors."

Boston was the perfect place to conduct such an experiment. Because they are rare, biopsies of childhood brain tumors are often hard to come by. Dana Farber and Boston Children's Hospital are so-called reference hospitals for all cancers. They had been accepting young patients referred from New England and other parts of the country for decades; consequently, they had a large supply of biopsies of even rare cancers from which Bergsagel could draw.

Garcea met with his protégé weekly, offering advice and encouragement. But he let Bergsagel design the experiments largely on his own. Bergsagel took this responsibility seriously. While he waited for the brand-new $10,000 PCR equipment to arrive, he secured tumor tissue and spent weeks reviewing his experiment protocols. One decision he made proved to be fateful.

Anxious not to waste the expensive chemical reagents needed to amplify the viral DNA, Bergsagel decided to design his experiment to maximize the number of experiments he could perform with each single PCR reaction. Because the polyoma viruses all belonged to the same family, Bergsagel knew that there would be long strings of their genetic code that would be nearly identical, regions that scientists refer to as "homologous" or "highly conserved." He knew that if he tested for these homologous sections of DNA, he could use just one primer reaction to find either JC or BK, killing two birds with one stone, as it were, and conserving his precious reagents. Then, if the primer showed a match, he would conduct further experiments using another primer unique to either BK or JC to distinguish between the two.

"I tried to use primers that would cross-react to try and save money and make it possible for me to do more experiments in less time," he says, looking back at his experiment design with the sheepish regard of one who would know better today. "A Ph.D.," he explains, "probably would have thought I needed to set up very specific experiments only looking for BK and only looking for JC." Bergsagel allows that he also had, in the back of his mind, the grand dreams of a young scientist who hopes to make his name by discovering a brand-new virus: "I thought: I'm going to look for these DNA sequences in the tumor, because I might not find BK virus or JC," but "I might find some similar human virus or some other polyoma virus which no one has ever found before."

Bergsagel's PCR machine finally arrived in the winter of 1988. There was no one to train him in its use, so Bergsagel "pulled out the manual and read it." He had spent four months in the computer lab designing an experiment protocol to test for the presence of portions of the virus that coded for large T-antigen, the tumor-inducing protein that had a similar genetic code in both the BK and JC viruses, and then set to work beginning many months of tedious days in the laboratory.

It wasn't long before Bergsagel began to accumulate data. He had managed to obtain twenty choroid plexus tumors and eleven ependymomas, thirty-one tumor samples in all. When he ran them against his primers, he found something strange. The primers were unquestionably detecting the presence of polyoma viral DNA in most of the tumors. But the "band" of dots on the X-ray film that signifies the presence of large T-antigen DNA reacting with the primers designed to detect it did not look like it was supposed to. "What was frustrating was that I was getting some DNA amplified that looked like it could be a polyoma virus. But it was not a nice, sharp clear-cut band like you should normally get with PCR," Bergsagel recalls. "PCR is an all-or-nothing thing. You get a beautiful band if what you're looking for is there and next to nothing if it's not. And I was getting hazy bands, and they were not as strong as they should be."

Bergsagel tried to figure out what was wrong. Perhaps he had failed to extract the DNA from the tumor samples properly. Perhaps some of the samples, more than twenty years old and stored in paraffin wax, had degraded. By the summer of 1989, he and Garcea realized that the only way to determine what they were detecting for sure was to sequence the DNA segments Bergsagel had amplified—employing the technique that would result in a list of the exact order for each of the individual nucleotides contained in the DNA segments. By sequencing the genetic code of the piece of the virus he had detected, they hoped to be able to pin down whether it was indeed JC or BK. It took Bergsagel a few more months to complete this task because he had to learn to sequence DNA, which at the time was fairly difficult. "I wasn't a very good scientist," Bergsagel says modestly, "so it took longer than average."

By the fall of 1989, Bergsagel had sequenced two of the specimens that had reacted to the large T-antigen primers. Because individual laboratories were not yet equipped with their own computers, Bergsagel had to go to the shared computer laboratory, wait his turn, and compare the sequence to the two polyoma viruses stored in the computer files. He was unsuccessful. "I tried to line it up with BK virus, and it didn't line up. I tried to line it up with JC virus, and it didn't line up," he recalls. Frustrated,

Bergsagel decided to try the National Institutes of Health Web site, which kept a record of all DNA nucleotide sequences known at the time. He sat before the computer and typed in the base pair sequence for his piece of viral DNA, all 127 pairs of letters, one pair at a time. Then he went off to do something else while the computer transmitted the information and NIH computers processed it. When he returned a few hours later, he was surprised at what he saw on the monochrome screen. The NIH computer had responded to his query unequivocally. This was not a new human virus, as he had secretly hoped, but a well-known monkey virus. "It matched up perfectly with SV40," Bergsagel recalls. "It was the one 'Eureka!' moment I had in my entire scientific career."

Bergsagel found that ten of the twenty choroid plexus tumors and ten of the eleven ependymomas tested positive for SV40 gene sequences. "I was in shock when I discovered that—because you don't find monkey viruses in humans," he says. Bergsagel went back and tested the samples again, this time with primers specific to SV40. The results were unequivocal. "In all, [in] sixteen of the twenty-one [positive] specimens we looked at [sequenced], the DNA sequences showed that it was SV40, not BK virus or JC virus," Bergsagel says. "It explained so many things about why my experiments were so frustrating. And even to me as a medical doctor, not a Ph.D. in virology, the fact that I'd discovered a monkey virus in all these human tumors was just astounding. Monkey viruses should not be present in a human brain tumor."

Today Bergsagel marvels at the discovery he made during his short tenure as a research scientist. Garcea, he says, deserves the credit as the "mastermind" of the experiment. But Bergsagel observes that it was his inexperience as a researcher that, ironically, helped lead to the quick breakthrough. "I made a lot of mistakes," he says, candidly. "Because I was a naive medical doctor, not a Ph.D., I looked for the viruses in a way which would find SV40 even though that's probably not the way a Ph.D. would set up the experiments. And also the way I prepared the DNA from some of the tumors was incorrect," he says, referring to his use of low molecular weight DNA as opposed to the preferred high molecular weight DNA. Often scientists employ protocols that call for the DNA to be extracted from a tumor specimen by "spooling" it. Much as one might wind spaghetti around a fork, the scientist twists long strands of DNA around a stick, leaving the short and broken pieces behind. The process captures high molecular weight DNA and avoids the low molecular weight or fractured pieces, which are sometimes considered less valuable. But SV40 is a low molecular weight virus and need not be part of long strands to be present and active in a tumor. "If he [Garcea] had been supervising me more closely or asking me about my technique, he would have probably had me isolate the DNA in such a way where I would have been very unlikely to have captured the fragments where the SV40 was found," Bergsagel says.

Bergsagel's discovery provided the first hard evidence that SV40 could be consistently isolated from human cancers using modern techniques. Co-incidentally, he had made it just a stone's throw from the Boston Children's Hospital laboratory in which John Enders had made his original tissue culture breakthrough. It was the Enders discovery that one could grow massive amounts of poliovirus in tissues—instead of in live monkeys—that had propelled Jonas Salk's discovery that rhesus monkey kidneys could be used to produce a vaccine and that, in turn, had led to the massive SV40 exposure. Now four decades later, the story had come full circle to Boston.

Bergsagel's discovery would eventually land him and Garcea in the *New England Journal of Medicine*—an outstanding publication venue for an aspiring research scientist. But to his consternation, Bergsagel's work was just beginning. From the moment the finding was made public, he was accused of having conducted a flawed experiment—specifically, of having accidentally contaminated his samples with the SV40 virus. "When I first delivered my results at a national meeting of the American Society of Clinical Investigators in the spring of 1989 or 1990, the very first question asked of me by a very respected scientist at the National Institutes of Health was: How can you be certain that your results don't just represent contamination by SV40?" Bergsagel recalls.

Bergsagel understood why such an accusation might be made. Because it is such a potent transforming agent, SV40 is widely used by cancer researchers. Dana Farber, as a prominent cancer research facility, "probably had more SV40 in it than most places," Bergsagel explains. And contamination of PCR samples is a recurring problem for anyone using the PCR technique. Yet, with the proper precautions, including control samples, it is possible to ensure that the results are not a result of contamination, or what scientists call artifact. Bergsagel took precautions that have since become standard practice among all scientists searching for the monkey virus: He extracted the DNA under a sterilized hood in a "clean" laboratory, ran the tests in a different laboratory, and carefully sterilized all PCR equipment after each use. "I was absolutely meticulous," Bergsagel recalls. "I ruined one PCR machine because I used so much household bleach on it." In response to the contamination concerns, Bergsagel extended his fellowship for an additional year and spent much of his remaining time at Dana Farber repeating the experiments to prove that his results were not a function of SV40 having accidentally contaminated his tumor samples.

Fear of contamination became "a huge, ongoing issue" that was frustrating to Bergsagel. He wanted to move on to other experiments that might one day bring relief to his young patients. When Garcea decided to launch a new project—looking for SV40 in several dozen bone cancers called osteosarcomas, which had tested positive for the monkey virus in rodent experiments—Bergsagel was initially interested. But he feared it would take ten years to perform the work to the satisfaction of those who would otherwise accuse him of contamination problems. "That's what led me to leave science, basically, and become a regular medical doctor," Bergsagel says now. His wife, who was from the South, was anxious to move back to that region of the country. And Bergsagel realized that whatever natural talent he might have lacked as a researcher, he made up for as a clinician. When Bergsagel was offered a job as a clinical pediatric oncologist at the Scottish Rite Hospital in Atlanta, he accepted the position. He still works there today.

Repeating their experiments to rule out contamination forced Bergsagel and Garcea to delay publishing their study results for a year. While the delay no doubt frustrated Bergsagel, the timing could not have been better for a young Italian researcher four hundred miles away in Bethesda. In April 1992, shortly after Carbone completed his second set of hamster experiments, he sat down in the reading room of his laboratory building, as he did routinely once a week, and began perusing the latest medical and scientific journals. One of them was a copy of the newly published April 9, 1992, edition of the *New England Journal of Medicine.* Surveying the contents, he noticed there was a report on an SV40 study performed by a team headed by scientists at the Dana Farber Cancer Center in Boston. Later that morning Carbone walked into Levine's office for their weekly Friday lab meeting carrying the magazine. Here, miraculously, was the evidence he needed to persuade Levine. Carbone showed him the article. A journal with the reputation of the *New England Journal of Medicine* was not likely to have published an article with incorrect data, Levine observed. Acquiescing, he told Carbone that he would not fund a study of human tumors, but he also wouldn't prevent Carbone from doing it.

Carbone was elated. But he quickly realized he had a second problem: Where would he find human mesothelioma samples to test? Moreover, would the samples even be suitable for DNA testing? How the tissue is preserved can affect the outcome of any such experiment. Generally, tissue samples come in two types: paraffin-embedded tissue and fresh-frozen tumor tissue. Embedding biopsy tissue in paraffin wax is the traditional method for preserving archival tissue samples. The pathologist drops the tissue sample into formaldehyde for twenty-four hours to "fix" it and then covers it with wax, essentially embalming it for eternity. Paraffin storage eliminates the need for refrigeration and ensures that the sample stays more or less as it was originally found, but small DNA viruses contained in the tumor sample, like SV40, can leach out from the tumor biopsy if it is soaked in formaldehyde too long, a possibility when samples are left to fix over the weekend or during a holiday. Paraffin samples thus have a drawback for any researcher looking for signs of viral DNA in a cancer specimen. In recent years, technology has developed to allow for the storage of tumors in the frozen state. Using this method, the surgeon takes a biopsy and immediately drops it into liquid nitrogen, then transfers it into a freezer where it is kept at minus 80 degrees Celsius, about four times as cold as a normal household freezer. As long as the tumor remains frozen, this storage method is often better than paraffin-embedded storage for research purposes.

Carbone asked everyone he knew where he might find the samples he needed to proceed. He obtained a couple of paraffin-embedded biopsy samples from Canada, but they were not enough for a full-fledged experiment. And then, one day while lunching in the NIH cafeteria with Diane Solomon, chief of cytopathology at the NCI, he told her about his unsuccessful quest. What a coincidence, she said. Didn't you know that one of the best collections of mesotheliomas resides right here at the NCI? It belongs to Harvey Pass, head of thoracic oncology at the NCI Surgery Branch. Pass's office, Solomon said, was right by hers. She offered to call him for Carbone. That afternoon, Carbone spoke to Pass on the telephone. They made plans to meet the next day, but Carbone could hardly contain himself. Tomorrow was too far away. Unable to wait overnight, a few hours after he hung up the telephone, Carbone strode into room 2B09, in Building 10, the laboratory belonging to Harvey Pass.

Pass had a national reputation as a lung surgeon and was fast acquiring a reputation as an expert in mesothelioma. At the suggestion of Helen Pogrebniak—the assiduous M.D. working in his laboratory who would later become his wife—he had diligently saved samples from each of the more than sixty mesothelioma surgeries he had performed. Pass had collected prime samples: not only fresh-frozen tumor specimens, but the peripheral blood and tissue samples from each of the patients necessary to make his collection a particularly outstanding research tool. By the time Carbone walked into his office, Pass was the possessor of what was, no doubt, one of the largest and finest frozen mesothelioma collections in the world.

Like Carbone, Pass was extremely self-assured. He was also a perfectionist, although no more demanding of those around him than of himself. In other respects, however, Pass was quite different from Carbone. With his flat, nasal voice, closely cropped hair, squat frame, and smooth, rounded features, Pass contrasted sharply with the wiry young Italian researcher ten years his junior who was standing before him. Whereas Carbone was easygoing and socially adept, Pass had a reputation as being temperamental and abrupt—the short-tempered, persnickety surgeon right out of central casting. Neither would have guessed that they would become close collaborators and friends.

Carbone was a junior researcher compared to Pass. Still, the surgeon, characteristically, couldn't resist trying to impress him. He led Carbone out of his laboratory into the hall. Like most of the hallways in NIH research buildings, it was crammed with freezers, file cabinets, and other equipment, in violation of building codes that for whatever reason go unenforced at the NIH. Pass threw open his freezer door, grandly revealing the sixty tumor samples within. As Carbone peered into the open freezer, Pass proudly informed the young doctor that he was the surgeon who performed more mesothelioma surgeries than, perhaps, anyone else in the world. "Well, it doesn't take much, does it?" Carbone replied cheekily, referring to the fact that the freezer contained, after all, not hundreds but only a few dozen samples.

If Carbone offended Pass, the senior scientist let it go. Something about Carbone was compelling. "Although he was cocky, I still felt I had to listen to this guy," Pass recalls. For the next forty-five minutes, Carbone explained his plan. Carbone needed some of Pass's mesothelioma biopsies, he said, because he had a hunch that the disease might be caused by a monkey virus, known as simian virus 40, or SV40, that had widely contaminated early doses of the polio vaccine, but that had long been considered harmless to human beings. Pass, who had never heard of SV40, listened, astonished, as Carbone explained the early history of the polio vaccine, what had happened to Bernice Eddy, and his own SV40 experiments with hamsters. Carbone told Pass that he wanted look for SV40 DNA in Pass's human mesothelioma samples, using the same sophisticated molecular technique Bergsagel had used, PCR, to extract tiny fragments of DNA from the tissue and then amplify and characterize them. Like Bergsagel, Carbone would take the amplified viral DNA and further confirm the result by performing a technique called Southern blot to verify the DNA sequences.

The more they talked, the more impressed Pass became with Carbone. The young scientist was energetic and extremely self-confident, something that Pass attributed to Carbone's surgical patrimony. Pass was also struck by Carbone's precautionary plans to avoid PCR contamination. Carbone planned to extract the tumor DNA in a laboratory that had never been used to characterize molecular DNA and then walk the sealed samples across the sprawling NIH campus to perform the DNA amplification experiments in another laboratory. This would allow him to avoid the possibility that any sort of so-called free-floating SV40 DNA from a previous experiment might contaminate Pass's samples, creating a false positive result. And he would use disposable test tube racks so that nothing from the PCR laboratory would ever return to the clean DNA extraction laboratory.

When Carbone had finished describing his proposed experiment, Pass realized that the implications were potentially significant. Only a handful of viruses had been directly associated with human cancers, and none of them were simian in origin. If SV40 was linked to mesothelioma in people, might it also cause bone and brain cancers in human beings, as it had done in hamsters? What if the monkey virus could spread from person to person? And if the virus could cause cancer in human beings, what was one to make of the fact that millions of Americans had been exposed to it as part of a government-sponsored vaccination program? Like every one of his peers specializing in thoracic cancer treatment, Pass knew that asbestos had been identified as the carcinogen that caused mesothelioma. Even though he felt there was no reason to doubt that fact, he decided to help Carbone. "He's got this wild-assed idea," Pass thought to himself, "If it's true, it's unbelievable. Even if it's not, I'm going to get a hell of an education in state-of-the-art molecular biology."

With Pass on board, Carbone had finally convinced an important scientist that his idea was worth pursuing, but he still had to overcome his own lingering doubts. Was it possible that his notion was as foolish as so many people around him seemed to think? Would the whole experiment be a waste of time and money, as others with more experience predicted? Carbone decided to confer with colleagues from within the brotherhood—

fellow pathologists who, he believed, could give him the benefit of their wisdom and experience. Talking with people was his way of working out ideas. He sought out two of the top pathologists in the country, Umberto Saffiotti, then chief of the NCI's Laboratory of Experimental Pathology, and Harold L. Stewart, former director of pathology at the National Cancer Institute. Both men listened as he told his story. Both men urged Carbone to follow his intuition. "Forget what people tell you," said the ninety-two-year-old Stewart, a widely respected pioneer in the field of experimental pathology. "They told me I was wrong all my life. Obviously I did something right to get where I did. If you want to do it, you should, or you will regret it."

Now Carbone had only one remaining obstacle. He could find no one at the NIH willing to assist him with the PCR tests of Pass's samples. His two postdocs needed to publish to advance their careers and were openly skeptical of his hypothesis. They couldn't risk spending six months working on an experiment that was likely to yield nothing, and then have nothing to publish. They declined to participate. Like Bernice Eddy thirty years before him, Carbone would have to undertake the experiments on his own time and with his own resources, since Levine wasn't going to provide additional funding for the work. Running out of options, Carbone prevailed upon his old friend Antonio Procopio, who was a professor of experimental pathology in Italy. He had tenure and wasn't under publication pressure like Carbone's postdocs. Moreover, he had worked for three years at the NIH and was familiar with all the protocols necessary for such an experiment. "I asked him if he was willing to do this crazy project with me. I told him I could not pay him or his expenses, and that the results would most likely be negative, in which case it would be over in two to three months and he could go home," Carbone recalls. A month later, Procopio arrived in Bethesda. "We had no money. He slept in my house for six months, and we worked day and night."

Carbone had promised Pass he would keep him informed of the experiment results day by day. Pass had heard similar promises before from scientists seeking lung tumor samples. More often than not, they disappeared with the specimens never to be heard from again. So it was with relief on Pass's part that a few weeks later Carbone burst back into his laboratory to report on some preliminary results. Pass, who has since become a proficient molecular researcher in his own right, had little knowledge of molecular diagnostic techniques at the time. Carbone threw the blot—the typing paper–sized sheet of film showing the SV40 DNA from the first of Pass's samples as a series of black splotches—up on Pass's light box.

"Here, look at this!" Carbone exclaimed, obviously electrified by the result. "Isn't this incredible?" At the time, Pass hadn't the faintest idea how to "read," or interpret, a blot. But he wasn't about to reveal that to the younger scientist.

"Wow!" said Pass, as he stared, uncomprehending, at the film that was so exciting to Carbone. "Unbelievable!" he added, trying to feign some knowledge of what he was looking at.

Then Pass had an idea. He knew that in any experiment, there had to be a positive control—in this case, a hamster tissue sample from a meso-thelioma that had been induced by SV40—to ensure that the primers being used in the experiment were able to detect the virus when it was present. "Which is the positive control?" he asked. Carbone pointed to an oblong black spot in one of the "lanes" on the far right side of the film. Pass could see that the same black splotch was present in many of the other "lanes" alongside it. Even to an untrained eye like his, he knew that meant that the tumor samples represented in those lanes all had tested positive. Suddenly, the scope of the experiment results became apparent. He could see that more than half the tumor samples contained SV40.

"Un-fucking-believable!" Pass howled.

This time he meant it.

It turned out that Pass's samples were loaded with the monkey virus: 60 percent of the mesothelioma samples contained SV40 DNA; the nontumor tissues from the same patients were negative. The patients suffering from mesothelioma appeared therefore to exhibit the virus only in the mesothe-lioma tumor and not in their normal healthy tissue. This was strongly suggestive that the virus was involved in causing the cancer. Of the forty-eight mesotheliomas Carbone tested, twenty-nine were positive for SV40 DNA, compared to one out of twenty-eight in normal-appearing back-ground lung tissue derived from the same patients. Importantly, none of the twenty-three nonmesothelioma lung tumors or other tumors Carbone tested was positive for SV40 DNA. Moreover, Carbone found that in most of the positive samples he tested, the monkey virus was active, producing proteins—suggesting to Carbone that the SV40 was not merely an oppor-tunistic "passenger virus" that had found a convenient hiding place in the malignant cells but was likely to have been involved in causing the cancer.

Within seconds of seeing the blot on the light box that afternoon, Pass recognized the enormous clinical ramifications of the experiment result. For years, clinicians confronted with a mesothelioma diagnosis could do little more than offer condolences. Surgery and chemotherapy might prolong life for a few months, but eventually the day came when Pass had to look virtually every patient in the eye and deliver the news that the best Western medicine had to offer was still no match for the pernicious malignancy, and that the patient had just a few months, in some cases, a few weeks, to live. All of a sudden, there was a chance that might change. The blot on the light box in his office provided Pass with a glimmer of hope. It meant a potential new avenue for mesothelioma research, and hopefully, one day, an effective therapy, at least for those individuals whose mesotheliomas were SV40-associated. If there was a virus at work in causing these cancers, there was, at long last, a target for a mesothelioma therapy—a potential bull's-eye for a precisely aimed magic bullet. It might take years to develop, but it offered more hope than anything else doctors currently had at their disposal.

In May 1994, Carbone, Pass, and Procopio published the results of their experiment in *Oncogene,* a leading cancer-research journal. It was the first time that researchers had systematically isolated SV40 in human mesotheliomas. In the conclusion of the paper, Carbone, the paper's lead author, proposed that SV40 might be a cocarcinogen with asbestos, somehow helping the mineral fiber cause cancer. He also observed that as many as half of the Americans diagnosed with mesothelioma each year have no history of asbestos exposure, and he speculated that SV40 might be able to cause cancer on its own. In the paper's final section, he reviewed the array of cancers SV40 had caused in hamsters and noted that Bergsagel's research had recently found SV40 in the human version of two such cancers, choroid plexus tumors and ependymomas. This was now a third instance. And while the Bergsagel and Garcea paper two years earlier had made a passing reference to the early SV40 contamination of the vaccine, Carbone was prepared to go a step further, asserting in the conclusion of his paper that the all-but-forgotten polio vaccine might cause cancer in human beings. "One must consider," he wrote, "that the increase in the incidence of mesotheliomas over the last thirty years not only parallels the expanding use of asbestos, but also coincides with the inadvertent inoculation of SV40 into the population when SV40-contaminated kidney cells were used in the preparation of polio vaccines." With that declaration Carbone turned thirty years of scientific dogma on its head and thrust himself into the center of a storm of controversy that was about to erupt all around him.

13

Don't Inflame the Public

CARBONE'S DISCOVERY THAT SV40 DNA was present and producing proteins in human mesothelioma biopsies—and his view that contaminated polio vaccine was involved with the tumors—was a direct challenge to thirty years of federal health orthodoxy. He, Pass, and Procopio had offered evidence that the virus the government had ignored since 1963 was now causing cancer. Worse, they were publishing their results in a major peer-reviewed scientific journal. Bernice Eddy's alarums about SV40 thirty years before had largely gone unnoticed, but *Uncogene* was a widely read, prestigious journal. Scientists from around the world were sure to learn of the discovery, and should the mainstream press learn of the new research, it might pose some embarrassing questions: Had the federal officials responsible for vaccine safety been derelict when they concluded that SV40 contamination of polio vaccine was inconsequential to human health? Were government-sponsored polio vaccines in some way responsible for the spectacular rise in mesothelioma cancer incidence from near zero in the mid-1950s to several thousand cases annually by the 1990s? Perhaps the most disturbing aspect of the whole situation was that Carbone had made his discovery in an NIH laboratory, making the finding that much weightier. Any public announcement about the discovery would appear to bear the imprimatur of the NIH.

It is common for important new NIH discoveries to be publicized by the respective media relations offices attached to each NIH institute, and

Carbone had no reason to think his experiment would be treated differently. He went to Levine with what seemed a logical request: Could he contact the National Institute of Child Health and Human Development media office and arrange for news coverage of the study results contained in his forthcoming paper? *Oncogene* had accepted Carbone's paper in early April and publication was scheduled for May. Carbone could arrange to have the media coverage coincide with the appearance of the journal. He approached Levine at the end of April, a few days before the magazine was set to appear. The two men stood in the NIH parking lot one evening as they were preparing to leave the campus. Levine was far more sensitive than Carbone to the political ramifications of the study. Extra publicity for this study was not something Levine wanted at all. "Let's pass," Carbone recalls him saying, that evening.

Harvey Pass, however, had decided to run the idea by his own superior at the National Cancer Institute, Steven Rosenberg, the NCI's chief of surgery. Each institute at the NIH is independent and has its own hierarchy. Just because NICHD didn't want press exposure, didn't mean that the NCI might not approve of the idea. Like Carbone, Pass felt the discovery was significant. Rosenberg agreed, and a few days after Levine turned Carbone down, the NCI press office arranged a daylong session of back-to-back media interviews for the following Monday, to coincide with *Oncogene*'s publication date. On the Friday before, Carbone drafted a press statement outlining the study results without, he felt, overstating the implications of their research. He wanted it to be clear that the findings they had published were preliminary. The draft statement, he says, did not even mention SV40's connection to the polio vaccine.

On Saturday, Carbone received a call from Levine. He was irate. Levine had received a call from his counterpart at the NCI, scientific director Bruce Chabner. Chabner and his boss, Sam Broder, director of the entire NCI, were concerned about the planned media event and did not want it to go forward. Levine told Carbone that the press event was canceled and that he and Pass were not to speak to the media under any circumstances. Instead of appearing before the press to discuss his findings that Monday, April 25, Carbone reported to Levine's office, where Levine expressed his views in no uncertain terms. Carbone recounted the events in a letter to Pass and Procopio that he wrote later that afternoon: Levine, he said,

> told me that he is worried that the media might exaggerate our findings and alarm the public. For the same reason, he ordered me not

to talk to the media. For the record, I wanted to have a press statement prepared through one or both of the Institutes, and to be able to talk to the media if contacted by them. I also believe that the public and the media have the right to ask us any question they wish once our work has been accepted by a peer review journal and that scientists should not decide what the media should or should not know . . . [Dr. Levine] told me that if I, or Harvey, talked to the press, against his wishes, we would be "punished." He also advised me that if Antonio wants to continue any collaboration with the NIH, he should adhere to his request . . .

Acquiescing to Levine's demands, Carbone promised not to talk to the media. The next day Carbone sent a memo to Levine informing him that he had advised Pass and Procopio not to discuss the paper. He also asked Levine for some guidance, "written, NIH guidelines not subject to personal interpretations" on how to deal with the media. Levine never responded to the request.

Pass was shocked at the uproar, particularly the threat. "I didn't think you got punished for science," he says. "There seemed to be a hysteria about what repercussions this could cause. Why would we be punished for talking about original findings in the laboratory?" Pass was in his eighth year as head of the Thoracic Oncology Section. In his mind, the association of SV40 with mesothelioma was one of the more exciting lung cancer studies to be published in his tenure at the NIH. "I thought this was incredibly novel data—to actually have a virus that was associated with a tumor that had never before been associated with this tumor. I thought this was a phenomenal thing that was going to reinforce, again, the type of science that is done at the NCI." Pass also felt that fears about what might occur at the press conference could have easily been addressed. "At scientific meetings when you have somebody junior talking about their findings, you sit down and go over the presentations with them and you say, 'They're going to ask you this, what are you going to say?' " Pass observes. "If they were concerned about our ability to communicate, they could have said, 'Okay, this is a very important press conference. Let's go over some guidelines.' There was none of that. It was: 'You're not going to talk about this and we're going to handle it.' "

Carbone was also upset, not only about losing the opportunity to speak publicly about his research, but by Levine's treatment of him. Levine had been a mentor, giving Carbone a laboratory of his own and helping guide his research priorities. He hadn't been overly supportive of the SV40 work, but he hadn't tried to hinder or discourage Carbone, either. He had already told Carbone that he could follow up on the SV40 question if he wanted to, even though it might not be a great career move. And, Carbone thought, Levine's desire to have his name on the *Oncogene* paper was a clear sign that his boss endorsed the findings. Suddenly Levine was toeing the NCI line with what Carbone felt was a belligerence that he had not seen in Levine before. "Arthur was not a friend anymore. He was very angry, very upset," Carbone recalls of their interaction at the time. "He told me that if anyone talked to the press it was going to be him or the scientific director of the NCI. It was not going to be me or Harvey Pass. And I told him, if somebody talks to the press it was going to be me. Because nobody talks to the press about my data. And that's more or less how we left each other."

Levine defends the decision to cancel the news conference on the basis of three concerns. One was that Carbone and Pass's findings might have been due to contamination. "Although I had gone over the data endlessly, to the point where I felt comfortable with the publication of the *Oncogene* paper, there was still in my mind the nagging possibility that those findings were due to contamination, since this was a laboratory that had used SV40 extensively and in fact was still doing so," Levine says. "I was reassured by the fact that some specimens had been dealt with in Antonio Procopio's lab [in Italy, where some of the experiments had been repeated], which I was told had never used SV40," but Levine still felt independent confirmation of the experiment was warranted. Levine also worried that Carbone had a touch of the "scientific evangelist" about him. "I was concerned that in a press conference he would be hyperbolic. The press, particularly the untutored and unsophisticated press, might have made more of the data than I thought was indicated at the time." As for the threat to punish anyone who did talk to the press without his permission, Levine says, he does not recall making a threat and that it is not his style to get angry. "I'm a devotee of Joe Kennedy Senior," he says. "Don't get mad, get even."

But the nub of Levine's concerns seems to have been that Carbone's research would reflect negatively on the polio vaccine. Levine says he and his NCI counterparts were concerned that publicity about the study would "inflame" the public's view of vaccines. "To have inflamed the public— made the public anxious about vaccines in general—would have meant that children to some extent would have gone without being immunized against infection that can harm and even kill them. So our public responsibility was profound," he says.

Evidently that responsibility included squelching publicity of a discovery linking SV40 with cancer. Even though Carbone's research implicated the Salk vaccine, which had not been used for decades—and even though Carbone was focused on SV40 and less inclined to talk about the polio vaccine—it seemed, once again, that official federal policy had not changed since the 1960s: Bad news about the polio vaccine was not going to be shared with the public. It had been thirty-four years since Bernice Eddy had approached her NIH superiors with the results of her hamster experiments. Back then, rather than engage in a discussion with her concerning the scientific merit of her experiments, they had ordered her to keep quiet. Now Carbone had been subjected to a similar gag order, this one emanating from high up within the federal health bureaucracy. It was as if the ghosts of Joe Smadel and Roderick Murray had returned to stalk the halls of the NIH, and were, once again, guiding federal health policy.

Despite Levine's threats—and despite Carbone's promise to adhere to his boss's wishes—Carbone did speak to a journalist about the *Oncogene* paper. In late May of 1994, a reporter from the British science journal *New Scientist* interviewed Carbone. She wrote an article about the research results entitled: "Mystery Virus Linked to Asbestos Cancer." In the interview, Carbone was careful to minimize the implications of his research, saying much more work needed to be done. "We do not know where the virus came from, we don't know if it's [authentic] SV40 or a related one, or even whether it is responsible for the tumor," he told the *New Scientist*. The article emphasized that Carbone's primary interest was in what his discovery might mean for fighting mesothelioma: "Carbone is less concerned with the origin of the virus than its potential to make mesothelioma treatable." It noted that Carbone thought attacking the large T-antigen was a potential therapy. "We have a target here and we can try to develop some kind of strategy," he told the journal. Curiously, Levine never reacted to the *New Scientist* article. Perhaps he felt the article was relatively insignificant. A report about SV40 and human cancer appearing in a smaller foreign journal was of little consequence; preventing that same kind of report from appearing in mainstream American media was far more important.

After the *Oncogene* paper appeared, Carbone began to make the rounds of scientific conferences to present his new research. He discovered that cancer specialists were not easily persuaded that SV40 was a possible human carcinogen. Brooke Mossman, director of the Environmental Pathology Program at the University of Vermont, remembers attending a conference of lung cancer experts in Paris in the spring following the publication of Carbone's *Oncogene* paper. Mossman is one of the world's foremost asbestos researchers; she is credited with identifying the mechanisms by which asbestos disrupts a series of interrelated cellular pathways within mesothelial cells, causing the cells to turn cancerous. Carbone attended the conference and made a presentation summarizing his paper. He was not particularly well received; the audience's response was, by and large, dismissive. Asbestos caused mesothelioma; that was a fact. The notion that a monkey virus might be the culprit was unbelievable, even bizarre.

After his presentation, Mossman sought out Carbone and offered him encouragement. She was intrigued by Carbone's mesothelioma research even if it challenged the accepted view of the disease's etiology. The opposition to his finding was, she felt, not based particularly on sound scientific reasoning but motivated by resistance to any finding that threatened the orthodox view. Everyone seemed to have a stake in blaming asbestos for the cancer's origin. "What made it controversial," she says of the early reaction to Carbone's theory, "is that people thought for years that only asbestos causes mesothelioma. That's a very attractive hypothesis for workers and for the asbestos abatement industry, because you can blame every cancer on asbestos exposure and somebody's responsible for that. This is a new mechanism. It's a novel hypothesis. And that is very unattractive to lawyers, to litigation, to the asbestos removal industry." Since that conference, Mossman has continued to be an important supporter of the view that SV40 is capable of causing mesothelioma in humans, especially in the presence of asbestos, consulting with Carbone on his studies of how the two carcinogens may work together to cause the cancer.

In Mossman, Carbone had won his first important scientific ally outside government circles, but back in Bethesda little had changed. In the spring of 1994, shortly after the publication of the *Oncogene* paper, Carbone was summoned to a meeting in Pass's office with three scientists, two of whom were employees from another section of the NCI called the Viral Epidemiology Branch (VEB).

The VEB was a group of about ten researchers. It was contained within a much larger division of the NCI, the Division of Cancer Epidemiology and Genetics, which was headed by Joe Fraumeni. The mission of the Division of Cancer Epidemiology and Genetics was to trace the possible genetic origins of cancer and the prevalence of cancers within certain populations. As a novice epidemiologist, Fraumeni had cut his teeth on SV40, but prior to the spring of 1994, his division had never researched the connection between SV40 and human cancer. Now, coincident with the publication of Carbone and Pass's *Oncogene* paper, his NCI branch was keenly interested in the monkey virus, and the VEB was primed to pursue the topic. The ostensible purpose of the meeting in Pass's office was to discuss collaborations between Pass and Carbone with the VEB on future SV40 research.

One of the VEB scientists who sat in Pass's office that day was James Goedert, a career Public Health Service veteran. Goedert's title was that of "tenured senior investigator," putting him on a par with Pass within the NIH hierarchy. Goedert has worked at the NCI for two of the three decades he has spent as a medical doctor. Thin and erect, with finely honed features and a carefully trimmed mustache, he looks and acts like he belongs in the crisp, military-style PHS uniform which he wears to the office for special occasions. In addition to being a medical doctor, Goedert is an epidemiologist. His subspecialty is the study of the epidemiology of diseases caused by two well-known viruses: HIV, which causes AIDS, and human papilloma virus, or HPV, which can cause genital warts and cervical cancer. The second VEB scientist was Howard Strickler, Goedert's protégé. Like Goedert, Strickler is a medical doctor and an epidemiologist. Lanky and balding, given to oversized suits and the occasional earring, Strickler speaks assertively and authoritatively. Strickler had joined the NCI in 1991. Like Carbone he was classified within the NIH hierarchy as a "staff fellow," a junior-level scientist.

Keerti Shah, the third scientist, was not a government researcher but a senior scientist at the Johns Hopkins University School of Public Health and Hygiene in Baltimore. Goedert and Strickler had asked Shah to attend because of his experience with SV40. Shah, who was born in India, had spent a number of years in the late 1960s examining various populations in India to try to determine whether people living near rhesus monkeys had higher levels of SV40 antibodies in their blood than those in other populations. His principal distinction was as author of a crucial 1976 survey on the state of SV40 research to that time. Much of the survey reviewed the history of SV40 contamination of vaccines. Shah's estimate was that 98

million Americans had been exposed to SV40-contaminated vaccines between 1955 and 1961. Shah concluded that anyone born between 1941
and 1961 had a high risk for exposure. Shah's study, which was funded by
the NIH, had become the basis for a number of assumptions about how
many people and what regions of the country had received SV40-
contaminated polio vaccines. Shah's own conclusion in 1976 was that all
the existing studies on SV40's relationship to human cancers had been
"limited" and were "not sufficient to exclude" the possibility that the virus
was responsible for human disease. In particular, he felt that there was a
need for comprehensive, long-term epidemiological follow-up of SV40-
exposed populations—something that still had not occurred as of 1994,
nearly twenty years later.

After the introductions were completed, the five men squeezed into Pass's
tiny office began to discuss the *Oncogene* paper. It quickly became apparent
to Carbone that Shah and the two VEB scientists were skeptical of his
experiment's results. Shah told Carbone and Pass that he had been unable
to find SV40 in tumor samples that he had examined in his past research.
According to Carbone, Shah suggested that perhaps the *Oncogene* study
findings were a result of contamination of Carbone's samples with SV40
DNA that was still in the laboratory from previous cancer experiments. In
Shah's view, even if minute quantities of the virus remained anywhere in
the laboratory, all of Carbone's samples could have been contaminated—
meaning the only thing Carbone had detected in Pass's tumors was false
positives.

Carbone explained the careful protocol he and Procopio had employed
to prevent just that sort of contamination, notably the decision to prepare
and seal all samples in a laboratory that had never been used for SV40
research. He noted that if the samples had been contaminated, his negative
controls would also have tested positive, and that they had not. Anxious to
reinforce his point, Carbone opened a notebook and began to leaf through
it, showing the original PCR data to Shah. "Shah was nice," Carbone remembers, but the Indian scientist rebuffed his efforts to show him the lab
data. Shah, Carbone says, insisted that if the virus was really present it
should be detectable by Southern blot.

Southern blot is a precise and reliable viral identification technique which
predates PCR, but it has a serious drawback. Unlike PCR, Southern blot
is an all-or-nothing proposition. If a scientist were searching for signs of a
virus in a tumor and happened to pick a few cells for Southern blot analysis

that contained very little virus, the technique might fail to detect it. PCR, on the other hand, can find minute fragments of viral DNA in a tumor and then amplify the fragments many millions of times, ensuring that the scientist has a large enough quantity for an accurate analysis. In modern laboratories, this is the point at which Southern blot is used—to precisely identify the virus recovered following the PCR portion of the investigation. This protocol was the one Carbone and Procopio had followed to confirm the presence of SV40 in Pass's tumors: PCR amplification to isolate the virus followed by Southern blot confirmation (followed by DNA sequencing to definitively confirm that the viral DNA matched the known genomic fingerprint base pair for base pair).

Carbone thought that Shah's preference for Southern blot over PCR was scientifically anachronistic, but at least Shah had extensive experience with SV40. On the other hand, Strickler and Goedert, who were also skeptical of his and Pass's SV40 findings, had no experience with the virus, epidemiologically or otherwise. Carbone felt the pair was unqualified to evaluate his laboratory technique. Neither was a virologist or molecular pathologist, and both were unfamiliar with the ins and outs of viral identification in a laboratory setting. And while Goedert had many research projects under his belt, Strickler's scientific experience was limited. Prior to 1994, he had published only one peer-reviewed research paper, a study of HIV in drug users. In contrast, Pass had published more than a hundred peer-reviewed papers by this time and authored more than thirty textbook chapters. Carbone had authored ten peer-reviewed papers (the *Oncogene* paper was his eleventh), with another dozen and a half shorter research treatments (known as "abstracts") to his credit. Carbone had also written two textbook chapters by 1994; Strickler wrote his first in 1997.

After their critique of Carbone and Pass's paper was finished, Strickler and Goedert proposed that Carbone and Pass collaborate with them on an elaborate study to "better understand the implications," as the pair termed it, of the SV40 findings in Pass's human mesotheliomas. They had two interrelated experiments in mind. In the first one, they would try to determine which techniques would best identify SV40 antibodies in human blood. The second part of the experiment called for employing the antibody assay technique that had been deemed most sensitive to engage in a massive effort to test for SV40 in blood samples collected from dozens of mesothelioma patients and their closest relatives. Goedert and Strickler said that from this experiment they hoped to determine whether the virus was being transmitted person to person within families of SV40-infected mesothelioma victims.

The study's design, however, glossed over a major shift in responsibility for this new avenue of SV40 research. The VEB—despite Goedert's and Strickler's limited expertise in SV40 research—would be very much in charge; Pass and Carbone would be relegated to supporting roles. They would not have the final say in determining which antibody techniques worked best in pinpointing the presence of SV40 and would have no input in picking the subjects and controls for antibody testing. In both studies, Strickler and Goedert would be responsible for final analyses of all experiments and preparation of the study for publication. They also would interpret the data and write the conclusions. As for Shah, his role in the experiment would be to test some of Pass's mesothelioma samples and see if he could find any SV40 in them in his Johns Hopkins lab. Shah would also be given blood samples which came from patients with tumors that Carbone and Pass had determined contained SV40, so that he could look for evidence of SV40 infection in the blood.

After some consideration, Carbone and Pass decided to accept the VEB proposal. True, their roles were limited and their collaborators did not seem to believe the mesothelioma study they had just published, but the truth was, as they both knew, that in science findings must be independently reproduced before they become accepted. Moreover, even with a mountain of molecular biological evidence that finds a virus again and again in a cancer, some skeptics contend that until one can show through epidemiological studies that exposure to the virus equates to increased cancer incidence, there is no proof that the virus is actually involved in causing the cancer. Here were two epidemiologists who seemed interested in pursuing this line of research with respect to SV40 and mesothelioma.

Within weeks Carbone and Pass began to reconsider the wisdom of their decision. First, Shah reported back that his laboratory had been able to identify SV40 antibodies in only one of the blood samples that Pass had provided, raising doubts in Carbone's and Pass's mind about his laboratory technique. Then, about two months after the initial meeting, the *New Scientist* ran a follow-up article to its May report about Carbone's *Oncogene* paper. The July 2, 1994, article was entitled: "U.S. Acts Fast to Unravel Viral Link to Cancer." It announced that "a major investigation is to be launched by government researchers in the U.S. into the apparent link between a virus and the cancer, mesothelioma."

The article provided some background about mesothelioma and Carbone's mesothelioma study findings—which was all well enough—but then came its penultimate sentence: "Howard Strickler and James Goedert at the National Cancer Institute are to head the new studies." When Pass read the sentence, he hit the roof. If the VEB scientists thought they were going to take over the research that he and Carbone had begun, they had better think again. Shah couldn't detect SV40 antibodies in the blood samples from patients that Pass had already determined were infected with the virus; and the two VEB scientists—and Shah—were openly skeptical about the presence of SV40 in human mesotheliomas. Why should he and Carbone assist them in trying to usurp their area of research? He withdrew his offer to share his specimens and dropped out of the experiment. Pass instead resolved to learn PCR and try to replicate the *Oncogene* experiment himself by looking for SV40 DNA using brand-new mesothelioma specimens. He completed this study successfully, publishing it in 1998.

Coincident with Pass's decision to withdraw from the collaboration with the VEB, Carbone had decided to leave the NIH. He was living with his future wife, Beth, and wanted to remain in the United States, but he was worried about his future. The encounters with NIH higher-ups about the press conference had confirmed his feeling that his wisest career move was to leave Bethesda. "They strengthened my resolve that in this world you need to be totally independent. You do not depend on the good mood of other people," he says of the incident. For true independence, Carbone realized that he needed, in addition to his medical license, the same board certification in pathology in the United States that he had obtained in Italy. That way, if it should ever come to pass that he couldn't find work as a researcher, he could practice medicine. Certification as a pathologist would also allow Carbone to perform and bill for pathology services, making him that much more valuable to a medical school or cancer institute.

In July 1994, Carbone left the NIH for the University of Chicago to complete his pathology residency so he could become board certified in the United States. Soon afterward, Pass also left the NIH, moving to Detroit to assume the position of professor of surgery and oncology at Wayne State University and chief of thoracic oncology and associate director for clinical research at the Barbara Ann Karmanos Cancer Institute.

The departures of Pass and Carbone did little to faze Goedert and Strickler, however. Soon after Pass walked out of the collaboration, the two VEB epidemiologists embarked on another SV40 plan, one with an entirely different agenda. Instead of an epidemiological study to see if they could measure the spread of SV40 among mesothelioma patients and their families, they decided to conduct a full repeat of the Pass and Carbone experiment—probing human mesothelioma samples for the presence of SV40 using PCR. By late summer 1994, Strickler and Goedert had finalized the design of their new study.

Because Pass was no longer providing them with tumor samples, the pair had been forced to locate another source of mesothelioma samples, the Armed Forces Institute of Pathology. But unlike Pass, who had an extensive collection of fresh-frozen tumor samples, the only mesotheliomas the Armed Forces Institute of Pathology was willing to make available in any quantity had been preserved in paraffin wax—a difference that would prove to be crucial. Moreover, because Strickler and Goedert had no experience in performing the PCR analysis or other viral identification work on the mesothelioma samples themselves, they would instead "contract" with Shah's laboratory to perform all the molecular work. To complicate matters further, Shah, who had already expressed doubts about the efficacy of PCR, would not perform the PCR work himself, but would relegate this most critical task to a technician in his laboratory.

With the study's rather unique protocol in hand, the three scientists began this second mesothelioma survey. Nine months later, on May 15, 1995, Goedert reported on the results in a memo to one of his superiors within the Division of Cancer Epidemiology and Genetics. Shah's laboratory, he said, had tested 50 mesothelioma samples from the Armed Forces collection but could not find any SV40 DNA sequences in a single one of them. Shah had also tried testing blood samples obtained from thirty-five mesothelioma patients that, according to Goedert's memo, Pass had said should contain SV40 antibodies up to 50 percent of the time. Shah had obtained positive results in only three of the thirty-five mesothelioma blood samples. Shah had also examined the blood from thirty-five patients with a bone cancer known as osteosarcoma, which had been linked to SV40 in hamster experiments, including Carbone's. Again, the results were poor. Only one of the thirty-five osteosarcoma blood samples tested positive for the virus.

Although Shah had been unable to find SV40 in any of the Armed Forces specimens, he had detected SV40 at least once during the experiment. One of Carbone's original mesothelioma biopsy samples, which Carbone had reported tested positive the previous year, had also tested positive for SV40 in Shah's lab. This seemed to provide some confirmation for the results that Carbone and Pass had published in their *Oncogene* paper. Goedert, however, omitted this salient point entirely in his report to his superior, failing to even mention this one positive biopsy. Shah's lab had also found SV40 in an osteosarcoma sample provided by Carbone. This, too, was not mentioned by Goedert in his memo. Instead, he recounted his and Strickler's "concern about possible contamination" of Carbone and Pass's laboratories as an explanation for the original positive findings. Indeed, the claim that laboratory contamination lay behind all positive SV40 findings in human tumors soon became de facto government policy.

Goedert concluded his memo by stating that he hoped to "summarize the negative . . . data from the mesothelioma study for publication, perhaps as a letter to the *New England Journal of Medicine*." (It would be a full year—June 1996—before the VEB study was printed. It did not appear in the *New England Journal of Medicine* as Goedert had originally hoped, but in a lesser-known journal called *Cancer Epidemiology, Biomarkers and Prevention.*) He added that now that this study was completed, "I do not expect SV40 to become a major focus of VEB research."

For anyone in Bethesda who had worried about how to respond to the findings of SV40 in human mesotheliomas by Carbone and Pass, Strickler and Goedert had delivered a ready-made present, all tied up and neatly wrapped. The two government scientists, with no experience in performing laboratory virology studies and no familiarity with SV40, had teamed with Shah, a scientist who doubted SV40 could be reliably identified with PCR. They had looked for SV40 in human mesotheliomas and found it absent. They had searched for evidence of SV40 in the blood of victims of cancers supposedly associated with SV40, and it was hardly ever there. There was now a direct contradiction to Carbone's *Oncogene* paper—a government study, with the authority of the entire NIH behind it, stating that there was no demonstrable connection between SV40 and human cancer.

Over the next several years, more and more independent laboratories around the world began to find SV40 in human tumors, but this lone negative study by Goedert, Strickler, and Shah, became the linchpin of federal efforts to cast doubt on SV40's association with human cancers. Should someone assert there seemed to be an awful lot of labs recovering the simian virus from human tumors, a federal spokesperson could always cite the VEB work and say, "Not necessarily so." For example, a 1999 consumer fact sheet from the Centers for Disease Control called "Questions and Answers on Simian Virus 40 (SV40) and Polio Vaccine" tackled the thorny issue of increasing reports of the simian virus in tumors this way: "Recently some researchers identified SV40 virus in the cells of some rare human cancers using modern techniques. However, other scientists have not been able to validate these findings and have not found the virus in similar cancers."

At the time the CDC prepared the fact sheet, more than two dozen published studies from more than fifteen different laboratories had found the monkey virus in human cancers. The only published negative study was the one performed by Strickler, Goedert, and Shah. Yet a casual reader would assume from the CDC phrasing that there had been many such studies and that they nullified all the positive ones. For the rest of the decade and beyond, the CDC and other health policy makers would employ the same strategy. Despite a tenfold difference between the number of positive and negative studies connecting SV40 with human tumors, they would cite the "inconsistency" in studies, successfully obscuring the fact that they were relying on a tiny number of mostly VEB-sponsored negative studies to contradict the multitude of positive studies produced in independent laboratories around the world.

Any comfort that federal health officials may have derived from Strickler and Goedert's negative mesothelioma study was, however, short-lived. In the same May 1995 memo in which Goedert reported on the VEB study, he stated that there was another positive SV40 study in the offing. This one was coming from the laboratory of the highly respected SV40 expert Janet Butel. As far as federal health officials were concerned, this was a most unwelcome development.

14

A Call to Turn Aside the Dogma

JANET BUTEL HAS been a constant presence at Baylor University's College of Medicine since 1963, rising in stature from a graduate student to head of the Department of Molecular Virology and Microbiology. Butel, who is in her sixties, has the appearance of a favorite grandmother, with comfortable eyeglasses and blond hair styled in a short, hair-sprayed fashion. She speaks calmly and deliberately. Butel's reputation as a virologist transcends even the political boundaries that separate those who support SV40 research from those who oppose it. Mention her name to a senior federal health official in Bethesda—even one who is skeptical of SV40 findings— and he or she will respond in respectful tones. Among her peers, Butel is known for her reliability. Experiments emanating from her laboratory are assumed to be careful and thorough and her conclusions completely documented. She has an equally strong reputation as a teacher and administrator. Listening to her present a paper at a scientific conference, it is easy to imagine how she has successfully guided countless struggling graduate students and medical doctors through the intricate world of molecular virology during her four decades at Baylor.

Still, her first love is research. Over the years, she has examined how the normal biochemical activity of certain viruses can lead to disease and tumors within "host" organisms. She has worked with adenoviruses, mouse mammary viruses, and mouse polyoma viruses. But her enduring focus has been the biochemistry of SV40. She published her first paper on the subject in

1964, one year after she arrived at Baylor. Today she is regarded as one of the leading SV40 experts in the world. Even after forty years, her enthusiasm for the subject is unmistakable; she can spend hours expounding on the science of SV40 with a level of clarity and precision unusual even in the world of pedagogy.

Butel was born in 1941 in Overbrook, Kansas, a prairie town astride the old Santa Fe Trail on U.S. Highway 56, about twenty-five miles south and east of the state capital, Topeka. Overbrook was, and still is, a small farming community. (The population was six hundred when Butel was growing up; four decades later it has yet to top a thousand.) Butel was born and raised on a farm, and farming had been a family occupation for several generations. As a youngster, Butel attended a one-room schoolhouse with ten students. It was at the local high school (twenty-five students were in her graduating class) that she was first exposed to science in chemistry classes. She recalls finding it "stimulating" and "challenging." After high school, Butel elected to stay relatively close to home, attending nearby Kansas State University in Manhattan, the same college at which her mother had studied architecture and engineering several decades before. (Butel says her mother was the only female student at Kansas State at the time.) While taking a bacteriology course, Butel fell in love with virology. "I was enchanted," she says, recalling that she was especially intrigued that viruses, while seemingly not "alive" in a classic biological sense, were nonetheless an entire class of discrete organisms. "I just thought they were the most fascinating things I had ever heard of."

Butel graduated summa cum laude from Kansas State in 1963 with a degree in bacteriology. Encouraged by some of her professors to take advantage of her scientific talents and attend graduate school, she elected to specialize in viruses. There were two possible choices for her at the time; one was at St. Louis University, which had the advantage of being relatively close to home in neighboring Missouri; the other was hundreds of miles away in Houston at Baylor University. The fact that one of her brothers, now an engineer, was in Houston at the time led Butel to Baylor.

When Butel arrived at Baylor, the virology department was headed by Joseph Melnick, one of the preeminent virologists of his day. A towering figure in the world of polio vaccine research, Melnick was considered one of the fathers of the polio vaccine because of his contributions to the science of polio and his role as an expert advisor on vaccine policy beginning in the 1950s. Soon after the discovery of SV40, Melnick obtained some samples of the virus from Maurice Hilleman, one of the two scientists who had originally isolated it. Samples in hand, Melnick went on to make important contributions to the early understanding of SV40. In 1962, for example, he published the first research to demonstrate that children who took SV40-contaminated oral polio vaccine were excreting live SV40 for weeks afterward—a finding that must have come as a shock to Albert Sabin, who had insisted since 1960 that if there was any SV40 in his vaccine it was being ingested and passed harmlessly through the digestive tract without ever multiplying and causing human infection. Melnick also demonstrated that monkeys could pass SV40 infections among each other through urine, suggesting that the kidneys were a natural reservoir of the virus. The SV40 strain that Hilleman gave Melnick was eventually sequenced by Baylor researchers and became known as the Baylor strain. Although Melnick himself devoted little of his own time to SV40 research after the early 1960s, his laboratory soon became famous for the quality of its work on SV40, cranking out study after study on the virus and how it worked in cell cultures and in animals. After she arrived at Baylor, many of those studies bore Butel's name.

By the end of the 1980s, Butel, who succeeded Melnick as head of the department, had coauthored more than a hundred virology papers, more than half of them concerning SV40. She had verified that SV40 caused cancer in rodents and was deeply involved in research that examined how it did so, yet, like most other SV40 experts of the day, she had failed to make a connection between the simian virus and human disease. This, even though throughout the 1970s and 1980s, the virus was being spotted in some unusual places.

In 1972, for example, a young Johns Hopkins University neurologist, Leslie Weiner, reported in the *New England Journal of Medicine* that, using antibody tests, he had isolated SV40 from the brains of two patients with the demyelinating disease, progressive multifocal leukoencephalopathy (PML). Weiner's results appeared to be a dramatic breakthrough, but his paper was greeted with widespread skepticism by the experts in the field. They said that he was a victim of his inexperience. Either he had confused the simian virus with one of the two human polyoma viruses, BK and JC, or, more likely, his lab was contaminated with stray bits of SV40 that had found their way into his PML samples. Weiner repeated the experiment three times, at one point essentially cleaning his lab from top to bottom to eliminate any possibility of accidental contamination. Each time he got the same results, but each time he encountered the same disbelief. Discouraged, Weiner dropped the subject entirely and never again investigated the possible relationship of SV40 to PML or to any other human brain disorder. (Ironically, Weiner's findings of SV40 in the brains of PML patients have been duplicated several times, including as recently as 2001.)

After Weiner's 1972 *New England Journal of Medicine* article, there were a few other odd SV40 sightings in human cancers—a melanoma, some bladder cancers, and a half-dozen studies that linked the virus to human brain tumors, including meningiomas, a frequent, but usually nonfatal brain cancer, ependymomas, and glioblastomas, a tumor of the nonneuronal tissue of the brain. But reaction to these studies from the virologists who worked with SV40 everyday in the laboratory was the same disbelief that greeted Weiner's 1972 PML paper. The studies were reported by scientists with no established background in the field—perhaps the findings were the result of confusion, contamination, or poor laboratory technique—and the studies were by and large never replicated. There was little reason to lend them much credence. Not linking SV40 to human disease had become "good science," just as not worrying about simian viruses in a vaccine had been "good science" when Salk, Sabin, and other vaccine pioneers were perfecting the polio vaccine. "I kind of ignored them like everyone else," Butel says of the early SV40 reports.

Beginning in 1990, however, Butel's attitude toward the possibility that the simian virus could be involved in human disease underwent a dramatic shift. That year, Bob Garcea approached her about the Bergsagel experiment that he was supervising. Garcea was a longtime acquaintance; like Butel, he was one of the "old SV40 crowd," as she puts it, and therefore had the qualifications to research the virus. When Garcea told her that Bergsagel had found SV40 in his human brain tumor samples, she was intrigued. Garcea was anxious to come up with another way to confirm Bergsagel's results and asked Butel if she could arrange for Milton Finegold, a pathologist at Baylor, to perform additional tests on the tumors in order to determine whether the SV40 was actively expressing proteins. Using antibodies Butel had created against SV40's T-antigen, Finegold tested eleven of Bergsagel's SV40-positive tumor samples. He found that in seven of them, large T-antigen was actively being formed in the tumor cells. This was a strong indication that the virus was not merely a "passenger"—using the tumor cells as a convenient hideout—but might actually be having an effect on the cells. In 1992, when Bergsagel's paper was published in the

New England Journal of Medicine, Butel and Finegold were both listed as contributing authors.

Bergsagel's study, exciting as it was, raised a critical question: What exactly had he found in the brain tumors—an SV40 variant or an entirely new virus? Viruses commonly have many different strains. Poliovirus, for example, has a few disease-causing varieties and many dozens that are harmless. Human papilloma virus has more than one hundred different strains, only a few of which have been associated with cancer. The same genetic variety exists within SV40 viruses. In 1978, the DNA of one of the SV40 viruses that Sweet and Hilleman had originally isolated in 1960 had been sequenced in its entirety. Now known as "776," it was considered to be the reference strain, or standard, against which all other SV40 viruses were measured. Scientists since had described several SV40 variants, including the Baylor strain, but none differed so dramatically from 776 that they could be classified as anything other than authentic SV40. They were, therefore, all the same virus that had originally come from monkey kidneys.

Whether this was true for Bergsagel's viruses was unknown. Bergsagel had used PCR to amplify sections of SV40 that coded for large T-antigen and then had run his DNA sequencing tests on these fragments. PCR is designed only to amplify such representative portions of a virus and not an entire virus. Except for T-antigen Bergsagel had not looked for other regions unique to SV40 DNA. Was it possible that the virus he had discovered was actually a genetic recombination between SV40 and one of the human polyoma viruses, BK or JC? Could his virus have coded for SV40's large T-antigen, but otherwise been different? If so, that would mean that Bergsagel had not found the SV40 that had been isolated from monkeys and contaminated the polio vaccine, but a chimera—perhaps a part-monkey and part-human virus. Or maybe it was simply a new, unknown human polyoma virus that had many similarities to SV40. No one would really know until his tumor isolates were studied in much more detail.

Butel was now interested in fully characterizing Bergsagel's virus. She decided to reexamine Bergsagel's brain tumor samples for herself. The first task was to repeat Bergsagel's experiments. A medical resident working in Butel's laboratory had been assigned the job of preparing PCR primers; the very first step was to prepare the necessary PCR controls. Scientists who use PCR to screen for the presence of a virus in tumor samples routinely set up both negative and positive PCR controls as a precaution to ensure that their results are genuine and not the result of artifact—or false in some way. A common negative control is water, or some other substance known to be negative for the virus. If a known negative control, such as water, tests positive, it is an indication that the laboratory is contaminated and that the PCR results on the tissue sample cannot be trusted. Confronted with such a result, the scientist would scrap the experiment and start over again. Scientists also run positive PCR controls. They test tissue samples known to be positive or that have been deliberately spiked with high levels of the virus. This helps them ensure that the primers they are using are sensitive enough to detect any virus that might be present in the tumor sample. Butel's medical resident was having difficulty getting the positive controls to work. It seemed that no matter how many times he ran the PCR reaction on his spiked samples, he found nothing. Until he worked out this glitch, he couldn't proceed to test the actual tumor tissue samples. Eventually, his study period ended in the laboratory and he departed.

Butel's experiment might have stalled at this point were at not for the expertise of a postdoctoral student named John Lednicky, who arrived in Butel's laboratory in 1992. Tall and athletic, with a receding hairline that is offset by a small goatee, Lednicky is an outdoors enthusiast, an expert scuba diver, and an avid soccer player. But he is also a virologist's virologist. "John is the only person I've ever met who can look at a series of DNA base pairs on a piece of paper and without even checking it against a key recognize exactly what section of viral code he is seeing," says Carbone. "It's like he's got a computer chip in his brain. It's absolutely amazing. He looks at the sequence—ATTGG etc.—and he can tell you what virus it is, what strain it is, what variant of the virus it is, what region of the genome it is. Really, I've never seen anything like it."

Lednicky had graduated from the University of Texas at Austin with a Ph.D. in microbiology and already had extensive experience with polyoma viruses. He was interested in the DNA transcription and replication of polyoma viruses—how they reproduce themselves and transfer genetic information to an RNA messenger molecule—and was attracted to Butel's lab by the prospect of exploring the biochemical properties of the large T-antigen. He was an expert in PCR, particularly the fine points of the technique when trying to detect SV40 and other polyoma viruses.

After the hapless medical resident had departed, Butel asked Lednicky if he could figure out what had gone wrong. Lednicky began from scratch. Whereas the resident had relied on Bergsagel's paper for information on the nucleotide sequences needed to prepare the control primers, it was Lednicky's policy never to begin an experiment without verifying all gene sequences required for the primer through Genbank, the massive international database of all publicly available DNA sequences. As soon as he consulted Genbank, the problem immediately became clear. In Bergsagel's published paper, one nucleotide sequence for a positive control had accidentally been transcribed backwards. Because the medical resident hadn't looked up the official sequence in Genbank, he hadn't seen the mistake. When Lednicky reversed the order, he was able to make the positive controls work.

With the primer glitch resolved, the actual work was ready to start. Garcea sent Butel and Lednicky seventeen of the brain tumor samples Bergsagel had tested in 1988 and 1989. All the samples were blinded, or masked, so that Lednicky and Butel had no idea whether they were positive or not. For the next several months, Lednicky was busy with PCR testing. In addition to the lengthy segment of the virus for which Bergsagel had tested, Butel and Lednicky also looked for nucleotide sequences representative of other regions of the SV40 genome.

When the results came in, Lednicky was chagrined. Like Bergsagel before him, he had harbored dreams of making a name for himself by discovering a brand new virus. Instead what he had detected was SV40, and only SV40. He and Butel looked at three distinct regions of the virus: the one that coded for large T-antigen, another which regulated viral replication, and a third which coded for one of the constituent proteins in the virus's capsid, or protective coating. All three regions were typical of the simian virus— not the human polyomas, JC or BK, or any other virus. There was no mistaking it: The virus present in Bergsagel's brain tumors had come from monkeys.

Butel's and Lednicky's PCR work also independently confirmed the accuracy of Bergsagel's original findings. All of the samples that Bergsagel had identified as positive did indeed contain SV40, they concluded. Moreover, when Lednicky examined fresh tumor tissue that had not been fixed in paraffin, he was able to extract a complete, infectious SV40 virus—a feat somewhat akin to pulling a needle out of a haystack. It was incontrovertible proof that the simian virus that had been presumed dead when present in the polio vaccine was alive and kicking, possibly causing cancer decades later in humans.

In July 1995, Butel and Lednicky, with Garcea and Bergsagel listed as coauthors on the paper, published the results of their SV40 viral sequencing in the well-known journal *Virology*. (Ironically, in 1960, Bernice Eddy had suggested to Joe Smadel that her original findings of cancer caused by rhesus kidney extracts be published in *Virology* because of its reputation and wide circulation among researchers. Smadel had rejected the idea.) The results, they said, were clear: The SV40 in the human brain tumors was "authentic"; it was "not due to laboratory contamination," and it was present in the same kind of human tumors that the virus could induce in laboratory animals. If Lednicky had been disappointed in the experiment's final outcome, Butel seemed taken aback. "The results reported here are somewhat unexpected," she wrote in the paper's concluding section, "because the dogma has been that SV40 infections of humans are very rare and harmless. These new data, together with reports from other laboratories, indicate that the dogma needs to reevaluated."

In Bethesda, Butel's call to turn aside the dogma that SV40 was harmless was received with consternation. For one thing, work emanating from Butel's laboratory could not be readily dismissed. It may have been tempting to write off Carbone as an overeager young scientist, publishing tendentious results in order to make a name for himself. But, given her stature in the world of virology, such a tactic would not work for Butel. For another, she and Lednicky had established there was no question that the virus in the Bergsagel brain tumors had originally come from a monkey. Logically, that meant the polio vaccine was the most likely source. Moreover, the positive brain tumor samples all came from children too young to have received contaminated Salk vaccines. That meant that either SV40 now was being transmitted within the human population or vaccine supplies since 1964 had still been contaminated at times.

Neither scenario was reassuring—a fact that was reflected by Goedert in the same 1995 memo in which he described the VEB-Shah failure to replicate Carbone's mesothelioma results. Goedert had apprised Andrew Lewis, Carbone's former lab chief, and now director of a laboratory in the Food and Drug Administration's Office of Vaccine and Research and Review, of the VEB's negative mesothelioma survey, but Lewis had also heard about Butel and Lednicky's just-completed brain tumor study. According to Goedert, Lewis was worried about the experiment's implications:

> . . . Dr. Lewis had already learned of our negative results from Dr. Shah. However, Dr. Lewis expressed continued concern about the report from the laboratory of Dr. Janet Butell [*sic*] of SV40 sequences in ependymoma tumor tissue in children, particularly because it would

imply SV40 transmission, presumably from the mothers of these children.

Goedert did see a silver lining to this unexpected storm cloud, however. He had heard through the scientific grapevine that the SV40 DNA Lednicky and Butel had characterized from the tumors was not identical to 776, Baylor, or other well-known SV40 strains used by laboratories around the world. That left an opening to discredit their work: "It should be added, however, that Dr. Strickler and I have heard a rumor that the DNA viral sequences from these ependymomas are all prototypical, suggesting possible laboratory contamination."

The "rumor" to which Goedert referred was true. Lednicky and Butel's DNA sequencing of the SV40 they found in Bergsagel's brain tumors showed slight variations in nucleotide sequences from SV40 used in most laboratories, including Butel's. But the implications were quite the opposite of Goedert's supposition: The slightly altered configuration of nucleotides proved that the SV40 they were finding could *not* be the result of laboratory contamination. The SV40 strain discovered by Butel and Lednicky in the brain tumors could not have gotten in their specimens as a result of contamination from a previous experiment, precisely because it had never before been used in their laboratory.

If SV40 was present in mesotheliomas and brain tumors, what about a third tumor in which it had been found in hamsters: bone tumors? Soon after completing the mesothelioma study, Carbone obtained some bone tumor specimens and began some initial SV40 experiments. When he left the NIH for the University of Chicago, he took the project with him. As had been the case with the mesotheliomas, Carbone found the human bone cancers did indeed contain SV40. The virus was showing up especially frequently in one particular kind of tumor: osteosarcoma, a cancer of the long bones of the body, and the identical bone cancer type that had been observed in SV40-exposed laboratory animals.

Wary of the skepticism that had greeted his mesothelioma study, Carbone decided to try to interest another scientist in the experiment to confirm his results. He picked up the telephone and called Bob Garcea at the University of Colorado, where Garcea now worked. It was the first time the two men had spoken. Carbone told Garcea about his newest experiment and asked if he could send the samples to Garcea for independent verification by his laboratory. Garcea, Carbone recalls, said, he had already performed a similar bone cancer survey (the one in which Bergsagel had decided not to participate), and he, too, had detected SV40 DNA. Instead of just exchanging samples, the two men decided to design a much larger collaborative study using "blinded" specimens to independently confirm their results.

The protocol called for four labs—Carbone's lab, Pass's new lab in Detroit, Garcea's in Colorado, and Procopio's in Chieti, Italy—to test bone cancer samples for the presence of SV40, "mask" the specimens, and then send them to the other partner labs. Once the partner labs received the "blinded" samples, they would test them, but they would have no inkling what the original laboratory had concluded about the samples until the completion of the experiment. If receiving laboratories reproduced the results obtained by the original testing laboratory, it would be strong proof that any positive SV40 findings were not the result of contamination, poor technique, or other laboratory error, but were bona fide.

Bone cancer samples from hospitals in the United States, Canada, Italy, and Germany were tested. The results for any one sample were not considered to be positive unless SV40 was confirmed by all four participating laboratories. When the specimens were unmasked at the end of the experiment, Carbone and Garcea discovered their collaboration had confirmed the earlier experiments they each had undertaken individually. Almost one-third of the osteosarcomas, 40 out of 126, were positive for SV40 large T-antigen DNA. Moreover, 14 of 34—or more than 40 percent—of a mixture of other bone-related tumors were also positive for the SV40 DNA. In 1996, Garcea, Carbone, Pass, and Procopio published the joint bone cancer survey results in *Oncogene*.

The 1996 study confirmed Carbone's hunch that SV40 was present in human bone cancers. The virus had now been connected to every human cancer that it had consistently caused in hamsters in the 1960s. The study also confirmed Bergsagel and Butel's mysterious finding that the virus was showing up in tumor tissues from patients who had not yet been born during the nine-year-long Salk vaccine contamination. Like the brain tumor biopsies, many of the osteosarcomas Carbone and Garcea tested were from young patients—too young, as the authors noted, to have been exposed to the SV40-contaminated vaccines in the 1950s and 1960s.

Clearly, if bone and brain tumors from children and young adults were now testing positive for SV40, there was a new public health question beyond whether SV40 was actually causing the cancers in which it was being found: How widespread was SV40 in the human population? Again, it was Janet Butel who decided to address this critical question, this time with two serological studies in which she examined blood samples to see if it was possible to determine SV40 prevalence within the population.

In the first study, Butel tested a group of 416 HIV-positive and HIV-negative men born after 1941. Twelve percent of the HIV-negative men showed evidence of SV40 infection compared with 16 percent of the HIV-positive group. The difference in SV40 antibody rates between the two groups, Butel concluded, was statistically insignificant. Therefore, the 12 to 16 percent range for the presence of SV40 antibodies among the men could be considered as an indication of the number of people in the United States who at one time or another have been exposed to SV40. Butel further broke down her data and examined just the men born after 1962, the year prior to the end of the use of SV40-contaminated vaccine stocks. Supposedly, almost all individuals in this group had no exposure to SV40 through contaminated vaccines, yet Butel found 10 percent of this group tested positive for antibodies to SV40.

Butel next tested sera from 337 Houston-area children born between 1980 and 1995, who had been hospital patients during the fall of 1995. Six percent of the children—despite birth dates twenty to thirty years after the supposed end of the SV40 contamination of vaccines—had antibodies to SV40. For thirteen of the children whose blood tested positive for SV40 antibodies, she tested tissue samples, if they were available, for the presence of SV40 using PCR and DNA sequencing. In most cases, the amount of tissue available for testing was extremely limited and Butel believed she had little chance of recovering any SV40, yet SV40 was found in the tissues of four children, all of them born after 1982—a finding she called "impressive" in her published paper on the study.

Butel's results indicated that SV40 was still getting into children, decades after the polio vaccine was supposedly cleaned up. Moreover, the 6 to 10 percent exposure rates that the two studies suggest, might just be the tip of the iceberg. Serological tests can only describe the *minimum* number of individuals who have been infected; they say nothing about the *maximum*. At best, they offer only an outline of viral exposure. After a while, an individual may stop making antibodies to a given virus, even if he or she had previously been exposed (hence the need for booster shots for certain vaccines). This is especially true for polyoma viruses like SV40, which can linger in the body in a latent state, causing long-term persistent infections.

While Butel's serological studies did not answer exactly how widespread the virus was in the human population, they clearly showed that the simian virus was no longer confined to those who had received contaminated vaccines during the 1950s and '60s—most of whom were baby boomers or older. Some of the children—and even the grandchildren—of the baby boom generation were now carriers of the virus as well. "I'm convinced that SV40 is able to cause infections in children," Butel said in a 1999 interview about her serology results. But why SV40 was spreading remained a mystery. Perhaps the virus was being transmitted from mother to child, as Andrew Lewis had feared—or through sexual contact. (In 1996, a team of scientists in Italy found SV40 in the sperm of healthy men.) Perhaps the polio vaccine was, somehow, still contaminated at times. Or perhaps SV40 virus had always been present in some small percentage of the population—for example, people in northern India exposed to rhesus monkeys—even before the polio vaccine introduced it into humans on a much more massive scale. One thing was clear from the Butel studies: SV40 had broken out from the original group of Salk vaccinees and was apparently here to stay.

15

On the Scientific Map

IN THE FALL of 1996, shortly before assuming his new position at Loyola University, Carbone heard from his NIH mentor, Andrew Lewis, that the federal government was going to hold its first-ever scientific conference devoted solely to discussion of SV40. The site of the two-day workshop was to be the NIH campus in Bethesda, Maryland, and it would occur that coming January. The proposed agenda suggested there would be a thorough discussion of the implications of SV40 findings in human tumors, including whether the virus was spreading among humans, and how it might possibly be causing the cancers in which it had been discovered.

Carbone was excited about the prospect of the conference. Interest in SV40 had been piqued by his mesothelioma and osteosarcoma studies along with the studies from Butel's laboratory. Several labs in Europe had begun to search for SV40 in human tumors, particularly mesotheliomas, and Carbone was in contact with some of them. The reports he was hearing supported his findings: The virus was turning up in the same tumors in which he had found it in his laboratory. The timing of the conference seemed ideal. This would be a chance to put SV40 on the scientific map, a public forum to present these new findings before the very federal officials who were responsible for cancer research and vaccine safety—and who could also come up with millions of dollars of funding needed to advance SV40 research, if they were so inclined. Perhaps within the NIH there had been a change of heart about SV40 and the resistance he and Pass had encountered had faded.

But Carbone was also wary. While the conference was a great opportunity
to be heard, given the event organizers, it was quite possible that the hearing
would be unsympathetic. Arthur Levine, his former boss at the NIH, was
assisting in conference preparations and was also scheduled to moderate the
portion of the conference that would discuss whether SV40 was circulating
among humans. It had been only two years since Levine and Carbone had
tangled over Carbone's attempts to publicize his first SV40 findings with
Levine quashing Carbone's press conference. Levine was hardly an ally to
the SV40 cause.

More worrisome was the role the Viral Epidemiology Branch was playing
in the conference. The proposed agenda listed the National Cancer Institute
as one of the primary organizational sponsors for the conference, but the
actual work had fallen to Joe Fraumeni's Division of Cancer Epidemiology
and Genetics, which included the VEB. In fact, the real driving force behind the conference appeared to be Howard Strickler and James Goedert.
Along with two FDA scientists, they were responsible for the crucial details
of the conference: the agenda, the topics that would be discussed, and
selection of the scientists who would sit on the various panels—determi-
nations that would shape the direction and tone of the conference.

Carbone's relationship with the VEB had become increasingly strained
since he had departed Bethesda. In the summer of 1996, Strickler had tried
to interest Carbone in a joint study, this time to search for SV40 in hundreds of brain tumor samples. But Strickler insisted Carbone first participate
in a "pilot phase," during which Carbone and Shah would each test fifty
tumor specimens in order, as Strickler termed it in a June memo, "to get
at the bottom of the conflict" between the positive findings emanating from
Carbone (and other laboratories) and the one negative VEB-Shah study.
The proposed collaboration quickly soured when Carbone learned that unless Strickler's doubts about this "discrepancy" (Strickler's word) were fully
resolved during the pilot phase, the VEB was prepared to cancel the larger
study and announce that Carbone's previous positive results were probably
due to laboratory contamination. Strickler, Carbone felt, was more interested in proving that Carbone's SV40 detection methodology was flawed
than in searching for the virus in human tumors.

Meanwhile, the VEB-Shah negative mesothelioma study had been published the previous June. Shah had told Carbone that at least one bone
tumor and one mesothelioma sample that Carbone and Pass had provided
had tested positive for SV40 in Shah's lab, but this fact had never made it

into the final report. In their conclusion, the government researchers had made a blanket statement that their results suggested there was no association between SV40 and mesotheliomas and osteosarcomas, completely ignoring the studies from Carbone, Pass, Butel, Garcea, and several other labs that had reached the opposite conclusion. It was clear to Carbone that the VEB scientists did not take his—or anyone else's—SV40 research seriously and the conference could likely as not serve as a forum for attacking, instead of advancing, SV40 research.

At 8:35 A.M., on Monday, January 27, 1997, Kathryn Zoon, director of the Center for Biologics Evaluation and Research (CBER), the FDA division charged with licensing vaccines, officially opened the conference, welcoming more than two hundred scientists from around the world assembled in the Natcher Auditorium on the NIH campus in Bethesda. More than half the attending scientists had positions within the NIH, CDC, or some other branch of the federal health bureaucracy. In addition to the federal scientists, researchers had come from across the United States and from a half-dozen foreign countries, as well: Britain, Canada, Spain, France, Sweden, Germany, and Italy. Representatives from the World Health Organization had signed up as well as public health officials representing vaccine regulatory agencies from the United Kingdom, Canada, and even the New York City Bureau of Immunization.

The event marked the first time all the major SV40 players were assembled under one roof. Butel and Lednicky, Bergsagel and Garcea, and Pass were all scheduled as speakers. So were Shah, Strickler, and others who were skeptical of any danger posed by the virus. There were also SV40 researchers of generations past in attendance. Anthony Morris, the NIH scientist, who had discovered in 1960 that SV40 caused low-grade infections when inhaled intranasally, was a panelist for Levine's session on whether SV40 was still present in humans. Andrew Lewis, whose career at the NIH spanned several decades, was to summarize his research on SV40 contamination of early adenovirus vaccines. Maurice Hilleman, who first isolated SV40 with Ben Sweet in 1960, would discuss his own recollections of the early days of SV40. The recognized "elder statesman" at the conference, Hilleman still served as a consultant to the Merck pharmaceutical company; at the conference, he was flanked by a pair of Merck handlers, who studiously shooed away reporters who approached him.

There was a large contingent of nonresearchers as well: thirty representatives from five different pharmaceutical companies, close to a dozen lawyers, a handful of vaccine watchdog activists, and a small cadre of news reporters, including CBC-TV from Canada, Channel Four from Britain, National Public Radio, and the Associated Press. In her opening remarks, Zoon pointedly asked the news media not to question any conferees while the conference was officially in session. Instead, there would be a press conference attended only by government scientists and panel chairmen at the end of the proceedings.

One of the first presenters of the morning was Keerti Shah. Standing underneath a projection of a larger-than-life rhesus monkey looming angrily down at the audience, Shah recapped SV40 research he had performed earlier in his career, including his 1976 review of exposure to SV40 through contaminated vaccines during the 1950s and 1960s. In this seminal review, conducted for the National Institutes of Health, Shah found that SV40 contamination of four different vaccines had occurred between 1954 and early 1963, "after which all vaccines on the market were probably free of SV40." Though he noted that the estimates were "very crude," they offered some indication of how many people were exposed to vaccine containing the simian virus.

By far, the largest group of Americans potentially exposed, Shah said, were those who received the Salk vaccine—almost one hundred million Americans between 1955, when the vaccine came on the market, and June 30, 1961, at which time all new lots manufactured had to be free of the virus. The second largest exposure was to 100,000 military inductees, who had received adenovirus vaccine between 1955 and 1961. About 10,000 people who had volunteered to try experimental oral vaccine during small trials that occurred between 1959 and 1961 were also exposed. (Shah noted that contaminated oral Sabin vaccine had been administered to millions of people outside the United States, notably in Russia beginning in 1959.) Finally, less than one hundred individuals had received SV40 as part of Anthony Morris's respiratory syncytial virus vaccine. Shah noted that the formaldehyde in the Salk vaccine "inactivated SV40, although not as completely as it did polio viruses."

In his presentation, Shah stressed that not all polio vaccine doses from that time contained live SV40. Sometimes formaldehyde killed all the SV40 in a dose, if the initial contamination level was low enough. Pooling monkey kidneys together, a common manufacturing procedure, increased the chances that vaccine batches were contaminated, he said, while doses that came from vaccine cultured on only one kidney were less likely to be.

Likewise, how tissue cultures were composed (kidneys could be minced by hand or chemically digested) also apparently influenced how much SV40 made it into the final vaccine. This much was clear: By 1961, 98 million people had received inactivated polio vaccine. This figure represented almost 90 percent of the nation's children and adolescents, 60 percent of those twenty to thirty-nine years old and 19 percent of those forty to fifty-nine years old. Some very large fraction of that vaccine had been contaminated with SV40, and anyone born between 1941 and 1961 had a high probability of exposure to live SV40 from contaminated vaccines. Presumably those who received the other vaccines produced on monkey kidneys during that period also had a high risk of exposure. Shah estimated that altogether 10 to 30 million people were exposed to live SV40—as opposed to inactivated SV40—although there is no real way of knowing how much of the monkey virus was killed by the Formalin. (For some reason Shah did not include in his estimates of SV40 exposure two other large groups of exposed individuals: the hundreds of thousands of children who had received contaminated vaccine as part of the Salk field trials in 1954, and anyone inoculated with contaminated vaccine between 1961 and 1963, when old lots of vaccine were finally used up. When these two groups are included, Shah's estimate of 98 million may undercount the number of Americans exposed to potentially contaminated vaccines by several million.)

After Shah, all the researchers who had recently published findings of SV40 in human tumors took the floor. Garcea described the work he and Bergsagel had completed in the early 1990s, detailing some of the extra steps and precautions they had undertaken to rule out contamination as the reason for their positive results. ("Contamination, of course, is going to be a major issue in our discussion," he told the audience, somewhat prophetically.) Butel followed, summarizing her Baylor work characterizing the various SV40 strains that she had encountered in tumors, including Lednicky's successful isolation of an entire, infectious SV40 from one of Garcea's and Bergsagel's brain tumors. Overall, their research, she said, "suggests strongly that authentic SV40 is present in at least a few human tumors."

After Butel came Carbone and a contingent of researchers from Europe, most of whom had begun working on SV40 only recently. Alan Gibbs, a researcher from Wales, in the United Kingdom, described how he and one of his colleagues, Bharat Jasani, had read Carbone's original mesothelioma paper with great interest. The hospital with which they were affiliated, Llandough Hospital in Cardiff, was where Chris Wagner, the scientist who first connected mesothelioma to asbestos exposure, had once worked. As a result, it had an archival store of several thousand mesothelioma samples. Jasani and Gibbs examined nine samples; four, Gibbs reported, were positive for SV40. Luciano Mutti, from the Salvatore Maugeri Foundation's Institute for Research and Care, in Pavia, Italy, was next. Mutti reported that he had found SV40 in three out of ten Italian mesotheliomas he had tested. Mutti was followed by another Italian, Antonio Giordano, a researcher at Philadelphia's Jefferson Medical College. Giordano described preliminary research indicating that in tumor cells SV40 may bind to certain proteins that normally suppress cancer growth—solid evidence that the virus could cause cancer once it invaded a cell. Mauro Tognon, from the University of Ferrara, described his laboratory's findings of SV40 in the same two brain tumor types as Garcea and Bergsagel had and in three more neural tumors—astrocytomas, glioblastomas, and neuroblastomas—as well as in osteosarcoma bone tumors. Tognon also tested peripheral blood samples (blood that is in the body's circulatory system as opposed to localized in a specific organ) and sperm from healthy volunteers. Twenty-three percent of the blood samples and nine of twenty sperm samples tested positive for SV40 DNA sequences, he said, suggesting SV40 might still be spreading.

The morning's most detailed presentation came from Carbone. Unlike Garcea and Butel, who had limited their discussion to whether SV40 was present in tumors, Carbone told the audience that he thought that SV40 was actually causing tumors, observing that his initial experiments showed that only the cancerous cells in Pass's mesothelioma samples contained SV40 T-antigen, while neighboring noncancerous cells from the biopsies did not. The next day, he promised, he would present more evidence that the simian virus was carcinogenic.

Carbone also broadly hinted that the only plausible source for the SV40 in human tumors was contaminated polio vaccine, something almost no one else was willing to assert publicly. And, now that it was settled, at least as far as Carbone was concerned, where the virus had come from and what it was doing, it was time to move on to treatment. If SV40 was causing tumors, then, in theory, attacking it could be a possible anticancer strategy. This avenue of research was, he admitted, "futuristic," and perhaps "too optimistic," but nonetheless, a "very exciting area." It was time, the Italian scientist was implying, to stop debating whether SV40 was present in tumors and start doing something about it.

It was nearing eleven o'clock and the first morning session was about to close. To Carbone and some the other SV40 researchers, it appeared they had gotten off to a good start—almost two straight hours of solid scientific evidence, all of which pointed to the presence of SV40 in tumors, as well as some strong suggestions that the virus was indeed causing the tumors. Audience reaction seemed to be positive, overall. However, the final speaker of the session was once again Keerti Shah. In the draft conference agendas that had been circulated, Shah had not been scheduled to speak a second time during this portion of the conference, but the conference organizers had subsequently inserted him into the tail end of the morning session, in effect allowing him an opportunity to rebut everyone who had preceded him.

Shah's rebuttal began with a review of his joint study with Strickler and Goedert. The negative results of that study, Shah asserted, seemed impossible to reconcile with the research that Carbone and the others had just presented. "From the results of previous speakers, we should have picked up at least twenty, twenty-five [SV40] positive specimens," out of the fifty they tested, Shah asserted. Moreover, he and the two VEB scientists were wrapping up a new study, in which they had examined urine samples from homosexual men for the presence of SV40. None of the urines tested positive for SV40. This latest negative study, Shah said, further called into question the morning's presentations. It just didn't make sense, he said, that so much of the research seemed to be finding SV40 in the tumors of individuals born well after the era of vaccine contamination, yet his urine samples were all negative. If SV40 were circulating in the population, why couldn't he find it in his urines, especially since in monkeys the kidneys were the natural reservoir of the virus?

Shah's presentation ended the morning session, but it only presaged the series of attacks on the SV40 researchers that was about to begin. After the lunch break, Shah and two European researchers, Robin Weiss, from Britain, and Ethel-Michele de Villiers, from Heidelberg, announced that, based on their own research, they believed the positive SV40 findings that had been discussed in the morning might have been the result of laboratory contamination. De Villiers could not find SV40 in tumors when she looked for it; Weiss had, but had since come to doubt the veracity of his own work. Shah then added his voice in support of the two European scientists' sentiments, again stressing his belief that positive SV40 findings could be explained away as contamination.

The moderator of the panel, Michael Fried, quickly followed up on Shah's remarks, suggesting that the panel should now fully explore why some labs could find SV40 while others could not, specifically whether the positive labs were using PCR methods that were, in fact, reliable. Suddenly, the focus of the conference had turned from a consideration of SV40 and its possible role in human tumors into a debate about whether any of SV40 researchers really knew what they were doing.

For an hour or so, the SV40 researchers defended the quality of their work, with most of the opposition coming from scientists like Weiss, Shah, Goedert, and de Villiers, all of whom, other than Shah, were papilloma virus or HIV experts and had limited experience with SV40 or other polyoma viruses. At one point, John Lednicky, speaking from the audience, offered a detailed presentation that suggested several plausible explanations for why Shah, Weiss, and others were having so much trouble detecting SV40 in human tumor samples. First, many of them had used DNA extracted from paraffin slides, which, Lednicky explained, is usually fragmented and degraded, making PCR more difficult to perform. When working with DNA from paraffin samples, Lednicky said, there was a need to repeat the PCR amplification process many times beyond the "standard" thirty or so cycles. Another problem, Lednicky said, was that many labs overrated the sensitivity of their PCR testing, missing the virus when it was present only at low concentrations. (Papilloma viruses are typically found in much higher concentrations in tumor cells than are polyoma viruses.) Shah's presentations during the conference had touted the sensitivity of his SV40 detection methods, yet as it later turned out, his were ten or more times *less* sensitive than Carbone's. Shah had also allowed two days to elapse between preparation of his samples and extraction of the DNA. Both facts, according to SV40 researchers who later reviewed his protocol, could explain why the Shah-VEB study was unable to detect any SV40 in their fifty paraffin samples.

But Lednicky's presentation was not persuasive. As the discussion dragged on, with neither the SV40 researchers nor their doubters giving ground, Fried suggested the only solution was to verify that the work from labs finding SV40 was "reproducible" through exchange and testing of blinded samples. Carbone observed that such an endeavor had been undertaken already, in the form of the blinded bone tumor study he had performed with Pass, Garcea, and Procopio, which had been just published in *Oncogene*. Shah took the floor as soon as Carbone had finished and offered Strickler his first opportunity to address the conference, a move that seemed as if it had been planned ahead of time:

"May I suggest? There's a strategy which has been proposed by Howard Strickler from the NCI, which I think really will address some of these problems, which will examine the different labs and the ability of the labs to reproduce their results. I think that would clarify much, and I wonder if Howard would comment on it?"

Strickler immediately took up the call:

"My suggestion was, in the face of the uncertainty of the data, that what we really need is an exquisitely controlled third-party study. The *Oncogene* [bone tumor] study was a very nice project involving four different laboratories, but it's somewhat difficult to follow exactly where DNA was extracted, who handled the samples, which laboratories worked with them."

It would turn out that the third party Strickler had in mind for his "exquisitely controlled study" was none other than himself. Suddenly one of the major objectives of the conference had become clear: VEB, the principal doubters of SV40 research, would coordinate a large multiple-laboratory study that would reexamine whether SV40 was actually detectable in human tumors. Securing consensus to proceed with the study was one of the chief aims of the conference organizers.

The last two presentations of the first day of the conference focused on the crucial question of whether there was any new epidemiological evidence linking SV40-contaminated vaccines to human disease. One presenter was Patrick Olin, a Swedish epidemiologist; the other was the VEB's Howard Strickler. Olin went first. SV40-contaminated vaccine, he said, was used for only one year in Sweden, 1957. By Olin's reckoning, around seven hundred thousand Swedes might have been exposed, most of them young children, between the ages four to eleven at the time. Olin had examined records from the Swedish National Cancer Registry, which dated back to 1960, and tried to determine whether the exposed children from 1957 had any higher risk of cancer. His own analysis, he said, showed that there was no increased risk for cancer overall, nor for the specific brain, bone, and lung tumors that had been linked to SV40 by the research presented by Carbone and the others in the morning. The results, he said were "reassuring from the Swedish public health perspective." As Olin took his seat, panel chair Dixie Snider, associate director of science for the CDC, introduced Strickler:

> "Thank you very much, Dr. Olin. Indeed, it sure is reassuring to Swedes. And now I'm sure we're all anxious to know about the U.S., and Dr. Strickler will get the last word of the day to speak on the epidemiology of cancers reported to contain SV40 DNA in the U.S.A."

Strickler strode to the podium. For the past several months, he had been preparing new data that he believed would quickly end the debate about whether contaminated polio vaccine was causing cancer. First, he briefly reviewed previous epidemiological studies on SV40 exposure, emphasizing the negative results of Fraumeni's 1963 study on Salk vaccinees and a 1990 German study by Erhard Geissler on East German children exposed to contaminated oral vaccine. Geissler had followed the children for twenty-two years after vaccination and like Fraumeni had concluded that there was no epidemiological evidence of any increased risk of cancer after contaminated vaccine exposure, he said.

Strickler then turned to the three lesser-known studies that had reached the opposite conclusion. Two had looked at children born to mothers who had received contaminated vaccine during pregnancy. Both of these had shown an increase in neural tumors. Another study, the 1968 one from Australia, had found that there was a correlation between inoculation with contaminated polio vaccine and the development of tumors among a group of hospitalized Australian children. Strickler dismissed all three studies, saying each had observed only a "small" number of children.

Strickler then began discussing his new data. Following a methodology similar to the one Fraumeni had employed three decades before, Strickler had selected cohorts of individuals and classified them by their supposed levels of SV40 exposure, although instead of dividing children by states as Fraumeni had done, Strickler categorized them by year of birth. Individuals born after 1964, when there was presumably no SV40 in vaccines, were classified as being at no risk of cancer from SV40 exposure. Individuals born between 1956 and 1962 were presumably vaccinated at infancy with contaminated vaccine, and thus were at high risk because of the immaturity of an infant's immune system. Individuals born between 1947 and 1952 were assumed to have received SV40-contaminated polio vaccine when they were grade-schoolers and were thus classified as at moderate risk.

For each of his three cohorts, Strickler had gone to the National Cancer Institute's Surveillance, Epidemiology, and End Results (SEER) database and looked at overall cancer incidence and mortality for a twenty-year period, 1973 to 1993. He then narrowed his search to examine those tumors in which the virus had actually been discovered, beginning with brain cancers of all types. He also looked at lymphomas and leukemias in this portion of his investigation, since recent research, like Tognon's, had found SV40 in peripheral blood cells. Strickler focused specifically on the three kinds of cancer that had been under discussion at the conference: mesotheliomas, osteosarcomas, and ependymomas. He even looked at ovarian cancers, he said, since occasionally mesotheliomas can be misdiagnosed as ovarian cancers.

Although Strickler reported he found a slight uptick in risk for ependymomas and a larger increase in risk for mesothelioma among the SV40-exposed cohorts, once he had subjected the numbers to more rigorous analysis, the increased risks were not statistically significant, he asserted. As for the other cancers, there was no measurable increased risk for osteosarcomas, no difference in overall cancer incidence, no difference in brain cancer risk, lymphoma risk, or leukemia risk. As slide after slide of graphs and charts appeared behind him, Strickler drove his point home. He and the two other members of his team at the VEB who had assisted him had conducted a thorough search, had sliced and diced the data every which way, and still could find nothing:

> "Cancers reported to contain SV40 were rare, and are rare. Ependymomas and osteosarcomas are remaining rare. Mesotheliomas and brain cancers are increasing, but mainly in the oldest [cohort], [and are] unlikely to be related to vaccine exposure."

Strickler finished his presentation by paying homage to the polio vaccine. A slide flashed up behind him demonstrating that polio rates in the United States since 1955 had plummeted from tens of thousands of cases annually down to zero by the 1970s, and had stayed there ever since. "I think it's important to remind all of us what happened to the number of polio cases in the United States after the introduction of the vaccines," he said soberly. "Thank you very much." As Strickler left the stage, Snider announced that the day's proceedings had concluded and the audience filed out of the auditorium.

Day two of the conference began with Carbone's former mentor Arthur Levine welcoming everyone back to the Natcher auditorium and gratuitously noting that the crowd had thinned from the day before because of "possibly having shed the lawyers and the reporters." As chairman of the morning panel, he then proceeded to give his take on the first day's events, in the process mischaracterizing what had occurred the day before as a draw between the thirteen labs who had found SV40 and the two (Shah and de Villiers) that had not. The only way to resolve the issue of these conflicting results, Levine said, would be an "appropriately blinded study," such as the one Strickler had already proposed. Levine concluded his day-one summary by noting that, based on the "strong epidemiological studies" of Strickler and Olin, there was "no evidence . . . that any apparent harm occurred as a consequence of the massive exposure to SV40 in the early era of the poliovirus vaccines." If the virus were harmful, "surely the rates of some cancers should have increased. . . . One might comfortably say that SV40, in fact, is not a human pathogen."

Levine's summary seemed to indicate that Carbone's preconference suspicions were justified. The entire event had been a pretense to dismiss him and the other SV40 researchers in a very public setting, and the proposed VEB study was likely as not an attempt to sidetrack, if not bury, further SV40 research. The second day of the conference allowed for almost no presentation of new data, although in the last session Carbone got to present the new research he had promised the previous day. He, Pass, and Procopio had tested fifty-two SV40-positive mesotheliomas; in thirty-one of them, the virus's T-antigen seemed to be interfering with p53, the body's crucial cancer-suppressing gene. This was the strongest indication thus far that SV40 was actively causing the tumors in which it had been found.

Other than that, most of the conference seemed to focus on Levine's order of the day: getting everyone to agree to the VEB's proposed study, although among the SV40 researchers only Pass had expressed any interest in the concept. But by the end of the conference it was a foregone conclusion: The only way to resolve the "conflicting" data between the large number of positive labs and the two negative labs was through a large multilaboratory study in which all the participants would exchange blinded samples and have to prove they could reproduce their own positive results. As one SV40 researcher at the conference remembers it, there didn't seem to be much choice in the matter. If you had found SV40, but indicated you weren't willing to participate in the proposed study, you would simply have been branded as uncooperative.

Strickler's epidemiological study succeeded in dominating all major news accounts of the conference. Indeed, the government position, that polio vaccine was safe, not causing cancer, and that what Carbone and others were discovering was likely contamination, permeated the most important mainstream press account to come out of the conference, an Associated Press story filed by Lauran Neergaard. The AP story, which appeared in many newspapers and in electronic media outlets like CNN, was probably the only news most Americans ever heard about the conference:

BETHESDA, Md. (AP) Scientists are dusting off a 40-year old medical mystery: Does a monkey virus that contaminated a polio vaccine millions of Americans took during the 1950s increase the risk of certain rare cancers? Government data suggest such fears are unwarranted, because the types of cancer involved do not appear to be increasing among people old enough to have gotten tainted vaccine. And the polio vaccine sold today is tested to ensure it is free of this monkey virus, called SV40.

Strickler's study was described in greater detail later in the article, and he was quoted as saying he did not feel any of the positive research presented at the conference by Carbone and the others "points us in a clear direction of whether the virus is causing cancer."

Although the AP story did note the SV40 findings of Carbone and the others, it counterbalanced these with the statement that "other scientists couldn't find the virus in human tissue at all, and questioned whether laboratory contamination was fooling their colleagues." The AP had thus given equal weight to the only two negative research reports that had been presented at the conference—the joint VEB-Shah mesothelioma study and de Villiers's research (which was not published)—as to the positive SV40 findings that had been presented and published in major peer-reviewed journals, which at this point represented nearly twenty different experiments from thirteen different laboratories.

National Public Radio offered a more nuanced presentation of the proceedings to its listeners, but it, too, used the Strickler data as a foil to any notion that SV40 was dangerous, allowing Strickler a chance to recapitulate his conference presentation:

STRICKLER: We don't see any increases in cancer risk in individuals who were exposed to the poliovirus vaccines during the period of time in which the vaccines were contaminated. The evidence has now been repeated in Germany. It's been repeated now in data from Sweden and the data I presented from here in the United States, representing 30-to-40 years follow-up time.

NPR REPORTER, JOE PALCA: Strickler's research has reassured most scientists that, if exposure to SV40 does pose any risk to human health, it appears to be a very small risk . . .

Palca's NPR story closed with a summary of remarks by Levine that it would be a "big, big mistake" to not get polio vaccine "because of a small hypothetical risk from an unknown virus."

Strickler's study (coauthored by Goedert and Fraumeni) formally appeared a year later, at the end of January 1998, in *JAMA*, the same publication that had published the Fraumeni's 1963 study. Press coverage in 1998 of the study's publication had the same tone as that which had emanated from the 1997 conference. A widely published account, again by the Associated Press (which had relied largely on an NCI-prepared press release), trumpeted the news with the headline: "No Cancers Tied to '50s Polio Vaccine." Strickler was quoted as saying the results of his study were "reassuring as it is likely that we would have observed an effect on cancer rates if one existed." It appeared that Strickler had authored the definitive, last word in SV40 epidemiology.

Or had he? As had been the case with Fraumeni's original 1963 study, there were serious limitations to Strickler's effort, although these were largely unknown to the media outlets that reported the study. The first was the same issue that had bedeviled Fraumeni thirty-five years before: It was impossible to really know with any specificity who received live SV40 from contaminated vaccine. Strickler's assumption that all the children in one age group were exposed to SV40, whereas all the children in another were not, was simply unsubstantiated.

Equally problematic was the presumption that Strickler's unexposed cohort had never been infected with SV40. If the research of Butel and Tognon is correct, either SV40 has been spreading among humans for decades, or polio vaccine at times has continued to be contaminated. That would mean that some of Strickler's "unexposed" cohort had actually been "exposed" to the simian virus. In effect, there is every reason to believe that it is not possible to construct with any certainty "exposed" and "unexposed" cohorts when it comes to SV40. (Strickler did not mention this limitation to his own study during his presentation at the conference. He also inaccurately described Fraumeni's 1963 study and Geissler's 1990 study as having escaped this shortcoming, when, in fact, both suffered from the same flaw as his.)

Another series of problems related to the specific cancers Strickler examined. For instance, because mesotheliomas are slow-developing cancers, it was still too soon to adequately measure whether vaccinated children were at higher risk—there simply had not been enough elapsed time. Susan Fisher, an associate professor in epidemiology and biostatistics, originally at Loyola, and now at Cornell University, examined the Strickler study in detail and submitted a letter to *JAMA* critiquing it. Given the actual mesothelioma data Strickler presented, the best Strickler could conclude, she wrote, is that "no conclusions can be drawn"—not that there was no statistically significant increase in risk for the lung cancers.

The relative rarity of the cancers Strickler examined was another problem, according to Fisher. One or two ependymoma cases in his data set could very easily have changed the conclusions regarding whether the increased risk Strickler observed was statistically significant.

But the biggest flaw in Fisher's mind was the way Strickler picked the three cohorts he compared: For the most part, their ages did not overlap. Since the development of cancer is age-dependent in general, this would tend to skew data. In her letter to *JAMA*, Fisher described Strickler's use of mismatched age groups as "possible . . . misuse" of statistical methods and "an error in judgment." Adding to the confusion of noncorresponding ages is that cancer reporting accuracy has increased over time, with more recent reports probably much more reliable than earlier ones. As an example, the oldest child in Strickler's childhood-exposed group turned twenty-six in 1973; the youngest child in his unexposed group did not turn twenty-six until 1995. During the intervening twenty-two years, there has been an explosion of knowledge in cancer detection. It is thus possible that cancers among the cohort Strickler classified as SV40-exposed could be underreported in the SEER data employed by Strickler.

In 1999, in the journal *Anticancer Research*, Fisher published her own epidemiological survey of SEER cancer data, using cohorts carefully matched in age. Her conclusion was that there *were* increases in cancer rates for children presumably exposed to SV40-contaminated vaccines, sometimes very large ones. Fisher reported a 2.3 percent rise in all cancer incidence among her exposed cohort. This broke down into a 37 percent increase specifically for ependymomas and choroid plexuses, with a 5 percent rise in the incidence of other brain cancer types. Osteosarcoma incidence, she found, was up 26 percent, with a 34 percent rise for all other bone cancers. And for mesotheliomas, Fisher observed an astonishing 220 percent rise in incidence. While her study did not offer any test of the statistical significance of the increased incidence rates—as Strickler's had done—Fisher notes that "it's hard to look at these numbers and turn around and say there is no evidence of an association."

In the end, this type of retrospective, population-based epidemiology may be an unreliable tool for answering one way or the other whether SV40 is causing cancer. In 2002, the Immunization Safety Review Committee of the Institute of Medicine reviewed every published epidemiological study on SV40. A sister organization to the National Academy of Sciences, the IOM functions as an independent advisory panel to federal health agencies. Its fourteen-member vaccine safety panel has taken up such controversial questions as whether hepatitis B vaccine is associated with neurological disorders and whether multiple immunizations are dangerous to the developing immune systems of children. Its pronouncements on health topics are viewed by federal health officials as definitive and are accompanied by extensive publicity.

All the SV40 epidemiological studies undertaken so far, the IOM panel concluded, were flawed in some fashion or another, and all, including Strickler's, were essentially inconclusive. The largest sticking point remains the inability to determine who received SV40 contaminated vaccines, and how much virus they were exposed to in those vaccines. The question whether the virus is still being transmitted is another problem. "The uncertainty of exposure makes interpretation of the epidemiological data very problematic," the IOM panel concluded. The panel then made a logical, yet astonishing recommendation—particularly in light of VEB's strenuous efforts to employ epidemiology as a vehicle for minimizing the perceived dangers of SV40: "Until some of the technical issues are resolved, the committee does not recommend additional epidemiological studies of people potentially exposed to the contaminated polio vaccine."

16

The Perfect War Machine

THE CARDINAL BERNARDIN Cancer Center at Loyola University, located in the outskirts of Chicago in Maywood, Illinois, is a multimillion-dollar monument to this nation's preoccupation with cancer. Opened in 1994, the sparkling 125,000-square-foot concrete-and-glass structure boasts that it is the only freestanding facility in Illinois dedicated exclusively to cancer research, diagnosis, treatment, and prevention. The center's primary patient treatment centers are situated on the ground floor of the building, surrounding a pleasant waiting area that is softened by plush magenta sofas and an airy atrium. The research laboratories encircle the atrium one story above, their proximity to the treatment clinics suggesting that any new scientific breakthroughs are sped to the suffering patients below. But the laboratories are largely hidden from the patients. To reach them you must enter an elevator or secluded stairwell, find your way up to the next level, push through a set of heavy firewall doors, and then continue down a maze of hallways. Here, sequestered in three-dozen laboratories, researchers are striving to unlock the molecular mysteries of cancer. Michele Carbone's office—jammed with ring binder notebooks, a microscope, and other research and writing accoutrements—is tucked into a corner of the building and overlooks a parking lot. In two tidy laboratories a few steps down the hall, he and his research team have begun to unravel the exact mechanisms by which SV40 causes cancer.

Carbone's lab is lively. His laboratory group includes scientists from

China, Pakistan, and Italy as well as the United States, and the whir of high-tech laboratory equipment is often punctuated by good-natured Italian banter. One section of the lab is taken up by Carbone's collaborator, Maurizio Bocchetta, who has made significant contributions to the understanding of how SV40 infection disrupts the normal functioning of regulatory genes inside mesothelial cells. The rest of the group has been led, until recently, by Paola Rizzo, who first teamed up with Carbone in 1993 when he sought her DNA-sequencing expertise during his initial experiments on Pass's mesotheliomas. It was Rizzo's DNA sequencing that provided the final confirmation that what was in the mesotheliomas could only have been SV40. Working with Rizzo, Carbone developed state-of-the-art PCR protocols specifically for SV40 detection in mesotheliomas that have been adopted by numerous other laboratories conducting SV40 research.

In one corner of Carbone's lab, photos of monkeys cut out of a magazine by a lab assistant stare down from a door; elsewhere an Italian-English magnetic word game plastered across the front of a freezer declares nonsensically: "*come, music, presente, passion, quest, inferno, tempest.*" But the rest of the laboratory has the appearance of an oversized space module in which real estate is at a premium: Every shelf is labeled and every piece of equipment has its designated place. Two three-foot-high incubators are stacked in a corner. In block letters penned across a swath of blue tape, the bottom incubator warns: "Do not open, virus!!" In the next room, another incubator admonishes, "No cells suspected to contain live viruses are to be lodged inside this top incubator."

Though the atmosphere is friendly, the work is exacting, with Carbone setting the example. On a warm July afternoon, Carbone is examining an SV40-infected cell culture plate under a microscope. His fingers hover over the focus knob, barely touching it, poised to fine-tune the view, as he searches the mesothelial cells for signs of cancerous transformation. He looks up from the microscope and speaks almost fondly of the virus he has studied so intensively for the past decade. SV40 is "the smallest perfect war machine ever," he murmurs. "He's so small. But he's got everything he needs."

Magnified fifty thousand times under an electron microscope, SV40 doesn't seem particularly menacing. In contrast to the portentous, wormlike shape of some more notorious viruses, such as Ebola, SV40 looks almost pretty—bluish snowflakes against a field of white. It owes its delicate appearance to its icosahedral triangular scaffolding, a geometric, twenty-sided protein skin that surrounds its lone circular double strand of DNA. Compact and efficient, the DNA strand contains only 5,243 base pairs—a lean life form compared to the four million base pairs of DNA contained in even a simple bacterium. SV40 is as simple as it is small. The human genome codes for 150,000 proteins while SV40 codes for just six (although some scientists believe they have recently discovered a seventh), three of which make up its protein skin. Of the remaining proteins, one regulates the virus's growth and the two others are the virus's tumor-causing proteins, hence the name: T-antigen, for tumor-causing antigen. The large T-antigen, distinguished by its capital T, is about 700 amino acids in length, while its sister protein, the small t-antigen, designated with a lower-case t, embodies 174 amino acids. Scientists often refer to these two tumor-causing proteins by the shorthand designations of "Tag," for the large T-antigen and "tag," for the small t-antigen. These tumor antigens, particularly the large T-antigen, are highly oncogenic. Carbone describes large T-antigen as "the most oncogenic protein ever discovered." It is unique, he says, in its ability to cause cancer when set loose inside certain types of cells.

To understand how a cell becomes cancerous, it helps to know something about the multilayered protections bequeathed by nature to help *prevent* cells from becoming cancerous. It is only when these protective mechanisms are breached that the cell takes its deadly turn toward immortality.

Simply put, for a cell to become cancerous three things have to happen. The first is that the cell has to lose the function of those genes that restrain cell growth and prevent malignancy—the cellular "brakes," so to speak. Secondly, the cell has to receive a stimulating signal from those genes—called oncogenes—that cause tumor cells to grow. Finally, the cell's normal limit on how many times it can divide must be overcome.

The first of these protections involve a series of tumor suppressor genes known as p53 and the Rb genes. Whenever a cell begins to divide, in the process known as mitosis, a small army of quality control agents goes to work. Running up and down the cell's DNA, like a band of frenetic electricians looking for loose wiring in an apartment complex, these genes and proteins work together in a succession of intricately linked mechanisms to scrutinize the DNA's integrity. If at any stage of cell division they detect DNA abnormalities, mitosis is halted and the damage is repaired. If the damage cannot be repaired, another set of genes is activated and the cell undergoes "apoptosis," the term for programmed cell death—the cell essentially commits suicide.

The principal in this elaborate regulatory dance is called p53. Arnold J. Levine, former president of Rockefeller University, in New York City, and one of the discoverers of p53, says that 60 percent of all cancers involve some sort of damage, mutation, or inactivation of the gene. "The p53 gene is central to human cancers," he explains, describing it as "the first line of defense against cancer formation." If p53 is not functioning properly, a cell with altered DNA may undergo mitosis instead of dying as it should. If the DNA alterations are such that the cell continues to reproduce wildly, that is the beginning of a cancer.

In July 1997, in two groundbreaking papers published in the journal *Nature Medicine*, Carbone and his collaborators examined how SV40's large T-antigen is able to strangle p53 and other crucial tumor suppressor genes in human mesothelial cells. One of the paradoxes about mesotheliomas is that human mesotheliomas are rich in normal p53, yet they are one of the most deadly human cancers. Why, if there is an abundance of this cancer-suppressing gene, is the cancer so aggressive? Carbone's experiments showed that in human mesotheliomas, large T-antigen attacks p53, binding to it so that it cannot function properly even though the gene is present in large quantities. In effect, it doesn't matter how much p53 is present in the mesotheliomas; SV40 produces enough T-antigen to disable all of it. In the companion *Nature Medicine* study, Antonio Giordano, then at the Kimmel Cancer Center in Philadelphia, described how large T-antigen inhibits a second series of anticancer proteins called Rbs, which together serve as the final gatekeepers in cellular division. They thus serve as a second layer of cellular protection against cancer. If p53 fails, the Rbs can step in and stop genetically defective cells from dividing. Giordano found that in mesotheliomas, SV40 T-antigen was crippling the Rbs.

Together, the Carbone and Giordano studies established that SV40 is uniquely oncogenic in human mesotheliomas. Using a single protein—large T-antigen—SV40 can disable two of the body's most important cancer suppressing systems simultaneously. No other cancer-causing virus has that capacity. For example, human papilloma virus, which causes cervical cancer, must produce two proteins, E6 and E7, to inactivate p53 and the Rbs respectively. SV40 needs only one—large T-antigen. For this reason, Arnold Levine calls large T-antigen "a remarkable protein."

But why mesotheliomas? With so many different cells and organs to choose from, why was SV40 turning up so frequently in this relatively rare cancer? Carbone reviewed the literature on the virus. He discovered that most studies of SV40's behavior in human cells had examined what happened when the virus invaded fibroblasts, specialized connective tissue cells. This was because large amounts of the tissue type were readily available to research laboratories in the form of human foreskin specimens. Mesothelial cells, however, are dramatically different from fibroblasts. They are the last remnants of the central embryonic layer called the mesoderm, and are a much more primitive cell type than fibroblasts. Carbone decided to conduct an experiment comparing SV40's infection of human fibroblasts with SV40 infection of human mesothelial cells. The results of the study completely changed the established view of what happens when SV40 infects human cells.

Viruses, such as SV40, enter a cell with the object of replicating, not causing tumors. In the normal life cycle of a virus, it invades a host cell, hijacks the cell's own reproductive machinery, and proceeds to make thousands upon thousands of copies of itself inside the cell. Eventually, the host cell becomes loaded with virus to the point that it can no longer hold all the invaders. The viruses either bud forth from the cell or burst the cell open, killing it in either case. Thousands of these newly liberated viruses then rush to attack other cells, and the infective process continues. In this scenario, the virus may make the host ill, but it doesn't cause cancer, because the infected cells die. This is exactly the situation that unfolds when SV40 infects a human fibroblast cell: The replication of SV40 eventually fills the cell with virus and causes it to burst and die. Because early SV40 studies centered on fibroblast cells, it was assumed the virus was harmless to human cells.

But mesothelial cells contain four to five times more p53 than human fibroblasts. Carbone discovered that in mesothelial cells, the large T antigen becomes preoccupied with binding to the excessive p53 present in the cells. This, in turn, dramatically retards the pace of SV40 replication—so much so, that the virus achieves a parasitic symbiosis with the mesothelial cells, in which it multiplies so slowly that it does not burst the cell. Now the mesothelial cell can divide unchecked. Carbone and his colleagues discovered SV40 caused mesothelial cells to become malignant at a rate 1000 times that of fibroblasts. "What we found was that SV40 does different things in different cells and organs," Carbone says. "In mesothelial cells, it doesn't kill them, but drives them to malignant growth." Whether this same process is at work in other SV40-related cancers remains to be investigated.

What makes a cell malignant? Once again, SV40 can serve as the source of the actual genetic changes that make normal cells cancerous. Again, the virus can do it in more than one way. One is through human chromosome damage—by adding or deleting whole sections of DNA or reshuffling the genes on the twenty-three pairs of chromosomes contained in the cell's nucleus. Joseph R. Testa, director of the Human Genetics Program at Fox Chase Cancer Center in Philadelphia, says that once SV40 is finished with a cell, "it looks like somebody set off a bomb inside the cell's nucleus, because of all these chromosomes rearrangements."

Another way SV40 induces malignancy is to accelerate cell growth. An Italian team of scientists discovered that T-antigen triggers an "activation" signal (or oncogene) in the cell called Met that stimulates growth factors. This causes the mesothelial cell to go from a resting phase to a replicating phase—essentially flipping the switch for cellular growth to fast forward. And just as cells have more than one brake (p53 and the Rbs), they also have more than one accelerator. Carbone's colleague, Bocchetta, discovered that SV40 can also activate a gene called Notch-1 that pushes the cell to divide. SV40 thus can inactivate two key cellular brakes and activate two key accelerators, all by itself.

Knocking out a cell's brakes and kicking on its accelerator is still not sufficient to produce unchecked tumor growth. Nature blessed the body with an additional anticancer feature: cells have a limited life span. A healthy cell will reproduce itself only a finite number of times before dying. That is because each time a cell divides, the telomeres, a spindle of microfibers on the ends of each chromosome, shorten a little bit. In classical mythology, three goddesses—the Fates—wove together the fabric of a person's life, determining how long he or she would live. Telomeres are literally the threads of life; they determine the natural life span of all cells. Each time a cell divides, a little piece of the thread gets used up, and the telomeres get shorter. Once they have shortened beyond a certain point, the cell— and all the daughter cells, which derived from it—have used up all their allotted thread. They cannot divide any longer, and they die. This is why most scientists believe that all human beings, no matter how healthy, have an upper limit to their life spans.

Interestingly, this phenomenon was discovered in the 1960s by Leonard Hayflick as he was perfecting his human cell substrate WI-38. During his work on WI-38, Hayflick discovered that after dividing forty to sixty times, his strain of human diploid cells inevitably died. Even if they had been frozen for years, once they were thawed and began dividing again, their total number of doublings never exceeded this preordained amount. Nature had programmed a natural life span, or senescence, into every cell. Today, the number of divisions a cell can undergo before dying is known as the Hayflick limit, in honor of the scientist whose discovery opened up an entire new field of inquiry—cell gerontology. Because of the Hayflick limit, even those cells in which p53 has been disabled or growth factors have been stimulated are still subject to this internal limit and usually enter so-called crisis and die after dividing forty or so times.

Carbone and Rudy Foddis, a postdoctoral student in his laboratory, found that SV40 activates telomerase, an enzyme that allows the telomeres to be elongated every time the cell divides instead of becoming shortened—in effect, allowing the mesothelial cells to divide endlessly. Ironically, it was the virus's contamination of the polio vaccine that led to the search for an alternative substrate by Hayflick, which in turn led to the discovery of the importance of telomeres. Now it turns out that it is SV40's interference with the natural behavior of telomeres that allows malignant cells to become immortal, instead of dying as they should.

"The idea of human cancer is that you need many different carcinogens, because different carcinogens do different things," Carbone explains. "Cancer is a multifactorial process." In essence, there is no such thing as a complete carcinogen—one substance that causes cancer by itself. Rather, a cell normally requires numerous "hits" or insults from various carcinogens before it can become cancerous. One will inactivate p53. Another will activate a tumor oncogene. Something else will cause chromosome damage. Still something else must occur to activate telomerase. Eventually the cell becomes a tumor cell. "There is no one thing that has been shown capable of doing all of these three things together," Carbone asserts, "except for SV40." SV40 can block the Rbs and p53. It can activate several oncogenes that stimulate the cell to grow. It can alter chromosomes and also induce telomerase activity. "Therefore SV40 by itself can do everything that is required to make a human cell malignant," he says. "It is one of the most potent human carcinogens that we know."

Cellular changes leading to cancer do not occur in a vacuum in the human body. Carbone notes that his SV40 findings are the result of cell culture studies—the only place in which SV40 infection can be safely and ethically tested on human cells. Because those studies take place in a test tube, not in the human body, they make no allowance for the defense of the human immune system. A healthy immune system generally seeks out and destroys invading viruses. The case of SV40 is no exception. Indeed, the fact that T-antigen is such a strong tumor inducer also means that in most cases it provokes a strong immune response. That is why, as with other carcinogens, not everyone who is exposed to the virus will become ill. Carbone suspects that, like other cancer-causing substances, SV40 usually works in concert with other carcinogens to cause disease. Whether the virus can sometimes cause cancer all by itself in human beings is still unknown.

"Human beings have devised many mechanisms to defend themselves against cancer," Carbone says. "This is one of the reasons that human beings live so long compared with other animals."

There are conditions, however, that militate against that response. One of them is the presence of an immunosuppressant, such as asbestos. Used widely as insulation material beginning in the 1950s, asbestos has been found in homes, schools, offices, factories, and shipyards around the world. The versatile mineral fiber was used in a variety of heat-sensitive applications, employed in everything from car brakes to lawn mowers, roofing materials to plumbing insulation. Over the last three decades, researchers have shown that asbestos fibers lodged in the lungs can act as an immune system depressant and trigger DNA damage that can lead to cancer. Debates about which types of asbestos are carcinogenic and whether the mineral fiber can always be traced to every case of the disease notwithstanding, thousands of mesothelioma victims have recovered damages from asbestos companies as a result of this research.

In his original 1994 *Oncogene* paper, Carbone hypothesized that SV40 and asbestos might act synergistically to cause cancer in some cases where either one alone would be less effective. Later, in a series of experiments, Carbone and his team set out to determine how the two putative carcinogens might interact in mesothelial cell cultures. First they deliberately mutated SV40 so that it could no longer produce small t-antigen. The mutant viruses seemed to have almost no ability to effect telomerase activity in mesothelial cells; consequently, the cells did not become malignant.

Next, they decided to see if adding asbestos to the mix had any effect. Interestingly, they discovered that when asbestos was added along with the SV40-mutant, they could now transform these same mesothelial cells. But asbestos by itself did not cause the mesothelial cells to become malignant. In a series of experiments conducted in 2003—this time not in tissue cultures, but with hamsters—Carbone and Pass reached essentially the same conclusion: SV40 and asbestos are co-carcinogens.

These recent experiments by Carbone and his team confirm some of the theories Carbone first advanced in 1994. One is that SV40 virus, with both of its tumorogenic proteins, appears capable of causing mesothelioma all by itself. "Clearly there are some cases of SV40-associated mesothelioma in which no history of asbestos exposure has been demonstrated," he says. Another is that in certain cases, asbestos and SV40 can interact together to cause the disease. Although the mechanisms by which asbestos and SV40 interact is still unclear, exploring this synergistic relationship opens an intriguing new dimension in cancer research—the possibility that viruses and environmental toxins are much more deadly in tandem when it comes to tumor induction. "Can you think of anything more different on earth than asbestos and a monkey virus?" Carbone says. "Yet you stick them together and they work together to be more deadly than either one of them is alone." The implications, Carbone says, are far-reaching. Traditionally, researchers have looked at only one variable when researching the cause of cancer. But if it is true that environmental toxins can interact with relatively common viruses to cause cancer, it may be time to reconsider what constitutes an "acceptable risk" for exposure to such carcinogens, says Carbone. The synergistic properties of two seemingly unrelated carcinogens may, when combined, raise the cancer risk to a substantially higher level than exposure to either one of them alone.

Meanwhile, other research shows that SV40 has additional cancer-causing tricks. Sometimes the virus sets off the chain reaction that leads to tumor formation, yet manages to leave no trace that it was ever present. In virology, this is described as a hit-and-run mechanism: The virus can cause so much damage that the cell perpetuates its own malignant growth long after the virus has disappeared.

A team of scientists from Bonn has demonstrated this mechanism in rats, showing that SV40 is able to inflict damage in cells and then vanish completely. The German team injected fetal rat brain cells that had been rendered cancerous by large T-antigen into the brains of adult rats. Eighty percent of the adult rats developed a brain cancer that is the rodent equivalent of human medulloblastoma, one of the pediatric brain cancers with which SV40 has been associated and the same type that afflicted Alexander Horwin. When the Bonn researchers searched for large T-antigen in the tumors, it was no longer present in some of the cells. Yet these particular sets of transformed (or malignant) cells appeared to be even more malignant than those that were still expressing the T-antigen—evidently because without the presence of T-antigen, the immune system could no longer recognize them as a threat. Thanks to SV40, the cancer cells were now able to escape notice by the body's disease-detection radar.

This finding may explain how SV40, and perhaps other viruses, can induce cancer and yet not be readily detectable once tumors start proliferating rapidly. Without the presence of an immunogenic protein like T-antigen, cancer cells are less prone to immune system attack. Thus, after a certain point in tumorogenesis, cancer cells that have rid themselves of the virus have higher survival rates than those that still contain SV40, eventually replacing SV40-infected cells as the dominant subset in some expanding tumors. Yet the ultimate source for the aggressive, "stealth" cancer was still SV40.

Studies from Italy support this novel hypothesis: SV40 is dangerous as long as it is in the right tissue, even if it is not actually present in every, or even most, cells. A team led by Luciano Mutti and Giovanni Gaudino discovered that a small number of SV40-infected mesothelial cells can induce malignancy in much larger numbers of nearby noninfected cells. Mutti and Gaudino found that once SV40 invades the mesothelial cells, the virus not only turns on the Met oncogene within the cells it has infected, it also stimulates those cells to send chemical signals to their neighbors, forcing them to turn on Met. Now these neighboring, uninfected cells have also been artificially switched on from a resting phase into an unnatural, hyperactive growth phase. Thus, even if only a few tumor cells contain SV40, growth factors produced by these cells will spur the malignant growth of nearby cells that do not contain the virus.

Mutti also found that once tumor formation is under way, SV40 subverts one more cellular regulatory system in order to ensure that the tumor continues to grow. SV40, Mutti discovered, stimulates mesothelioma cells to produce vascular epithelial growth factor or VEGF. VEGF is a chemical that promotes blood vessel growth. Mutti found that in mesothelioma biopsies that tested negative for the presence of SV40, little VEGF is produced, while tumor cells that contained SV40 manufacture high levels of the growth factor. In this way, SV40, by encouraging blood vessels to grow toward the tumor, helps secure for the burgeoning cancer an ample supply of blood and nutrients.

Mutti's data may offer a reason why mesothelioma is such a difficult cancer to cure—the SV40 helps maintain the malignant state of the cancerous cells and its nearby sisters with very little effort. Not surprisingly, Mutti found that patients whose tumors contained the virus had shorter life spans than those whose mesotheliomas were caused for other reasons.

Some of the strongest evidence that SV40 causes mesothelioma has come from the labs of two self-proclaimed SV40 skeptics. David Schrump, a boyish-looking researcher with round glasses and sandy hair, succeeded Pass as the head of the Thoracic Oncology Division of the NCI after Pass left the NCI in 1996. He had by his own admission "no interest" in looking for SV40 and had "a very skeptical eye on what had been previously published" about the association of SV40 with human tumors. In his experiment, he and his team established a series of mesothelioma cell lines that tested positive for SV40. They then devised a genetic "magic bullet"—a strand of RNA called an antisense that would bind onto SV40's T-antigen and disarm it. Doubtful that SV40 played any role in causing mesotheliomas, Schrump expected that his antisense would have no effect on the malignant cell cultures. Instead, to his surprise, Schrump found that disarming T-antigen stopped the mesothelioma cell lines that contained SV40 from growing. The results of his experiment completely contradicted the working hypothesis Schrump had constructed before he began his experiment. Not only was SV40 involved in making the cells malignant, but disabling the virus in effect halted the malignant growth.

The unexpected results of his antisense experiment changed Schrump's thinking about the virus. "I find it hard to believe that if SV40 gets into these cells that it does not do something that's bad," he says. "It's so disruptive of cell physiology." He also lends much greater credence to the work of those who are recovering the virus in human tumors than he did before his experiment. Researchers such as Strickler, Goedert, and Shah who cannot find SV40 are using "far less sensitive techniques," he says, than the ones that Carbone and others have perfected. Since 1999, Schrump has published two papers suggesting that deactivation of T-antigen has potential as a therapy for mesothelioma victims. He and the NCI have also applied for a patent on the antisense mechanism, in the hopes that it might some day prove useful as a therapy for mesothelioma.

One of the most important experiments supporting SV40's causal role in mesothelioma formation was conducted by another self-described SV40 skeptic, Adi Gazdar, a former head of the Tumor Cell Biology Section of the NCI. Today, Gazdar is professor of pathology and deputy director of the Hamon Center for Therapeutic Oncology Research at the University of Texas Southwestern Medical Center in Dallas, where he has amassed a collection of more than twenty-five hundred tumor specimens. Gazdar, a native of India, has a medium build and silver-gray hair. He is soft-spoken and unassuming and one might be forgiven for failing to recognize him as one of the world's leading cancer researchers. But there is no mistaking his credentials. Gazdar has published more than five hundred articles on human cancer and its causes. His accomplishments include the creation of some four hundred cell lines (cultures of cloned tumor cells) from different types of human cancers, more than two hundred of which have been deposited with an international organization that makes them available to scientists conducting cancer research. Not only have cell lines initiated by Gazdar been distributed more widely than those of any other researcher, but he also has the distinction of creating the cell line used by NCI researcher Robert Gallo to continuously propagate the HIV virus for the first time, thus enabling blood tests to be developed to identify HIV conclusively.

When Gazdar first heard about Carbone's research, he found it unconvincing. "I read some of Carbone's written works and, frankly, I just didn't believe them," he recalls. "Here's a monkey virus suddenly popping up in the middle of a rare tumor. I was suspicious. I was skeptical of the data, whether the work was performed correctly, whether the conclusions were right, so forth. Then I thought: I've got the perfect tool to either prove or disprove it—and I certainly thought I was going to disprove it—and that was to microdissect the samples."

Gazdar used an exacting technique called laser microdissection, to examine a series of mesothelioma samples. He meticulously separated the cancer cells, one by one, from nearby noncancerous cells. "If one can find the virus in both [types of] cells, then almost certainly it's very likely to be some sort of contamination or artifact. But if I found it specifically in the tumor cells and not in the adjacent nonmalignant tissue, than it was likely to be an association" between the virus and the cancer, Gazdar says. "When I did that, to my amazement I found the virus was specifically associated with the tumor cells." In his microdissections, Gazdar found that SV40 was present in more than half of the malignant cells in the mesotheliomas he examined. He also found the virus in some precursor cancer cells within the tumor masses. Significantly, more than 98 percent of the cells from adjacent, nonmesothelial lung tissue were negative for SV40. "That rules out any contamination," he says, "because if a specimen were contaminated [with the virus] . . . it would be in all parts of the specimen, it wouldn't whomp down on the mesothelium alone." The fact that SV40 is in the precursor cancer cells is also strong evidence it is causing the tumors, Gazdar says. "The virus is in the right type of cells for many years before they become malignant." Gazdar, who published his results in 1999, has completely reversed his position on SV40's ability to cause tumors in human beings. "I went from an agnostic to a skeptic to a believer to a zealot," Gazdar says. "I'm convinced. I've gone 180 degrees."

With even former doubters becoming zealots, it is not surprising that there has been an upsurge in SV40 research efforts. Between 1997 and early 2003, more than twenty-five new studies were published demonstrating the presence of SV40 in human mesotheliomas; sixteen others found the virus in brain, bone, and various other cancers, as well as in the kidneys and peripheral blood. Apparently the efforts of Carbone and others at the 1997 NIH conference to garner widespread interest in the virus have paid off. Since 1997, study of the simian virus has become a global phenomenon. As of 2003, researchers had found SV40 in human tumors in China, Japan, New Zealand, Australia, Spain, Portugal, France, Switzerland, Italy, Germany, Sweden, Norway, Belgium, England, Scotland, Wales, the United States, Canada, and Brazil.

Many of the studies suggest there is a geographic correspondence between the location of the SV40-positive tumors and the distribution of contaminated polio vaccine. Rates of SV40-positive tumors seem to be particularly high in the United Kingdom, United States, and Italy, all of which had large mass programs of immunization with the contaminated Salk vaccine. On the other hand, in countries that did not use the contaminated vaccine or had only small campaigns, the rate of SV40-positive tumors appears to be extremely low, in some cases negligible. For instance, more than eighty mesotheliomas from Finland and Turkey were tested for SV40 in three separate studies. Every tumor was SV40-negative. Neither country used contaminated polio vaccine. (Today, Finland has one of the lowest mesothelioma rates in the West, half the U.S. per capita rate and one-third of the United Kingdom's.) The authors of all three studies pointed to lack of contaminated vaccines in their countries as the most plausible explanation for their negative findings. Similarly, Finnish brain tumors have also tested negative for SV40, while those from Italy, the United States, and other countries that used Salk vaccine frequently test positive.

One of the most significant new SV40 findings has come from the labs, once again, of Janet Butel and Adi Gazdar. Working independently of each other, the two scientists found SV40 at high rates in a group of cancers that are known collectively as "non-Hodgkin's lymphomas"; they occur more frequently than any other types of lymphoma. Gazdar reported he had found SV40 in 43 percent of the non-Hodgkin's lymphoma samples he examined, and Butel had found SV40 in 42 percent of her samples. Lymphomas, interestingly, are a fourth tumor type that hamsters sometimes contract when exposed to SV40, a discovery made in the 1970s.

Like mesotheliomas and pediatric brain cancers, lymphomas have been increasing steadily in incidence in recent years, and non-Hodgkin's lymphomas are the most common of all lymphomas. Five percent of all cancers diagnosed in the United States annually are now lymphomas of one sort or another. Unlike mesotheliomas or pediatric brain tumors, non-Hodgkin's lymphoma cannot be described as a rare cancer: 54,000 Americans are diagnosed with the disease every year, and 30,000 die from it annually. Non-Hodgkin's lymphoma incidence has risen 3 percent annually since the 1970s; risk increases as one ages.

Gazdar has also linked SV40 to leukemia. In 2003, Gazdar detected SV40 DNA in seven of twenty-four leukemia samples he checked, or 29 percent of the time. When he tested another set of samples, the incidence of the virus increased to slightly above 30 percent. He found that SV40 was completely absent in the bone marrow cells, lymph nodes, and blood of patients without the cancer. "That proves the association," Gazdar says. SV40 is "clearly associated with both chronic and acute leukemias of several types."

Gazdar discovered that SV40 appears to behave the same way in leukemias and lymphomas as it does in mesotheliomas and brain tumors. The virus attacks the cells' anticancer defenses. In many of the SV40-positive lymphoma and leukemia samples, Gazdar found the virus had disabled a series of seven different tumor-suppressing genes.

Although he states SV40 is not sufficient or necessary for leukemia and lymphoma development, he is convinced that the virus is present and facilitating cancer in the leukemias and lymphomas he has examined. "The data is so striking that there's just no way it could be by chance," he says.

"It's got to be there, and it's got to be having a biological effect. It's specific to lymphoma and leukemias. It's not present in controls [those who do not have the disease] and so that proves association. The part that proves causality to me is the fact that it is knocking out tumor suppressor genes— remarkable tumor suppressor genes." That, says Gazdar, is consistent with how other tumor-causing viruses work.

Gazdar, the former SV40 skeptic, believes the public health response to the simian virus must change. The different types of cancers with which it is involved, the numbers of victims, and the increasing evidence that it causes cancer, all demand a serious federal effort to study it. "Look how many people were potentially contaminated with the virus," he says. "The potential health issues are mind-boggling."

Unfortunately, the NIH does not appear to agree. Since 1997, the federal government's primary response to SV40 has been to dispute almost all the research associating the virus with human tumors. The centerpiece of that effort was the large so-called reproducibility study that Howard Strickler and Keerti Shah had suggested at the January 1997 NIH conference. It was launched by Viral Epidemiology Branch in mid-1997. The inconclusive study dragged on for four years, wasted hundreds of thousands of dollars, and tied up some of the world's top SV40 researchers in a largely fruitless effort. In the process, it set off a round of bitterness and recrimination rarely seen in the world of science.

17

A Study Marred by Strife

ON JULY 1, 1997, at 8:30 in the morning, eighteen government scientists and private researchers crowded into a small conference room on the NIH's Bethesda, Maryland, campus to debate the future of the federal government's involvement in SV40 research. The scientists present represented the full range of opinion on SV40. There were believers: Carbone, Butel, Lednicky, and Pass. There were the prominent naysayers: Goedert, Strickler, and de Villiers. And there were some scientists who were ostensibly neutral. Dubbed the SV40-PCR Working Group, the disparate lot had been summoned by Andrew Lewis, Carbone's former boss at the NCI, who was now head of the Laboratory of Virology in the FDA's Office of Vaccine Research and Review.

At the January 1997 NIH SV40 conference, Carbone and the others in the SV40 camp believed they had made a convincing and scientifically valid case that what they were finding was genuine SV40 and not PCR contamination. The VEB felt just the opposite and believed it had been given a mandate at the conference to press ahead with the so-called reproducibility study that Strickler and Shah had proposed. Strickler had recruited some potential participants—two labs in Britain and one in France—and had already begun to design the study. The goal was to see whether PCR could "reliably" detect SV40 in human tumor samples. To do this, Strickler conceived of a study in which multiple laboratories would be given blinded tumor samples and controls *in duplicate* so that the labs would have to prove not only that they could detect the virus when it was present (and not detect it when it was not present), but achieve the identical results twice. Lewis now wanted this group of scientists to achieve consensus on whether to implement Strickler's proposed design and hoped to secure agreement from all of them to participate.

Carbone and some of the other SV40 researchers were pleased that Lewis was chairing the meeting. He had solid credentials as a researcher, and a strong background in SV40, and unlike the VEB scientists, he was not predisposed against the possibility that the simian virus was associated with human cancer. When the meeting began, one researcher remembers being hopeful that the two opposing camps could resolve their differences. "Wow, maybe we're going to get to the bottom of this," the scientist thought.

Nothing, as it turned out, could have been further from the truth. As the day wore on, it became clear that there were still many simmering resentments left over from the January conference. The researchers who had successfully detected SV40 DNA felt that they were being patronized and that when they pointed out legitimate scientific shortcomings in the proposed VEB protocol, they were not taken seriously. Worse, they felt that their own research was once again under attack by scientists who were not qualified to pass judgment upon it. Strickler and Goedert, the VEB duo, had never even performed PCR tests. Yet they were going to lead an entire study on the issue of whether PCR could detect SV40 and, in the process, render a definitive determination on the reliability of everyone else's PCR work.

Just as it had in January, the discussion often circled back to funding. As Strickler outlined his proposed experiment, Carbone and several other U.S.-based scientists pointed out that it necessitated hundreds and hundreds of PCR tests over many, many months, an unbelievable expense for labs already stretched thin. The financial support the VEB was offering each participating lab—$15,000 to $25,000—needed to be double, triple, perhaps ten times as much, especially if the study went on as long as it appeared it would.

By the end of the meeting, which Strickler would later describe in a memo as "very contentious," the mistrust between the two groups was palpable. (It took three months for the participants just to agree on the minutes.) Just before the meeting broke up, Strickler proposed a study coordinator, someone who was a papilloma virus expert, a suggestion that was angrily rejected by the SV40 scientists. About the only thing the two factions could agree on was that instead of using ependymomas for an SV40 survey, as Strickler had proposed, fresh-frozen mesotheliomas were the better choice.

After the meeting, several of the American researchers felt that they had been trapped. The two British labs and the one French lab were on board to go forward with Strickler's plan, and the VEB had made it plain that it would simply proceed without the U.S. scientists if they refused to cooperate. Some worried that if they didn't participate, their refusal would be interpreted as a sign that they feared their own work was unreliable. On the other hand, the VEB's study design was complex, expensive, and contained ample room for error, especially since the VEB organizers seemed to understand so little about the biology of SV40. Moreover, interpretation of the experiment results was being granted to Strickler. Wasn't it a conflict of interest, they wondered, to make Strickler, who had authored the only published negative study, the organizer of a study that was to determine once and for all which side was right?

Carbone, for one, felt the whole exercise was unnecessary. Two months earlier, he had agreed to participate in a study directed by one of the world's leading investigators in the areas of mesothelioma treatment and basic research, Joseph R. Testa, of Philadelphia's Fox Chase Cancer Center. Testa had told Carbone up front he was highly doubtful of the SV40-mesothelioma association but would oversee a search for the virus in mesothelioma biopsies at the request of the International Mesothelioma Interest Group, an organization of researchers and clinicians.

The plan called for four laboratories to be given blinded samples from the same twelve mesothelioma biopsies. Only those samples in which all four laboratories found SV40 would be considered positive for the purpose of the study. In addition to Carbone's lab, there would be two labs that had never worked with SV40 before, and a Finnish lab that tested for SV40 in mesothelioma samples from a population that hadn't received contaminated vaccine and failed to find the virus. A strict protocol was in place to minimize any possibility of PCR contamination. All mesothelioma specimens were to come from the Sloan Kettering Cancer Center, which was unaffiliated with any of the participating labs. Mesothelioma specimens from this hospital had never before been tested for SV40—so there was no chance the specimens could be contaminated at their point of origin. DNA from all the specimens would then be extracted in Testa's lab. Not only had Testa's Fox Chase facility never worked with SV40 before, it had never even worked with DNA viruses before. Given the rigid protocol, the possibility that positive results from this experiment could be attributable to contamination was nil. (In 1998, Testa published the results of the study in *Cancer Research*. Four labs found SV40 in at least nine of the twelve mesotheliomas. After the experiment, Testa became convinced about the association of SV40 with mesotheliomas. He has since gone on to do further research on the topic.)

The only difference Carbone could see between the experiment that he had commenced with Testa and the one Strickler was now proposing was that Strickler wanted everyone to test an enormous number of mesothelioma samples—ninety-five—and he wanted every mesothelioma biopsy to be tested twice. Still, like all the other U.S.-based researchers, Carbone had told Lewis he would participate in the study.

Three months after the July meeting, Carbone had a severe run-in with Strickler. On October 2, 1997, Strickler sent a memo to all twelve would-be study members saying that, because securing frozen mesotheliomas was proving difficult, he was prepared to use paraffin-embedded tissues as a fallback. Strickler also indicated that he and the VEB would be in charge of decisions concerning the DNA extraction techniques. Carbone fired off an angry letter to Lewis immediately, which he copied to Strickler and every other study participant. Strickler, Carbone asserted, was an epidemiologist; he was unqualified to make decisions about what type of specimens to use and had no right to assume unilateral control of the investigation:

> I have just received the enclosed fax from Howard Strickler. I do not understand the tone of this fax since the only job of Dr. Strickler was to provide appropriate specimens. . . . Furthermore, you are the person who is coordinating this panel. . . . I do not see why Dr. Strickler who does not work in a lab, who does not perform PCR experiments, who is not a molecular biologist or virologist, would be the one to decide what type of experiments and procedures should be performed.

But what Carbone didn't know was that a decision had already been made at the highest levels of the NCI sanctioning the VEB as the study's coordinator. Then-NCI Director Richard Klausner, in a 1999 interview, said he personally had decided that the VEB shoud lead the study, and not another NCI branch with more experience in DNA extraction, sequencing, and characterization—even though the study's principal goal was to assess the reliability of PCR, a molecular technique. "Their expertise in viruses and virus-associated disease makes [the Viral Epidemiology Branch] really the right place to do it," Klausner insisted. "As an expert in doing this sort of work, I feel that I can make that decision and I feel very comfortable with the decision," he said.

Strickler, meanwhile wasted no time in responding to Carbone's challenge to his authority. In a memo sent the same day to all the study participants, he reminded them that this was the VEB's study and that there was limited room for dissent:

> No one individual or laboratory should be allowed to hold this important topic hostage . . . trying to hammer out a single study plan . . . has only lead [sic] to hostility and delayed important research. . . . VEB has been the promoter of this project for more than a year, the group writing the protocol, putting in all aspects of the study design . . . to make the study a reality. Therefore, all comments should be returned to VEB for response.

Strickler closed by noting that while "all possible, reasonable requests" to change the protocol would be considered, there was only so far the VEB would go in accepting suggestions. "A final protocol will be adopted soon and everyone will need to make their own decisions regarding participation," he wrote.

On November 3, Lewis sent a revised draft protocol to all the potential participants. In the letter that accompanied the protocol, Lewis made an oblique reference to the fact that the VEB was "taking the lead role in developing the study." In fact, three weeks previous, Lewis's boss at the FDA, Kathryn Zoon, had agreed that the VEB had "a clear mandate" to run the study and was "in control of the investigation." Despite what the SV40 scientists might have believed initially, the VEB, not FDA, was in charge. Lewis's letter was the first notice to most of them of this apparent substitution in leadership roles.

In a November 9, 1997, letter to Lewis, Carbone expressed his vexation at this turn of events. Strickler's protocol, he wrote, contained a major shortcoming: No one had tested whether the commercial DNA extraction kit Strickler wanted to use was effective in capturing SV40 DNA from tumor specimens. Another problem was the VEB's unwillingness to pay the labs for the true costs of the necessary PCR tests. This would lead to short-cuts, Carbone said, that "will not serve the best interests of science but increase enormously the risk of mistakes." His biggest complaint, however, concerned Strickler himself, who Carbone asserted was openly prejudiced against SV40 research:

> Dr. Strickler and his collaborators [at the VEB] are biased. This [has] emerged every time they have spoken about this issue and it is also obvious in the first 2 pages of the draft [protocol] . . . which contains gratuitous and unnecessary biased comments. It should be Dr. Lewis—as we were initially led to believe—who coordinates this project and who decides the final protocol, not scientists with an already preformed opinion about the issue.

Eleven days later, Butel and Lednicky both wrote to Lewis to air many of the same complaints about Strickler's protocol. They, too, questioned the DNA extraction kit Strickler had chosen, and they, too, felt the opening section of his draft protocol, which suggested contamination was the reason for previous SV40 findings, indicated the VEB scientist was far from objective. The opening paragraph of the protocol, the pair said, "sets a distrustful and biased tone and should be rewritten."

Strickler, however, was firmly in control of the study and soon began to exercise his new prerogatives. One of the first things he did was set about cleaning house. On December 10, 1997, in a carefully crafted letter, Strickler essentially "uninvited" Carbone from the study, ostensibly because of the amount of funding Carbone said he required to participate. ("We were disappointed to find your correspondence indicates that you will not be able to participate in the study without sufficient time to train a new technician . . . and without funding for 2–3 years," Strickler wrote. "As you know unfortunately training time and the $300,000 plus indirect [expenses] you require both go substantially beyond the study plan. . . .") Pass received a similar letter the same day. He, too, had estimated his costs as far higher than the VEB was willing to accommodate. Butel and Lednicky had also announced their intention to withdraw, but unlike Carbone and Pass, they were coaxed into remaining.

Interestingly, soon after the loss of the Carbone and Pass labs, Strickler changed the study design. Instead of testing ninety-five samples, only twenty-five would be required. This, of course, dropped the costs per laboratory considerably, cutting them to a fraction of what each lab had originally projected. Strickler also suddenly raised the compensation the VEB was offering to each participating lab. Pass and Carbone, however, were never informed of the change in remuneration nor given a chance to reestimate their costs based on the lower number of samples. The VEB study would not include the labs of two of the world's recognized authorities on SV40 and human cancer. Strickler replaced Pass and Carbone with two labs of his own choice that had far less experience with SV40 and human tumors.

The VEB study finally commenced in the spring of 1998. Its purpose, according to the final protocol, was to "assess the sensitivity, specificity, and reproducibility [of] SV40 PCR assays." Nine laboratories were on board. As a requirement for their participation, all had been asked to sign statements saying they had agreed to the protocol and that the study could be published listing them as coauthors. Four of the labs had detected SV40 previously in human tumors, two others had not (one was Shah's, the other de Villiers's). Robin Weiss's lab was also participating. He had once found SV40, but he had written off the finding as contamination. Two other labs that had never searched for SV40 were also on the team. One of these was associated with David Sugarbaker, a well-known mesothelioma surgeon from Brigham and Women's Hospital in Boston, who had expressed doubt that there was an association between SV40 and mesothelioma.

Sugarbaker was also providing the twenty-five mesothelioma specimens that everyone was to test twice. After Sugarbaker prepared the specimens, they were sent to a commercial lab near the NCI offices for DNA extraction. Strickler, in his role as study coordinator, had picked the contractor, who in turn had picked the DNA extraction kit. None of the participating labs had any input into these critical decisions.

Throughout most of 1998, things were quiet as the labs received their masked samples and ran their PCR tests. On December 11, 1998, Strickler reported that all the labs had finished and the data had been tabulated. Strickler's memo outlined the preliminary results. Six of the nine laboratories, he said, were able to detect SV40 DNA in at least one of the twenty-five samples. Three labs reported no SV40 in any of their samples. Four found one only one sample to be positive. Two labs had better results. One had found SV40 in ten samples, or 40 percent, of Sugarbaker's samples, while the other had found SV40 in 20 percent of its mesotheliomas.

Overall, the SV40 positive rate seemed quite low; the Sugarbaker samples apparently contained little SV40. (Or, as it later developed, they might have contained a significant amount, but the viral DNA was lost during the extraction process.) There had also been an unexpected glitch, Strickler reported. Almost all of the first set of negative controls had tested positive for SV40. The commercial contractor Strickler had hired to extract the DNA from the Sugarbaker samples had neglected to adequately clean its biosafety hood after preparation of the positive controls and had inadvertently contaminated all of its negative samples. The company was forced to prepare a new batch of negative controls and send them out for testing a month later.

In the same memo, Strickler noted that he was about to leave the NIH to assume a new position at Albert Einstein College of Medicine, in New York, but promised that he would soon be sending off a draft manuscript for everyone's review and that even with his new nongovernmental position, everyone should "rest assured . . . I will continue to work on as before." Strickler left the NIH a few days later and headed for New York and began to draft his manuscript. In early 1999, he sent it out to the study participants for their comments.

For Carbone, "dismissal" from the multilaboratory study meant more time to pursue other avenues of research—ones he felt were more important and considerably more promising than simply proving once again that PCR was a reliable tool for detecting SV40 in human tumors. One thing in particular had nagged at him over the years. It seemed indisputable that the only source for the SV40 that he and the others were discovering in human tumors was contaminated vaccines. But he had no proof. Absent such proof, skeptics like Strickler continued to suggest polio vaccine was not the source.

The skeptics had come up with any number of theories to explain away the SV40 that was appearing in human cancers. Strickler and the VEB repeatedly suggested laboratory contamination was the reason, an argument that frustrated Carbone and the other SV40 researchers, because they felt they had answered it. Each year brought more and more labs finding SV40 in human tumors. Many of them had never worked with the simian virus before. Moreover, detection techniques had expanded well beyond PCR to include techniques such as immunohistochemistry, the demonstration of specific antigens in tissues by the use of fluorescent markers or enzymes. That technique ruled out contamination.

But the skeptics had other theories. Maybe all the SV40 in humans had come from monkey bites. How rhesus monkeys biting people in northern India could transmit SV40 so widely that it was now appearing in tumors in North America and Europe was never explained. Still, the weakness of their arguments did nothing to dissuade the doubters. Strickler, for example, commented on the state of SV40 research in 1999 by declaring: "Show me the slightest proof that these cancers have any connection with the polio vaccine." Until Carbone or someone else could demonstrate that the SV40 being recovered from human tumors was the same as what was in contaminated polio vaccine, the doubters would continue to insist the vaccine was not at fault.

Carbone had tried for a number of years to find old vials of vaccine. He wanted to use PCR to see if they contained SV40 and, if so, what type. But how could he get his hands on archival vaccine? Carbone first approached the FDA. The agency responded that it no longer had vials dating back to the contamination era in the late 1950s and early 1960s. In the early 1990s, coincident with the new round of SV40 research that Carbone and others had begun, a decision had apparently been made at FDA to discard the old lots of vaccine. Carbone next wrote to every one of the six manufacturers who had produced Salk vaccine in the 1950s and 1960s. None had vials for him to test; they had discarded their old stock years, even decades, ago. Where could Carbone find vaccine to test? Stumped, he decided to call on Herbert Ratner, an elderly doctor he had met while attending the 1997 SV40 conference in Bethesda. Ratner had served as the public health officer during the 1950s in—of all places—Oak Park, Illinois, the very community in which Carbone resided. Ratner had been hoping to hear from the young Italian scientist who had impressed him at the 1997 conference; he had something very special he wanted to give him.

Within a week of the April 12, 1955 announcement of the success of the Salk field trials, cases of Parke, Davis vaccine had arrived at Ratner's offices in Oak Park. Ratner was supposed to start inoculating local school children immediately as part of the National Foundation's free immunization campaign. But Ratner was the rare public health official in 1955 who was not eager to distribute the newly licensed Salk vaccine. He was concerned that the Salk inactivation process was inadequate, and he was also concerned about viral contaminants. Ratner refused to administer the vaccine. Parents were angry, and Ratner was practically run out of town. Then the Cutter incident broke, and Ratner suddenly appeared to be very perspicacious. After the Cutter incident had blown over, Ratner remained suspicious of the vaccine. Instead of injecting the young children of Oak Park with the vials he deemed unsafe, he stored them away in his refrigerator, where they remained, unopened, for more than forty years. The eighty-seven-year-old Ratner offered them to Carbone to test. "I would have gone all the way to Alaska to find this stuff, and here it was three miles away," Carbone says, holding a tiny vial of vintage vaccine between his gloved thumb and forefinger.

Carbone and Rizzo used PCR to test Ratner's vials in the summer of 1999. Their first discovery was that the 1955 Parke-Davis vaccine did indeed contain SV40, but it was a variant of the simian virus that virologists refer to as slow-growing, because it replicates at a much slower rate than most SV40 strains used in laboratories. Carbone's discovery was significant because it marked the first time such an SV40 variant had been recovered from polio vaccine. Earlier researchers, including Sweet and Hilleman, had only found fast-growing SV40 when they had searched contaminated vaccines. Both kinds of SV40 occur in human tumors, but until Carbone tested the Parke, Davis vaccine, there was no proof that the slow-growing SV40 found in humans had come from polio vaccine. Carbone's finding debunked claims that the virus the researchers were finding in human tumors came from another source. Even if some small amount of exposure to SV40 was due to monkey bites, SV40 researchers now widely agree there is no question that the vast exposure of millions of Americans to the monkey virus occurred through contaminated vaccines. "This proves that the SV40 that was present in the polio vaccine is identical to the SV40 we are finding in these human tumors," Carbone says of his finding.

Why did Hilleman's and Sweet's SV40 isolated from vaccine during the 1960s contain only the faster growing versions of SV40? Both kinds, Carbone says, occurred in the monkey kidneys used to grow the vaccine. "It's mixed. It's purely a matter of chance. . . . No one knows for sure whether those 1960 . . . [samples Sweet and Hilleman tested] just coincidentally failed to contain the slower strain or whether the faster growing strain had an advantage in the cell cultures and somehow edged out its slower growing siblings."

Faster growing strains of SV40 are more often recovered from mesotheliomas, while slower growing variants generally are found in brain and bone cancers. Carbone hypothesizes that the large amount of p53 in mesothelial cells allows them to withstand fast-growing SV40 without bursting, while brain and bone cells can only withstand the slower growing versions of the virus. He and Lednicky also believe that the slow-growing version might have an advantage in tumor formation because it would be less likely to be detected by the immune system.

Not only was the slow-growing variant detected by Carbone in the Ratner vaccine the same type found in human brain and bone cancers, but in a surprising turn of events, three years after Carbone's polio vaccine study, Janet Butel isolated from a human lymphoma biopsy a virus identical to the one Carbone had extracted from the vaccine. As part of the non-Hodgkin's lymphoma study she published in the *Lancet*, Butel sequenced portions of the SV40 virus she had isolated from her patients. Three of her sequenced viruses lined up identically with one of the strains Carbone had found in Ratner's vaccine vials. Here was the definitive answer to the charge that "artifact" or "contamination" was the reason for the SV40-positive tumors that Carbone and so many other researchers had identified during the previous decade. Butel's lymphomas biopsies contained the exact SV40 variant that was in a vial of commercially distributed polio vaccine. Moreover, no lab, including Butel's had ever worked with this variant before, so she could not have possibly contaminated her tumor samples with it.

The last piece of the puzzle about SV40's origin had fallen into place. The virus in the tumor had been lined up against the virus in the vaccine; the two had been measured against each other base pair by base pair. The two viruses, the one in the tumor and the one in the vaccine, were a perfect match, reflections of each other—so much alike they were virtually indistinguishable. There was only one significant difference between them. The one from Ratner's refrigerator had never escaped from the vial that imprisoned it. Stuck for forty years in a glass bottle with a yellowing label, it had slowly fragmented in a soup of poliovirus, cellular debris, and chemicals. Its twin, on the other hand, had been liberated, perhaps decades ago, an unnoticed passenger in a shot of polio vaccine. Eventually, it had found a secure place to hide, some tissue where it was not noticed, some cell that it could slowly subvert. It had found a human host, and it was causing cancer.

18

Wasted Time, Wasted Money

RIGHT AROUND THE time Carbone began his search for vials of polio vaccine to test, Strickler began circulating his draft of the multilaboratory study results. One of the scientists to whom Strickler sent his draft manuscript was Bharat Jasani.

Jasani is a friendly and outgoing scientist. In his mid-fifties, he is trim and neat, with a large forehead and short black hair streaked with gray. He is gentlemanly almost to a fault. Jasani, who is of Indian descent, was born and raised in Kenya and moved to the United Kingdom as a young man. Like Carbone, he is a board-certified pathologist who graduated from a well-respected medical school (Britain's Royal College of Medicine) and also holds a Ph.D. (in immunology). He has a broad-ranging intellect. After college, he took a year off from hard science to take courses in math and philosophy, which he describes as "the queen of the sciences." Jasani, who is head of Histopathology at the University of Wales College of Medicine in Cardiff, first read about Carbone's research in the 1994 article in the *New Scientist.* "I felt there was something important about it," he said of Carbone's and Pass's first mesothelioma paper.

He and his boss, Alan Gibbs, decided to repeat the experiment themselves. Forty-five percent of the archived mesothelioma samples he examined from the Wales College of Medicine's extensive collection tested positive for SV40. After that Jasani surveyed mesotheliomas from sixty patients just from the 1990s; 70 percent of these biopsies were positive. Many of the tumors were also expressing T-antigen. Then Jasani decided to test the peripheral blood of some of the patients whose tumors were SV40-positive; he found SV40 was frequently circulating in their blood. Like Carbone, Jasani is interested in learning exactly how the virus works at the cellular level. He has been focusing on whether SV40 interferes with intracellular communications by blocking or altering "channels" that cells use to pass molecular messages back and forth to each other.

Jasani's office is small and crowded with medical texts. Through the window, you can hear the sound of the traffic on the nearby M-4 highway, mixed with the occasional screeching of seagulls. An Olympus microscope with five objectives sits on his desk. It was on this desk that Strickler's draft write-up of the multilaboratory study results arrived in 1999. Jasani began to read it.

Jasani had entered into the study in good faith. He had attended the July 1997 meeting and had assumed, like the other SV40 veterans, that the FDA, not Strickler and the VEB, was going to direct the effort. He had been chagrined by the bickering and the disagreements that accompanied the start of the study, but felt it was still wiser to go along with the effort, if that was what U.S. officials felt was needed. Even at this late date, he still believed that he and the other SV40 researchers could convince these federal health officials that the association between the virus and human cancer was significant. Now, as he read Strickler's manuscript, however, he worried that his decision to participate in the VEB had been naive. The more closely he examined the study draft, the more troubled he became. There were problems with the DNA extraction and preparation, problems perhaps with the way the tumor samples had been prepared and selected, but equally important, there were serious problems with Strickler's overall tone and conclusions. Strickler was prepared to dramatically overstate the findings and infer that since so few of the Sugarbaker samples were positive, SV40 findings in previous studies should now be doubted.

In 1998, Jasani had reviewed the 1995 Strickler, Shah, and Goedert study, focusing on their experimental protocols. He had been struck by the inadequacies in their technique and had written a detailed critique of their paper. (The trio's lab technique was so bad, Jasani says, that it seemed like the "work was almost conducted to ensure that [they were] going to get a negative result . . . and scientifically, [their] methods were extremely loaded against getting a positive result.") As he contemplated how to respond to Strickler's manuscript, he reached a decision. He was not going to let his name appear on a flawed study, but he would see if he could work with the VEB to fix the study's shortcomings.

On March 16, 1999, Jasani, with the support of Gibbs, initiated what would become a two-year effort to try and address the flaws in Strickler's study and his manuscript. Butel and Lednicky also took up the fight. At times pressure on the four American and British researchers to relent would become intense, but they did not yield. The struggle between them and the federal government would, in the description of one FDA official, become "fatiguing" for all concerned.

The battle was joined in a seemingly innocuous fashion. Butel and Lednicky and several other laboratories had written to Strickler in the early winter with a series of technical questions about procedures. Strickler had replied near the end of February. Jasani had "read with great interest," as he now wrote, some of the comments from participating laboratories, as well as Strickler's responses:

> This has helped to bring into a sharp focus in my mind the fact that what is the major strength of this study may also be its major weakness. . . . The study was conducted primarily to check out whether SV40 DNA found in mesotheliomas is a contaminant or not. The DNA therefore was organised to be extracted by a neutral agency which had not previously handled SV40 DNA in any capacity whatsoever.

This was Strickler's private contractor, who had contaminated an entire set of negative controls. That, in and of itself, was a strong indication that there were serious problems with the quality of the contractor's work. Here was the nub of the problem:

> Whilst this approach may have helped towards resolving the question of contamination at the DNA extraction level, it has unfortunately left the question of efficiency of DNA extraction not adequately attended. This is mainly because the efficiency of DNA extraction claimed by [the contractor] does not seem to have been quantitatively assessed.

Beneath the cordial language, Jasani was saying that he did not trust that Strickler's private contractor lab knew what it was doing. The contractor had never worked with SV40 before, and the commercial DNA extraction kit it had chosen was of unknown efficacy for extracting SV40 DNA. None of the labs that were experienced with SV40 had relied on the kit before, and Strickler was offering no reassurance that efforts had been made to determine if the kit actually worked. As Jasani reviewed the contractor's own tests on the kit, he realized that it was quite conceivable that the contractor could have falsely, albeit unknowingly, reported that its methodology was sufficient to recover a large volume of SV40 DNA from human tumors, when it fact it could not. This would mean that if the Sugarbaker samples *had* contained SV40, it was possible the contractor had been unable to extract it at all—hence the small number of positive samples. Strickler had skirted the entire issue in his write-up by asserting that the kit was of "high efficiency" without giving any figures to back up the assertion.

Eight days after Jasani's letter, Butel and Lednicky weighed in on the issue, repeating Jasani's critique of the DNA extraction in even greater detail. They raised several other technical shortfalls as well. Their biggest concern lay with a curious statistic buried in the tables that accompanied the manuscript. According to Strickler's compilation of the labs' reports, by the end of the experiment Shah's lab had become the most sensitive at detecting SV40 DNA in the positive controls, able to find it at much lower concentrations than any of the other labs. Inexplicably, Shah's ability to detect SV40 in positive controls had also dramatically improved between the start of the experiment and its conclusion. This seemed to make no scientific sense and Lednicky and Butel pressed for an explanation for Shah's sudden improvement in SV40 detection. Strickler's initial explanation was as follows:

> Keerti explains that they were disappointed in the sensitivity of their results during the pretrial testing . . . which was [less sensitive] than in previous testing and took steps to make improvements . . . before the investigation began. They conducted repeat testing of some specimens [control samples] when it was necessary.

Strickler's explanation astounded Butel and Lednicky. One of the purposes of the study was to assess each lab's technique. Why was Shah suddenly being given a chance to "make improvements" in his lab's technique?

We are seriously concerned by your response to our questions about the data from laboratory 7 (Shah laboratory). . . . It strains credulity to suggest that they retested when necessary. How would they know which samples should be retested . . . ? We think sensitivity, reproducibility, and reliability cannot be measured from this laboratory's results.

If Shah's laboratory had compromised a primary purpose of the experiment, as Butel and Lednicky suspected, it should be removed from the study.

The Baylor scientists, like Jasani, were also disturbed by the tone of Strickler's conclusions as contained in the draft write-up he was circulating:

Our major disagreement with the . . . draft manuscript is the effort to extrapolate from this study [the] answer once and for all [to the question of] the possible association of SV40 with human mesotheliomas. Just as one positive study cannot prove etiology [causality], one negative study cannot disprove other positive studies. . . . [A]ll that can be concluded from this study is that in this set of 25 mesotheliomas collected from a group of patients in Boston . . . SV40 DNA was not detectable [within the limits of the PCR assays used by each lab]. . . .

Strickler now had a trans-Atlantic contretemps on his hands. To complicate matters, the two dissenting laboratories had an unlikely ally in the FDA's William Egan, the acting head of the Office of Vaccines Research and Review. After an internal FDA committee had reviewed Strickler's draft manuscript in February 1999, Egan wrote a lengthy letter to Strickler criticizing it.

Strickler, in the opening section of his draft manuscript, had written that epidemiological studies had "repeatedly failed" to detect any statistically significant increases in cancer incidence among those exposed to contaminated vaccines. Egan reminded Strickler that there had been some studies that *had* found increases in cancer incidence (the ones that Strickler had dismissed at the 1997 NIH conference as irrelevant because of size) and suggested that he tone down the conclusory language and include references to the positive studies. Strickler, in a written response to Egan, said that he was willing to replace the offending adverb ("repeatedly"), but was not willing to undertake any discussion of positive epidemiological studies in his article. He reminded the FDA official (and all the other study participants) that this section of the manuscript had already been circulated prior to the experiment. Discussion about its contents was now closed unless it was "to correct clear inaccuracies . . . shown to be essential."

Egan next noted that portions of Strickler's manuscript appeared to "imply, unintentionally so, that the positive results [of SV40 in tumors] that have been reported [by other scientists] are due to laboratory contamination; I do not think that this should be implied." Strickler responded that, contrary to what Egan had assumed, the implication was intentional, not accidental: "This study would not have been conducted if there was not some doubt. That point must be made and made clearly."

Egan also took exception to Strickler's statement that "the presence of SV40 in human mesotheliomas has remained controversial." Said Egan: "The meaning and implication of this sentence are not clear. I personally think that the evidence for the presence of SV40 in these tumors is reasonably good." Egan added that whether the virus caused the tumors, however, was still uncertain in his mind. Later Egan chided Strickler about another section of his draft, which stated, "This multi-institutional study failed to demonstrate the reproducible detection of SV40 in human mesotheliomas." Egan wrote:

> More exactly, it failed to demonstrate SV40 sequences in *this set* of mesotheliomas. This is not inconsistent with SV40 being found by others previously. Indeed, the fact that laboratories that previously found SV40 in their samples do not now find SV40 in these samples (and get the study controls correct) only lends credence to their previous findings. . . . These laboratories are able to find SV40 when it is there, and do not find it when it is not there.

Strickler's response was that he "disagree[d] strongly" with Egan's point. The other positive studies, he asserted, must have been mistaken: "The results of this study directly bring into question the detection of SV40 DNA reported in other investigations."

Strickler next wrote to Butel, Lednicky, Gibbs, and Jasani. In a mid-April 1999 memo, he addressed their concerns point by point. First, he responded to Butel and Lednicky's criticisms that Shah's laboratory had been given an opportunity to change its SV40 detection methods. His earlier explanation, Strickler said, was a "paraphrasing" of Shah's work and that any "misunderstanding" he had created had been "unfortunate." All Shah had done, Strickler asserted, was simply take any positive controls that had tested positive and run them through additional PCR cycles. A two-paragraph letter from Shah was attached in which Shah made clear his reluctance to discuss the matter much further. ("I am not sure that there is any point in any of us going into great details about the tests in the individual laboratories.") Strickler then turned to the questions that had been raised about the contractor's DNA extraction capabilities. Letters from the contractor were provided explaining its procedures more fully, and Strickler professed confidence in the lab's competence. And as to the concerns about the tone and conclusions, Strickler's response to the two labs was essentially what he had told the FDA: he was writing the manuscript, not they.

It was at this point that relations between the two labs and Strickler (and the VEB) began to rapidly deteriorate. Over the next several months, there followed a flurry of correspondence full of accusations and counteraccusations. In one letter, from the spring of 1999, Butel and Lednicky complained to Strickler about his continued refusal to heed their suggestions on the manuscript:

> We feel that our comments about data interpretation are being dismissed and ignored. Your intransigence about the interpretation of the data and the conclusions of the study have forced us to admit that the collegiality and the scientific collaboration that was the basis of this study is very strained.

On the same day, the pair wrote to Egan and Lewis directly, asking for FDA intervention because of our "concerns about data analysis and interpretation, and concerns about preparation of the manuscript."

Jasani and Gibbs, meanwhile, took Strickler to task in a strongly worded, single-spaced, six-page letter. Strickler, the pair said, had engaged in "a studied effort to . . . side-step the many flaws in this study rather than engage in meaningful, good-faith, exchange and resolution of legitimate scientific issues." As a result, the study's integrity was now in jeopardy and its "flaws and unresolved scientific issues . . . have become so cumulative as to outweigh any positive scientific benefit which might be derived from the publication of this study." Strickler, they said, was trying to color the study's findings to fit his contamination theory, even if the data did not support such a conclusion:

> It cannot be that all of these laboratories are contaminated and that contamination always happens in mesotheliomas, osteosarcomas and brain tumors, while the negative controls are always negative. Contamination is a random event.

Increasingly perturbed at the tone of Strickler's manuscript and his open hostility to any questions concerning its content, Jasani and Gibbs said that the situation had deteriorated to the point that Strickler should simply step aside:

> You seem to have unilaterally assumed exclusive control of the study organization, the method of the study, as well as the wording of the manuscript. These developments have . . . given rise to so many questions, discrepancies and issues of scientific significance that we strongly feel the scientific integrity of the study has been seriously undermined and is need of an evaluation by a neutral third party.

The reply to this letter from Jasani and Gibbs did not come from Strickler, but from Strickler's former mentor, the VEB's Jim Goedert, who made it clear he was responding on behalf of his "colleague and former post-doctoral fellow." "I was quite taken aback by the tone of your letter," he wrote, in a letter dated May 26, 1999. "The notion of bias on our part is without basis." In essence, the four-page letter said, all of the pair's complaints were unfounded, and Goedert demanded that the two scientists "personally apologize" to Strickler, "an extraordinarily capable physician and researcher, [who] has done nothing to merit the insults contained in your letter." Jasani and Gibbs responded to Goedert a few weeks later. While they apologized for the tone of their letter to Strickler, they did not recant its contents. Instead, they pointedly renewed their criticisms of the study and the draft manuscript and suggested that the only way out of the impasse would be to reconvene the entire study group and perhaps start the whole experiment all over again.

Frustrated by the continuing objections, Goedert and Strickler considered taking what is in science a highly unusual and uncollegial step: They made preparations to publish the study without the permission of the dissenting scientists. Strickler drafted a letter to the other study participants in which he described the objections of Butel and Lednicky and Jasani and Gibbs as "outrageous," and described them as "a partisan minority," which was holding the project "hostage." The VEB was going ahead without them, he told the other labs. Enough was enough. "We intend to move forward," Strickler wrote. "We plan to submit the manuscript without further testing or delay."

At this point, Goedert contacted NCI deputy director Alan Rabson for advice—the same Rabson who had performed SV40 experiments on rodents in the 1960s and who was also married to NIH acting director Ruth Kirschstein. Rabson, the number-two person within the entire NCI bureaucracy, apparently had become involved with how the VEB was handling the manuscript controversy, an indication that the VEB study was of paramount concern within the top echelons of the NIH. In a June 1999 e-mail to Strickler, Goedert reported that Rabson had outlined a series of specific steps for the pair to take in response to the Baylor and Cardiff labs, including submission of the manuscript with or without the labs' approval. Rabson, Goedert wrote to Strickler, "agrees we should no longer negotiate, but should send it in." According to Goedert, Rabson had also agreed on their choice of a journal and had even offered the name of a specific scientist they should contact who could sponsor the submission.

But any plan to publish without the consent of all the study's participating labs was scientifically suspect and perhaps even legally risky. Goedert's e-mail reveals Rabson was well aware of these perils. According to Goedert, Rabson had advised that, before Goedert and Strickler submitted the study, they first check with the NCI's Office of General Counsel "to assure that we/the government is unlikely to be sued." Goedert himself was worried about personal liability. "If there is legal action, how much can/will [the Office of the General Counsel] help us?" he wrote to Strickler, and added, "Is there any reason to think we need coverage from claims of misconduct?"

Goedert closed his e-mail by noting that Rabson offered his personal sympathies to Strickler: "Alan also said 'poor Howard!' but advised that you hang in there." (When questioned about the incident, Rabson states that he remembers few details from the episode and doesn't recall advising Goedert about how to get the study published.)

Before the NCI could move ahead with its plan to submit the study unilaterally, the FDA stepped in. A neutral panel of government scientists was convened to examine some of the technical problems that had befallen the study, and an FDA scientist, Phil Krause, was appointed as a mediator to rewrite portions of the study manuscript. For a while, the hostile back-and-forth subsided, although Strickler did draft one letter to Jasani and Gibbs in which he termed their apology "simply obnoxious and pointless," accused them of "ridiculous" "attempts to seem intimidating," and suggested they resign from the study. (Goedert advised not sending the draft and Strickler sent a considerably toned down version.) Krause circulated a new draft of the manuscript to all participants during the fall, and in February 2000, the manuscript was submitted to *Cancer Research* in hopes that the prestigious journal would accept it for publication.

At this point, another controversy broke out, this one involving Carbone and Pass. The two had long been interested in an immunogenic therapy to target T-antigen in patients whose mesotheliomas tested positive for SV40. They had begun working with a Michigan University researcher, Martin Sanda, who had devised an anti-T-antigen vaccine and had tested it in mice with SV40-induced tumors. The vaccinated mice outlived the controls. Pass and Carbone now wanted backing for what are known as Phase I clinical trials, which would test the safety, but not the efficacy, of their T-antigen targeted approach in humans. In February 2000, at about the time the VEB's study was submitted to *Cancer Research,* they applied to the National Cancer Institute for assistance. Their application, they believed, was strong and the research supporting it sound. The two felt they had an excellent chance of approval.

On May 5, 2000, they received a notice that they had been rejected. Grant applications at the NIH are reviewed by small panels of scientists from outside the NIH who are considered experts in a particular field of study. Generally, only two of the panel's members review any given grant in detail; these reviewers submit written recommendations to the entire panel, whose members then score each proposal. All panel members' scores are then compiled, and only the highest scoring grants receive funding. Thus, for each grant application, the two written reviews carry substantial weight. The letter rejecting the Pass and Carbone NCI grant listed the review panel's final score for their application and noted it was too low to merit government support. Accompanying the rejection letter were the reports of the two reviewers who had been assigned to examine Pass and Carbone's application in detail, although, in accordance with NIH grant review policy, the identities of the two reviewers were not revealed.

The first reviewer had given the application a priority ranking of "excellent," saying that "the proposal has many strengths" and "the hypothesis is strong . . . SV40 virus has been implicated as being a co-factor (along with asbestos) in the etiology [cause] of human cancers such as mesothelioma, osteosarcoma and some brain cancers. . . . This is a sound approach that may benefit patients."

The second review was as hostile as the first one was enthusiastic. The reviewer felt there was a flaw in Pass and Carbone's approach (there might not be sufficient T-antigen in the tumor cells to serve as a target for the vaccine). But his main thrust was not a critique of their approach; instead he used most of his page-and-a-half review to discredit the notion that SV40 was associated with human tumors. "The major concern regarding this application relates to the question of whether SV40 . . . is truly etiologically related to or even expressed in human mesotheliomas or other human cancers," the reviewer stated. "There are roughly an equivalent number of investigators who failed to find SV40 . . . in human tumors as investigators who have claimed to find them." At the time of the application, there were more than forty papers connecting SV40 to human cancers and three that had not; this assertion was simply false.

The reviewer was just warming up. All of the studies so far that had detected SV40 were fundamentally flawed. None had included blinded samples in which positive results had been verified by other laboratories (another false statement); none had included what the reviewer called "gold standard assays of proof," such as use of Southern blot and other confirmatory molecular techniques (again, false). There was only one worthy study in the reviewer's mind: the VEB's multiple-laboratory study. "This is the one study in which samples were tested in a completely blinded fashion among multiple laboratories and in duplicate and with appropriate positive and negative controls. This study therefore stands as the most definitive," the reviewer opined. Then came the kicker—the VEB study "shortly to be reported in *Cancer Research*" failed to find SV40 in mesotheliomas. In short, there was no worthwhile evidence associating SV40 with cancer.

Carbone and Pass were shocked when they read the review. The entire NIH grant application process is predicated upon reviewer neutrality, but this reviewer, far from being neutral about SV40, had worn his bias, blatantly, on his sleeve. The reviewer had grossly misstated the status of current SV40 research. Who could have written such a prejudiced review? The VEB's manuscript had not yet been published, yet the author knew about its contents. Whoever had written the review had inside knowledge of the results of the study and was mimicking the VEB line on the study, over-interpreting the study's results to suggest that all previous SV40 work was suspect. For good measure, the reviewer had thrown in an ad hominem remark about Carbone and Pass, claiming that they had "refused to partic-ipate" in the VEB study, when in fact, both Carbone and Pass felt the facts showed they had been ejected from the study.

The first thing Carbone and Pass did was to determine the status of the *Cancer Research* submission. Contrary to the reviewer's assertion, the VEB paper was not about to go to print. In fact, it was about to be rejected. (The study's fatal flaws, according to *Cancer Research*, included the contam-ination of the negative controls by Strickler's contractor and the imprecision of the DNA extraction: the very technical flaws that Jasani, Butel, and Lednicky had been citing for months. Thus, a crucial assertion in the neg-ative review—that an outstanding study was about to appear in a major journal casting doubt on the validity of previous SV40 findings—had been false.)

Now Carbone and Pass were outraged. They requested an internal NIH investigation and asked that the reviewer be identified publicly. They also filed a lengthy response to the scientific objections raised in the review and asked for a new review of their application. The NIH often rejects such requests; in this case, however, the new review was granted and their NCI application was subsequently approved. Carbone and Pass's request, how-ever, that the NCI reveal the identity of the negative reviewer, was denied. In a letter to the pair, Robert E. Wittes, then-director of the NCI's Division of Cancer Treatment and Diagnosis, urged them to "let this matter rest," saying that the peer-review process required maintaining reviewer anonym-ity. Wittes acknowledged that the reviewer "did not act according to the usual standards we expect from reviewers," adding that, "There is evidence of carelessness, or bias, or both in the review." He promised that the NCI would "not ask this individual to participate in the review of . . . future . . . applications [of grants for the specific NCI program to which Carbone and Pass had applied]" and that he would also "recommend" the person be excluded from review panels for other types of NCI grants.

In November 2003, the authors of this book concluded their own investigation and identified the negative reviewer as Dr. Drew Pardoll. Pardoll is a prominent Johns Hopkins University cancer immunologist and a colleague of Keerti Shah's, whom he has known for about ten years. Pardoll insisted that he and Shah do not work together closely but acknowledged that Shah was a coinvestigator with him on one of his NIH-funded grants. Pardoll said Shah was the source for his statement about the imminent publication of the VEB's multilab study in the journal *Cancer Research*, a comment that Pardoll concedes was a "mistake" due to his having "misheard or misinterpreted" Shah on that point.

Despite the many mischaracterizations of SV40 research in the review, Pardoll said his review was objective and non-baised and that, with the exception of the *Cancer Research* statement, he stands by every word. Three years after the controversy, Pardoll still insists that the multilaboratory study "is to this day the one and only study" to attempt to address the question of whether SV40 is actually present in human tumors. And what of Wittes's pledge to Carbone and Pass that because of his "carelessness" and "bias" the author of the negative review would be removed from future NCI grant panels? Pardoll says he was never reprimanded by the NCI and continued to serve on NCI grant panels until his appointment expired at the end of 2002—two full years after Wittes offered his assurance that Pardoll would be removed.

The rejection of the Strickler manuscript by *Cancer Research* set off one final round of squabbling among the study participants. Almost as soon as he had received notice that *Cancer Research* had turned down the submission, Strickler proposed sending it right back out to another publication, *Cancer Epidemiology, Biomarkers and Prevention*. This was the same small journal that had accepted the original negative mesothelioma study he, Goedert, and Shah had performed back in 1995. Strickler indicated that he thought the journal would "very likely" accept the study under what he termed "expedited review." (In the minds of the Cardiff and Baylor labs, this meant less scrutiny than the normal peer-review process used at most scientific journals.) Strickler's thinking, apparently shared by the FDA, was that there was no need to address any of the failures that had caused the rejection by *Cancer Research*—no new experiments, no new manuscript.

Once again Jasani protested. "Not only is the study flawed but it is also now obsolete," he wrote in late August 2000 to the FDA's Phil Krause.

While the multilab participants had fought for two years over the conclusion of their study, the Testa-Carbone multilab study, in which a series of blinded samples had been exchanged, had been published nearly two years previously. That study, Jasani said, definitively answered the VEB's questions about contamination. (Ironically, the Testa-Carbone study had appeared as a lead article in *Cancer Research,* the same journal that had just found the VEB work inadequate.) Jasani also criticized the U.S. officials for being scientifically slothful and wanting to "take the easy path of submitting the paper without any revision to a friendly journal of lesser scientific relevance."

Around the same time, Lednicky expressed similar sentiments in a letter addressed to Pass and Carbone, which he copied to Krause. There was something else bothering Lednicky. Lednicky said Butel had recently received a call from Andrew Lewis. Lewis, according to Lednicky, had told them that in Bethesda there was "intense pressure" to get the Strickler manuscript out the door. He was encouraging the Baylor scientists to drop some of their objections so the study could get published sooner. Lednicky, in his letter, made it plain he resented being pushed to publish a study which he felt remained fundamentally flawed:

> I do not believe that the interests of Public Health and Science are served by hastily submitting the flawed manuscript to a journal *known in advance to be favorable to the wishes of the proponents* of the flawed data. We should not succumb to pressure being exerted at the executive level and surrender our duty to inform the public and scientific community with reliable data. (Lednicky's emphasis.)

When Jasani a few weeks later wrote to Krause to complain that he, too, felt there was "pressure . . . com[ing] from the executive level" of the NIH to publish the study without any changes, Krause blew up. "There is and has been no intent to 'pressure' anybody into doing anything," he wrote testily, "your direct and implied accusations of ethical misconduct . . . is unfounded and distasteful."

In May 2001, the study was finally published. After negotiations, the dissenting labs had agreed to Strickler's preferred venue, *Cancer Epidemiology, Biomarkers and Prevention,* but won a significant victory in return. Butel and Jasani, not Strickler or Goedert, prepared a thoroughly revised manuscript for submission. Gone was the Strickler overreading of the results; gone was the suggestion that previous SV40 findings were "controversial"; and gone were the intimations that labs reporting SV40 were possibly contaminated. Butel and Jasani had instead added language that said contamination was an unlikely reason for previous positive SV40 findings. They also noted several possible reasons why the Sugarbaker mesotheliomas seemed to be devoid of SV40. One of these was the possibility that the DNA extraction kit simply was inadequate.

There was one final chapter to the study saga. On June 24, 2002, Keerti Shah spent all day in a Baltimore attorney's office giving a deposition. Shah was deposed because he had been listed as an expert witness for Lederle, the manufacturer of oral polio vaccine, which was a defendant in a vaccine injury case. Donald MacLachlan, one of the plaintiffs' attorneys, spent more than four hours questioning Shah. There were two surprising admissions by Shah during the course of the deposition. The first was that he had signed on as a scientific consultant with one former manufacturer of inactivated polio vaccine, Merck, four to five years previously. Shah also testified that he had become a consultant for a second former IPV manufacturer, Pfizer, in early 2002. He was serving each company as an advisor regarding SV40 and human disease. Given his prominence as the leading researcher in the anti-SV40 camp, Shah's allegiance to the former Salk vaccine manufacturers had, at the very least, the appearance of a conflict of interest. He was being paid by the drug companies at the same time that he was deeply involved in research that could exculpate those very companies if it was found that SV40 had not caused disease in humans.

The second admission from Shah was even more startling. Prior to the start of the replicability study, Shah *had* been given positive controls in advance of the other labs, just as Butel and Lednicky had suspected back in 1999. This was a clear breach of the study's integrity. According to Shah's deposition, before the experiment began Strickler sent Shah some unidentified controls and Shah tested them. Shah had not been able to detect SV40 in all the samples and reported this to Strickler. Strickler then told Shah that the samples Shah had received were all supposed to be positive. This left no doubt that something was wrong with his assay. Shah went back and changed his technique to improve the sensitivity of his SV40 assay until he could detect SV40 in the controls. The second time around, his positive controls came out positive. At last, here was the explanation why Shah's lab had become so much better at detecting SV40 over the course of the study. Strickler and he had tampered with the study's protocol. In effect, Shah had been given the answers ahead of time and allowed to "refine" his technique until it worked properly.

In late 2002, MacLachlan published a synopsis of Shah's deposition in the form of an article that appeared in the scientific journal *Anticancer Research*. As MacLachlan's article made clear, the ramifications of Strickler's and Shah's conduct were numerous. By unmasking the positive controls, they had compromised the entire study design. One goal of the study supposedly had been to assess whether the PCR techniques being used by the various labs that had searched for SV40 in human tumors, including Shah's, were reliable. Yet, by covering up Shah's initial inability to detect SV40 in the positive controls, they had made such a determination impossible. Moreover, any notion that Shah's PCR techniques for SV40 detection were "sensitive, specific, and reproducible" (as the study's protocol had termed it) had been entirely debunked. (When questioned about MacLachlan's allegations, Shah stated that his financial relationship with the vaccine manufacturers did not in any way influence his research. He declined to discuss the charges that he and Strickler had compromised the integrity of the multilaboratory study.)

In the end, Shah's admission may explain his inability to find SV40 in the original mesothelioma study he performed with Goedert and Strickler in 1995. While labs all over the world were using PCR to detect SV40 in tumors, it appeared that, just as Carbone, Jasani, and others had said all along, his lab methods at the time were so poor that he would have missed the virus had it been present. Until Strickler had allowed him a chance to tinker with his assay, Shah's SV40 detection abilities were apparently sub par. Yet, based almost entirely on this single, poorly executed study that he had conducted at the behest of Strickler and Goedert at the VEB, federal health officials had been able to insist for several years that SV40 findings in numerous laboratories from around the world were to be distrusted. Based largely on this one, negative study, they had also been able to insist on the need for their multilaboratory replicability study, which had cost more than $300,000, was itself hopelessly flawed, and tied up some of the most important SV40 researchers for several years. The result had been, MacLachlan said, "simply tragic. . . . So much time and money has been expended to address the serious flaws of the multicenter study," he lamented, instead of on research that could have further explored the virus's relationship to human tumors, research that could potentially save human lives.

19

No Funding, No Research

On a beautiful spring weekend in April 2001, there was a reprise of the NIH's 1997 SV40 conference. The meeting was a chance for many of the same SV40 investigators who had first met four years before in Bethesda to catch up, exchange notes, and present their latest research. Scientists from across the United States and Western Europe traveled to Chicago for the meeting; also attending were researchers from more far-flung locations such as Turkey, China, and New Zealand. The sponsors of this SV40 gathering, however, were not the federal health bureaucracies that had convened the previous gathering; they were Loyola University and the University of Chicago, the two academic institutions at which Carbone had taught since he left the NIH five years before. This time it was Carbone and the other SV40 researchers who set the agenda; Carbone himself served as one of the two conference chairmen.

The two-day affair was a celebration of sorts for all those who had been working on the connection between SV40 and human cancer since 1997. With typical Carbone élan, the weekend featured much fine food and wine—a catered reception at a friend's Frank Lloyd Wright house in Oak Park, an elaborate four-course banquet at an art museum, and a conference-closing dinner at Carbone's house for fifty guests at which he cooked all the food.

Behind the festive air of the conference lay much serious science, almost all of it further strengthening the connection between SV40 and human

cancer. There were more than forty presentations of additional findings of
the virus in human tumors. While much of the new research concerned
mesotheliomas, presentations focused on other SV40 cancer types as well.
A researcher from Philadelphia's Hahnemann University Cancer Center
reported that when looking for the human polyoma virus JC in medulloblastoma brain tumors (the type that had afflicted Alexander Horwin), she
had found SV40 expressing large T-antigen in more than 25 percent of her
twenty-three samples. A Chinese team reported it had found SV40 in seven
different brain cancer types and that it had demonstrated that the virus was
knocking out p53 and the retinoblastoma proteins in the tumors, the same
two critical anticancer agents it disables in mesotheliomas. Three researchers
from Lyon, France described how they had searched for SV40 in two hundred different brain tumor samples, finding it in 35 percent of the tumor
samples, which together encompassed eleven distinct types of brain cancers.
Employing the same microdissection technique that Gazdar had used in his
mesothelioma study, the French researchers found that SV40 was present
in the tumor cells but not in the adjacent nontumor cells, strongly suggesting that the virus was implicated in causing the brain cancers.

The virus had also been found in new locales. An NCI researcher, Jeffrey
Kopp, said that he found SV40 in the kidneys of patients with a particular
form of kidney disease known as idiopathic focal segmental glomeruloscle-
rosis (FSGS), a disease that had been relatively rare in the 1960s but now
afflicts up to ten thousand people a year. Among them is Alonzo Mourning,
the professional basketball player, who was forced to retire prematurely in
November 2003 after he contracted FSGS. Kopp's survey found that almost
half of the FSGS patients he sampled and 10 percent of the patients with
other kidney diseases had SV40 in their urinary cells. He concluded that
SV40 infects humans and that human kidneys in particular can serve as a
"viral reservoir," with the virus being shed at times in urine, perhaps suggesting a way the virus could be transmitted from person to person.

Many of the researchers at Carbone's conference said they had moved
beyond mere proof that the virus was present in tumors and were now
concentrating on its molecular properties inside human cells. Several described new experiments demonstrating that SV40 can activate oncogenes
in cells, stimulating the out-of-control growth that leads to cancer. During
the closing panel that summarized the results of the conference, George
Klein of the Karolinska Institute in Stockholm, former chairman of the
Nobel Assembly and a world authority on tumor viruses, said that "the

presence of SV40 in human tumors had been convincingly demonstrated" and that there was stronger and stronger evidence that the virus causes cancer. Other prominent scientists not directly involved in SV40 research agreed.

Carbone pointedly invited scientists who were dubious about the connection between SV40 and human tumors to come to the Chicago event. Shah and de Villiers both attended and each made presentations. Shah, acknowledging that he would "strike the first discordant note in the conference," recapped his negative findings of the past seven years and expressed his continued doubts about the validity of the SV40 findings of many of the scientists in the room. After he was finished, he was peppered, albeit politely, with questions from several of the leading SV40 researchers in the audience about his own techniques. (At one point, as Carbone was about to ask a question, Shah made a rueful aside to the audience. "I was dreading this," he said.) In response to a later question from Carbone, Shah was forced to admit that the DNA extraction method used in some of his negative studies was "very crude."

Carbone's conference invitations to SV40 doubters also included Strickler and Goedert. Both declined to come to Chicago. Perhaps the refusal of the Viral Epidemiology Branch representatives reflected a disinclination to be subjected to the same scrutiny Carbone had received at the 1997 conference. One thing is clear, their absence at the event was indicative of the NIH's response as a whole to the dozens of studies linking SV40 to human cancer since the 1997 Bethesda conference. By 2003, researchers had repeatedly isolated the virus in all four tumor types that it causes in hamsters (brain, bone, lymphomas, and mesotheliomas). In the case of mesotheliomas and at least five different types of brain tumors (medulloblastomas, ependymomas, choroid plexus papillomas, astrocytomas, and glioblastoma multiformes), repeated studies had demonstrated the virus was not just present in the tumors, but was playing a cancer-causing role. Gazdar's work suggested it was doing the same in non-Hodgkin's lymphomas and some acute and chronic leukemias. Meanwhile, several studies had reinforced Carbone's and Garcea's 1996 bone tumor surveys. In addition to osteosarcomas, the virus had been detected in at least two other bone tumor types, giant cell tumors and chondrosarcomas. And then there were any number of experiments which had detected SV40 in other tumors including: thyroid cancers, prostate cancers, AIDS-related lymphomas, Wilms' (kidney) tumors, and meningiomas, pituitary and several other brain cancer types—

although there was no indication yet whether it was playing a cancer-causing role or was merely a bystander in these cases. Finally, the virus was also turning up in some noncancerous disorders, such as FSGS and the demyelinating disease PML. Yet, despite this abundance of research associating the simian virus with human disease, SV40 has remained a low priority within the NIH.

Nowhere is this attitude more evident than in the level of government support for independent SV40 researchers. It is negligible. A check of NIH grant databases reveals that in fiscal years 2001 and 2002 combined—the two most recent years for which figures are available—less than $2 million was awarded for research connecting SV40 to human cancer. Numerous grants have been awarded to investigators examining the basic biochemistry of the virus or using SV40 as a tool in other areas of cancer research, but almost no funding has been granted to examine the critical question of whether or how the polio vaccine contaminant is causing human disease. By comparison, funding directed by the NCI to outside researchers working on human papilloma virus topped $75 million for the same two-year fiscal period. Almost all of the 135 NCI grants to several dozen outside investigators were for research on how HPV is causing cancer and how to fight it. Meanwhile, only Carbone and two or three other independent researchers have successfully obtained grants specifically to conduct experiments on SV40's role in human tumors.

The impressive array of research on SV40 and human cancer during the past few years has come despite, not because of, government support and interest. American researchers in particular have been forced to cobble together funds from a variety of sources to support their SV40 work. Butel, for instance, had received regular NIH grant support throughout her early tenure at Baylor, but her SV40 grants dried up once she turned her focus away from how SV40 acted in laboratory animals and began to concentrate on whether the virus caused human cancer. Her important 2002 study finding SV40 in non-Hodgkin's lymphomas was only possible because she accessed a piece of an AIDS research grant Baylor had already received and combined it with funding derived from another unusual source, NASA's National Space Biomedical Research Institute. Similarly, Gazdar, because he helps direct an entire cancer center, has access to funds that ordinary cancer researchers do not. With so little federal support, it is, perhaps, understandable that many of the more recent SV40 discoveries have occurred outside the United States.

NCI deputy director Alan Rabson says that he finds nothing surprising about the low level of support his agency has directed toward SV40 researchers. The funding discrepancy between SV40 and HPV is appropriate, he says. "HPV happens to be a known cause of one of the major cancers in the world," says Rabson, who remains skeptical about the role SV40 plays in human cancers. "There's certainly not an epidemic of [SV40 cancers] sweeping the world."

Gazdar dismisses that excuse as "bogus," noting that the NCI often funds research on rare cancers that affect only small numbers of people. "The NCI has backed all sorts of things on much less evidence than this, and I'm just amazed that they keep taking this line," says Gazdar. "The NCI studies rare diseases as well as common diseases." He cites NCI funding of the virus HTLV-1 as an example. HTLV-1 stands for human T-cell lymphotropic virus type I, which has been associated with adult T-cell leukemia/lymphoma, and a handful of other unusual diseases. It is one of a half dozen viruses known to cause cancer in human beings (among them are the hepatitis B and C viruses).

NCI funding for independent researchers studying HTLV-1 surpassed $10 million in fiscal years 2001 and 2002—five times that of SV40 funding for researchers studying the virus in human tumors for the same two-year period. Yet rates of infection with HTLV-1 in the American population are extremely low. Only 0.025 percent of American blood donors, or 25 individuals in 100,000, test positive for the virus. Research on HTLV suggests that among those who are seropositive, only 4 percent will ever develop an HTLV-related cancer or other disease. Taken together, the two statistics indicate that as of mid-2003, there are less than three thousand Americans at risk of ever developing an HTLV-1 associated cancer or disease in their *entire lifetime*—about the same number of Americans who are diagnosed *each year* with mesothelioma, one of the cancers associated with SV40 exposure. "In any case," says Gazdar, Rabson's argument "doesn't apply anymore because SV40 is associated with [the more common cancers] lymphoma and leukemia. I think to ignore something such as this is crazy. They're not doing themselves a service—nor the public. Frankly it's their business to serve the public and I'm not sure they're doing this. In fact, I'm certain they're not."

The picture is not much better within other branches of the NIH. With the exception of the completed mesothelioma investigations of NCI Thoracic Oncology head David Schrump and the kidney investigations of Jeffrey Kopp, there have been no studies on the virus emanating from within the NIH—with one exception: the cascade of negative studies conducted under the auspices of the Viral Epidemiology Branch. Howard Strickler left the VEB at the beginning of 1999 but has remained associated with some of its SV40 work. James Goedert still heads the branch. Eric Engels, who replaced Strickler, has coordinated a number of studies, all negative, in which researchers have failed to associate the virus with cancer rates.

In one recent study, Keerti Shah and Eric Engels reported that they were unable to find evidence of SV40 in brain tumors from individuals living in northern India, where, presumably, the proximity to the natural habitat of rhesus monkeys would lead to high SV40 exposure. (Shah undertook this research while he was consulting for Merck and Pfizer, although this fact was not mentioned in the published study.) That study was deemed so flawed that an international group of eleven different researchers took the unusual step of signing a joint letter that was published in the same journal that had originally reported the Engels-Shah work. The letter writers cited numerous problems with the Engels-Shah methodology and the pair's interpretation of their data. In another study, Strickler and Goedert reexamined mesothelioma incidence and concluded that the only group in which they had detected increased incidence of the lung cancer was not likely to have been exposed to contaminated polio vaccine. That study also provoked published responses from both Butel and a team of Italian researchers. The Italians pointed out that even a very few cases either way would have altered the VEB's conclusions.

Epidemiology studies remain at the core of the VEB's response to SV40. Three were published just between the fall of 2002 and the spring of 2003. In each one the VEB authors concluded they had again demonstrated there was no link between SV40-contaminated vaccines and cancer. But how valid are these epidemiological studies?

When the National Academy of Sciences' Immunization Safety Review Committee of the Institute of Medicine took up the SV40 issue in the July 2002, it was impressed by the dozens of biological studies—that is, studies of how the virus works on the cellular level—conducted by Carbone and other investigators around the world. Based on these studies, the IOM committee concluded that "that the evidence is strong that SV40 is a transforming virus" (that is, it can transform healthy cells into cancerous ones) and "the evidence is of moderate strength that SV40 exposure could lead to cancer in humans under natural conditions." These were unexpectedly strong conclusions coming from the normally conservative advisory panel, and SV40 researchers hailed them as a major confirmation of their work.

When it came to evaluating the SV40 epidemiology studies, however, the committee said the data was inconclusive. The committee found that the population-based studies—all of them, whether they showed an increase in cancer among vaccinated individuals or not—were inherently unreliable. Looking back in time, it is essentially impossible to determine who was exposed to live SV40 in contaminated vaccines. Furthermore, the IOM found there are questions about whether the virus is still spreading. Thus, constructing any study that tries to measure cancer incidence in a group of SV40-exposed individuals versus cancer incidence in another group that was supposedly unexposed is simply an unworkable proposition.

Why does one small lab, the Viral Epidemiology Branch, insist on spending so much money and effort on SV40 epidemiology despite the severe limitations inherent in any retrospective population studies of the virus? The answer seems to be partially one of predilection. The VEB is part of the NCI's Division of Cancer Genetics and Epidemiology, whose mission is to research the possible genetic origins of cancer. The head of that division is Joe Fraumeni, the author of the crucial 1963 epidemiological study that found SV40 had no role in cancer. According to Al Rabson, Fraumeni is the NCI's resident SV40 expert among its upper echelon of administrators, and it was only natural that he should spearhead any NCI effort to research the virus.

Fraumeni defends the work of his Viral Epidemiology Branch, despite the appearance to so many SV40 researchers that the VEB is biased against an association between SV40 and cancer. If the VEB lab uncovered positive results suggesting an association between the virus and cancer, "I'd be the first person to support publication of a finding," Fraumeni says. "Negative studies are not our specialty."

But what about the criticisms raised by the Institute of Medicine and others that it is virtually impossible to perform accurate population-based retrospective studies to evaluate the carcinogenicity of SV40? The VEB has repeatedly attempted such studies since the mid-1990s. Yet, if the populations assumed by VEB *not* to have been exposed to the virus actually *have* been exposed to the virus (or the reverse), aren't all the calculations and comparisons of cancer risk that the VEB had presented in these studies inaccurate? Doesn't that mean the data is worthless? "I wouldn't say it's worthless," Fraumeni says. "I'd say it's limited." If the VEB published studies contain conclusions that are based on incorrect assumptions, aren't they misleading? "I wouldn't say misleading," Fraumeni says of the VEB studies, "I'd say they have limitations."

Others disagree. If the data is inherently flawed, the conclusions from that data are at best worthless; at worst they are deceptive. Even the IOM took the unusual step of recommending that, in light of the difficulty in discerning exactly who was exposed to the virus and who was not, there be a cessation to all such retrospective population-based SV40 studies. That recommendation, however, has not stopped the NCI and Centers for Disease Control public affairs offices from continuing to cite the VEB studies as evidence that there is no link between the virus and cancer. Both agencies have relied heavily on the VEB's population studies and molecular studies to reassure the public that exposure to the simian virus has no consequences for human health.

An example is the official NCI statement on SV40, dated April 3, 2003, and posted at the Institute's "News Center" on its Web site. After citing twenty-one studies that have found "traces of the virus" in human tumors (the actual number of published studies at the time that had connected SV40 to human tumors or human disease was in excess of eighty), it cited fourteen studies to the contrary. Six were authored by the VEB, including the discredited multilaboratory study directed by Strickler. A seventh was directed by a sister lab to the VEB within Fraumeni's NCI division. Of the remaining seven cited by the NCI, two were not actually studies but letters to the editors of journals, critiquing published positive SV40 research. Another so-called study was the report given by the German researcher de Villiers at the 1997 NIH conference, which was never published and so never peer-reviewed; another was also a non-peer-reviewed report, published in the form of a letter to the editor. Only three of the negative studies cited were by independent, non-government researchers and subject to peer-review prior to publication. One of these was by Sugarbaker's lab in Boston, the source of the negative mesothelioma samples during the VEB's multilaboratory study, and another was a 1997 British study that was the subject of an extensive critique by Bharat Jasani because of the poor DNA extraction and PCR methodology employed.

More than half of the NCI statement on SV40 was devoted to a detailed review of the Engels-Shah study of human brain tumors. The NCI statement did not mention the peer-reviewed letter from the eleven independent researchers that was published in response, nor other published critiques of VEB research, including the two written by Butel and the Italian researchers. Susan Fisher's detailed criticism of Strickler's 1998 epidemiological study—the one he had presented to great effect at the 1997 NIH conference—was also not mentioned. CDC fact sheets on SV40 have contained a similar bias, consistently implying that the number and quality of studies not associating SV40 with human cancers is at least equal to, if not outweighing, the many more that have.

The danger of such publicity is not only that it misleads the public. By becoming, in effect, official public pronouncements on the virus and its role in human cancers, it misleads the scientific community as well, including the individuals who serve on grant-awarding panels and make decisions about funding research.

While Fraumeni is candid about the limitations of all government epidemiology to date on SV40, including his own 1963 study, the fact remains that simply by publishing a half dozen of these "limited" studies since 1995, the VEB (and the NCI) have influenced the overall scientific response to SV40. For scientists and policy makers who have not kept abreast of the latest molecular biological research on SV40, the cumulative message of all the VEB's studies is that SV40 is not a public health threat. Scientists evaluate many factors in considering whether a substance is causing a disease, but in the classical public health model, epidemiology trumps all other disciplines. Despite all the molecular studies that have overwhelmingly demonstrated SV40 association and causation in human cancer, in the minds of those who make the funding decisions precedence is given to the VEB's epidemiological studies. Essentially, one branch of the NCI churns out the "limited" epidemiology and another branch uses the conclusions of that epidemiology to discourage serious funding of SV40 research.

To Carbone and many other SV40 investigators, the only way out of this dilemma is to sidestep the epidemiologists. He, Butel, and Gazdar are now lobbying for the inclusion of SV40 in the official list of likely carcinogens maintained by the International Agency for Research in Cancer, an arm of the World Health Organization. In March 2003, Butel argued in an essay in the *Lancet* that using epidemiology to deny SV40 plays a role in causing human cancers made little scientific sense given all the SV40 findings in tumors and recent research on how the virus causes those tumors. She followed that essay with a study appearing in June 2003 surveying

every finding ever published in which researchers looked for SV40 in human tumors and had employed controls, including those in which they
found no trace of the virus.

Using a technique known as meta-analysis, she lumped together all the
results from all the studies—which together summed to almost 1,900 tumor
samples and more than 1,650 controls—and attempted to make a statistical
determination whether, overall, the virus was more likely to be associated
with tumors than not. The results were expressed in terms of a number
called the odds ratio, which serves as an indication of the strength of the
association between the virus and a particular type of tumor. Butel found
the odds ratio demonstrated a clear, statistically significant association between SV40 and all the tumor types in which researchers have found the
virus over the years. For lymphomas, the odds ratio was five, for brain
cancers it was four, while for mesotheliomas and bone cancers it was much
higher: seventeen and twenty-five respectively. "To put things in perspective," Butel says of her results, "it was an odds ratio of about ten that linked
smoking with cancer."

When there is this kind of evidence, Carbone says, it is a mistake for
public health officials to insist that there be indisputable epidemiological
evidence of SV40's carcinogenicity before acting. "New molecular techniques allow us to see exactly how carcinogens disrupt cells. Yet we are
continually held back by epidemiology. We had to wait for more than a
decade while epidemiologists studied thousands of women to confirm what
molecular biology had already proved—that HPV causes cervical cancer in
women—time that, no doubt, cost many lives. The same was true for
asbestos. Now it's happening again with SV40," he says. Gazdar concurs,
vociferously so. "Do you want to wait for ten more years?" he says of federal
officials' reluctance to act until they have more epidemiological evidence.
"I think that's crazy. How can we afford to wait ten more years and let
people get cancer and do nothing about it?"

Aware of the growing criticism of population-based studies, the VEB
has embarked on a different kind of epidemiological study. Two outside
laboratories are under contract with the VEB to develop a serological assay
that they hope will allow researchers to determine from a blood test whether
or not an individual has been exposed to SV40. Using the blood assay, the
plan is to see whether there is any difference in tumor incidence between
the carefully defined nonexposed and exposed groups. So far, SV40 experts

like Butel, Carbone, and Lednicky have not been invited to participate in the VEB's serological assay design.

Engels is spearheading the effort, which will examine hundreds of blood samples from non-Hodgkin's lymphoma patients for SV40 antibodies. The samples will then be compared with blood samples from a control group that does not have the cancer. Fraumeni says that if the people with non-Hodgkin's lymphoma have a higher positivity rate of SV40 antibodies in their blood than people who do not have disease, then it can be said that SV40 might be contributing to the disease. Engels is contracting with researchers at the Fred Hutchinson Cancer Center in Seattle and Johns Hopkins Medical School in Baltimore to conduct the study. Researchers at Fred Hutchinson conducted a preliminary test looking at blood samples from osteosarcoma patients in the Washington area. As of July 2003, they had found no sign of SV40. Whether this is a reflection of the absence of SV40 antibodies in the blood samples or the many difficulties inherent in creating an accurate test for measuring antibody activity to SV40 remains to be seen.

Researchers involved with the Engels study have described their technique as the most definitive to date for measuring blood response to the SV40 virus. But Butel says such characterizations are misleading because of the complexities of the human immune system. "It's not definitive," says Butel. "They may say that, but until more is known about how humans respond to SV40 infections, that may or may not be the definitive test." Butel, who conducted her own antibody tests, finding SV40 infection ranging between 6 to 16 percent of the population, says antibody tests for the monkey virus are very complicated because they can cross-react with the human polyoma viruses BK and JC, which infect an estimated 80 percent of the population. Yet tests to rule out BK and JC may obscure the presence of SV40. "In a nutshell," Butel says "we know very little about the human immune response to SV40 infections. I would say it's a black box. It's possible that the human immune response is very poor to SV40 infections. And at this point I would just say that the absence of a detectable humoral [immune system] antibody response [in a given study] does not prove that there was no infection ever in the past—or even currently." Butel also stresses that in one of her investigations, on hospitalized children in Houston, she was able to find SV40 in the tumor tissue of the same patients who also had circulating SV40 antibodies in their blood. "I believe those were truly SV40 antibodies we detected," she says.

Bharat Jasani, who participated in the multilaboratory study, may have found a way to bypass the problems plaguing traditional serological studies. Jasani is conducting research on immune reactions to SV40 in mesothelioma patients. He is developing new evidence and insight as to how the virus provokes the immune system, particularly with respect to recognition of certain large T-antigen peptides by T-cells, the specialized killer lymphocytes that roam the body seeking out foreign invaders. Jasani describes his research as offering the potential for "a powerful new approach to identify SV40 immune reactions in people who harbor the virus." Jasani says he hopes the approach will lead to ways to stimulate the immune system to fight the virus. "My interest is to develop treatment strategies. If you tell people 'you've got a virus,' then they'll say 'what can you do about it?' You have to have an effective treatment."

Butel supports the type of research being conducted by Jasani and calls for much more basic investigation of the virus and how it infects human beings. "There's still a lot we don't know about the basic biology of the virus in human infections, including what tissues it infects, how it is transmitted, and when people become infected with it," Butel says. The more scientists understand about how SV40 infects human beings, how it is distributed throughout the infected host, how it interacts with different cell types, and how the host reacts immunologically to this infection, the better serology assays will be, she says. In the summer of 2003, Butel learned that the NCI had approved a grant for her to study some of these questions. In particular, she says, "We want to understand how the virus gets spread around in the body, and how it interacts with the lymphoid system, which is important in the immune response as well as the development of lymphomas."

Although the Butel grant is welcome news, many researchers feel the federal government has created a vicious circle with respect to SV40 funding, one that seems to serve their own purposes: As long as senior federal officials insist there is no epidemiological evidence linking SV40 with rising cancer rates (and, in some cases, continue to deny the presence of SV40 in human tumors), grant review panels will be unlikely to deem research into SV40's role in human tumors worthy of funding. And without funds, scientists cannot develop new data about SV40. In the absence of new data, federal officials can continue to insist that there is little research showing the virus plays a role in causing tumors. Therefore, they assert, there's no need for more funding of SV40 studies. Eventually, the absence of funding will discourage scientists from the field and younger investigators will once again have the idea that prevailed throughout most of the 1960s, '70s and '80s: Research on SV40 is a career dead end. "Well, that's absolutely been true and that's why you haven't seen an influx of a lot of people doing these kinds of experiments," says Butel. "People can't do work that they're not funded to do."

May Wong, the NCI official charged with administering the NCI's grant program for independent researchers, agrees that there has been a longstanding disincentive to submit grants for SV40 research. "Not many people apply . . . and I know in the past [it is] because it's been shot down and people are not receptive [on the grant review panels] so people say 'why should I bother?' " Wong says she believes funding SV40 research is imperative, given the massive exposure to the monkey virus. "I agree. We should. I am trying," she says. She said she was hopeful SV40 research would become a higher priority, but acknowledged she had not received any directive from the officials within the senior NCI hierarchy to fund more SV40 research.

Arnold J. Levine, the former Rockefeller University president, says that it is time for these senior federal health officials to support a serious research effort. "If it's part of the cause of a disease, it has significance in public health and I think we ought to find that out," says Levine. "That's a good reason to spend taxpayers' money: to do science to find out whether the public health is really monitored properly here." To properly study SV40, Levine says, the NCI should issue a RFA, or Request for Applications, the formal process by which the federal agency identifies a major research initiative and invites scientist to apply for funds. "That would stimulate people to come in and design experiments and replicate these things," he says.

Who initiates the RFA process? Members of the NCI's Executive Committee, a select group of high-level managers who wield great power over the NCI budget, grant programs, and long-range strategic planning. Both Fraumeni and Rabson serve on the NCI's Executive Committee. Both men have been involved with SV40 since it was first discovered in the 1960s; given their powerful positions both men could easily initiate the RFA process. Neither has suggested doing so.

Asked why not, Fraumeni draws a blank, saying he thought an SV40 RFA was issued as a result of the 1997 SV40 conference in Bethesda. He says he would support an RFA and suggests contacting May Wong about it. Rabson is even more vague, lobbing the ball into May Wong's court, implying that she makes the decision. But Wong says that only members of the Executive Committee can set the wheels in motion for an RFA. "I'm just a peon," Wong responds, with a nervous laugh. Wong is correct. As powerful members of the senior NCI bureaucracy, it is up to Fraumeni, Rabson, and other top NIH officials to determine whether the exposure of millions of Americans to a carcinogenic monkey virus will ever be fully investigated. Thus far, their attitude has been "not on my watch."

SV40 researchers say it is imperative for the NCI to reverse its course on SV40 and fully support comprehensive research efforts on the virus. The agency's mission to research and fight cancer demands such a response. "Because when all is said and done, at the end of the day, this research is about helping patients," Carbone says. "There are people out there who are suffering because of this virus. It's time we figured out how to treat them."

20

Alexander's Tumor

ON AN UNUSUALLY hot July afternoon in Detroit, Harvey Pass is in the middle of his weekly lung clinic at the Wayne State University Barbara Ann Karmanos Cancer Institute, where he is chief of thoracic surgery. Mesothelioma patients from across the Midwest and neighboring Ontario come to see Pass, attracted by his reputation as one of the premier lung surgeons in North America. The former NCI thoracic surgery chief slaps a CAT scan of the lungs of his next patient onto an X-ray light box. He points his two residents to signs that the cancer is progressing despite a recent chemotherapy regimen. A few minutes later, they crowd into a small, bleak examining room. He is telling the patient and his wife, a trim well-educated and young-looking couple in their fifties, that there is nothing to do for now except drain, or tap, fluid from the lungs when the man's symptoms become uncomfortable. The wife, wearing jeans, a T-shirt with neatly rolled up sleeves, and Teva sandals, has a large black ring binder on her lap crammed with the latest clinical studies available on the Internet. Her blond hair is tied back in a bun held by a green comb. Her husband, tall and thin, a Ford plant worker, seems unusually good-natured, almost embarrassed that his disease is causing everyone around him so much discomfort. The two of them seem very much in love.

"If the frequency of taps increases, then we'll discuss possibilities," says Pass, as the visit draws to a close.

"So you see nothing out there for him?" the wife asks. She is on the verge of tears.

"No, there's plenty out there for him—with very, very low response rates," Pass responds. One such drug, Pass says, is Adriamycin. "You're going to lose your hair, you're going to be nauseated, and it affects your heart." Moreover, says Pass, "It only has a 12–15 percent response rate . . . That's lousy." Without being explicit, the implication of Pass's remarks, is obvious to everyone in the room: For a patient who has already endured the debilitating, sometimes agonizing side effects of toxic chemotherapy with little response to show for it, there comes a time to stop. "There are very few patients who, once their tumor's recurred after therapy, are salvaged to live a long life with second [chemotherapy] agents," he explains later. Better to live the last few months of one's life without the added misery of a treatment that won't work.

As a mesothelioma expert, Pass is involved in innovative laboratory and clinical research, including gene therapy and new forms of chemotherapy and photosensitive therapy. But Pass knows his arsenal is limited. Of the more than 250 people he has treated for the disease, few have survived more than five years. Many have died within twelve months of diagnosis, no matter how spirited the fight was to keep them alive. That is the nature of the disease. And even though 2,500 cases of mesothelioma diagnosed a year is a small number relative to the epidemic rates of so many other cancers, Pass knows that these are not just statistics. Every one of those numbers represents an individual: someone's father or mother, someone's child, someone's husband, wife, or lover—a human being, whose loss, to those who love him, or are dependent on her, seems unbearable, a human being who is often healthy in other respects and might normally live many more years.

After years of working with conventional treatments and finding them largely ineffectual, Pass does see some reason for optimism. From the very beginning of his collaboration with Carbone, he has been spurred on by the intriguing possibility that SV40 could be a potential target for treating mesothelioma. With research suggesting that as many as four out of five mesotheliomas in the United States test positive for the simian virus, the goal for the two physicians was always to find a therapy—perhaps, ironically, a vaccine—that would target SV40's T-antigen and prevent or reverse the pernicious disease. For that reason, Carbone and Pass fought hard to reverse the negative decision on their grant proposal to test in humans the regimen that had worked against mesothelioma in mice. They are now working on preparations necessary to begin Phase 1 clinical trials in which they will test the safety of the drug in human subjects. If the drug is deemed safe, they will proceed to the next step, testing its efficacy.

But, as research indicates, mesothelioma is not the only cancer associated with SV40. And it is not just the individuals potentially exposed to contaminated vaccine between 1954 and 1963 who are developing SV40-positive tumors. An estimated eighteen thousand Americans—three thousand of them children—were diagnosed with brain tumors in 2003. The incidence of childhood central nervous system tumors rose 35 percent between 1973 and 1994. And even though some of the increase may be attributed to better diagnosis, and brain tumors are still considered rare, their high rates among children make them particularly insidious. Nearly a dozen different types of brain tumors have been found to contain SV40, in varying percentages depending upon the study. If the overall numbers seem small in comparison to other, more common cancers, they are far too great to the families affected. No one knows that better than Raphaele and Michael Horwin.

In August 1998, when the Horwins learned that their only child, Alexander, had medulloblastoma, their world was turned upside down. The next few months were a living nightmare as they watched Alexander die slowly before their eyes. Two operations had successfully removed the entire tumor from Alexander's brain, and the Horwins were hopeful that Alexander would recover, but Alexander's doctors said the brain tumor would come back unless he had further treatment: chemotherapy or radiation. Radiation was ruled out—because of Alexander's young age it would lead to mental retardation. That left chemotherapy. Neither parent wanted to subject Alexander to the highly toxic blend of chemicals that would be used during chemotherapy. They had found a doctor in Houston who had been successful treating young cancer patients with an experimental, nontoxic therapy that had received a favorable review from an NCI investigator, but the Food and Drug Administration, which oversaw the doctor's protocol, refused to let the Horwins enroll Alexander in the alternative treatment unless they had first tried conventional treatments. "They told us that young children do extremely well on chemo. They told us that, without a doubt, chemo would prolong Alexander's life," Mike Horwin recalled. Raphaele Horwin recalls weeping quietly as she held Alexander while a technician attired from head to toe in a biohazard suit hooked him up for his first intravenous chemical "drip."

Three rounds of chemotherapy confirmed the Horwin's worst fears. The chemotherapy treatments caused unbearable suffering for the two-year-old child. In addition to losing his hair there was vomiting and high fevers that forced extended stays in the hospital. There were blood transfusions to replace the blood cells the chemotherapy had killed, hearing tests to see if chemotherapy was destroying Alexander's hearing, tests to see if Alexander's kidneys and liver were still functioning under the stress of so many toxic chemicals. All of the suffering, all the tests, all the endless weeks in the hospital were to no avail. Soon after the three rounds of chemotherapy, Alexander began to complain of pain. An MRI showed he had developed more than thirty aggressive tumors throughout his brain and spine.

On January 31, 1999, Alexander died in his mother's arms in a hotel room in Texas; they were on their way to the Houston doctor to begin the nontoxic therapy. The experience of watching their son suffer needlessly left the Horwins angry. "Without chemo, Alexander wouldn't have been poisoned. He wouldn't have had to spend his last months on earth suffering in a hospital," Mike Horwin observes. Because of the chemotherapy, Alexander died the very kind of death Harvey Pass was trying to avoid for his mesothelioma patient.

When Carbone informed them that Alexander's tumor biopsy contained SV40, they wondered, where had Alexander contracted the simian virus? One possible source was the Horwins themselves. Theoretically, a parent could have been infected by SV40 from an early dose of contaminated polio vaccine and then transmitted the virus to Alexander. The Horwins tested themselves for signs of an SV40 infection—their blood, their urine, and Mike's semen. Both parents were negative for SV40. They tested Alexander's cord blood, the blood taken from his umbilical cord at the time of birth. It, too, was negative. Alexander was born SV40 free and had contracted the virus sometime during his first two years of life—but not from his parents. That left the polio vaccine Alexander had received as a toddler as the most plausible source. Like almost every child in America, Alexander was vaccinated against polio at an early age. He had received two doses of inactivated vaccine before he was six months old, and then in November 1997, at age seventeen months, Alexander received a dose of Orimune, manufactured by Lederle Laboratories. He was diagnosed with medulloblastoma nine months later.

Could the dose of oral polio vaccine Alexander received have been contaminated? The Food and Drug Administration insists that such a scenario is not possible: In accordance with its regulations, they say, no vaccine produced since June 1961 has contained SV40, and after 1963, when all the old stocks of SV40-contaminated vaccine were finally used up, no polio vaccine consumed in this country has contained SV40. The FDA officials cite two different studies, which they say address the question directly. In one study published in 2000, FDA scientists used PCR to look for SV40 DNA sequences in samples from oral polio vaccine batches released in the United States between 1972 and 1996. Their conclusion was that "SV40 sequences were not found in any of the vaccine lots tested." In another study, British researchers looked for evidence of SV40 in vaccine samples from lots released in that country after 1962. The British team also concluded there was no evidence of SV40 contamination in the vaccine samples they tested.

Lederle, meanwhile, has consistently denied that any post-1961 doses of its vaccine have ever been contaminated. In May 1996, when asked if it was possible that oral polio vaccine produced after 1961 ever contained SV40 or other contaminating viruses, Audrey Ashby, a spokesperson for Lederle, said that the company had "complete faith and confidence" in its vaccine and took "complete safety precautions" in the manufacturing process.

In September 2003, Natalie de Vane, a spokesperson for Wyeth, the parent company of Lederle, issued an even more pointed denial that its modern vaccine had been contaminated. Her statement was made in response to allegations of SV40 contamination made by Philadelphia lawyer Stan Kops. Kops has decades of experience litigating against Lederle on behalf of victims in polio vaccine injury cases. Until oral polio vaccine was removed from the market in January 2000, every year about eight to ten people contracted polio and became paralyzed from the vaccine itself when one of the three types of attenuated poliovirus in each dose reverted to virulence, a fact that was particularly disturbing because wild polio was eradicated from the United States back in 1979. As a result of his legal fights against the company, Kops has amassed thousands of pages of internal Lederle documents relating to the company's vaccine manufacturing process. He had an opportunity to present some of those documents publicly on September 10, 2003 when the House Subcommittee on Human Rights and Wellness held a hearing on SV40 and the polio vaccine. Among others who testified at the ninety-minute hearing were a New Jersey mother whose son had developed brain cancer after inoculation with oral polio vaccine, consumer activist Barbara Loe Fisher, SV40 researcher Adi Gazdar, and the Viral Epidemiology Branch's James Goedert. Kops said that his collection of documents "tell a frightening story of contamination of live oral polio vaccine with a monkey virus known as SV40" and termed Lederle's assurances over the years that the vaccine had been tested for the presence of SV40 "factually incorrect and intentionally misleading." De Vane sharply disagreed with Kops's assessment, telling a reporter, "These claims don't have any validity." She added, "We have always conducted extensive screening and testing of our products." As proof that Lederle's vaccine has always been free of SV40, de Vane specifically cited the FDA's negative results from its tests of samples from old batches of Lederle vaccine, terming the FDA's tests "the most advanced methods of testing available."

Carbone has closely examined the negative FDA study cited by de Vane and does not think the study's results are as definitive as the FDA and Lederle claim. He is critical of the FDA's methodology, which differed considerably from the one that he and other SV40 researchers employ. The FDA researchers, Carbone says, did not run enough PCR cycles during their tests and failed to use Southern blot to confirm their results. They also used a PCR primer that was designed only to detect very large fragments (574 base pairs or more) of SV40 DNA, whereas, in Carbone's experience, the size of the SV40 DNA fragments that are recoverable from old vaccine samples is much shorter, between 100 to 200 base pairs in length. Carbone believes that altogether the shortcomings in the FDA protocol were significant enough that if SV40 was present in the vaccine samples tested, the FDA's tests could have missed it. "If they really want to be sure that these vaccines do not contain SV40, they need to repeat the experiments using the correct primers, the correct number of PCR cycles, and Southern blot analysis following PCR," he says.

Carbone has even harsher words for the other study the FDA cites—the British study, which "concluded that there were not [any] detectable SV40 sequences" in old British oral vaccine samples. That statement is misleading, he says. A close reading of the paper shows that some of the vaccine samples the British scientists tested actually were positive for the presence of SV40, but the authors ascribed their positive results to laboratory contamination, a conclusion that Carbone feels was unjustified. In fact, Carbone says, the positive PCR results the authors report are not at all suggestive of contamination but are instead much more likely to be indicative of low levels of SV40 in the vaccine samples tested. "Technically they cannot be accused of falsifying their data—because they report their results. But then they give a very subjective and very questionable interpretation of their results," Carbone says. "Their own data do not support their conclusions. And if it is true that they contaminated [their own] samples, the whole paper is unreliable."

If the studies that conclude oral polio vaccine has never been contaminated with SV40 are as scientifically unreliable as Carbone asserts, then they appear to provide little clarification of the issue. The documentary evidence, however, seems to provide a clearer picture. Internal Lederle and government documents offer strong support to the theories of Kops and others that oral vaccine produced and released in this country since 1961 has at times contained live SV40.

One possible source for SV40 in the oral vaccine that Alexander (and possibly others) received could have been the kidneys of the African green monkeys used as a vaccine substrate since the early 1960s. U.S. manufacturers switched from rhesus to African greens by 1963 because, unlike rhesus, the African green monkeys do not naturally harbor SV40. However, they can become infected through contact with other monkeys, and internal memos from Lederle, the sole supplier of polio vaccine in the United States from 1977 to 2000, show that at times the manufacturer experienced SV40 problems with African greens as well.

In November 1961, seven months after the directive that no SV40-contaminated vaccine would be released, Lederle reported in a memo that three of the fifteen lots of oral vaccine it had produced contained SV40. In the same memo, Lederle reported that ten percent of the African green monkeys it had planned to use for vaccine production were testing positive for SV40. (The African greens had likely been infected by close contact with rhesus monkeys during shipment from Africa or while at Lederle.) Another memo, this one from 1962, indicates that Lederle experienced widespread SV40 contamination of its laboratory facilities at the time and that the virus may have contaminated the vaccine.

Indeed, viral contamination of its monkey kidney substrate was a recurring headache for the company. In an internal 1983 report, Lederle compiled a thirteen-year survey of 2,239 "harvests"—the term used to describe the poliovirus-containing fluid that each monkey kidney tissue culture yields within seventy-two hours of inoculation with the poliovirus seed. Almost half the harvests for the thirteen-year period had been scrapped because of viral contamination. Simian cytomegalovirus, the monkey version of human cytomegalovirus, and a virus that has been associated by some scientists with chronic fatigue syndrome and malaise, was the leading cause of rejection, accounting for 38 percent of the rejections. But the 1983 report cites a laundry list of other contaminants that also forced rejection of vaccine harvests, including simian foamy virus, measles virus, and occasional SV40 contamination.

The problem was so acute that Lederle was forced to set up a special segregated colony of African greens for polio vaccine production. The animals were carefully isolated from other monkeys likely to transmit SV40 or any other virus. After the 1980s, the contamination problems appear to have ceased. Moreover, FDA regulations required extensive testing of the kidneys used as vaccine substrate for the presence of SV40 prior to the start of the manufacturing process. This would seem to suggest the kidneys were not the source of the SV40 in Alexander's 1997 oral vaccine.

That leaves another possible source of SV40 contamination of the oral vaccine: the poliovirus seed used to infect the kidney cultures during the vaccine manufacturing process. In order to grow the billions of copies of poliovirus needed for the oral vaccine, the manufacturer first "seeds" the monkey kidney cultures with a small amount of poliovirus. Once added to the African green monkey kidney cultures, the seed poliovirus reproduces itself, multiplying millions of times, allowing the manufacturer to "harvest" billions of copies of the poliovirus it needs to make final vaccine.

The sources for this viral seed are the same attenuated strains of poliovirus that Albert Sabin first cultivated in the 1950s on rhesus monkey kidneys. Every batch of oral polio vaccine produced in this country since 1961 originates from each of the three original Sabin strains (Type I, II, and III). All of Sabin's strains were heavily contaminated with SV40. That was the discovery made by Ben Sweet and Maurice Hilleman in 1960 when they tested stores of Sabin's strains at Merck. After that discovery, Sabin's strain material for each of the three polio types had supposedly been neutralized for SV40 by treating it with an SV40 antiserum. Over the years, Lederle has used the original Sabin strains and, at times, their derivatives, to periodically make small amounts of so-called working seed or production seed for each of the three poliovirus types. This working seed is stored in a deep freeze and thawed each time the company initiates a new batch of vaccine. A small amount of each of the three working seed types is then inoculated into a monkey kidney substrate and the poliovirus begins to replicate. Once a large volume of each type of poliovirus is produced, the virus is harvested from the kidney substrate and the large volumes of each virus type (now called a monopool) are combined to form a bulk batch of final vaccine. Assuming the Sabin strain material and all the working seeds produced from each strain type over the years contained no viable SV40—and that throughout the entire vaccine production process there was no other exposure to SV40-contaminated tissues—there should be no possible SV40 contamination of the final oral vaccine.

But how well had the neutralizing process worked? At the time, the only way to know if SV40 was still present in the master strains or their derivatives would have been to test each one by growing it in a cell culture and looking for signs of SV40's characteristic cytopathic effect—vacuolating holes in the cells. Such a process would require observing the cell cultures for a certain number of days—enough time to allow the virus to grow out and destroy the cells and, in this way, be visible. But another set of internal memos from Lederle laboratories show that the oral polio vaccine master strains provided to the company by Albert Sabin and used to manufacture working seeds of virus may not have been adequately tested for SV40 and that the working seeds derived from these Sabin strains were also never tested for the presence of SV40.

In October 1962, Sabin mailed Lederle five milliliters (5 ml) of Type III virus master strain. In an attached letter, Sabin warned that even though the tests carried out by Maurice Hilleman at Merck on the master strain he was sending Lederle were negative for SV40, "he [Hilleman] told me at the time the tests were made they were not observing the cultures for as long as they are now and he could not be certain that there may not be a trace of SV40 virus in this material." In effect, Sabin was putting the company on notice that the neutralization process for this strain material, as likely as not, had not worked. Such an uncertainty would seem to demand serious efforts to test for the virus every time the strain was used or working seed made from the strain was used.

Apparently, such tests did not occur. In a deposition taken in 1988 for a court case, Mary Ritchey, the Lederle vice president of operations, said that she could find no documentation indicating that all of the company's polio vaccine production seeds were tested for SV40. Indeed, evidence suggests that such tests were not performed. In an internal memo dated March 14, 1979, a Lederle official, commenting on the poliovirus production process, wrote:

It should be made clear that Lederle did not test the original Sabin seeds for extraneous agents or neurovirulence since only 50 ml or less of each seed were provided by Dr. Sabin. It was presumed that if progeny [final vaccine monopools] of these seeds proved to be free of extraneous agents and have satisfactory neurovirulence, the parent seeds were satisfactory.

Instead of testing the Sabin master strains or the working seeds, the company tested each harvest, the type I, II, and III virus monopools that, combined, made a final batch of vaccine. In these tests, a portion of each lot is inoculated into cell cultures and allowed to grow for fourteen days. Then a subculture is made of the fluid from the first culture and it, too, is allowed to grow for fourteen more days. The presumption is that at the end of each of the fourteen-day periods, any SV40 present would have burst the cells and become apparent to whoever was screening the cultures. This assumption was based on the analysis Paul Gerber had performed in the early 1960s on SV40 growth in cell culture. The federal government continued to rely on Gerber's analysis decades later, despite warnings from Anthony Girardi in the late 1960s that it could take up to thirty-five days for SV40 to grow out (become visible) in tissue culture.

In 1999, when Carbone tested his vials of 1955 vaccine for SV40 and realized he had detected slow-growing SV40 variants, he became curious. Suppose a slow-growing SV40 variant were present in the oral vaccine. Were current FDA regulations, which required only fourteen-day cell culture cycles, adequate to detect all SV40 types, including SV40 that was slow growing? Carbone conducted his own test. He discovered that the slow-growing strain of SV40 that he had recovered from Herbert Ratner's 1955 vaccine took nineteen days to grow out—or become apparent in tissue cultures. That meant FDA-mandated tests as likely as not would have failed to detect it or other slow-growing variants present in a vaccine.

Using the FDA's testing protocol, here's what might have happened in the case of the slow-growing variant of SV40 such as the type Carbone found in his 1955 vaccine vials: A sample of a lot from which the final trivalent vaccine batch was derived would have been inoculated into a test culture and held for fourteen days. Because the virus contained in the lot was Carbone's nineteen-day, slow-growing type, after fourteen days, little, if any, of the virus would have infected cells and replicated to the point where it would burst the cells and release SV40 into the fluids that surround the tissue culture cells. There would be no apparent sign of viral growth and this primary culture, therefore, would be regarded as negative. On the fourteenth day, the fluids that surround the cell culture would be inoculated into a second culture, the subculture. But these fluids from the first culture (primary culture) still contained either no SV40 or only a very small amount of the virus. If there were no SV40 in the fluids from the first culture, this second subculture, too, would be negative. In the event that some SV40 actually was in the fluids of the primary culture, the subculture would still appear to be negative, even after fourteen days of observation, since this particular slow-growing SV40 variant takes nineteen days to grow out. Thus, an SV40-contaminated lot would pass the one safety test designed to catch the virus, and it would be released.

Slow-growing SV40 happens to be the type most often found in brain and bone cell tumors—tumor types that often afflict children, including the brain cancer that killed Alexander Horwin. (Faster-growing variants of SV40 have been found in these tumor types as well.) Carbone's tests on his vintage vaccine support the theory that if slower-growing SV40 was present in the lots used to make the oral polio vaccine administered to Alexander, it might not have been detected following the test protocols required by the FDA. It is certainly scientifically possible, therefore, that Alexander's dose of oral vaccine was a possible source for the SV40 in his medulloblastoma.

On January 31, 2000, one year to the day after Alexander died, Raphaele and Michael Horwin filed a lawsuit against Lederle in U.S. District Court in Los Angeles. Their San Francisco legal team of Marte Bassi and Fred Blum was joined by Donald MacLachlan, the New Jersey lawyer who uncovered that Shah was being paid by two vaccine manufacturers to advise them on SV40, and Stanley Kops, who lent his expertise on polio production.

In their complaint, the Horwins alleged that the oral polio vaccine that Alexander received on November 7, 1997, was contaminated with SV40 and that the virus caused Alexander's medulloblastoma. The expert witnesses for the Horwins included some of the scientists who have made the biggest SV40 breakthroughs in recent years: Adi Gazdar from the University of Texas, Southwestern Medical Center, Bharat Jasani from the University of Cardiff, and John Lednicky, now at Loyola. During the pretrial exchange of pleadings, motions, and depositions, lawyers for Lederle argued that the virus was not a carcinogen and that Alexander did not contract it from their polio vaccine, in effect repeating the same argument some federal health officials have offered over the years. They offered several alternative sources for the virus, theorizing that Alexander Horwin could have contracted the virus from his babysitter or from monkeys while riding on his father's back during a visit to the San Diego zoo. They also suggested that Alexander might have contracted the virus from one of the two inactivated polio vaccine shots he received during the first six months of his life. (Lederle did not sell inactivated polio vaccine. The supplier of inactivated vaccine in this country is a North American subsidiary of the giant European vaccine house Aventis Pasteur.)

John Lednicky, one of the Horwins' expert witnesses in the case, dismissed all three Lederle theories, saying there was no evidence "whatsoever" that the babysitter became infected and then "would somehow infect only Alexander and not also infect Alexander's mother or father." Nor was there evidence to support the monkey hypothesis, especially since there had been no physical contact with any monkeys during the zoo visit.

Lednicky also stated that there was no evidence indicating that the current version of the inactivated polio vaccine (IPV) was contaminated with SV40. The Pasteur vaccine given to Alexander was produced on fully characterized simian cells—not fresh monkey kidney tissues. Like WI-38, the substrate is free of viral contaminants. According to the FDA's Office of Vaccine Research Review, PCR tests for the presence of SV40 have been conducted on the IPV seeds for the vaccine administered to Alexander and for the only other IPV currently licensed in the United States, also manufactured by Pasteur. Both seeds have proven negative. "All of the medical articles I have reviewed indicate the IPV is [now] manufactured in a way which would eliminate SV40," Lednicky stated in court filings.

In a 102-page declaration filed in the case, Lednicky summed up the case against Lederle. He said that the evidence pointed strongly in the direction of the Lederle vaccine as the SV40 source, with all other exposure routes proposed by the company as implausible. All the tests confirming the presence of the virus in Alexander's tumors had been checked and double-checked. Positive tumor results from Carbone and Jasani's lab had been confirmed by Adi Gazdar, who had performed laser microdissection. Gazdar found that SV40 DNA was present in Alexander's tumor tissue, but absent in the adjacent nonmalignant brain tissue. Tests performed on separate sets of slides after a two-year interval yielded the same result. "These findings exclude the possibilities that the results were due to accidental contamination of the specimen with the virus," Gazdar concluded.

"The presence of SV40 sequences in the tumor tissue and its absence in adjacent nonmalignant brain tissue indicates a very specific association between a highly transforming virus and the tumor cells . . . These findings provide powerful evidence that the virus played a role in the causation of the tumor."

Lednicky next assessed the effectiveness of Lederle's SV40-neutralization of the Sabin master strains. The procedure's basic flaw was that neutralization—like the formaldehyde used in Salk's vaccine—was not necessarily 100 percent effective against SV40. Moreover, since it was originally designed to fight specific SV40 strains, the process, Lednicky said, might not always be effective against all occurring SV40 variants:

> In my opinion, the neutralization process described by the vaccine manufacturer thus far would have left a distinct possibility of infective SV40 viral particles surviving the neutralization process. In light of the lack of adequate information received from the vaccine manufacturer, it is my opinion that it would be more likely than not that some viable SV40 viral particles survived the neutralization process and propagated [multiplied and grew] during the subsequent manufacturing process.

Lednicky also examined whether SV40 could have been in the vaccine dose Alexander received. The virus subtype found in Alexander's tumor was slow growing. It was the very type of SV40 that could have been missed in safety tests conducted according to FDA guidelines. He reviewed the safety tests performed by Lederle for the presence of SV40 in the harvest used to make the polio vaccine from which Alexander's dose had originated. He concluded the company's testing procedures would have detected only relatively high levels of the virus if it had contaminated the batch. Smaller amounts could have slipped through.

The most damning information Lednicky found was readily apparent in the company's own records. The manufacturer *had* detected a monkey virus in a harvest used in the production of Alexander's vaccine. During the Lederle tissue culture tests to detect the presence of SV40, a harvest used to make the batch of vaccine that was the source for the dose which Alexander received had failed—not once, but twice. When samples of the Type I harvest (No. 7596) that became part of the vaccine administered to Alexander Horwin were injected into tissue cultures of African green monkey kidney cells, the harvest produced discernable cytopathic effect during the second fourteen-day tissue observation period in two separate tests—a clear sign of SV40 contamination. Yet vaccine using the suspect Type I lot had been released by the company anyway.

Lederle's lawyers countered Lednicky's assertion by admitting that while it was true that Type I harvest 7596 had failed the African green monkey culture test, it was not necessarily true that SV40 was the culprit. The company's own tests, they suggested, were not precise enough to determine which virus had caused the cytopathic effect. It could have been one of the other common contaminants the African greens harbor, such as cytomegalovirus, or foamy virus. But Lednicky tested Alexander's tumor for cytomegalovirus and found none. Moreover, other tests by Lederle on harvest 7596 in other tissue culture types (rhesus monkey and rabbit cells)—tests specifically designed to detect the presence of foamy virus—were negative. During these tissue culture tests, there was no evidence of viral contamination. The only failing tests were in the African green monkey kidney tissue cultures—the tissue culture test the DBS had mandated back in 1961 because it was the most reliable tissue culture test for detecting SV40. Based on Lederle's own tests, Lednicky opined, the only virus contaminating the harvest was SV40.

Why would a polio vaccine manufacturer release vaccine that failed the one safety test designed to screen for SV40? Perhaps because the federal government itself seems to have been inconsistent, if not slipshod, when it came to enforcing safeguards devised to protect the public from exposure to the virus. Despite all the panic SV40 caused among vaccinologists outside of Bethesda, there seems to have been, at times, a cavalier attitude within the federal agencies charged with vaccine safety. The 1961 memo in which a Lederle official noted that three lots of the company's oral vaccine contained SV40, also reported that the head of the Division of Biologic Standards, Roderick Murray, had allowed these lots to pass. The Lederle official even wondered if the company should consider voluntary withdrawal of the lots—a step the company apparently decided not to undertake. All three lots were included within the company's original DBS license for oral polio vaccine—meaning they were distributed, sold, and consumed in the United States during the 1960s.

In another example, as we have seen, Murray delayed almost two years after the discovery of live SV40 in Salk's vaccine—until March 1963— before imposing a regulation that would require manufacturers to ensure their virus pools were SV40-free *prior* to inactivation (instead of relying on formaldehyde to kill it). This was the change that finally spurred a wholesale switch by manufacturers from the contaminated rhesus to the SV40-free African green monkeys. Yet, in a 1964 memo from Murray to vaccine manufacturers, the DBS chief writes, "The DBS views with considerable concern . . . [that manufacturers are] still submitting for release lots of vaccine . . . inactivated prior to March 1963." Murray adds that, from now on, the DBS will not pass any such lots. Apparently, up until the writing of this memo, Murray had allowed such lots to be released, in effect, extending the exposure of Americans to SV40-contaminated vaccine beyond 1963 by at least one additional year.

In 1967 came another potential SV40-exposure event. After several European vaccine workers had died during the Marburg virus crisis, most of the world stopped the production of polio vaccine. At the time, it was assumed that the United States had done so also—even the *New York Times* reported the cessation of vaccine production. But unbeknownst to the newspaper, the American public, and most scientists, oral polio vaccine production in this country did not halt during the Marburg scare. At the November 1967 NIH conference on viral vaccine substrates, the one at which Hayflick and his supporters argued in vain for abandonment of monkey kidneys in favor of WI-38, Murray made the surprising announcement that he had not ordered a halt in vaccine production in the United States in response to the Marburg virus outbreak. Instead, he said, polio vaccine production temporarily had been switched back to rhesus monkeys. What steps the DBS had undertaken, if any, to ensure that SV40 would not once again contaminate polio vaccine was not mentioned by Murray at the conference. Here was a third time the government had sanctioned a potential exposure to SV40 in vaccines—all the more incredible when one considers the backdrop for the Murray decision. Marburg was a monkey virus that was so deadly that lab technicians who never had any direct contact with the infected African green monkeys, their kidneys, or the kidney tissue cultures—but had washed glassware that had been used during the tissue culture process—became ill and died. Yet the DBS response to the Marburg crisis was not to insist, at long last, that vaccine production be switched to clean, virus-free substrate, such as WI-38, but instead to consent to a return to the use of rhesus monkey kidneys—a substrate that Murray knew was almost always contaminated with SV40.

In 1977, another Lederle memo reveals a different type of government failure—this time, a missed opportunity to make the vaccine safer. Just before Christmas 1977, Lederle officials traveled to Bethesda to meet with Murray's successor, Harry Meyer. (The DBS by this time had been renamed the Bureau of Biologics, or BoB.) At issue were continuing problems the company was having with Type III attenuated poliovirus. Lots of the Type III virus were frequently reverting to virulence, a problem traceable to the original Type III Sabin strain, which was notorious in this regard. Meyer could have required the company to find a less virulent Type III strain, but he did not. Instead, according to the Lederle memo, Meyer offered to water down the regulations to make it easier for the company's Type III lots to pass:

> Dr. Meyer asked us to bear with him in their efforts to change regulations which may be accomplished by mid-1978. . . . Dr. Meyer said the regulations must be changed in a way that will not be interpreted as a "softening" of BoB and yet allow the manufacturer to be able to produce with current seeds since establishment of a new Type 3 seed will be very expensive and time consuming.

If Meyer, who subsequently left the BoB to assume a high-paying executive position with Lederle, had actually required his future employers to change the Type III strain material, not only would he have helped reduce the neurovirulence problem, he also would have eliminated one potential source of SV40 contamination. Unlike the original Sabin Type III strain, a new Type III strain could have been produced on a substrate that was free of SV40.

More recently, even though much more sophisticated tests for screening viruses, such as PCR, have been available for two decades, federal vaccine safety regulations remain unchanged. The regulations still only require the use of relatively crude viral screening tests (tissue culture observation along with ordinary light microscope examination) for the detection of the presence in SV40. In essence, despite the widespread availability of sensitive tests, the government-mandated testing methodology has barely evolved since the days of Bernice Eddy and Ben Sweet. Lederle, ironically, used that fact—that its tissue culture tests were not sophisticated enough to discern whether the virus in Alexander's vaccine was SV40 or another virus—to excuse its failure to reject the contaminated batch of vaccine.

Horwin attorney Stanley Kops says the situation is even worse than the government's failure to take advantage of opportunities to make the vaccine safer or require the use of better SV40 screening tests. He says that his collection of manufacturer documents shows that there were repeated instances where Lederle used rhesus monkey kidneys—despite the fact that the animals frequently harbor SV40—during crucial stages of the vaccine manufacturing process. During his September 2003 testimony before the House Subcommittee on Human Rights and Wellness, Kops placed into evidence a series of Lederle's manufacturing protocol documents. The protocol documents, he said, proved that between 1961 and 1980, the company produced seven different working Type I and II poliovirus seeds on rhesus monkey kidney cell tissue cultures—thus, providing an opportunity for SV40 contamination of any vaccine made from monopools that had been initiated with these seeds. These particular seeds, Kops asserted, were never tested for the presence of SV40. Kops told the House subcommittee that his documentation on these working seeds belied assertions by a Lederle spokesperson made during the January 1997 NIH SV40 conference that the company had prepared "all subsequent working seed strain . . . in [African green monkey] cells and screened [them] to assure they are free of SV40 virus."

Kops also revealed to the House Subcommittee company documents showing that an entire Type II monopool—not just a working seed—was grown on rhesus monkey kidneys during the 1980s. This Type II monopool was released in 1986; conceivably, any dose of vaccine that contained Type II poliovirus from this monopool could have also contained live SV40. In one final surprise, Kops placed into evidence a January 15, 1990 letter from Lederle's director of quality control to Paul Parkman, the head of FDA's Center for Biologics, Evaluation and Research, the FDA agency responsible for licensing vaccine. In the letter, Lederle asks for permission to release monopools of all three poliovirus types "produced in Rhesus primary monkey kidney cells" between September 1984 and April 1987, which "represent several million doses of trivalent oral polio vaccine." In the letter, the Lederle official seems to indicate that it is of little consequence that the vaccine in question had been grown on fresh rhesus monkey tissues, noting that "live oral polio vaccine was once routinely produced in Macaca [rhesus] primary monkey kidney cell cultures" and that monkeys used to produce the vaccine the company now sought to release had been "domestic-bred . . . in Lederle-controlled monkey colonies." (How this lessened the chance for SV40 infection of the animals was not specified by the Lederle official.)

It infuriates Kops that despite its public statements to the contrary Lederle continued to use rhesus monkey kidneys in vaccine manufacture during the 1960s, '70s, and '80s. "My feeling is that this is the biggest cover-up in the history of vaccine production in the United States. Regulations were made after years of debate. They were explicit. They were prepared to protect the American child who was receiving the vaccine. The safety regulations were not followed," Kops says. "The purpose of vaccines is to fight a war against a crippling disease. But even in war there are rules of engagement. This vaccine manufacturer broke the rules knowingly and decided that it was above the law. That is a travesty."

In April 2003, Kops, MacLachlan, and the Horwins' other lawyers faced off in U.S. District Court in Los Angeles against Lederle's legal team for a two-week preliminary hearing to determine the admissibility of the scientific evidence to be presented in the Horwins' lawsuit. Lednicky and Gazdar appeared as expert witnesses for the Horwins. Lederle presented its own experts. The hearing resulted in a transcript of more than two thousand pages. In May 2003, a U.S. district judge in Los Angeles ruled that based on the evidence presented at the hearing, he had concluded that SV40 was a cancer-causing virus, that one of the cancer types it causes is brain tumors, in particular medulloblastoma, and that Alexander Horwin's medulloblastoma was caused by SV40. Although he agreed that there was indeed "a possibility that the dose of Orimune given to Alexander was contaminated" with SV40, the judge sided with Lederle on the crucial question of what exactly had caused the failure in the African green monkey tissue culture test. In his ruling, he found that there was insufficient "direct evidence" to definitively conclude that the virus was SV40, and not some other virus—essentially adopting the Lederle point of view that the company's tests were simply too unsophisticated to tell exactly what the contaminant was in Alexander's vaccine. Ironically, it seems that the federal government's failure to require that manufacturers use a readily available, reliable, and sensitive SV40 detection assay, such as PCR, allowed the company to avoid liability in this case. The ruling effectively dismissed the Horwins' lawsuit against Lederle.

There are now several more lawsuits pending in U.S. courts against Lederle alleging death or disease caused by SV40 in contaminated vaccines. The Horwins, meanwhile, have become lay experts on the subject of SV40 and cancer. They want the federal government to require SV40 testing as a standard diagnostic procedure for children with cancer—*before* they start chemotherapy or radiation treatments. Based on their own reading of the scientific literature, the Horwins believe that Alexander's chemotherapy not only produced horrific side effects but actually hastened his death—and would do the same for any other child (or adult) with an SV40-positive tumor. Both chemotherapy and radiation, they contend, rely on p53 to initiate apoptosis—cellular suicide—and thereby trigger tumor cell death. But if SV40 in a tumor were binding p53 and other tumor-suppressor genes, then chemotherapy or radiation would be useless and potentially harmful. The SV40 would immobilize the p53, allowing the tumor cells to survive. These cells would, in turn, become even more malignant because of genetic mutations caused by the treatments. The Horwins believe that is why Alexander suffered more than thirty tumors when his cancer recurred. It is imperative, they believe, for federal regulators to acknowledge the presence of SV40 in certain tumors and to test for it prior to treatment in order to spare those diagnosed with SV40-related cancers even more suffering.

The Horwins' theory has never been tested in a laboratory setting and so remains just a hypothesis. But scientists say it is a reasonable hypothesis for tumors that contain SV40 that is actively binding to p53. Perhaps it explains why victims of mesothelioma—the most investigated SV40-associated tumor—have such poor response rates to standard cancer treatments. It also highlights yet another scientific enigma about SV40. Paradoxically, standard therapies that are effective against other tumors may render SV40-related cancers even more pernicious. When it comes to responding to this deceptively simple virus, scientific orthodoxy, it seems, may not only be misguided, but also deadly.

Conclusion

JONAS SALK DIED in 1995, Albert Sabin, in 1993. Both men lived long enough to witness research linking SV40 to cancer, but both men had long before decided the virus was harmless. Both men, it seems, could never reconcile themselves to the prospect that their vaccines might have been tainted in any fashion. Despite the visionary capabilities they had displayed in discovering and perfecting their respective vaccines, when it came to considering the virus that contaminated their discoveries, they remained mired in scientific dogma.

Hilary Koprowski, another of the early polio vaccinologists, responded to SV40 in the opposite fashion. In 1960, he had declared that he thought any viral contamination of a vaccine, including SV40, was most likely inconsequential, but after learning of Bernice Eddy's experiments, he changed his mind. Throughout the 1960s, his Wistar laboratory was the source of some of the most important early research on the simian virus's oncogenic potential, and after Leonard Hayflick's, his was one of the loudest voices lobbying for a switch away from the "dirty" kidneys. Today Koprowski is experimenting with the use of plants as a vaccine substrate, which he believes could eliminate the risk of vaccine contamination by potentially dangerous foreign animal viruses and cellular debris. Unlike Salk and Sabin, Koprowski's encounter with SV40 completely changed his scientific thinking and caused him to shed his preconceived notions.

After the polio vaccine was licensed, the responsibility for its safety passed from the vaccinologists to the federal regulators. Here, too, scientists remained firmly entrenched in the dogma about SV40, unmoved by any experimental evidence that challenged their established view of the virus. As Bernice Eddy learned, such evidence was extremely unwelcome. Joseph Smadel, with the full support of his superior, Roderick Murray, sentenced Eddy to a lifelong internal exile within the Division of Biologics Standards because she dared suggest that she thought the polio vaccine contained a dangerous contaminant.

Murray, for his part, never reevaluated the simian virus's putative harmlessness and instead, on all questions regarding the polio vaccine, manifested a bureaucratic instinct for self-preservation that was the hallmark of his tenure at the DBS. At every point at which he was confronted with a reason to change polio vaccine policy, he either took no action or stalled until the last moment. Confronted with the news in 1961 that Salk's vaccine contained SV40, Murray neither recalled the contaminated vaccine nor required any change in the manufacturing process. It was not until 1963 that he enacted regulations that forced manufacturers to stop using SV40-contaminated rhesus monkeys. And even then he wasn't willing to enforce them rigorously. Because of Murray's foot-dragging, millions of Americans were needlessly exposed to SV40 for at least three additional years.

When it came to WI-38, Murray's approach was the same: Change was the enemy. In response to the overwhelming evidence that Hayflick's diploid cell substrate was far safer than the contaminated monkey kidneys, Murray, for years, adopted a position whose tortured reasoning strained scientific credulity. Yes, the kidneys were contaminated, but at least that glaring deficiency was known, therefore it could presumably be controlled. WI-38, on the other hand, was new; to embrace it would have required Murray to countermand previous DBS policy. This would have implied errors in judgment, perhaps even negligence.

With Murray, the blueprint had been established for evaluating SV40 research; it would remain unaltered even decades after he had left the federal government. Federal health officials who had previously opined that the virus was harmless were the ones given the authority to evaluate the merits of independent research that challenged that conclusion. Not surprisingly, they reaffirmed their own previous wisdom that the virus was harmless.

That position endures today. Even as the number of independent, peer-reviewed studies linking SV40 to cancer approaches one hundred, federal officials persistently maintain that there is no proof the virus is carcinogenic.

The reasons for such persistence are not difficult to discern. It is easier to ignore (or distort) the ever-growing body of scientific evidence on the dangers of SV40 than to confront the inescapable implications of that evidence: Forty years after it was declared harmless, SV40 is causing cancer in humans. Accepting such a proposition—that SV40 is a human carcinogen—requires that health officials answer any number of troubling questions: What is the proper government response to a cancer-causing simian virus that was released into the human population by a government-sponsored vaccination program? Would it be a coordinated and extensive search for SV40 in other kinds of tumors, coupled with far greater efforts to study how the virus causes tumors, as almost every SV40 investigator believes is necessary? A crash SV40-screening program among populations most likely to have been infected, as some researchers are calling for? Is there a need for an anti-SV40 vaccination campaign? Each of these steps could require a huge new government health initiative, with the need to explain to elected officials and to the public why they were necessary. Undertaking any of them would be an acknowledgment that the original polio vaccine contamination was an enormous blunder, far more serious than has even been admitted, and that not responding to it in a more concerted effort sooner was shortsighted, negligent, and a serious failure in fulfillment of the basic mission of the NIH and its sister agencies, the CDC and FDA—to protect public health. Given the enormous consequences that would inevitably follow an acknowledgment that SV40 is carcinogenic, it is no wonder that some SV40 researchers question whether they will ever receive an honest evaluation of their research in Bethesda.

There is another consequence that follows from such a determination, one which is also highly problematic to policy makers. If SV40 causes cancer, that implies there has been a catastrophic failure in the government's oversight of a vaccine program. Universal immunization is one of the cornerstones of this nation's public health policies, and the reputation of vaccines has long been a concern among federal health officials. But the story of SV40 calls into question whether protecting the reputation of vaccines at times has been more important to these health officials than actually ensuring they are safe.

Vaccines lie at the heart of the SV40 controversy. It is the virus's connection to America's miracle vaccine, the one that wiped out the nation's scourge, which makes SV40 research controversial. Indeed, a common refrain from within the NIH is that associating SV40 with human tumors will scare people away from the polio vaccine and other vaccines.

While that apprehension is understandable—certainly it would be a disastrous turn of events if vaccine-preventable epidemics returned—it obscures a larger issue. Vaccines are the only product manufactured by a private industry whose universal consumption is mandated by the government (as a prerequisite for attending public school or college). By and large, consumers have no choice about the vaccines they receive. A physician prescribes, and a patient—often a child or an infant—is inoculated. Consumers are usually uninformed about the vaccines they are told to take. It is the rare parent who asks a physician whether there are different versions of a vaccine, whether one has side effects while another is safer, whether different vaccines might interact with each other if administered simultaneously. And when confronted with those questions, many, if not most, pediatricians would not know how to respond beyond repeating information provided by the Centers for Disease Control. Most physicians, like most consumers, rely on the government to ensure that vaccines are safe. They assume that federal licensing and regulation are reliable assurances that the vaccines we receive are effective, pure, and potent, and that federal officials have explored all the issues connected with a given vaccine's safety before it is sent to market.

SV40 contamination of the polio vaccine and the continued reluctance of federal officials to deal with the consequences calls into question whether this system always works. Lederle continued to experience contamination problems during polio vaccine production with various viruses, including SV40, and yet some of those lots were released—often with the complicity of the federal officials who regulated the vaccine. And history shows that polio vaccine has not been the only vaccine to suffer from contamination headaches. Over the years, viral contamination of vaccine substrates of all kinds—duck eggs, dog kidneys, beef serum, hen's eggs—have forced manufacturers to scrap lots of vaccines of a variety of types, from rubella to measles. Government health officials stress that advances in vaccine substrate production have significantly reduced the threat of viral contamination during the past twenty years, but it remains true that the federal government still does not mandate state-of-the-art virus detection technology to search for possible viral contaminants in vaccines. Sophisticated techniques for viral identification, such as PCR, immunoflourescence, and immunohistochemistry, have been part of the typical virologist's tool kit for two decades. Yet federal regulations require only that vaccine manufacturers screen for viruses by observing tissue cultures under an ordinary light microscope, a technique that has advanced little since the early twentieth century. Moreover, there is no routine testing of these vaccines by the government itself.

Consumer activists like Barbara Loe Fisher, cofounder of the National Vaccine Information Center in Vienna, Virginia, can recite dozens of other examples of how federal regulators have fallen short in their duty to protect the public from dangers associated with vaccines. One concerns the use of thimerosal, a mercury-based preservative used for many years in several common vaccines, including the combined diptheria-pertussis-tetanus (DPT). Mercury poisoning causes irreversible brain, liver, and kidney damage. Yet it was not until 1997 that the FDA reviewed whether exposure to thimerosal from vaccines was dangerous. The agency found that it was possible that infants receiving routine vaccinations during the first six months of their lives could be exposed to levels of mercury in excess of Environmental Protection Agency–recommended safety guidelines. The agency's review also found that the mercury-based preservative had been associated in at least one study with development of attention deficit hyperactivity disorder. The FDA and CDC response to the thimerosal issue was to "urge" manufacturers to reduce or eliminate the preservative from their vaccines. In March 2001, the FDA licensed a thimerosal-free DPT vaccine, although there is still no requirement that all vaccines be free of the preservative. In a redux of the failure to recall SV40-contaminated polio vaccine in 1961, old stocks of DPT containing thimerosal were never recalled. (Not were old stocks of DPT that were more likely to cause brain injury, despite the introduction of DaPT, a new formulation designed to decrease the chances of seizures and other vaccine reactions in susceptible children.) At many doctors' offices, unless consumers knew enough to ask for the safer formulations, there was no guarantee that they received it.

Given examples like these, it is perhaps understandable that there has been a rise in the past two decades in the number of parents who now resist inoculating their children with the increasing number of vaccines mandated by state health departments. Fisher and others who represent such parents say they are not opposed to vaccination, but instead advocate safer products and informed consent: If the government proposes injecting something into a child or adult that they cannot guarantee is absolutely safe, the consumer should make the final decision whether the risk is acceptable, not the government. This is particularly true, they say, given the documented conflicts of interest between many of the scientists who advise and receive money from pharmaceutical companies and also often sit on panels that advise federal regulators on decisions concerning which vaccines to make mandatory.

Moreover, they say, however lofty and altruistic the public health goals behind the discovery of a particular vaccine, the manufacture of vaccines is still big business. Profits are king. As the story of SV40 shows, when it comes to protecting those profits, safety and best practices do not always come first during vaccine manufacturing. Lederle's resistance to WI-38 did not stem only from a self-protective interest in preservation of its market share against a competitor. There was also the problem that if Hayflick's substrate caught on and Pfizer's vaccine became preferred by American physicians, the company itself might have had to retool its manufacturing process and move to a characterized cell substrate, a considerable expense. As it was, absent any competition after 1977 and any regulation that required change, the company never altered its basic manufacturing methods. Until oral polio vaccine was removed from the market in January 2000, every dose of vaccine manufactured by Lederle Laboratories, the sole oral polio vaccine supplier in the United States from 1977 onward, began with slaughtering a monkey, removing its kidneys, and using the minced kidneys to start a tissue culture to support the growth of the poliovirus.

In this context, the long delay in removing thimerosal from vaccines and the continued refusal to use PCR to screen against possible viral contamination is not particularly remarkable. The Lederle polio vaccine history suggests that until the federal agencies that license and regulate vaccines require enhanced safety measures, vaccine manufacturers are not necessarily going to institute them on their own initiative. Indeed, in the case of Lederle's vaccine, the government (the DBS) aided the company's resistance to a safer substrate, actively fighting the Pfizer alternative, in part because it could not abide public criticism of its previous decisions.

In fact, the change in the United States to the safer, Pasteur inactivated polio vaccine grown on a characterized, virus-free cell substrate is only happenstance; it was not the result of a deliberate government decision to demand a safer substrate. The switch occurred because, by the mid-1970s, polio had been eradicated from North America yet, every year, eight to ten Americans were unnecessarily paralyzed by the live vaccine, a situation that federal regulators finally deemed unacceptable. And so, by accident, in January 2000, three decades after many European vaccine regulators concluded that monkey kidneys were unsafe—and long after their Canadian counterparts had reached the same conclusion—America's vaccine regulators finally made available to the public a polio vaccine that was not grown on fresh monkey kidney tissues.

Since the events of September 11, 2001, vaccines have assumed a new role in U.S. health policy. They are now regarded as a crucial line of defense in the war against terrorism. There has been a demand for wide dissemination of vaccines against smallpox and anthrax and for the development of vaccines against other potential bioterrorism agents. There has been an insistence that the nation be prepared to engage in quick, massive immunization campaigns against such potential health threats. New laws have been contemplated giving public health officials sweeping powers to enforce compulsory vaccination in the event of possible bioterrorist activities. As a price for supplying new and updated vaccines, pharmaceuticals have lobbied to be absolved of any liability for their products. Citizens, in turn, are asked to rely on the judgment of federal regulators and public health officials and to take whatever steps they deem necessary under such circumstances.

The story of SV40 invites us to take pause. The decisions of our health policy makers, even when well intentioned, are not always enlightened. And sometimes those decisions are not even well intentioned. Sometimes they are based on bias or inadequate scientific evidence. Sometimes they are influenced by the close relationship between the pharmaceutical industry and the government health officials who are charged with regulating that industry. Moreover, sometimes even the best scientists can make mistakes. The safest medical products can have unforeseen side effects. Things do occasionally go wrong, sometimes dreadfully wrong, during even the most noble of scientific endeavors. For that reason, individuals, not governments, must maintain the right to control what medical procedures they and their children undergo and what pharmaceuticals they consume. As long as medicine in general, and pharmaceuticals in particular, remain for-profit industries, it may be reasonably asked whether safety isn't, at times, subservient to the bottom line.

Ultimately, the story of SV40 and the polio vaccine is a cautionary tale, a coda to the remarkable health century we have just completed. Medical knowledge leapt forward at a dizzying pace during the twentieth century. Heading into the twenty-first century, researchers promise us even greater leaps in medical advancement, offering visions of life spans that are measured in tens of decades, routine replacement of worn-out limbs, genetic manipulation of food supplies and, perhaps, human beings. We live in an age when scientists talk of substituting human organs with those from animals, and when the promise of the biotech revolution includes splicing genes from one species to another in the service of designer medicines and exotic food stuffs. But the story of the virus and the vaccine compels us to reconsider our headlong rush to meddle with the basic mechanics of life. It suggests that we ask what Pandora's box we may open in the process. In an era when our ability to manipulate biology seems at times to outstrip our rational and ethical capabilities, we would be wise to ask not only how to accomplish such advances, but whether all such advances are truly in the interests of humankind, indeed, of life as a whole. We would be wise to ponder how the unintended consequences of even the most admirable scientific advances can live on long after the problems that stimulated them have been solved.

Notes and Sources

A NOTE ON SOURCES

Our goal throughout the research and writing of this book was to rely on primary source material. The greater part of the book is the result of original research, including extensive, documented interviews with most of the major living figures mentioned in the book and a review of hundreds of scientific articles, newspapers, periodicals, transcripts of hearings and scientific meetings, and other original documents. Except where noted, all interviews were conducted by the authors either in person or by telephone. Affiliations are noted only for those not already identified in the book.

The events in this book fall roughly into two time periods. The first ten chapters relate events that, by and large, occurred decades ago. We were able to interview some of the surviving participants in those events, but given the time frame covered, we relied as much on traditional historical sources, including books, periodicals, and transcripts, all noted in what follows here. The second half of the book, which relates contemporary events, relies more on personal interviews with participants in the events described and on the authors' personal observations of many of these events—although documents, memoranda, and other sources were also used. For both past and contemporary periods, published scientific research is one of the most important sources for information concerning SV40 and is cited throughout the book. In addition to specific citations in each chapter, we have provided a separate Appendix A, "Scientific Research on SV40 and Human Tumors," which is a comprehensive list of scientific studies concerning the association of SV40 with human tumors through fall 2003. Internal government and vaccine manufacturer documents, as well as correspondence and memoranda, are also extensively cited in the book. We have listed these in separate appendices with notes about the contents of the documents as appropriate.

CHAPTER 1: THE PARALYZED PRESIDENT

General Background. In this chapter we relied on several books for the early history of polio and the story of how Roosevelt contracted and coped with polio: John R. Paul, *A History of Poliomyelitis* (New Haven, Conn.: Yale University Press, 1971), pp. 1–9; Richard Carter, *Breakthrough: The Saga of Jonas Salk* (New York: Trident Press, 1966) pp. 8–11; Michael B. A. Oldstone, *Viruses, Plagues, and History* (New York: Oxford University Press, 1998), pp. 92–96. John Rowan Wilson, *Margin of Safety* (Garden City, N.Y.: Doubleday, 1963), pp. 36–37, provided general background, primarily on the science and history of polio. Richard Thayer Goldberg, *The Making of Franklin D. Roosevelt: Triumph over Disability* (Cambridge, Mass.: Abt Books, 1981), pp. 13–46, 71, 104, 105–110, 122, 137–138, 140–142, 160–167, was a source primarily about Roosevelt. Other authors providing background on polio and FDR included: Aaron Klein, *Trial by Fury* (New York: Scribner's, 1972), pp. 6–9, 85–87, and Nina Gilden Seavey, Jane S. Smith, and Paul Wagner, *A Paralyzing Fear: The Triumph over Polio in America* (New York: TV Books, 1998), pp. 19–24.

Two background sources used for this (and other chapters) are particularly noteworthy: Jane Smith, *Patenting the Sun: Polio and the Salk Vaccine* (New York: Morrow, 1990), pp. 34–35, 43, is an eminently readable account of the history of America's fight against polio, beginning with the epidemic of 1916 and Roosevelt's paralysis. *FDR's Splendid Deception*, by Hugh Gregory Gallagher (New York: Dodd, Mead, 1985), pp. 1–10, 59–95, is an excellent and intimate look at how polio shaped the life and character of America's thirty-second president, including detailed examples of the difficulties that a crippled FDR faced—unexpected falls, severe pain each time he took a train ride, and some of the ways he coped with his paralysis, such as use of a specially modified automobile that could be operated without foot pedals.

Public Chronology. Nina Gilden Seavey, director, provided a documentary history of the era in *A Paralyzing Fear: The Story of Polio in America* (PBS, 1998). Newspaper articles also provided general background: Leonard Engel, "Polio: New Weapons and New Hope," *New York Times Magazine,* May 31, 1953, pp. 11 ff.; Leonard Engel, "Climax of a Stirring Medical Drama," *New York Times Magazine,* Jan. 10, 1954, pp. 7–10; "Disease Ancient, Its Study Modern," *New York Times,* Apr. 13, 1955, p. 21; "Famous Victims Withstood Polio," *New York Times,* Apr. 13, 1955, p. 21; and "Health Aide Cites '16 Polio Epidemic," *New York Times,* May 1, 1955, p. 56.

CHAPTER 2: A NATION AT WAR WITH POLIO

Interviews. We drew upon an interview with Albert Sabin, conducted by Edward Shorter, Dec. 15, 1986 (available from the History of Medicine Division of the National Library of Medicine, Washington, D.C.) as an additional source for the history of early polio research efforts, particularly the NIH decision to cede to the National Foundation supremacy in this area.

General Background. For the establishment of the National Foundation for Infantile Paralysis and its efforts to fight polio, we relied on Carter, *Breakthrough,* pp. 11–25, 131; Gallagher, *FDR's Splendid Deception,* pp. 34–51, 150–151; Goldberg, *Making of Franklin D. Roosevelt,* pp. 74–104, 130–137, 153–160; Paul, *History of Poliomyelitis,* pp. 253–262; Smith, *Patenting the Sun,* pp. 52–59, 73–75, 82, 86, 161, 170–175, 249; Wilson, *Margin of Safety,* p. 62; and Otis L. Graham and Meghan Robinson Wander, eds., *Roosevelt, His Life and Times: An Encyclopedic View* (Boston: G. K. Hall, 1985), pp. 298–299, 331–333.

Public Chronology. Additional general background was derived from Engel, "Polio: New Weapons and New Hope," *New York Times Magazine,* May 31, 1953, pp. 11 ff. (general history of National Foundation, discovery of gamma globulin); "Gamma Globulin Bank,"

Newsweek; Dec. 22, 1952, p. 67 (on discovery of gamma globulin); "$7,500,000 Set Aside for Injections," *New York Times,* Sep. 21, 1953, p. 13. The obituary of Basil O'Connor (*New York Times,* Mar. 10, 1972, p. 40) and an account of his funeral (*New York Times,* Mar. 14, 1972, p. 45) provided background information.

The text makes reference to these articles: "This Won't Hurt Much," *Newsweek,* Jul. 14, 1952, p. 86 ("blackest [summer] . . ."); "Panic Triumphant," *Newsweek,* Sep. 7, 1953, p. 76 (occupation of health department offices by Queens parents); "Polio Unit Plans Emergency Drive," *New York Times,* Jun. 25, 1954, p. 12 (National Foundation fund-raising and spending in 1954).

Transcript. A transcript of Basil O'Connor's lecture, with its insights into his character, may be found in Louis Finkelstein, ed., *Thirteen Americans: Their Spiritual Biographies* (Port Washington, N.Y.: Kennikat Press, 1953), pp. 219–229. The lecture, delivered before the Institute for Religious and Social Studies of the Jewish Theological Seminary of America, reveals that he thought government had an obligation to ensure the health of its citizens and take a much more active role in fighting disease. He had been publicly maligned, he said, for suggesting a much more active government role in the provision of health care. In 1955, O'Connor testified before Congress that he believed Salk's newly licensed polio vaccine should be provided for free to every American child, something the Eisenhower administration was unwilling to do.

Other. The authors visited Warm Springs and FDR's Little White House (Apr. 20, 2002). Materials from the Georgia Department of Natural Resources were an additional source of background information.

CHAPTER 3: A YOUNG MAN FROM PITTSBURGH

Interviews. Maurice Hilleman, May 24, 2002. Hilleman recalled for us the great difficulties of working with monkeys to make and test vaccine. Once the monkey was sacrificed, all its blood was removed by tapping into the carotid artery and pumping formaldehyde through the circulatory system. Bone forceps would then be used to pull the animal's spinal cord out of its body, a procedure that Hilleman recalled would tax the stamina of even healthy young research assistants after it was performed several times in one day. Dozens of cross-sections of the spinal cord would then be prepared for microscopic examination. The slides for each monkey had to include ones that isolated the exact spot where the monkey had originally been injected with the vaccine preparation—the needle track had to be visible on the slide—making the monkey work painstaking as well as physically exhausting.

General Background. The primary source for the history of Salk and his vaccine work, here and in later chapters, was Carter, *Breakthrough,* pp. 28–44, 46–61, 64, 67–68, 72–77, 90–94, 105–107, 114–115, 128–129, 132, 142–143. This work is perhaps the definitive account of Salk's discovery of polio vaccine—at least from Salk's point of view. Other works, including Klein, *Trial by Fury,* pp. 28–41, 72–73, 86; Paul, *History of Poliomyelitis,* pp. 373–375; Seavey, Smith, and Wagner, *A Paralyzing Fear,* pp. 191–193; Smith, *Patenting the Sun,* pp. 47, 97, 102–127, 130–133, 144, 191; and Wilson, *Margin of Safety,* pp. 12–31, provided useful background. Material on the manufacture of the vaccine is found in Alton L. Blakeslee, *Polio and the Salk Vaccine: What You Should Know about It* (New York: Grosset & Dunlap, 1956), pp. 23–26, and in Edward R. Murrow's *See It Now* (CBS television, Feb. 22, 1955, courtesy of CBS Archives). Logan Clendening, ed., *Source Book of Medical History*

(New York: Dover Publications, 1942, 1960), pp. 388–392, tells the story of Pasteur's discovery of the rabies vaccine.

Public Chronology. For our description of the progress toward a vaccine, we used the contemporary accounts: "Polio in Test Tubes," *Newsweek,* Sep. 10, 1951 (Enders's tissue culture discovery); "The End of Polio Is in Sight at Last," *Life,* Oct. 27, 1952, pp. 115–121 (pre-Salk vaccine research efforts); Robert Coughlan, "Tracking the Killer," *Life,* Feb. 22, 1954, pp. 121–135, which offers a thorough review of Salk's efforts to create a vaccine and the science that supported it, including Enders's discovery. Leonard Engels, "Climax of a Stirring Medical Drama," *New York Times,* Jan. 10, 1954, pp. 7–11, also offers a thorough review of Salk's vaccine work. A series of articles in the *New York Times* on Apr. 13, 1955 (pp. 21 and 23) provided information and history concerning virology and vaccinology and were also the source of Salk's description of himself as a "perfectionist," who "read everything he could lay his hands on." A *Time* magazine cover story, "Closing In on Polio," Mar. 29, 1954, pp. 55 ff., provided an in-depth look at Salk's vaccine work, including his use of monkeys as well as details concerning National Foundation efforts to ensure a steady supply. "Polio Prize," *Time,* Nov. 1, 1954, p. 77, reported on the Nobel Prize awarded to Enders and his team.

Transcripts. The details of Enders's tissue culture discovery are found in John Enders, Frederic Robins, Thomas Weller, "The Cultivation of the Poliomyelitis Viruses in Tissue Culture," Nobel Lecture, Dec. 11, 1954, pp. 448–467.

Scientific Articles. The papers referred to in this chapter are listed below. (For a more complete list of scientific articles on SV40 and human tumors see Appendix A.)

Enders. J. F., Weller, T. H., Robbins, F. C. "Cultivation of the Lansing Strain of Poliomyelitis Virus in Cultures of Various Human Embryonic Tissues." *Science* 109:85–87 (Jan. 28, 1949).

CHAPTER 4: THE VACCINE THAT OPENED PANDORA'S BOX

Interviews. Leonard Hayflick, Dec. 16, 2001; Julius Youngner, May 29, 2002; Maurice Hilleman, May 3 and 24, 2002. We also drew upon an interview of Maurice Hilleman, conducted by Edward Shorter, Feb. 6, 1987 (available from the History of Medicine Division of the National Library of Medicine, Washington, D.C.) as an additional source, specifically for Hilleman's statement that "You didn't worry about wild viruses. It was good science at the time." For another example of the attitude at the time concerning possible contamination of Salk's vaccine, see Carter, p. 218, relating Basil O'Connor's reaction to a report in February 1954 (which was false) that the vaccine Salk was preparing to field-test was contaminated with tuberculosis. "I was sure the vaccine was free of tuberculosis, even if somebody had spat in the vat," Carter reports O'Connor as saying. "The Formalin would have killed the germ."

General Background. The primary general background source for this chapter was Carter, *Breakthrough,* pp. 75–76, 108, 112, 125, 142–146, 156–166, 185–186, 194–198, 208–211, 218, 220–225, 247–251. Carter reports that on Mar. 10, 1949, Salk wrote his National Foundation sponsor, Harry Weaver, to thank him for sending him a copy of a Sabin article on a researcher who died from monkey B virus. Salk wanted to know whether the National Foundation would pay for life insurance for his lab assistants "who will be engaged in this extra-hazardous work [of handling monkeys]." Weaver wrote back five days later, saying that the NF did not consider Salk or his workers employees and that he should take up the matter with the University of Pittsburgh. (See Carter, pp. 75–76, for text of the letters.)

Other works providing background for this chapter include: Paul, *History of Poliomyelitis,* p. 419; Seavey, Smith, and Wagner, *Paralyzing Fear,* pp. 179–190; Smith, *Patenting the Sun,* pp. 129, 143–149, 179, 183–187, 221–223, 250–253; and Wilson, *Margin of Safety,* p. 98.

Public Chronology. From early 1953 through the spring of 1954, stories about Salk, his vaccine work, the promise that the vaccine might be the long-awaited answer to polio, and the 1954 field trials of the vaccine were almost daily news items, as evidenced in newspapers such as the *New York Times* and periodicals such as *Time, Newsweek,* and *Life.* The prominence Salk achieved is reflected in his appearance on the cover of *Time,* "Closing In on Polio," Mar. 29, 1954, pp. 55 ff., two *New York Times Magazine* pieces, Leonard Engels, "Climax of a Stirring Medical Drama," Jan. 10, 1954, pp. 7–11; and Engels, "Battle of the Labs," Mar. 27, 1955, pp. 63–65, a lengthy piece in *Life,* Robert Coughlan, "Tracking the Killer," Feb. 22, 1954, pp. 121–135, as well as numerous appearances on the front page of the *New York Times* (see, for example, Dorothy Barclay, "New Antipolio Vaccine Ready for Mass Tests on Children," Oct. 9, 1953, p. 1; and William L. Laurence, "Lasting Prevention of Polio Reported in Vaccine Tests," Mar. 12, 1954, p. 1). Sabin's public attacks on Salk can be found in Foster Hailey, "Doctor Criticizes Polio Vaccine Use," *New York Times,* Mar. 12, 1954, p. 22, which reports on a speech by Sabin before a meeting of the Michigan Medical Society. Other background articles include Huntly Collins, "The Man Who Changed Your Life," *Philadelphia Enquirer,* Aug. 30, 1999, which provided a biography of Maurice Hilleman, and a CNN news report, "Researcher Dies after Contracting Virus from Monkey," Dec. 11, 1997, reporting the death of the Yerkes researcher from monkey B virus.

The text makes reference to these articles: Robert K. Plumb, "New Polio Vaccination Treatment Offers Hope in Curbing Paralysis," *New York Times,* Jan. 27, 1953, p. 1 ("leak" of news about Salk's early vaccine tests), "Closing In on Polio," *Time,* Mar. 29, 1954, pp. 55 ff. ("Why did Mozart compose music?" and doubts by virologists concerning his abilities); Robert Coughlan, "Tracking the Killer," *Life,* Feb. 22, 1954, pp. 121–135 (Salk would assume "personal responsibility" for his vaccine's safety; and "it can't be safer than safe"). For our description of Salk's appearance on Edward R. Murrow's *See It Now* (CBS television, Feb. 22, 1955), we viewed a tape at the CBS studios in New York City, courtesy of CBS Archives.

Congressional Hearings. Between 1955 and 1963, Congress held several hearings on the status of polio vaccines. Our text references the following:

The testimony of NIH Director William Sebrell is taken from "Hearings before House of Representatives Subcommittee on Interstate and Foreign Commerce on Poliomyelitis Vaccination Assistance Legislation," May 25, 1955 (Washington, D.C.: GPO, 1955), pp. 44–50.

The testimony of Jonas Salk is taken from "Hearings before the Committee on Interstate and Foreign Commerce, House of Representatives, Scientific Panel Presentation on Poliomyelitis Vaccine," Jun. 23 and 25, 1955 (Washington, D.C., GPO, 1955), pp. 150 ff.

The testimony of Leonard Hayflick appears in "Hearings before Subcommittee on Executive Reorganization and Government Research of the Committee on Government Operations, United States Senate," Apr. 20, 21; May 3, 4, 1972 (Washington, D.C.: GPO, 1972), pp. 30–38, and Exhibit 4, pp. 119–127. A portion of Hayflick's testimony follows: "[S]electing monkey kidney cultures as a substrate for polio vaccine production . . . in retrospect was a questionable choice. Each monkey is a universe unto itself; therefore the thousands of different kidneys going into polio vaccine production provides the ultimate in an unstandardized, heterogeneous tissue culture medium. The scope of this problem can be appreciated if one realizes that each lot of vaccine may require the sacrifice of several hundreds of monkeys whose kidneys are a veritable storehouse for the most dangerous kinds of contaminating viruses. In fact, monkey kidney is, in this sense, the 'dirtiest' organ known . . ."

Transcripts. Speech by Hilary Koprowski, Jun. 29, 1961 speech to annual meeting of the American Medical Association, as printed in *Journal of the American Medical Association* 178(12):1151–1155 (Dec. 23, 1961). In the speech he said this: "The material used for growing polioviruses in tissue culture consists of living cells obtained from the freshly harvested kidneys from monkeys . . . monkeys are subject to viral infections, which are more often than not dormant in the intact organism but go on a rampage when infected tissues are removed soon after the animal's death and the virus is left to an unmitigable growth in culture . . ."

Stanley Plotkin's reference to debating with Sabin as being "very much like getting into a bear pit" is taken from International Conference on Rubella Immunization, Feb. 18–20, 1969, as printed in *Diseases of Children* 118(1) 372–380 (Aug. 1969).

Other Documents. "United States Public Health Services Technical Report on Salk Poliomyelitis Vaccine," United States Department of Health, Education, and Welfare (officially submitted by Surgeon General Leonard Scheele to President Dwight D. Eisenhower), June 1955, Washington, D.C., Appendix B.

"Arrangements with India concerning Rhesus Monkey," Department of State Bulletin, United States Department of State, Washington D.C., Sep. 5, 1955, p. 398. The need for a continued, uninterrupted supply of monkeys for vaccine production was a foreign policy issue for the United States well into the 1960s. See, for example, "Red Tape Tangles India's Monkeys," *New York Times,* Mar. 2, 1958, which reported that Hindu reverence for the monkey god, Hanuman, made it difficult for the government to allow for the export of monkeys, especially smaller ones. The same article noted that the National Foundation was importing 100,000 monkeys a year for research and vaccine purposes.

Scientific Articles. The papers to which reference is made in this chapter include those listed here. (For the titles of related scientific articles on viral contaminants of vaccines, including monkey B virus, see Appendix A.)

Cox, H. "Viral Vaccines and Human Welfare." *Lancet,* Jul. 4, 1953, 1–5. Cox headed up the Lederle Laboratories live polio vaccine research team. In this article, Cox argued against the use of monkeys for vaccine production. Cox noted one drawback to monkeys was the possibility of vaccine contamination by simian viruses dangerous to humans. He specifically cited monkey B virus and speculated that there were possibly others. Ironically, despite his publicized fears of 1953, Cox and Lederle Laboratories decided in August 1960 to begin production of Sabin's live polio vaccine, which was cultured on monkey kidney tissues. For years afterward, the company struggled with ongoing simian viral contamination of vaccine batches. (See chapters 10 and 20 and the notes for those chapters.)

Hayflick, L. "Human Virus Vaccines: Why Monkey Cells." *Science* 176:813–814 (May 19, 1972).

Hull, R., Minner, J., and Smith, J. "New Viral Agents Recovered from Tissue Cultures of Monkey Kidney Cells." *American Journal of Hygiene* 63:204–215 (1956). This was the first of Hull's seminal articles on the problem of viral contamination of the monkey kidneys used to produce polio vaccine. Interestingly, immediately preceding this article in the same issue of the *American Journal of Hygiene* was one by Salk and his chief collaborator, Julius Youngner. Hull's article details that the simian viruses had first been encountered by manufacturers beginning in January 1954 during preparation of vaccine for the Salk field trials. Given Hull's presentation in April 1955 before the NIH Special Committee (see chapter 5) and this journal article, one must assume that, early on, Salk was well aware of Hull's viral identification work and the monkey virus contamination problems manufacturers were having during production of his vaccine. Moreover, around the same time, Salk received a letter (Dec. 18, 1956) from Leonora V. Brown, M.D., thanking him for the use of material she used for an experiment, which she wrote up for the *American Journal of Hygiene.* (Brown's letter is found in the files of Salk's papers at the Mandeville Special Collections Library at the University of California, San Diego.) Brown, who was aided by a grant from the National Foundation, reported that she found viruses infecting her cell cultures of rabbit cells after she introduced "normal" monkey kidney tissues into them. This was another instance in which the discoverer of the polio vaccine was put on notice that the kidneys used to produce it often contained viral contaminants.

Hull, R., Minner. J., and Mascoli, C. "New Viral Agents Recovered from Tissue Cultures of Monkey Kidney Cells III." *American Journal of Hygiene* 68:31–44 (1958).

Sabin, A., and Wright, A. "Acute, Ascending Myelitis Following a Monkey Bite, with the Isolation of a Virus Capable of Reproducing the Disease." *Journal of Experimental Medicine* 59:115–136 (1934).

"Fatal Cercopithecine Herpes virus 1 (B Virus) Infection Following Mucocutaneous Exposure and Interim Recommendations for Worker Protection." *MMWR Weekly* (publication of the Centers for Disease Control) 47(49):1073–1076, 1083 (Dec. 18, 1998).

National Institutes of Health Fact Sheet on B-Virus Infection, 2001.

CHAPTER 5: TRIUMPH AND DISASTER

General Background. Sources for the information in this chapter included: Blakeslee, *Polio and the Salk Vaccine,* pp. 35, 43; Carter, *Breakthrough,* pp. 216–217, 257–282, 303–313, 329–332; Klein, *Trial by Fury,* introduction, pp. 111–117; Paul, *History of Poliomyelitis,* p. 433; Smith, *Patenting the Sun,* pp. 305, 325–328, 356; Wilson, *Margin of Safety,* pp. 98–99, 103–104, 110, 232; Shorter, *Health Century,* pp. 47–76; and Robert Branyan and Lawrence Larsen, *The Eisenhower Administration, 1953–1961: A Documentary History* (New York: Random House, 1971), pp. 432, 575–586. Branyan and Larsen recount some of the political fallout that resulted from the Eisenhower administration's ineptness when faced with problems related to polio vaccine during the spring and summer of 1955. These were not limited to its response (or lack thereof) to the deaths and paralysis caused by Cutter's vaccine. Another public relations disaster was its lack of planning to ensure there would be an adequate supply of Salk's vaccine once it was licensed. Despite the fanfare accompanying the Salk field trials in 1954 and the universal assumption that, as soon as it was available, every parent and every doctor would want Salk's vaccine, the administration took no steps to ensure an adequate supply or fair distribution when it became available. There was a severe vaccine shortage in 1955 throughout the spring and the early summer, just as the polio season was getting underway. In one memorable gaffe, HEW Secretary Oveta Culp Hobby, while testifying before Congress about her agency's failure to anticipate and ease the 1955 vaccine shortage, stated: "No one could have foreseen the public demand for the vaccine"—a statement that appeared patently absurd given the years of public demand for a vaccine. Afterward, critics began to refer to her as Oveta "Culpable" Hobby.

Personal data on Roderick Murray was obtained from the Public Health Service, including application for employment, Feb. 24, 1949; curriculum vitae; notice of appointment to assistant chief of Laboratory of Biologics Control, Apr. 28, 1953. Information concerning the history of Cutter Laboratories was provided by Bayer Corporation publicity materials (Web site), copyright 2000, and National Register of Historic Places nomination, prepared by John Edward Powell (Twining Laboratories, original site of Cutter Laboratories). Biographical information for Surgeon General Scheele was based on "Former Directors of the National Cancer Institute, Leonard Andrew Scheele, M.D.," a summary posted at National Institutes of Health Web site, history section, and an article by former Surgeon General David Satcher, "The History of the Public Health Service and the Surgeon General's Priorities," *Food and Drug Law Journal* 54:13–18 (1999).

Public Chronology. Throughout the spring and early summer of 1955, Salk's vaccine was in the news on an almost daily basis, usually on the front page. For the last two weeks in April 1955, coverage was decidedly adulatory. For example, the Apr. 13, 1955, *New York Times* devoted most of its front page to the announcement of the success of the 1954 field trials. Inside, five full pages were given over to articles about Salk, the polio vaccine, and the scientific background of the vaccine. Newspapers and periodicals around the country and throughout the world provided similar coverage lauding the vaccine and Salk. (See also "A Hero's Great Discovery Is Put to Work," *Life,* May 2, 1955, p. 105; and "A Quiet Young Man's Magnificent Victory," *Newsweek,* Apr. 25, 1955, pp. 64 ff.) After the Cutter incident broke in late April, the barrage of news about the vaccine continued, though its tone altered dramatically. (See, for example, "Premature and Crippled," *Time,* Jun. 20, 1955, which suggested it had been a mistake to use Salk's vaccine so soon; and "The Dark Polio News," *Newsweek,* Aug. 22, 1955).

The text makes reference to these articles: William Laurence, "Polio Fund Buying Salk Vaccine for 9,000,000 Children, Women," *New York Times,* Oct. 19, 1954, p. 1, and "Polio Gamble," *Time,* Nov. 1, 1954, p. 77 (both articles detailing the National Foundation's 1955 free immunization campaign for schoolchildren); Bess Furman, "Six Vaccine Makers Get U.S. Licenses," *New York Times,* Apr. 13, 1955, p. 1 (how the delay in the Licensing Committee decision caused HEW Secretary Hobby to lose press coverage); "281,853 Eligible for Vaccine Here," *New York Times,* Apr. 13, 1955, p. 1 ff. (Mayor Wagner's comment on Salk's being a City College graduate); "Salk to Be Given Award by Mt. Sinai," *New York Times,* Apr. 13, 1955, p. 21; "Eighteen Senators Back a Civilian Medal," *New York Times,* Apr. 20, 1955, p. 28; and "The President Congratulates Dr. Salk As a 'Benefactor of Mankind," *New York Times,* Apr. 23, 1955, p. 1 (all three articles reporting on awards Salk received); Bess Furman, "One Firm's Vaccine Barred: Six Polio Cases Are Studied," *New York Times,* Apr. 28, 1955, p. 1 (first public news of polio caused by Cutter vaccine, and Scheele's statement of "complete faith" in Salk's vaccine); Morris Kaplan, "All Banned Cutter Vaccine Here Found; 219 Got Shots," *New York Times,* Apr. 29, 1955, p. 1 (Van Riper's assertion that Cutter victims may have had polio before receiving Cutter vaccine); "Possible Link Indicated," *New York Times,* May 5, 1955, p. 21 (Carl Eklund, chief of Public Health Services laboratory links Cutter vaccine to Idaho polio cases); Bess Furman, "U.S. Halts Flow of Polio Vaccine Pending a Study," *New York Times,* May 7, 1955, p. 1 ff. (Scheele's statement that "we have to have a lot more evidence" before Cutter vaccine was found to be the cause of polio; and source that after Apr. 12, 1955, commercial vaccine was cleared for use by NIH in as little as twenty-four hours, based solely on review of manufacturer's protocols); "Polio Shot Delay Is Asked by U.S.; May Last a Month," *New York Times,* May 8, 1955, p. 1 (decision by Scheele to halt all Salk vaccine inoculations); William M. Blair, "Eisenhower Sees Polio's Early End with Salk Shots," *New York Times,* May 12, 1955, p. 1 (Eisenhower states he "couldn't be happier" that his grandson has been inoculated); "Halt!" *Time,* May 16, 1955, p. 57 ("nationwide program of vaccination . . . ground . . . to a sickening halt"); "This Is the Polio Picture," *Newsweek,* Aug. 1, 1955, p. 43, and "The Dark Polio News," *Newsweek,* Aug. 22, 1955, p. 62 (reporting on drop-off in participation in National Foundation's free immunization program and cancelation of program by some states); "Vaccine and the Law," *Time,* May 6, 1957, and "Cutter in Court," *Time,* Jan. 27, 1958, p. 38 (both articles reporting on lawsuits filed against Cutter by vaccinees).

Congressional Hearings and Transcripts of Scientific Meetings. "Transcript of Proceedings, National Institutes of Health, National Microbiological Institute, Ad Hoc Committee on Poliomyelitis Vaccine, Bethesda, Maryland, Apr. 29 and 30, 1955," unpublished document, from the National Institute of Health reference library. Day 1: pp. 1–33, 41–70, 75–88, 92–97, 102–108, 114–126, 131–143, 161–167, 175, 178–180, 206–208, 213–214; Day 2: pp. 20–26, 31–36, 40–42, 45, 52–60, 65, 71, 81–84, 96, 99–100. During these meetings of NIH officials and polio vaccine experts convened to respond to the Cutter incident, William Sebrell, director of the NIH, professed total ignorance of the science underlying vaccinology, stating, "I don't know anything about virology."

 Hearings before the Committee on Interstate and Foreign Commerce, House of Representatives, Poliomyelitis Assistance Legislation, May 25 and 27, 1955 (Washington, D.C.: GPO, 1955), pp. 20–24, 28, 40, 44–50, 54–56, 84–98, 109–111, 122–123,

 Hearings before the Committee on Interstate and Foreign Commerce, House of Representatives, Scientific Panel Presentation on Poliomyelitis Vaccine, Jun. 22 and 23, 1955 (Washington, D.C.: GPO, 1955), pp. 131–133, 137, 140–153, 158–177, 177 ff. This hearing featured testimony from a National Academy of Sciences (NAS) select panel of vaccine experts, including Salk and Sabin, on the causes of the Cutter incident. Several remarkable statements were made. Salk (p. 153 of hearing transcript) once again asserted that his vaccine was tested "to rule out the presence of extraneous viruses that might come from the monkeys from which the material is originally prepared," an assertion that Robert Hull was already disproving. Joseph Smadel (p. 148) claimed that he had little concern about any possible harm from exposure to monkey kidney tissue that might remain in a vaccine. "I personally don't care very much about the idea one way or another of having antibodies to monkey tissue in me. I already have them. I have been immunized with monkey material." His dismissive attitude toward the issue may serve to partially explain his equally dismissive attitude toward Bernice Eddy when, five years later, she concluded there was every reason to be worried about immunization with monkey material. Finally, Dr. Wendell Stanley, a Nobel Prize winner (pp. 171–172), stated that in his opinion as a chemist, formaldehyde would not always kill live viruses if they were present in a vaccine and that tests which reported complete viral inactivation by formaldehyde were simply too insensitive to detect the small amounts of live virus that remained after "inactivation" was supposedly complete. The accuracy of Stanley's assertion was proven six years later when it was discovered SV40 was not always killed by the formaldehyde inactivation process.

 On June 23, 1955, on the second day of the House Interstate Commerce Committee hearings, after the individual NAS scientists had finished testifying, there followed an impromptu vote by the NAS panel on a Sabin proposal to suspend the nation's polio vaccination program immediately. The vote was eight to three in favor of continuation of the program. Of the eight scientists voting to continue with the program, four had a strong connection to Salk or his vaccine. One was Salk's mentor, Thomas Francis, whose analysis of the field trials led to the licensure of the vaccine, another was the National Foundation's Rivers, and two more were NIH officials responsible for licensing the vaccine and ensuring its safety. Only four of the NAS scientists who did not have a direct connection to Salk's vaccine favored its continued use that afternoon. Aside from Salk, three other scientists on the NAS panel abstained from the vote that day, but during their testimony before the

House Subcommittee, all three had made it apparent that they thought Salk's vaccine, as then formulated, was dangerous. If the votes had been changed to exclude those with an obvious tie to Salk's vaccine and include the sentiments of the abstainers, Salk's vaccine probably would have been removed from the market, perhaps permanently. One change that resulted from the public criticisms of Salk's vaccine by the NAS panel members was a reformulation of the vaccine by Salk to replace the "Mahoney" Type I strain of polio he had used in the vaccine with a less virulent Type I strain.

Other Documents. United States Public Health Services Technical Report on Salk Poliomyelitis Vaccine, June 1955, United States Department of Health, Education, and Welfare (officially submitted by Surgeon General Leonard Scheele to President Eisenhower), Washington, D.C., 1955, pp. 1–4, 7–8, 9, 12, 15, 17–28, 34–40, 45, 48–60, 67–80, 88, 90–91, Appendixes A through F.

Scientific Articles. The following paper is specifically referred to in this chapter.

Nathanson, N., and Langmuir, A. "The Cutter Incident: Poliomyelitis Following Vaccination in the United States during the Spring of 1955. I. Background, II. Relationship of Poliomyelitis to Cutter Vaccine, III. Comparison of the Clinical Character of Vaccinated and Contact Cases Occurring after Use of High Rate Lots of Cutter Vaccine." *American Journal of Hygiene* 78: 16–81 (1963).

CHAPTER 6: DOES ANYONE KNOW WHAT'S IN THIS VACCINE?

Interviews. Maurice Hilleman, May 24, 2002; Ruth Kirschstein, Jul. 23, 1999. Also, interviews of Bernice Eddy, Dec. 4, 1986, Alan Rabson, Dec. 5, 1986, and Maurice Hilleman, Feb. 6, 1987, conducted by Edward Shorter (available from the History of Medicine Division of the National Library of Medicine, Washington, D.C.).

General Background. American Men of Science: A Biographical Directory, 10th ed. (Tempe, Ariz.: Jacques Cattell Press, 1961), p. 3775, and C. Moritz, ed., *Current Biography Yearbook* (New York: H. W. Wilson, 1963), pp. 390–391, provided general biographical information in this chapter. Additional information was obtained from the National Academy of Sciences and Nobel Foundation Web sites for biographies of NAS members and Nobel laureates.

   Insight into Smadel's character and accomplishments was provided in several scientific articles by Joseph Smadel, including: Pond, W., and Smadel, J., "Neurotropic Viral Diseases in the Far East during the Korean War," and Smadel, J., Goodner, K., and Woodward, T., "The Control of Plague" (both presented on Apr. 28, 1954, to the Course on Recent Advances in Medicine and Surgery, Army Medical Service Graduate School, Walter Reed Army Medical Center, Washington, D.C.). Further biographical information about Smadel was obtained from T. E. Woodward, "Joseph E. Smadel, 1907–1963," *Transactions of the Association of American Physicians* 77 (1974): 29–32. Two *New York Times* articles, "Biochemist and Virologist Win Lasker Awards," Oct. 17, 1962, p. 31, and Morris Kaplan, "Sarnoff Predicts Electronic Aid to Treat Sick Astronauts Aloft," Nov. 17, 1962, p. 41, provided background on Joseph Smadel and on his discovery that typhus could be treated with antibiotics. An article from *The Bulletin: University of Maryland Medical Alumni Organization* (spring 2000) described the career of Peyton Rous. Biographies of Bernice Eddy and Sarah Stewart were obtained from Elizabeth Moot O'Hern, *Profiles of Pioneer Women Scientists* (Washington, D.C: Acropolis Books, 1985), pp. 151–169, and E. Shorter, *The Health Century,* pp. 55–57, 196–199. Eddy's "Obituary of Sarah Elizabeth Stewart," *Journal of the National Cancer Institute* 59(4): 1039–1040 (1977), provided biographical information about her and about Stewart. George Klein, "The Strange Road to the Tumor-Specific Transplantation Antigens (TSTAs)," *Cancer Immunity* 1:6 (Apr. 9, 2001) recounts Macfarlane Burnet's dismissal of the role of viruses in tumors as "nonsense."

Eddy's personnel file, obtained from the U.S. Public Health Service, included: an application for employment (1964); curricula vitae (two) from same time period; "Experience and Qualifications Statement," Apr. 27, 1959; letter of nomination for Bernice Eddy, Oct. 31, 1931. The file also contains a letter from W. H. Sebrell, director, NIH, to Eddy, Oct. 26, 1953, with an official notice of her receipt of the NIH's Superior Accomplishment Award for her work on gamma globulin.

Huntly Collins, "The Man Who Changed Your Life: Maurice Hilleman's Vaccines Prevent Millions of Deaths Every Year," *Philadelphia Enquirer,* Aug. 30, 1999, provided further general background for this chapter.

Public Chronology. The text makes reference to and drew upon "Cornering the Killers," *Time,* Jul. 27, 1959, pp. 52 ff. (a cover story on cancer research at the NCI that prominently featured Eddy and Stewart).

Congressional Hearings. The testimony of Joseph Smadel appears in *Hearings before the Committee on Interstate and Foreign Commerce, House of Representatives, Scientific Panel Presentation on Poliomyelitis Vaccine,* Jun. 22 and 23, 1955 (Washington, D.C.: GPO, 1955), pp. 139–143, 145, 148–149, pp. 177 ff.

Other Documents. A complete listing of the memos between Bernice Eddy, Joe Smadel, and Roderick Murray and other documents relative to events as told in this chapter is found in Appendix B, "Bernice Eddy's Correspondence with Joseph Smadel and Roderick Murray."

Scientific Articles. The following papers were referred to in this chapter.

Eddy, B. E., et al. "Tumors Induced in Hamsters by Injection of Rhesus Monkey Kidney Cell Extracts." *Proceedings of the Society for Experimental Biology and Medicine* 107: 191–197 (1961). This was the report of Eddy's original work demonstrating that some unknown "substance"—which she suspected was a virus and later proved to be SV40—caused cancer in hamsters.

Eddy, B. E. "Simian Virus 40 (SV-40): An Oncogenic Virus." In J. Homburger, ed., *Progress in Experimental Tumor Research* (Cambridge, Mass.: Karger, 1964), 4:1–26.

CHAPTER 7: THE VIRUS DISCOVERED

Interviews. Anthony Girardi, Dec. 26, 2001; Maurice Hilleman, May 3 and 24, 2002; Ruth Kirschstein, Jul. 23, 1999; Ben Sweet, Jul. 23, 1999, and Oct. 26, 2001; Anthony Morris, Nov. 19, 2001. Also, interviews of Ruth Kirschstein, Nov. 21, 1986, Alan Rabson, Dec. 5, 1986, and Maurice Hilleman, Feb. 6, 1987, conducted by Edward Shorter (available from the History of Medicine Division of the National Library of Medicine, Washington, D.C.).

General Background. For this chapter Carter, *Breakthrough,* pp. 357–393 (contains reference to the "polio gap"), and Wilson, *Margin of Safety,* pp. 190–234, were sources for some of the events portrayed, particularly details of the race to develop an oral vaccine and Sabin's field trials in the USSR.

E. J. McMurray, ed., *Notable Twentieth-Century Scientists* (New York: Gale Research,

International Thompson Publishing, 1995), pp. 532–533, provided biographical information on Renato Dulbecco. "Three Share in Nobel Prize for Work on Viruses and Genes," *New York Times,* Oct. 17, 1975, p. 12), provided additional information about Dulbecco.

Maurice Hilleman published three autobiographical sketches in scientific journals: "Six Decades of Vaccine Development—A Personal History," *Nature Medicine* 4:507–514 (Supplement) (May 1998); "Discovery of Simian Virus 40 (SV40) and Its Relationship to Poliomyelitis Vaccine," *Developments in Biological Standards* 94: 183–190 (1998); and "Personal Historical Chronicle of Six Decades of Basic and Applied Research in Virology, Immunology, and Vaccinology," *Immunological Reviews* 170:7–27 (1999); these provided biographical background on Hilleman and the discovery of SV40 at Merck. Huntly Collins's "The Man Who Changed Your Life," previously cited, was also useful in this chapter.

As one of our sources concerning events that occurred at Merck at the time SV40 was discovered, we used a portion of Louis Galambos (with Jane Eliot Sewell), *Networks of Innovation: Vaccine Development at Merck, Sharp and Dohme and Mulford, 1895–1995,* (Cambridge: Cambridge University Press 1995), pp. 79–83. This history of Merck includes the actions and reactions of Hilleman and Merck officials to the discovery of SV40 and cites internal company documents.

Public Chronology. The text makes reference to or relied upon these specific articles: "New Anti-Polio Vaccine Being Tried on Convicts," *New York Times,* Jan. 18, 1955, p. 13; Robert Plumb, "Polio Immunity for Life Sought," *New York Times,* May 4, 1955, p. 1; "New Live Virus Polio Vaccine, Taken Orally, to Get Mass Test," *New York Times,* Oct. 7, 1956, p. 1; "Tests by Russians Back Live Vaccine," *New York Times,* Jun. 25, 1959, p. 31; Leonard Wallace Robbins, William Laurence, "Polio Vaccine Composed of Live Virus Is Reported to Be Successful," *New York Times,* Jun. 28, 1959, p. E9; "Polio Progress," *Time,* Jul. 13, 1959, p. 34; "Polio's March," *Time,* Aug. 3, 1959, p. 49; "Now the Sabin Vaccine for Polio," *New York Times Magazine,* Sept. 6, 1959, p. 10 ff.; "Better than Salk?" *Newsweek,* Jan. 18, 1960, p. 50; "400 Babies Given Live Polio Virus," *New York Times,* Feb. 9, 1960, p. 33; Too Many Polio Vaccines?" *Time,* May. 2, 1960, p. 68; "Live-Virus Vaccine," *Time,* Jul. 4, 1960, p. 57; "Get Ready . . . Get Set . . ." *Newsweek,* Aug. 29, 1960, p. 83; "O.K. for Live Vaccine," *Time,* Sep. 5, 1960, p. 41; "Third Polio Vaccine Licensed by U.S.," *New York Times,* Mar. 28, 1962, p. 1.

Congressional Hearings and Transcripts of Scientific Meetings. The following are referred to in the text:

Second International Conference on Live Poliomyelitis Vaccines, Washington, D.C., Jun. 6–10, 1960, Scientific Publication No. 50, Pan American Health Organization (PAHO), pp. 66, 79–89. This transcript is the source for Hilleman's remarks at the PAHO conference, as well as at other events that took place at the conference

Department of Health, Education, and Welfare, National Institutes of Health, Division of Biologic Standards: Conference on Production and Testing and Requirements for Live Poliovirus Vaccine, Aug. 18–19, 1960, Day 1: pp. 16–22, 89–92, 94, 101; Day 2: pp. 44–54, 58, 60–69, 97–112. It was during this conference that Sabin successfully argued for essentially weakening the safety standards for detection of contaminating viruses in vaccines. The transcript, however, makes it clear that Sabin's view was not shared by all the virologists in attendance at the conference. Joseph Melnick, for one, presciently argued that a fourteen-day observation period for the presence of SV40 (or other possible viral contaminants) in oral vaccine was too short and urged the regulations be strengthened to require at least a twenty-eight-day observation period.

Hearings before a Subcommittee of the Committee on Interstate and Foreign Commerce of

the House of Representatives: Developments with Respect to the Manufacture of Live Poliovirus Vaccine and Results of Utilization of Killed Virus Polio Vaccine, Mar. 16 and 17, 1961 (Washington, D.C.: GPO, 1961), pp. 4, 21, 43, 48 ff., 187, 189 ff., 263, Appendices I and K. This hearing was our source for some of the specific information concerning Sabin's vaccine, his field trials, and polio incidence in the United States at the time. Appendix K contains the final DBS regulations for oral vaccine production, and includes the change Sabin had sought in the 1960 draft. The final regulations required only the exclusion of those extraneous agents that were both "demonstrable" and "viable."

Other Documents. A complete listing of all the documents relative to the events described in this chapter, including the memos between Bernice Eddy, Joseph Smadel, and Roderick Murray, will be found in Appendix B, "Correspondence between Bernice Eddy, Joseph Smadel, and Roderick Murray."

Scientific Articles. The following papers are specifically referred to in this chapter.

Eddy, B. E., et al. "Identification of the Oncogenic Substance in Rhesus Monkey Kidney Cell Cultures as Simian Virus 40." *Virology* 17:65–75 (1962). This was the study that Eddy began in early 1961, even as she was being pressured by Smadel and Murray to drop her research. This study proved that the "substance" from her rhesus kidney cell cultures that caused cancer in her hamsters was indeed SV40.

Koprowski, H. "Tin Anniversary of the Development of Live Virus Vaccine." *JAMA* 174 (5): 972–976, Oct. 22, 1960. This article is the reprint of Koprowski's remarks at the June 1960 PAHO conference, in which he suggested the discovery of SV40 in polio vaccine was not a cause for alarm. At the time, Koprowski and almost every other vaccinologist assumed that until there were some obvious disease caused by the simian viruses, which they all knew were contaminating live vaccines, there was simply no basis for concern.

Melnick, J. L., and Stinebaugh, S. "Excretion of SV40 Virus (Papova Virus Group) after Ingestion as a Contaminant of Oral Poliovaccine." *Proceedings of the Society for Experimental Biology and Medicine* 109:965–968 (April 1962). Melnick's paper was the first to definitively contradict Sabin's assertions during the early 1960s that SV40 in his vaccine did not multiply in vaccines. Melnick found that infants fed SV40-contaminated Sabin vaccine excreted SV40 in their stools for four to five weeks.

Morris, J. A., et al. "Clinical and Serological Responses in Volunteers Given Vacuolating Virus (OSV40) by Respiratory Route." *Proceedings of the Society for Experimental Biology and Medicine* 108:613–616 (1961). Morris presented the preliminary results of this study during the August 1960 NIH conference on regulations for oral polio vaccine. It was the first proof that SV40 was infectious for humans.

Sweet, B., and Hilleman, M. R. "The Vacuolating Virus, SV40." *Proceedings of the Society for Experimental Biology and Medicine* 105:420–427 (1960). This is the first announcement to the scientific world of the discovery of SV40.

CHAPTER 8: "WE WERE SCARED OF SV40"

Interviews. Maurice Hilleman, May 3 and 24, 2002; Anthony Girardi, Dec. 26, 2001; Ben Sweet, Jul. 23, 1999. Also, interview with Maurice Hilleman, Feb. 6, 1987, conducted by Edward Shorter (available from the History of Medicine Division of the National Library of Medicine, Washington, D.C.).

General Background. One of the sources for a description of events at Merck and Co., here as in chapter 7, is a book chapter from Louis Galambos, with Jane Eliot Sewell, *Networks of Innovation,* pp. 79–83, which cites company documents prepared at the time of the discovery of SV40. "Viruses and Cancer, A Public Lecture in Conversational Style," delivered by Albert Sabin, May 28, 1965, at the University of Newcastle upon Tyne, provided background on Sabin's views at the time on the role of viruses in cancer. A transcript of the "Conference on Cell Cultures for Virus Vaccine Production" (Nov. 6–7, 1967, National Institutes of Health, Bethesda, Md., *NCI Monographs,* No. 29, p. 475), is the source of Francis's public rebuke of Maurice Hilleman's fear of SV40.

Public Chronology. "A Note on Polio," *Saturday Review,* Apr. 1, 1961 as reprinted in *Hearings before a Subcommittee of the Committee on Interstate and Foreign Commerce of the House of Representatives: A Bill to Assist States and Communities to Carry Out Intensive Vaccination Programs . . . ,* May 15 and 16, 1962 (Washington, D.C.: GPO, 1962), p. 115. This article was the source for the details on the Cuban polio epidemic and the Kennedy administration's response.

Congressional Hearings. The following hearings are referred to in the text. *Hearings before the Committee on Interstate and Foreign Commerce, House of Representatives, Scientific Panel Presentation on Poliomyelitis Vaccine,* Jun. 22 and 23, 1955 (Washington, D.C.: GPO, 1955), p. 174, contains Tom Rivers's reference to formaldehyde as an "old friend." ("Many things will kill or destroy or inactivate viruses, but at the same time the products are no good as vaccines because they will not immunize you. So formalin is an old friend among vaccine makers and, so far as I know, it is the best substance yet found.")

Further notes about hearings cited in this chapter will be found in Appendix C, "Documents and Articles Concerning the Discovery of SV40 in Salk's and Sabin's Vaccines."

Other Documents. A complete list of all Technical Committee documents with notes will be found in Appendix C. In addition, the text refers specifically to this document:

28 Federal Regulations 2109, effective Mar. 5, 1963, Part 73-Biological Products, "Safety Standards; Poliomyelitis Vaccine, Adenovirus Vaccine." Formal adoption of change in polio vaccine manufacturing process to require testing for SV40 prior to inactivation of the virus pools.

Scientific Articles. The articles that were referenced in the text in this chapter are included in Appendix C.

CHAPTER 9: "THE WORST THING IN THE WORLD"

Interviews. Joseph Fraumeni, Jul. 23, 1999; Anthony Girardi, Dec. 26, 2001; Leonard Hayflick, Dec. 16, 2001; Maurice Hilleman, May 3 and 24, 2002; Hilary Koprowski, Jan. 10 and Feb. 15, 2002; Ben Sweet, Oct. 26, 2001; Julius Youngner, May 29, 2002; also, interview with Maurice Hilleman, Feb. 6, 1987, by Edward Shorter (available from the History of Medicine Division of the National Library of Medicine).

General Background. As with the previous two chapters, the events at Merck and Co. are derived from Louis Galambos, with Jane Eliot Sewell, *Networks of Innovation,* which cites company documents prepared at the time of the discovery of SV40, pp. 79–83. A Channel 4 (British television) documentary from the program *Dispatches,* "Monkey Business" (Impact for Investigative Media Production, 1997), provided additional background for this chapter.

Curricula vitae of Hilary Koprowski and Anthony Girardi also provided background for this chapter.

Robert Hull's *The Simian Viruses* (Vienna: Springer-Verlag, 1968), pp. 44–50, provided the details on Hull's own SV40 experiments with hamsters and was the source of Hull's quote that Eddy's paper "was disturbing to many people."

Edward Hooper, *The River* (Boston: Little, Brown, 1999), pp. 324–326, provided background on SV40 contamination of the Soviet Union's Sabin vaccines. Hooper relates an interview he conducted with Victor Grachev, a Russian scientist who was an official in the Biologicals Unit of the World Health Organization at the time of the Hooper interview. During the Sabin vaccine trials in the Soviet Union in the late 1950s and early 1960s, Grachev worked closely with Sabin's chief Russian collaborator, Chumakov. According to Hooper, Grachev said that after the discovery of SV40, the Soviets, realizing that the oral vaccine they were using was almost certainly contaminated, tested the scientists and technicians involved in oral polio vaccine production. Both groups, Grachev said, showed that they had been infected with very high amounts of SV40. (Hooper interviewed Grachev in 1993. In 2000, the authors attempted to contact Grachev. He had left his WHO position by this time and did not respond to inquiries directed to him at the forwarding address provided by WHO.) One of the mysteries about SV40 is the extent to which there was any follow-up by the Soviet Union of the tens of millions of people exposed to SV40 during the Sabin field trials. A review of the scientific literature reveals nothing published on the subject in English. An East German researcher, Erhard Geissler, did attempt to review whether East Germans believed to have received SV40-contaminated Sabin vaccine were more likely to develop tumors than those who were vaccinated with presumably SV40-free vaccine. (We discuss this later, in chapter 15.)

Public Chronology. The following articles were specifically referenced in the text: "Two Companies Halt Salk-Shot Output," (AP story) *New York Times,* Jul. 26, 1961, p. 33; "The Great Polio Vaccine Cancer Cover-up," *National Enquirer,* Aug. 6–12, 1961, cover, pp. 14 ff.; Earl Ubell, "Polio Vaccine Virus Puzzles Scientists," *Chicago Sun-Times,* Apr. 16, 1962 (as reprinted in "Hearings before a Subcommittee of the Committee on Interstate and Foreign Commerce of the House of Representatives: A Bill to Assist States . . ." May 15 and 16, 1962, previously cited, p. 116); "Viruses and Cancer (Cont'd)," *Time,* Apr. 27, 1962, p. 68 (Eddy's SV40 study is highlighted in the article); "New Studies Link Cancer and Virus," *New York Times,* Aug. 10, 1962, p. 21; Walter Sullivan, "Cancer-Like Role of a Virus Traced, *New York Times,* May 25, 1963, p. 52; "Public Reassured on Polio Shots; U.S. Finds No Links to Cancers," Aug. 30, 1963, "Cancer Research Implicates Virus," *New York Times,* Apr. 19, 1964, p. 51.

Scientific Meetings. The text of H. Koprowski's June 29, 1961, speech before the annual meeting of the American Medical Association is reported in H. Koprowski, "Live Poliomyelitis Virus Vaccine: Present Status and Future Problems," *JAMA* 78 (12):1151–1155 (Dec. 23, 1961).

Further notes about additional hearings cited in this chapter will be found in Appendix C, "Documents and Articles Concerning the Discovery of SV40 in Salk's and Sabin's Vaccines."

Other Documents. Documents referenced in the text, along with notes, are found in Appendix C.

Scientific Articles. The text makes specific reference to these articles:

Farwell, J. R., et al. "Effect of SV40 Virus-Contaminated Polio Vaccine on the Incidence and Type of CNS Neoplasms in Children: A Population-based Study." *Trans-American Neurological Association* 104:261–264 (1979). This study surveyed the Connecticut Tumor Registry and identified all children born between 1956 and 1962 who developed central nervous system tumors. Surveying ninety of these, the authors concluded there was a statistically significant correlation between *in utero* exposure to SV40 (mothers who were vaccinated with Salk vaccines during pregnancy) and development of two specific types of brain tumors during childhood: medulloblastomas and glioblastomas. A follow-up study by Farwell ("Medulloblastoma in Childhood: An Epidemiological Study," *Journal of Neurosurgery* 61:657–664, 1984) reached the same conclusion. Both of these epidemiological studies contradict the 1963 Fraumeni study's conclusions (see Fraumeni, Ederer, and Miller, below).

Fraumeni, J., Ederer, F., and Miller, R. "An Evaluation of the Carcinogenicty of Simian Virus 40 in Man." *JAMA* 185:713–718 (Aug. 31, 1963). This was the "negative" epidemiological survey by the National Cancer Institute that effectively discouraged further research into whether SV40 could cause cancer in humans.

Gerber, P. "An Infectious Deoxyribonucleic Acid Derived from Vacuolating Virus (SV40)." *Virology* 16:96–97 (1962).

Gerber, P. "Patterns of Antibodies to SV40 in Children Following the Last Booster with Inactivated Poliomyelitis Vaccines." *Proceedings of the Society of Experimental Biology and Medicine* 125:1284–1287 (1967). Gerber's study included a group of seventeen children who initially had developed antibodies to SV40 within a month of injection with Salk vaccine. Eleven of the seventeen still had detectable antibodies to SV40 three years later. This suggested to Gerber "a continual antigenic stimulus to maintain the constant levels of antibodies to SV40" in these children—in other words, a fairly constant and high level of live SV40 circulating in the bodies of these eleven vaccinees for several years after inoculation with contaminated vaccine.

Gerber, P., and Kirschstein, R. L. "SV40-induced Ependymomas in Newborn Hamsters." *Virology* 18:582–588 (1962).

Girardi, A. J., et al. "Tumors Induced in Hamsters Inoculated with Vacuolating Virus, SV40." Abstract presented at 53rd Annual Meeting of the American Association for Cancer Research and published in *Proceedings of the American Association for Cancer Research* 3(4):323 (1962). This paper, presented by Girardi in April 1962, prompted Koprowski to recruit him away from Merck. It was during this presentation that Girardi announced that SV40 could transform human cells.

Heinonen, O. P., et al. "Immunization During Pregnancy Against Poliomyelitis and Influenza in Relation to Childhood Malignancy." *International Journal of Epidemiology* 2(3): 229–235 (1973). This survey of 50,897 American pregnancies found a statistically significant increase in childhood brain tumors among offspring of mothers vaccinated with Salk vaccine while pregnant; it contradicts the 1963 Fraumeni study's conclusions.

Innis, M. D. "Oncogenesis and Poliomyelitis Vaccine." *Nature* 219:972–973 (1968). This survey of 810 hospitalized Australian children found significant association between immunization with Salk vaccine and childhood cancer; it contradicts the 1963 Fraumeni study's conclusions.

Jensen, F., et al. "Autologous and Homologous Implantation of Human Cells Transformed *in vitro* by Simian Virus 40." *Journal of the National Cancer Institute* 32(4): 917–932 (1964). This Wistar experiment showed SV40-transformed cells induced precancerous lumps when injected into humans. The protocol for this experiment is one that today would be regarded as unethical. (The volunteers were all terminally ill cancer patients.)

Koprowski, H., et al. "Transformation of Cultures of Human Tissue Infected with Simian Virus SV40." *Journal of Cellular Comparative Physiology* 59:281–292 (1962).

Morris, T. A., et al. "Occurrence of SV40 Neoplastic and Antigenic Information in Vaccine Strains of Adenovirus Type 3." *Proceedings of the Society of Experimental Biology and Medicine* 122:679–684 (1966). This study showed it was impossible to separate SV40 DNA from adenovirus DNA in experimental adenovirus vaccines. Eddy is a coauthor of this study. Ironically, Smadel had appointed Morris to take Eddy's position in July 1961 after he had forced her out because of her alarms about SV40. However, Morris soon became convinced the dangers of SV40 were real. After he left the NIH in the 1970s, Morris was one of the few scientists willing to publicly state that he did not believe it had been demonstrated that SV40 was harmless.

Rabson, A., et al. "Papillary Ependymomas Produced in *Rattus (Mastomys) Natalenis* Inoculated with Vacuolating Virus (SV40)." *Journal of the National Cancer Institute* 29(4): 765–787 (Oct. 1962).

Rabson, A., and Kirschstein. R. L. "Induction of Malignancy *in vitro* in Newborn Hamster Kidney Tissue Infected with Simian Vacuolating Virus (SV40)." *Proceedings of the Society of Experimental Biology and Medicine* 111:323–328 (1962).

Rabson, A., et al. "Simian Vacuolating Virus (SV40) Infection in Cell Cultures Derived from Adult Human Thyroid Tissue." *Journal of the National Cancer Institute* 29:1123–1145 (1962).

Shein, H., and Enders, J. F. "Transformation Induced by Simian Virus 40 in Human Renal Cell Cultures." *Proceedings of the National Academy of Sciences* 48:1164–1172 (1962).

CHAPTER 10: WHY NOT A SAFER VACCINE?

Interviews. Tony Girardi, Dec. 26, 2001; Leonard Hayflick, Dec. 7 and 16, 2001; Maurice Hilleman, May 3 and 24, 2002; Hilary Koprowski, Jan. 10 and Feb. 15, 2002; Arnold J. Levine, Sep. 8, 1999; Stanley Plotkin, Dec. 31, 2001; Robert Stevenson, Jan. 31, 2002.

General Background. In addition to the interviews cited above, the authors relied on several sources for information concerning Leonard Hayflick's career. Several were writings authored by Hayflick himself, including his curriculum vitae; L. Hayflick, *How and Why We Age* (New York: Ballentine Books, 1994), pp. 111–136; L. Hayflick, "The Coming of Age of WI-38," *Advances in Cell Culture* 3:303–316 (1984); L. Hayflick, S. Plotkin, and R. E. Stevenson, "History of Acceptance of Human Diploid Cell Strains As Substrates for Human Virus Vaccine Manufacture," *Developments in Biological Standards* 68:9–17 (1987); L. Hayflick, "Evolving Scientific and Regulatory Perspectives on Cell Substrates for Vaccine Development," *Developments in Biologicals* 106:5–24 (2001). Other sources for information concerning Hayflick's career were: W. Shay and W. E. Wright, "Hayflick, His Limit, and Cellular Aging," *Nature Reviews* 1:72–76 (October 2000); S. Rattan, "'Just a Fellow Who Did His Job . . .': An Interview with Leonard Hayflick," *Biogerontology* 1:79–87 (2000); Lisa Chippendale, "Dr. Leonard Hayflick, Towards a Fountain of Health, Not Youth," *Infoaging News,* produced by the American Federation of Aging Research, posted on AFAR Web site (2001); and H. F. L. Mark, "Leonard Hayflick, an Interview," *Journal of the Association of Genetic Technologists* 27(1):11–15 (2001).

J. A. Witkowski, "Cell Aging in Vitro: A Historical Perspective" (review article), *Experimental Gerontology* 22:231–248 (1987), provided further background on the history of WI-38. Examples of Hayflick's proselytizing on behalf of WI-38 in the scientific press are numerous. Some examples include: L. Hayflick, "Cultured Cells and Human Virus Vaccines," in M. Saunders and E. H. Lennete, eds., *Applied Virology* (compilation of papers presented at the First Annual Symposium on Applied Virology, December 1964, Boca Raton, Fla.); L. Hayflick, "An Analysis of the Potential Oncogenicity of Human Virus Vaccine Cell Substrates," *Proceedings of the Symposium on Oncogenicity of Virus Vaccines* (paper presented at Yugoslav Academy of Sciences and Arts, Zagreb, 1968); and L. Hayflick, "Human Virus Vaccines: Why Monkey Cells?" *Science* 176:813–814 (May 19, 1972).

Background on the Marburg virus outbreak came from G. A. Martini and R. Siegert, eds., *Marburg Virus Disease* (New York: Springer-Verlag, 1971), preface and pp. 97, 161–165. A Centers for Disease Control fact sheet posted on the CDC Web site, "Disease Information, Viral Hemorrhagic Fever," was a source for information concerning filoviruses. H. D. Klenck and W. Slenczka, "Marburg and Ebola Viruses," in *Encyclopedia of Virology Plus,* ed. R. Webster and A. Granoff (New York: Academic Press, 1995), was a further source on Marburg virus.

A three-part news series by reporter Nicholas Wade in *Science* ("Division of Biologics Standards: Scientific Management Questions," Mar. 3, 1972, pp. 966–970; "DBS: Officials Confused Over Powers," Mar. 10, 1972, p. 1089; "Division of Biologic Standards: The Boat That Never Rocked," Mar. 17, 1972, pp. 1223–1230) detailing criticisms of the DBS within the scientific community, and specifically of Roderick Murray's leadership of the agency, was also used as a source for this chapter. Wade notes that the DBS under Murray acquired a reputation as unwilling to change because "of the importance attached to presenting an unruffled surface to the public" rather than take decisive action when confronted with problems with vaccines. Wade writes that DBS critics (including Hayflick) listed the biggest shortcomings under Murray's tenure as its failure to recall contaminated SV40 stocks in 1961 and its decade-long delay in licensure of WI-38 as cell substrate for vaccine production.

The widespread use of SV40 as a biological and cancer research tool is well documented throughout the scientific literature. A Medline search, for example, lists tens of thousands of experiments in which the virus has been employed or studied. This chapter refers to some of the breakthrough discoveries about viruses and cancer made by studies of and with SV40. These are summarized in a review: A. F. Gazdar, J. S. Butel, and M. Carbone, "SV40 and Human Tumors: Myth, Association or Causality," *Nature Reviews/Cancer* 2:957–964 (2002). The use of the virus in early biotechnology experiments is also described by E. Shorter in *The Health Century* (New York: Doubleday, 1987). Some examples of early studies on SV40's cancer-causing capabilities include: G. Todaro, H. Green, and M. R. Swift, "Susceptibility of Human Diploid Fibroblast Strains to Transformation by SV40 Virus," *Science* 153:1252–1254 (September 1966); S. A. Aaronson and G. Todaro, "Human Diploid Cell Transformation by DNA Extracted from the Tumor Virus SV40," *Science* 166:390–391 (Oct. 7, 1969); G. T. Diamondopolous, "Leukemia, Lymphoma, and Osteosarcoma Induced in the Syrian Golden Hamster by Simian Virus 40," *Science* 176:173–175 (Apr. 14, 1972); and C. M. Croce, et al., "Genetics of Cell Transformation by Simian Virus 40," *Cold Springs Harbor Symposia on Quantitative Biology* 39 Pt. 1:335–343 (1975). Arnold J. Levine's role in discovering p53 in part through experiments using SV40 was described to the authors by Levine personally. His biographical sketch at the Rockefeller University Web site also references his 1979 discovery.

A Channel 4 (British television) documentary from the program *Dispatches,* "Monkey Business" (Impact for Investigative Media Production, 1997), was the source of the J. Anthony Morris quote that appears at the end of the chapter. A review, S. Kops, "Oral Polio Vaccine and Human Cancer: A Reassessment of SV40 as a Contaminant Based upon Legal Documents," *Anticancer Research* 20:4745–4750 (2000), was a source for Lederle's market share for oral polio vaccine, as was a May 24, 1996, letter to the authors from Audrey Ashby, Director of Public Relations, Wyeth-Ayerst Laboratories.

Public Chronology. In this chapter, the following were referenced to or relied upon: Harold Schmeck, "Human Cell Role Given in Vaccines," *New York Times,* Nov. 12, 1966, p. 36 (another example of Hayflick promoting the use of WI-38 over monkey cells); Jane Brody, "Cell Bank Is Suggested for Every Person at Birth," *New York Times,* Apr. 3, 1967, p. 25 (further Hayflick promotion efforts); "No Yellow Fever in Frankfurt," *New York Times,* Aug. 25, 1967, p. 5 (Marburg outbreak); "Two More Germans Die from Monkey Virus," *New York Times,* Sep. 5, 1967, p. 2 (Marburg outbreak); Richard Lyons, "Diseases Carried by Pets Increase," *New York Times,* Oct. 26, 1967, p. 24 (Marburg outbreak); Jane Brody, *New York Times,* "Vaccine Produced in Human Cells," Mar. 8, 1972, p. 18 (Diplovax announcement); Harold Schmeck, "Report Allays Fears on Carcinogenic Vaccine," *New York Times,* Dec. 27, 1981, p. 22 (news account of epidemiological survey of oral vaccine recipients). See also Scientific Articles, notes to this chapter.

Scientific Meetings. The following are referenced in the text.

Conference on Cell Cultures for Virus Vaccine Production, Nov. 6–7, 1967, National Institutes of Health, Bethesda, Md., *NCI Monographs,* No. 29, pp. 83–89 (Hayflick presentation); pp. 474–475 (Murray quote); pp. 495–497 (Perkins quote). During this conference, held just months after the Marburg outbreak, there was a clear division among the participants about the continued wisdom of using monkey tissues when there was a "clean" cloned cell alternative (WI-38) for vaccine production. One supporter of Hayflick's noted that given the obvious risks associated with monkey kidneys, a switch to WI-38 or a like cell substrate would surely occur in the near future. In the future, he predicted, vaccinologists would look back on the crude production then in use and "remember this period as the end of the 'horse-and-buggy' days of vaccines." He optimistically (or perhaps naively) believed that such a time would only be five years later. In fact, more than three decades would pass before American polio vaccines were no longer produced on monkey kidney tissues.

International Conference of Rubella Immunization, National Institutes of Health, Feb. 18–20, 1969, reported in *Diseases of Children* 118: Jul.-Aug. 1969, pp. 372–381. This portion of the conference turned into a debate between Stanley Plotkin, who was already using WI-38 to produce vaccines at Wistar, and Sabin, who opposed the substrate's use. Plotkin told us that he (and many other scientists attending the conference) found Sabin's arguments against WI-38 to be irrational to the point that they were almost ludicrous. Sabin's position on WI-38, Plotkin says, was like "the creationist argument. It was impossible to prove it didn't happen." (At the 1969 conference, Plotkin referred to Sabin's position as "theology.") Irrational or not, Sabin's public aspersions of WI-38 clearly hampered the substrate's acceptance. As Plotkin and others remember the events, Sabin's opposition was "influential" in delaying licensure of WI-38 in the United States.

Documents. The following were referenced or relied upon for this chapter:

John Rose, Lederle Laboratories, to Dr. P. J. Vasington, Mr. S. A. Flaum, Mr. R. Oppenheimer, Lederle Laboratories, memo, Nov. 15, 1971. Subject: "The commercial importance of seeing that the Academy Committee . . ." This memo details Lederle plans to lobby the American Academy of Pediatrics (AAP) against recommending use of Diplovax (Pfizer's polio vaccine produced on WI-38 cells).

John Rose, Lederle Laboratories, to Dr. P. J. Vasington, Mr. S. A. Flaum, Mr. R. Oppenheimer, Lederle Laboratories, memo, Nov. 16, 1971. This memo details further Lederle plans to lobby AAP.

Dr. P. J. Vasington, Lederle Laboratories, to Mr. R. A. Schoellhorn, Mr. J. H. Rose, G. J. Sella, Jr., Dr. W. M. Sweeney, Mr. D. Wallis, Lederle Laboratories, memo, Nov. 29, 1971. Details Lederle conversation with Dr. Sam Katz of AAP, who, according to memo, states that AAP will not recommend Pfizer vaccine, but merely let doctors know an alternative to Lederle's is available.

R. J. Vallancourt, Lederle Laboratories, to Mr. G. P. Bywater, Dr. F. E. Fontane, Mr. H. Perlmutter, Dr. P. J. Vasington, memo, Jan. 31, 1972. "The tissue which was used to develop what is now designated WI-38 was considered to have oncogenic potential in the beginning . . ." The memo also suggests that Lederle begin development of a simian diploid cell line (monkey version of WI-38) for vaccine production and move away from fresh monkey tissues—a change the company did not undertake.

"Corrections: Some Facts about Oral Polio Vaccine," Lederle Laboratories press release, Apr. 12, 1972. "Several recent public communications concerning the use of a human diploid cell substrate have given the erroneous impression that vaccine prepared from such cells is safer than presently-available oral polio vaccine."

"The New Era: Diplovax, Poliovirus Vaccine, Live, Oral Trivalent (Sabin Strains) the First U.S. Licensed Polio Vaccine Prepared in Human Diploid Cells. A Cell Substrate That Is Free of Known Adventitious Agents," promotional brochure prepared by Pfizer Laboratories, Pfizer, Inc., New York, N.Y. (courtesy of Leonard Hayflick).

"Q/A—Diplovax/Orimune," Lederle informational packet, 1972.

P. Stessel to Mr. R. A. Schoellhorn, Mr. H. Perlmutter, Mr. J. Rose, Mr. G. J. Sella, Jr., Dr. R. J. Vallancourt, Dr. P. J. Vasington, Lederle Laboratories, memo, Apr. 26, 1972. "Received a call from the DBS Information Office informing us that they have finally decided to take strong action in opposing Dr. Hayflick's allegations concerning monkey tissue vaccines . . ."

R. J. Vallancourt, Lederle Laboratories, to Mr. D. Carroll, Mr. H. Perlmutter, Lederle Laboratories, memo, Aug. 4, 1972. Memo, while discussing contamination problems Lederle was having with African green monkeys during vaccine production (see notes, chapter 20), suggests the federal government will not sanction the company because "unless and until Pfizer's Diplovax is in abundant supply, the [DBS] cannot risk Lederle being off the market."

Stanley Harrison, M.D., American Academy of Pediatrics, to Julius J. Weinberg, M.D., Nov. 29, 1972. This letter notes that AAP believes Diplovax "has some slight advantage over the old [Lederle] vaccine because of the elimination of the risk of transmission of simian virus." The letter also notes that Pfizer's vaccine is not readily available in the United States and that this fact "should not deter the practitioner from going ahead and continuing to use the vaccine produced on monkey kidney cells."

Scientific Articles. The following scientific articles were specifically referenced in the text:

Hayflick, L., and Moorhead, P. S. "Serial Cultivation of Human Diploid Cell Strains." *Experimental Cell Research* 25:585–621 (1961).

Hayflick, L., Plotkin, S. A., Norton, T. W., and Koprowski, H. "Preparation of Poliovirus Vaccines on Human Fetal Diploid Cell Strains." *American Journal of Hygiene* 75(2):240–258 (Mar. 1962).

Hayflick, L., Jacobs, P., and Perkins, F. "A Procedure for the Standardization of Tissue Culture Media," *Nature* 204:146–147 (1964).

Mortimer, E.A., et al. "Long-Term Follow-up of Persons Inadvertently Inoculated with SV40 as Neonates." *New England Journal of Medicine* 305(25):1517–1518 (Dec. 17, 1981). Study of 925 oral vaccine recipients referred to in text. This study and an earlier one published in 1970 (Fraumeni, J. F., Stark, C. R., and Lepow, M. L., "Simian Virus 40 in Polio Vaccine: Follow-up of Newborn Recipients," *Science* 167:59–60 [1970]) followed one small cohort of infants. All were born at one Cleveland hospital in 1959 and 1960 and fed SV40-contaminated Sabin (experimental) oral polio vaccine shortly after birth.

This is the only group of American oral polio vaccinees ever included in an epidemiological study on the effects of SV40 ingested orally. It has always been assumed that there was no exposure to SV40 in the United States from Sabin vaccines other than the small numbers of individuals who ingested Sabin's pre-1961 experimental doses. (We discuss the validity of this assumption further in chapter 20.)

Scherp, H. W., et al. "Continuously Cultured Tissue Cells and Viral Vaccines: Report of a Committee on Tissue Culture Viruses and Vaccines" (presented to Dr. James A Shannon, Director, National Institutes of Health). *Science* 139:15–20 (Jan. 4, 1963). Report of the NIH committee, which included Smadel and concluded that despite viral contamination problems with monkey kidneys, including SV40, there was no reason to switch to cloned cells for viral vaccine production.

CHAPTER 11: EVERYONE KNOWS SV40 DOESN'T CAUSE CANCER

Interviews. Carmine Carbone, M.D., Aug. 13, 2001; Italietta Carbone, Aug. 10, 2001; Michele Carbone, Sep. 25, 1996, Oct. 19, 1997, Nov. 1, 1997, Mar. 18, 1999, Jul. 17, 18, 1999, Feb. 12, 2000, Apr. 13, 2002; Elizabeth Chambers Carbone, Nov. 14, 2002; Arthur S. Levine, Jan. 3, 2003; Andrew Lewis, Dec. 12, 2002; Harvey Pass, Dec. 24, 1998, Jul. 16, 1999; Sep. 6, 2002; Antonio Procopio, Apr. 20, 2002; Paola Rizzo, Feb. 3, 2003; Janet Rowley, Jun. 8, 1999; Giovanna Tosato, Jul. 28, 2003.

General Background. Beginning with this chapter and throughout the second half of the book, a number of concepts relating to molecular biology and virology are discussed. In addition to our interviews and visits to the laboratories of scientists whom we describe in this book, we relied upon a number of sources to better understand and explain these concepts in layman's terms.

For an appreciation of the modern technology used in molecular biological experiments, we used as a source Joseph Sambrook and David Russell, *Molecular Cloning: A Laboratory Manual,* 3d ed. (New York: Cold Spring Harbor Laboratory Press, 2001), particularly chapter 8, "In Vitro Amplification of DNA by PCR," which includes a history of the discovery of the technique as well as details about actual technique; chapter 6, "Preparation and Analysis of Eukaryotic Genomic DNA," chapter 11, "Preparation of DNA Libraries and Gene Identification," and chapter 12, "DNA Sequencing." Benjamin Lewin, *Genes VII* (Oxford: Oxford University Press, 2000), provided an overview on DNA, RNA, genes, etc., in particular, parts 1, 4, and 6. James Watson, Michal Gilman, Jan Witkowski, Mark Zoller, *Recombinant DNA* (New York: Scientific American Books, 1992), was an additional source for descriptions of some of the molecular biological techniques and basic molecular genetics described throughout. David Spector, Robert Goldman, Leslie Leinwand, *Cell: A Laboratory Manual* (New York: Cold Spring Harbor Laboratory Press, 1998), particularly chapter 15, "Apoptosis Assays," chapter 98, "Preparation of Cells and Tissues for Fluorescence Microscopy," and chapter 102, "Introduction to Immunofluorescence Microscopy," provided us with further insight into experimental molecular biology.

For an overview of general concepts in virology we relied on Wesley A. Volk, David C. Benjamin, Robert J. Kadner, J. Thomas Parsons, *Essentials of Medical Microbiology,* 4th ed. (Philadelphia: Lippincott, 1991), particularly pp. 35–130. B. N. Fields, D. M. Knipe, et al., eds., *Fundamental Virology,* 2d ed. (New York: Raven Press, 1991), provided additional background on viruses, including polyoma viruses (chapter 29) and herpes viruses (chapter 33). Ironically, the third edition of Field's text provides a typical example of the accepted wisdom about SV40 that was imparted to most medical students after SV40's discovery in the early 1960s:

> SV40 is one of several viruses identified by screening for viruses in the secondary rhesus monkey kidney cell cultures used for production of poliovirus vaccines. Although SV40 does not produce a visible cytopathic effect in rhesus monkey kidney cells, Sweet and Hilleman noted a pronounced cytopathic effect when African green monkey kidney cells were infected with extracts from the rhesus kidney cell cultures. Soon afterward, it was discovered that tumors were induced by injection of SV40 into newborn hamsters. Many lots of poliovirus vaccine were contaminated with SV40, raising concern that this virus, which is oncogenic for newborn hamsters, might also be oncogenic for humans. *Fortunately, studies to follow the incidence of cancer in those inadvertently inoculated with SV40 during poliovirus vaccination indicate that SV40 does not cause tumors in humans.* (p. 1998, italics added.)

Frank Netter, *Atlas of Human Anatomy* (Summit, N.J.: CIBA-GEIGY, 1989), and B. M. Pugh, ed., *Stedman's Medical Dictionary,* 27th ed. (Philadelphia: Lippincott, 2000), were two sources used throughout for basics in medicine and anatomy. H. zur Hausen, "Viral Oncogenesis," in J. Parsonnet, ed., *Microbes and Malignancy: Infections As a Cause of Human Cancer* (New York: Oxford University Press, 1999), pp. 107–130, was a source on the role that some viruses, including SV40, play in tumor induction.

A useful overview on mesothelioma and SV40 is contained in Giuseppe Barbanti-Brodano et al., eds, *DNA Tumor Viruses: Oncogenic Mechanisms* (New York: Plenum Press, 1995), chapter 5, "Association of Simian Virus 40 with Rodent and Human Mesotheliomas," by Michele Carbone, Paola Rizzo, and Harvey Pass. Some of the statistics relating to the incidence of the disease, causality, etc., can be found in these scientific articles: B. T. Mossman and D. C. Gruenert, "SV40, Growth Factors, and Mesothelioma: Another Piece of the Puzzle," *American Journal of Respiratory Cellular Molecular Biology* 26:167–170, (2002); A. Powers and M. Carbone, "The Role of Environmental Carcinogens, Viruses, and Genetic Predisposition in the Pathogenesis of Mesothelioma," *Cancer Biology and Therapy* 1(4):350–355 (2002); and B. Price, "Analysis of Current Trends in United States Mesothelioma Incidence," *American Journal of Epidemiology* 145:211–18 (1997), as well as Carbone's first SV40 and human cancer study (see notes to chapter 12).

Basic information about the structure of the National Institutes of Health was derived from a visit to the NIH campus on July 23, 1999, and from the NIH Web site: www.nih.gov/about/. Statistics about the budget of the National Cancer Institute can be obtained at http://plan.cancer.gov/budget/2004.htm and from the NCI Press Office. Statements about Michele Carbone's background and youth were based on conversations with members of his family and friends in Calabria in August 2001. We also used Carbone's curriculum vitae as well as documentation of his various academic degrees and honors as additional background sources.

The stories that Carbone heard about NIH scientists contracting cancer after working with SV40 were true and were taken seriously by the health bureaucracy. In 1991, Alan Rabson, deputy director of the National Cancer Institute, and four other scientists sent the following letter to the *New England Journal of Medicine*. It was published in the Feb. 14, 1991 issue, p. 491:

> During the past five years, two established molecular virologists, each of whom had performed many experiments with the SV40 virus and SV40-transformed cells, died of cancer. One had a malignant lymphoma . . . and the other had an adenocarcinoma of the colon. Since both were relatively young, the question of whether SV40 played

a role in causing these tumors was raised. As a result, the National Cancer Institute formed a committee to investigate this possibility.

The letter further explains that studies undertaken on tumor samples from the two researchers could find no SV40 DNA and that therefore "we conclude that there is no evidence that SV40 played a part in causing these tumors."

Scientific Articles. The papers to which reference is made in this chapter include those listed here. (For a more complete list of scientific articles concerning SV40 and human tumors, see Appendix A.)

Cicala, C., Pompetti, F., and Carbone, M. "Simian Virus 40 Induces Mesotheliomas in Hamsters." *American Journal of Pathology* 68:3138–3144 (1993). This paper contains Carbone's first hamster experiment showing that SV40 induces mesothelioma.

Fraumeni, J. F., Stark, C. R., and Lepow, E. A. "Simian Virus 40 in Polio Vaccine: Follow-up of Newborn Recipients." *Science* 167:59–60 (January 1970). A study of 925 recipients of SV40-contaminated oral vaccine. One of the two studies Fraumeni performed on one small cohort of oral vaccinees. (See notes to chapter 9.)

Haddada, H., Sogn, J. A., Coligan, J. E., Carbone, M., Dixon, K., Levine, A. S, et al. "Viral Gene Inhibition of Class I Major Histocompatibility Antigen Expression: Not a General Mechanism Governing the Tumorogenicity of Adenovirus Type 2, Adenovirus Type 12, and Simian Virus 40 Transformed Syrian Hamster Cells." *Journal of Virology* 62:2755–2761 (1988). This paper is an example of the type of work that Carbone was doing with Lewis and Levine before he began his own SV40 experiments.

Lewis, A. M. "Experience with SV40 and Adenovirus-SV40 Hybrids," in A. Hellman, M. N. Oxman, and R. Pollack., eds., *Biohazards in Biological Research* (New York: Cold Spring Harbor Laboratory Press, 1973), pp. 96–113. Lewis's original review of SV40 exposure and early research on the virus, which he gave to Carbone to read.

Mortimer, E. A., et al. "Long-Term Follow-up of Persons Inadvertently Inoculated with SV40 as Neonates." *New England Journal of Medicine* 305 (25):1517–1518 (Dec. 17, 1981). Further follow-up on 925 recipients of SV40-contaminated oral vaccine. (See Fraumeni et al., 1970, above.)

CHAPTER 12: "A WILD-ASSED IDEA"

Interviews. Daniel J. Bergsagel, Feb. 25, 2002; Janet Butel, Aug. 2, 1999, Mar. 15, 2002; Michele Carbone, Sep. 25, 1996, Jul. 15–16, 1999, Apr. 13, 2002, Apr. 22, 2002; Stanley Kops, Aug. 15, 2003; John Lednicky, Oct. 23 and 25, 2002, Arthur R. Levine, Jan. 3, 2003; Harvey Pass, Dec. 24, 1998, Sep. 6, 2002, Sep. 24, 2002; Dec. 28, 2002; Antonio Procopio, Apr. 20, 2001; Paola Rizzo, Feb. 3, 2003; Umberto Saffiotti, Apr. 20, 2001; Diane Solomon, Sep. 17, 2003.

General Background. The story of how Bernice Eddy and Sarah Stewart collaborated in discovering mouse polyoma virus is contained in O'Hern, *Profiles of Pioneer Women Scientists,* pp. 151–169. A letter from Michele Carbone to the authors, Sep. 24, 1996, provided a detailed account of his decision to seek advice from renowned experimental pathologist Harold Stewart, who is now deceased. A description of Dana Farber including its role as a research and "reference" hospital can be found at http://www.dfci.harvard.edu/. Background on the discovery of JC and BK virus and tumors with which they are associated can be found in S. D. Gardner et al., "New Human Papovavirus (B.K.) Isolated from Urine after

Renal Transplantation," *Lancet* 1:1253–7 (1971); B. L. Padgett et al., "Cultivation of Papova-Like Virus from Human Brain with Progressive Multifocal Leukoencephalopathy," *Lancet* 1:1257–60 (1971); L. P. Weiner et al., "Isolation of Virus Related to SV40 from Patients with Progressive Multifocal Leukoencephalopathy," *New England Journal of Medicine* 286(8): 385–389 (Feb. 24, 1972); and K. Shah and N. Nathanson, "Human Exposure to SV40: Review and Comment," *American Journal of Epidemiology* 103:(1):1–12 (1976).

The text references that only a "handful" of viruses have been directly associated with human cancer. The International Agency for the Research on Cancer (IARC), an arm of the World Health Organization, has designated six human viruses as "probably carcinogenic to humans." These are: human papillomavirus, types 16 and 18 (cervical and anogenital cancers), hepatitis B virus (liver cancer), hepatitis C virus (liver cancer), Epstein-Barr virus (Burkitt's lymphoma, Hodgkin's disease, uncommon types of non-Hodgkin's lymphoma, nasopharyngeal carcinoma, sinonasal angiocentric T-cell lymphoma), human T-cell lymphotropic virus type I (adult T-cell leukemia/lymphoma), and human immunodeficiency virus type I (non-Hodgkin's lymphoma, Kaposi's sarcoma). It had not formally evaluated the association of SV40 with human cancer, as of the preparation of this manuscript. For more information on IARC, visit the IARC website at: www.iarc.fr/.

Scientific Meetings. Simian Virus 40 (SV40): A Possible Human Polyomavirus, U.S. Department of Health and Human Services—CBER, NCI, NICHD, NIP, NVPO—Workshop, Jan. 27–28, 1997, transcript pp. 36–45, contains an account by Robert Garcea of aspects of pediatric oncology resident Daniel J. Bergsagel's serendipitous discovery of SV40, although our account of that discovery relies primarily on our interview with Bergsagel.

Scientific Articles. The papers to which reference is made in this chapter include those listed here. (For a more complete list of scientific articles concerning SV40 and human tumors, see Appendix A, "Association of SV40 with Human Disease.")

Bergsagel, D. J., Finegold, M. J., Butel, J. S., Kupsky, W. J., and Garcea, R. L. "DNA Sequences Similar to Those of Simian Virus 40 in Ependymomas and Choroid Plexus Tumors of Childhood." *New England Journal of Medicine* 326:988–993 (1992). This is the paper in which Bergsagel and Garcea announced their findings and which Carbone used to convince Arthur Levine to allow him to look for SV40 in human mesotheliomas.
Carbone, M., Pass, H. I., Rizzo, P., Marinetti, M., Di Muzio, M., Mew, et al. "Simian Virus 40-Like DNA Sequences in Human Pleural Mesothelioma." *Oncogene* 9:1781–1790 (1994). Carbone's first paper on SV40 in human mesotheliomas.

CHAPTER 13: DON'T INFLAME THE PUBLIC

Interviews. Michele Carbone, Apr. 13, 2002, Apr. 22, 2002, Apr. 23, 2002; Joseph Fraumeni, Jul. 23, 1999, Jun. 4, 2003; James Goedert, Jul. 23, 1999; Richard Klausner, director, National Cancer Institute, Jul. 23, 1999; Arthur R. Levine, Jan. 3, 2003; Brooke Mossman, Mar. 17, 1999, Aug. 6, 1999; Harvey Pass, Sep. 6, 2002, Sep. 24, 2002, Dec. 28, 2002; Alan Rabson, Jul. 16, 1999; Joan Schwartz, assistant director, NIH National Office of Intramural Research, Aug. 15, 2002; Keerti Shah, Aug. 22, 1996, Jul. 18, 2003; Howard Strickler, Jul. 21, 1999.

General Background. For our description of "Research Fellow Program" we relied upon an NIH Web site: www.od.nih.gov.oir.sourcebook/prof-desig/research-fellow.htm. Background on the Division of Cancer Epidemiology and Genetics (DCEG) and the Viral Epidemiology Branch (VEB) was obtained from a review of DCEG and VEB publicity materials, a review of studies published by DCEG and VEB researchers, and interviews with DCEG director Joseph Fraumeni. The meeting between Michele Carbone, Harvey Pass, James Goedert, Howard Strickler, and Keerti Shah in Harvey Pass's office was based on the recollections of Carbone and Pass, the only two participants who would discuss the meeting with us.

We relied on the curricula vitae of several of the participants in this chapter as a source for statements about careers, credentials, publication history, and positions within the NIH at the time, among them Harvey Pass, James Goedert, Michele Carbone, Arthur S. Levine, and Howard Strickler. Concerning Strickler's curriculum vitae, there is some controversy. For most of his career at the National Cancer Institute, Strickler referred to himself as a "senior clinical investigator," using that title on letters and memos he wrote. The official title of the highest position Strickler held while at the NCI was actually that of "staff fellow," a designation given to postdoctoral researchers by the NIH, which indicates a status that the agency describes as "junior-level scientist." (Postdoctoral fellows have completed an advanced science degree such as an M.D. or Ph.D. and are continuing their training in order to gain biomedical research experience. At the time of the events portrayed in this chapter, Carbone also was a staff fellow.) According to Joan Schwartz, assistant director of the NIH's Office of Intramural Research (which supervises collaborative research among NIH branches), "senior clinical investigator" is a nonexistent status within the NIH. (The NIH designation of "senior investigator," which closely resembles the term Strickler used to describe himself, is a designation reserved for scientists who have achieved tenure at the NIH.) Schwartz said that, in her view, Strickler's use of such a title was inappropriate and comparable to the practice of an assistant professor at a university referring to him- or herself as a full professor. Goedert states that Strickler used the title with Goedert's permission, but that Strickler's position was that of a staff fellow.

Public Chronology. The following articles were referenced in the text: Phyllida Brown, "Mystery Virus Linked to Asbestos Cancer," *New Scientist,* May 1994, and P. Brown, "U.S. Acts Fast to Unravel Viral Link to Cancer," *New Scientist,* July 1994.

Documents. The following, obtained through the Freedom of Information Act and other sources, were either referred to or relied upon in writing the text of this chapter:

Michele Carbone to Harvey Pass and Antonio Procopio, Apr. 25, 1994. On his conversation with Arthur S. Levine. (". . . told me that he is worried that the media might exaggerate our findings and alarm the public.")

Michele Carbone to Arthur S. Levine, Apr. 26, 1994. On his conversation about SV40 research. Carbone is seeking "written NIH guidelines not subject to personal interpretations."

Michele Carbone to Arthur S. Levine, May 2, 1994. Concerning his conversation about SV40 research.

James Goedert and Howard Strickler to Harvey Pass and Michele Carbone, memo, Jun. 6, 1994, through Viral Epidemiology Branch Chief, Dr. Blattner. On possible collaboration. This memo summarizes the original experiment that Goedert and Strickler proposed to Pass and Carbone in the spring of 1994. Concerning the experiment's protocol, the memo states that:

> You [Carbone and Pass] would be responsible for providing sera from your mesothelioma cases. . . . We [Goedert and Strickler] would be responsible for identifying appropriate control subjects and providing the control sera, for recoding your sera (to assure blinding . . .) and for compiling the results and performing preliminary analyses. Final

analysis and manuscript preparation would be primarily our responsibility. . . . Authorship. . . . [I]t seems to us that we would put in the major effort and that we (or our designees) should be first and last authors. . . .

Howard Strickler and James Goedert to Keerti Shah and Richard Daniel at Johns Hopkins and William Travis and Miriam Flemming at Armed Forces Institute of Pathology, memo, Aug. 8, 1994. This memo describes the protocol that was used in the Strickler-Shah-Goedert negative mesothelioma study. It notes that DNA recovery will be performed by Shah and another Johns Hopkins scientist. Strickler and Goedert "will be responsible for sectioning of tumor specimens and coordination between laboratories."

Chief, AIDS and Cancer Section (James Goedert), to Associate Director for Epidemiology and Biostatistics, Division of Cancer Epidemiology, NCI, memo, May 15, 1995. On study results obtained by Keerti Shah. Goedert writes that he hopes to "summarize the negative . . . data . . . for publication, perhaps as a letter to the *New England Journal of Medicine.*"

Michele Carbone to Howard Strickler, M.D., MPH, Viral Epidemiology Branch, Jun. 18, 1996. Carbone notes that Strickler and Shah have both told him that neither Strickler, Shah, nor Goedert performed the PCR tests on the fifty mesothelioma samples, which all tested negative. Carbone also states that Shah has told him that one mesothelioma sample tested positive at least once during the experiment, but this result was not included in the published paper.

CDC Fact Sheet, "Questions and Answers on Simian Virus 40 (SV40) and Polio Vaccine," 1999. "Recently some researchers have identified SV40 virus in the cells of some rare human cancers . . . .However other scientists have not been able to validate these findings. . . ." (From: http://www.cdc.gov/nip/vaccinesafety/sideeffects/SV40.htm.) The same 1999 CDC fact sheet also implies that all the studies that had found SV40 had failed to use "standardized procedures necessary to confirm new discoveries." At the time the CDC published this fact sheet, most researchers who had isolated SV40 from human tumors had also used standard confirmatory methodologies to ensure the accuracy of their work, including negative controls. A Carbone experiment that found SV40 in bone tumors (see chapter 14) and another mesothelioma study (see chapter 18) both included the exchange of masked samples between labs, another procedure that provides strong confirmation of the accuracy of any positive results. The CDC, however, failed to note this; nor did it mention any of the positive studies in its reference section attached to its fact sheet. Instead, the only study it listed concerning SV40 and human tumors was the negative one by Strickler, Shah, and Goedert. In a 2001 update of its fact sheet, the CDC termed the results of studies on the association of SV40 with human tumors as "inconsistent." The reference section for this 2001 CDC fact sheet, again, failed to list any of the several dozen studies detecting SV40 in human tumors that had been published by this time.

Scientific Articles. Papers to which reference is made in the text are listed here. (For a more complete list of scientific articles concerning SV40 and human tumors see Appendix A.)

Shah, K. V., and Southwick, C. H. "Prevalence of Antibodies to Certain Viruses in Sera of Free-Living Rhesus and Captive Monkeys." *Indian Journal of Medical Research* 53:488–500 (1965). One of Shah's early studies on whether human populations living near wild rhesus monkeys had SV40 antibodies.

Shah, K. V., Goverdhen, M. K,, and Ozer, H. L. "Neutralizing Antibodies to SV40 in Human Sera from South India: Search for Additional Hosts of SV40." *American Journal of Epidemiology* 93:291–297 (1971). Another such Shah study.

Shah, K., and Nathanson, N. "Human Exposure to SV40: Review and Comment." *American Journal of Epidemiology* 103 (1):1–12 (1976). This is the 1976 survey in which Shah included the estimate that 98 million Americans had been exposed to SV40-contaminated vaccines between 1955 and 1963.

Strickler, H. D., Goedert, J. J., Fleming, M., Travis, W.D, Williams, A. E., Rabkin, C. S., et al. "Simian Virus 40 and Pleural Mesothelioma in Humans." *Cancer Epidemiology, Biomarkers and Prevention* 5:473–475 (1996). The Strickler-Shah-Goedert negative mesothelioma study. Between 1994 and 2001, more than fifty new studies were published documenting SV40's presence or cancer-causing activity in relation to human tumors. During the same period only Strickler's and two other studies were published that failed to find the virus in human tumors.

CHAPTER 14: A CALL TO TURN ASIDE THE DOGMA

Interviews. Janet Butel, Aug. 21, 1996, Aug. 2, 1999, Mar. 15, 2002, Jul. 8, 2003; Michele Carbone, Apr. 22, 2002, Apr. 23, 2002; Anthony Girardi, Dec. 26, 2001; John Lednicky, Feb. 3, 2001, Feb. 26, 2002, May 17, 2002, Nov. 21, 2002, Jan. 25, 2003; Joseph Melnick, Apr. 17, 1996; Harvey Pass, Dec. 24, 1998, Apr. 24, 2002, Oct. 28, 2002; Leslie Weiner, Feb. 5, 2002.

General Background. Background on Joseph Melnick came from a variety of sources, including interviews listed above (Girardi and Butel, in particular), Klein's *Trial by Fury,* press accounts from the early years of the development of the polio vaccine, a biographical sketch of Melnick posted at the Baylor College of Medicine Web site, and an obituary of Melnick in the newsletter of the American Society for Tropical Medicine and Hygiene, Jun. 14, 2001. The curriculum vitae of Janet Butel, as well as materials from the Baylor College of Medicine (College of Medicine catalog and "Baylor College of Medicine, 1900–2000; 100 Years of Service"), provided additional background on Butel and Melnick. Some of the background on Butel's hometown came from the Kansas State Library. Butel's reputation as an internationally respected SV40 researcher is borne out by her publication record and her frequent appearances at scientific conferences. The authors' interviews with researchers on both sides of the question of the association with SV40 with human tumors also evidenced the respect with which Butel is regarded. The American Cancer Society, "Cancer Reference Information," is a source for some of the scientific information concerning human papilloma virus (HPV) that appears in this chapter. Some of the history concerning the various strains of SV40 and their sequencing was provided by John Lednicky and also by R. A. Stewart, J. A. Lednicky, and J. S. Butel, "Sequence Analyses of Human Tumor-Associated SV40 DNAs and SV40 Viral Isolates from Monkeys and Humans," *Journal of NeuroVirology* 3:1–12 (1997). See also Robert Hull, *The Simian Viruses,* pp. 44 ff., in this regard. Background information concerning Genbank was obtained from the NIH Web site on the genetic sequence database.

Public Chronology. "Simian Virus 40 DNA Found in U.S. Children," Reuters, Aug. 26, 1999.

Documents. The following documents were referred to or relied on in this chapter.

James Goedert, Chief AIDS and Cancer Section, to Associate Director for Epidemiology and Biostatistics, Division of Cancer Epidemiology, NCI, memo, May 15, 1995. ". . . Dr. Lewis had already learned of our negative results from Dr. Shah. . . ."

Scientific Articles. In this chapter, the following papers were cited. (For a more complete list of scientific articles concerning SV40 and human tumors see Appendix A.)

Bergsagel, D. J., Finegold, M. J., Butel, J. S., Kupsky, W. J., and Garcea, R. L. "DNA Sequences Similar to Those of Simian Virus 40 in Ependymomas and Choroid Plexus Tumors of Childhood." *New England Journal of Medicine* 326:988–993 (1992).

Brandner, G., et al. "Isolation of Simian Virus 40 from a Newborn Child." *Journal of Clinical Microbiology* 5(2):250–252 (1977). SV40 found by researchers from Freiburg, Germany, in child of Spanish guest worker who died in infancy.

Bravo, M. P., et al. "Antibodies to Simian Vacuolating Virus 40 in Bladder Cancer Patients." *Urologica Internationalis* 42(6):427–430 (1987). SV40 found in bladder cancers.

Bravo, M. P., and Del Rey-Calero, J. "Association between the Occurrence of Antibodies to Simian Vacuolating Virus and Bladder Cancer in Male Smokers." *Neoplasma* 35(3): 285–288 (1988). SV40 found in bladder cancers.

Butel, J. S., Arrington, A. S., Wong, C., Lednicky, J. A., and Finegold, M. J. "Molecular Evidence of Simian Virus 40 Infections in Children." *Journal of Infectious Diseases* 180: 884–887 (1999). Butel serological study.

Butel, J. S., Jafar, S., Wong, C., Arrington, A. S., Opekun, A. R., Finegold, M. J., et al. "Evidence of SV40 Infections in Hospitalized Children." *Human Pathology* 30:496 (1999). Butel serological study.

Carbone, M., et al. "SV40-like Sequences in Human Bone Tumors." *Oncogene* 13: 527–535 (1996). Blinded, four-laboratory study that found SV40 in bone tumors.

de Fromentel, C., et al. "Epithelial HBL-100 Cell Line Derived from Milk of an Apparently Healthy Woman Harbours SV40 Genetic Information." *Experimental Cell Research* 160: 83–94 (1985). SV40 found in breast milk.

Ibelgaufts, H., and Jones, K. W. "Papovavirus-Related RNA Sequences in Human Neurogenic Tumors." *Acta Neuropathologica* 56:118–122 (1982). Eleven of 23 brain tumors screened (48 percent) contained SV40.

Krieg, P., et al. "Episomal Simian Virus 40 Genomes in Human Brain Tumors." *Proceedings of the National Academy of Sciences, USA* 78:6446–6450 (1981). Eight of 35 brain tumors (22 percent) screened contained SV40.

Lednicky, J. A., Garcea, R. L., Bergsagel, D. J., and Butel, J. S. "Natural Simian Virus 40 Strains are Present in Human Choroid Plexus and Ependymoma Tumors." *Virology* 212: 710–717 (1995). Experiment confirming true SV40 was isolated in original Bergsagel study.

Martini, F., et al. "SV40 Early Region and Large T-Antigen in Human Brain Tumors, Peripheral Blood Cells and Sperm Fluids from Healthy Individuals." *Cancer Research* 56: 4820–4825 (1996). Italian study that found SV40 in sperm and circulating blood of otherwise healthy individuals.

Meinke, W., Goldstein, D. A., and Smith, R. A. "Simian Virus 40-Related DNA Sequences in a Human Brain Tumor." *Neurology* 29:1590–4 (1979). SV40 found in glioblastomas.

Melnick, J. L., and Stinebaugh, S. "Excretion of SV-40 Virus (Papova Virus Group) after Ingestion as a Contaminant of Oral Poliovaccine." *Proceedings of the Society for Experimental Biology and Medicine* 109:965–968 (1962). Melnick found that infants fed SV40-contaminated Sabin vaccine excreted SV40 in their stools for four to five weeks.

Scherneck, S., et al. "Isolation of a SV40-Like Papovavirus from a Human Glioblastoma." *International Journal of Cancer* 24:523–531 (1979). SV40 found in brain cancers.

Soriano, F., Shelburne, C. E., and Gokeen, M. "Simian Virus 40 in a Human Cancer." *Nature* 249:421–424 (1974). SV40 found in malignant melanoma of a retired plumber.

Stoian, M., et al. "Investigations on the Presence of Papovavirus in Certain Forms of Human

Cancer. Note 2. Brain Tumors." *Revue Roumaine de Médicine—Virologie* 35:127–132 (1984). SV40 found in brain tumors.

Tabuchi, K., et al. "Screening of Human Brain Tumors for SV40-Related T Antigen." *International Journal of Cancer* 21:12–17 (1978). SV40 found in brain cancers (ependymomas).

Weiner, L. P., et al. "Isolation of Virus Related to SV40 from Patients with Progressive Multifocal Leukoencephalopathy." *New England Journal of Medicine* 286 (8):385–389 (Feb. 24, 1972). First published report finding evidence of SV40 in humans. Examples of studies since Weiner's that have linked SV40 to PML include S. Scherneck et al., "Isolation of a SV-40-Like Virus from a Patient with Progressive Multifocal Leukoencephalopathy," *Acta Virology* 25(4):191–198 (July 1981); J. D. Martin, "Regulatory sequences of SV40 Variants Isolated from Patients with Progressive Multifocal Leukoencephalopathy," *Virus Research* 14(1):85–94 (1989); and M. Tognon et al., "SV40 as a Potential Causative Agent of Human Neurological Disorders in AIDS Patients," *Journal of Medical Microbiology (Virology)* 50(2):165–172 (2001).

Weiss, A. F., et al. "Simian Virus 40-Related Antigens in Three Human Meningiomas with Defined Chromosome Loss." *Proceedings of the National Academy of Sciences, USA* 72(2): 609–613 (1975). SV40 found in brain cancers.

CHAPTER 15: ON THE SCIENTIFIC MAP

Interviews. Michele Carbone, Jan. 26, 1997, Jan. 27, 1997, Feb. 5, 2003; Susan Fisher, Jul. 16, 1999; Antonio Giordano, Jan. 26, 1997; Bharat Jasani, Aug. 27, 1999, Mar. 5, 2001; Allen Gibbs, Mar. 5, 2001; John Lednicky, Feb. 23, 2001, Nov. 26, 2002, Jan. 24–25, 2003; Luciano Mutti, Jan. 26, 1997, Jun. 12, 1999, Jun. 14, 2000; Apr. 21, 2001; Antonio Procopio, Jan. 26, 1997, Apr. 21, 2001; Paola Rizzo, Jul. 17, 1999; Mauro Tognon, Jan. 26, 1997, Apr. 21, 2001.

General Background. The description of the events at the 1997 NIH SV40 conference was based on the authors' observations while attending the conference, with the aid of the full transcript. (See notes this chapter.) The authors obtained copies of the agendas and schedules that had been prepared prior to the conference (documents dated Jan. 13, 1997: "Tentative Agenda, Simian Virus 40 (SV40): A Possible Human Polyoma Virus, CBER-NCI-NICHD-NCID-NI-NVPO Workshop, Jan. 27 and 28, 1997"). Concerning the conference organizers, in addition to the preconference and conference materials that the authors reviewed, of interest is the "official" NIH account of the conference, "Simian Virus (SV40): A Possible Human Polyomavirus," Jan. 27 and 28, 1997, published in *Developments in Biological Standards* (Basel: Karger, 1998). The cover page for the volume lists three workshop organizers: Andrew Lewis, James Goedert, and Howard Strickler. We also interviewed two government officials who wish to remain anonymous concerning the events in this chapter; they provided additional background information concerning the NIH workshop. The 2002 Institute of Medicine meeting in Washington, D.C., described in this chapter was attended by the authors. The authors engaged in an e-mail correspondence with Michael Innis during 2002 and early 2003; the correspondence provided background material for this chapter. We also relied on the curriculum vitae of Susan Fisher for background for this chapter.

Public Chronology. The following were specifically referenced in the text: Lauren Neergard, "Monkey Virus Stirs Debate," Associated Press, Jan. 29, 1997; Joe Palca, "Polio Infected," National Public Radio, Jan. 29, 1997; "No Link Found between Contaminated Polio Vaccine and Cancer" media advisory from the American Medical Association, Jan. 27, 1998 (announcing publication of Strickler epidemiology study); "No Cancers Tied to '50s Polio Vaccine," Associated Press, Jan. 28, 1998 (news story on Strickler epidemiology study).

Scientific Meetings. The following meetings are referred to in the text:

U.S. Department of Health and Human Services—CBER, NCI, NICHD, NIP, NVPO—Simian Virus 40 (SV40): A Possible Human Polyomavirus. Workshop, Jan. 27 and 28, 1997. The entire transcript has been used as a source. In particular, Day 1: pp. 5–8 (Zoon); 24–35 (Shah); 36–49 (Garcea); 50–60 (Butel); 60–72 (Carbone); 72–77 (Gibbs); 77–80 (Mutti); 80–84 (Giordano); 84–97 (Tognon); 97–103 (Shah); 171–176 (Weiss); 176–180 (de Villers); 188–192 (Shah); 192–202 (Lednicky); 202 ff. (debate on reproducibility of SV40 researchers' work); 223–225 (Shah's invitation for Strickler to speak; Strickler); 315–322 (Olin presentation); 322–323 (Snider); 323–342 (Strickler presentation). Day 2: pp. 5–15 (Levine); 266–273 (Carbone).

K. Stratton, D. Almario, M. McCormick, eds., "Immunization Safety Review: SV40 Contamination of Polio Vaccine and Cancer" (Washington D.C.: National Academies Press, 2002). Report from Institute of Medicine Immunization Safety Review Committee, released Oct. 22, 2002, of its review of scientific evidence concerning association between SV40 and human tumors. The passage we have quoted, recommending cessation of SV40 epidemiological studies, appears on page 13 of the executive summary.

Documents. The following were either referred to or relied upon in the text of this chapter, specifically with regard to the VEB-Carbone collaboration proposed by Strickler in the summer of 1996, which never occurred:

Howard Strickler, M.D., MPH, to Michele Carbone, memo, Jun. 6, 1996, regarding possible collaboration. Strickler suggests that Carbone and Shah's laboratory engage in a new study in which they would each test fifty choroid plexus tumors and ependymomas for the presence of SV40. "The primary goal of this collaboration is to get at the bottom of the conflict between the positive findings in your laboratory and the negative findings in our work with Keerti Shah's laboratory. . . ."

Howard Strickler, M.D., MPH, memo, to Michele Carbone, Aug. 15, 1996, regarding possible collaboration to search for SV40 in ependymomas. Study has changed from Jun. 6 proposal: 688 ependymomas from different regions of the country to be tested for SV40. VEB would then attempt to statistically determine whether SV40-positive tumors appeared more frequently in regions of country that had supposedly received contaminated vaccine.

Howard Strickler, M.D., MPH, Viral Epidemiology Branch, to Joseph Fraumeni, Director of Division of Cancer Epidemiology and Genetics, NCI, memo, Sep. 11, 1996. Strickler writes concerning recent attention to SV40 in the lay media, his recent study initiatives, and requests Fraumeni's input. Strickler tells Fraumeni that the VEB wishes "to understand the conflicting laboratory results" (the negative VEB-Shah study versus all the other positive studies) and that the VEB will act as "honest brokers" on the issue. Strickler's resolution to the "conflict" involves another change to the study's protocol. Prior to the large ependymoma survey, he tells Fraumeni, there will be a "small pilot phase." "If . . . positive results in the Carbone lab can not be replicated, we will report that the previous results in [the Carbone] laboratory might have been due to artifact [contamination] and the study would end." This statement seems to be at odds with Carbone's understanding of the purpose of the proposed collaboration (see the following note).

Michele Carbone to Howard Strickler, Oct. 16, 1996. Carbone gives his views on Strickler's proposed ependymoma study protocol. Carbone is particularly upset about the new "pilot phase" portion of the protocol Strickler has added. "What is the purpose of this blind test? I am not sure, but I suppose it is to see if in my new laboratory in Loyola, I am still able to produce reliable results. . . ." Carbone states that with several new positive SV40 papers either published or in press there is strong evidence that SV40 is in human tumors. ("Therefore, I hope we *all* agree that SV40 sequences *are* present in some human specimens.")

Howard Strickler to Michele Carbone, Oct. 18, 1996. Strickler responds to Carbone's "surprising [Oct. 16, 1996] correspondence," which "showed that there is a misunderstanding between us, that I hope will be corrected by this letter." Regarding the proposed ependymoma study, Strickler writes that before it will take place, the reason for the "discrepancy" between Carbone's positive mesothelioma results and Shah's negative ones must first be addressed by showing that Carbone's results are "reproducible" in Shah's lab and an NCI lab.

Michele Carbone to Howard Strickler, Oct. 21, 1996. On the goals of the ependymoma study. Carbone makes it clear in his letter that he believes he has no obligation to duplicate his positive results and that the effort will be "very expensive and *very time consuming.*" He directly addresses the intimation that his (and others') results are the result of contamination: "Labs all over the world, which had never worked with SV40 are finding these [SV40 DNA] sequences in human specimens. I do not know what it means . . . but it cannot be that the entire world is SV40-contaminated!"

Scientific Articles. All of the papers relating to SV40 and human tumors presented at the 1997 NIH conference on SV40 are listed in Appendix A. With one exception, we include in the notes for this chapter only those papers related to the epidemiological discussion that occurred during the conference.

Farwell, J. R., et al. "Effect of SV40 Virus-Contaminated Polio Vaccine on the Incidence and Type of CNS Neoplasms in Children: A Population-Based Study." *Trans-American Neurological Association* 104:261–264 (1979). Epidemiological study that demonstrated a link between SV40-contaminated Salk vaccine and cancer. (See notes to chapter 9.) A follow-up study by Farwell, "Medulloblastoma in Childhood: An Epidemiological Study," *Journal of Neurosurgery* 61:657–664 (Oct. 1984), reached the same conclusion. Farwell's work was criticized by Strickler during the 1997 NIH conference for following only a small number of children.

Fisher, S. "SV40 Contaminated Poliovirus Vaccine and Childhood Cancer Risk." Letter to the Editor, *JAMA* 279(19):1527 (May 20, 1998). Letter in which Fisher critiqued Strickler epidemiological study presented at 1997 NIH conference, particularly for using cohorts with little or no correspondence in age.

Fisher, S. G., Weber, L., and Carbone, M. "Cancer Risk Associated with Simian Virus 40-Contaminated Polio Vaccine." *Anticancer Research* 19:2173–2180 (1999). Fisher's retrospective study that concludes there is a correlation between exposure to SV40-contaminated Salk vaccine and several types of cancer.

Fraumeni, J. F., Ederer, F., and Miller, R. "An Evaluation of the Carcinogenicity of Simian Virus 40 in Man." *JAMA* 185 (9):713–718 (Aug. 31, 1963). Original Fraumeni epidemiology study on SV40 exposure through Salk vaccine; referred to by Strickler during his presentation at 1997 NIH conference on SV40 as employing cohorts where it was possible to determine who had been exposed to SV40-contaminated vaccines and who had not. See chapter 9 for our analysis of this study's methodology.

Geissler, E. "SV40 and Human Brain Tumors." In J. L. Melnick, ed., *Progress in Medical Virology* (Basel: Karger, 1990), vol. 37, pp. 211–222. Retrospective survey of East German recipients of oral polio vaccine that concluded no correlation between exposure to presumably contaminated oral vaccine and brain tumors. This study was referred to by

Strickler during his presentation at 1997 NIH conference on SV40 as employing cohorts in which it was possible to determine who had been exposed to SV40-contaminated vaccines and who had not. Similar to Strickler's own study, Geissler's underlying assumption was that the only East Germans exposed to SV40 were those who received oral polio vaccines prior to the early 1960s, while all those who were vaccinated after this time were not exposed to SV40. As is explained throughout this book, and as the Institute of Medicine concluded in 2002, such an assumption appears to lack scientific validity.

Heinonen, O. P., et al. "Immunization during Pregnancy against Poliomyelitis and Influenza in Relation to Childhood Malignancy." *International Journal of Epidemiology* 2(3):229–235 (1973). Survey of 50,897 American pregnancies that demonstrated a link between SV40-contaminated Salk vaccine and cancer. (See notes chapter 9.) During his presentation before the 1997 NIH conference on SV40, Strickler criticized this study because it only followed a small number of children.

Innis, M. D. "Oncogenesis and Poliomyelitis Vaccine." *Nature* 219:972–973 (1968). Survey of 810 hospitalized Australian children that demonstrated a link between SV40-contaminated Salk vaccine and cancer. (See notes chapter 9.) During his presentation before the 1997 NIH conference on SV40, Strickler criticized this study because it only followed a small number of children.

Jasani, B., et al. "Simian Virus 40 Detection in Human Mesothelioma: Reliability and Significance of the Available Molecular Evidence." *Frontiers in BioScience* 6:12–22 (Apr. 12, 2001). This paper includes a critique of the methodology employed by Shah, Strickler, and Goedert during their 1995 negative study of mesothelioma biopsies. Jasani notes that because Shah's DNA detection technique was much less sensitive than Carbone's, the specimens Shah collected from the mesothelioma biopsies would have needed to be significantly larger than Carbone's (and most other researchers') in order to detect any SV40 present in a sample. Jasani states that using Shah's own estimate of the sensitivity of his assay, Shah and the VEB researchers required specimens ten to twenty times larger than they actually used in order to ensure that they recovered a quantity of SV40 DNA sufficient to be detectable using Shah's assay. (See chapter 19 and notes for further discussion of Shah's detection technique.)

Shah, K., and Nathanson, N. "Human Exposure to SV40: Review and Comment." *American Journal of Epidemiology* 103(1):1–12 (1976). This is the 1976 survey that included the estimate of 98 million Americans exposed to SV40-contaminated vaccines between 1955 and 1963. (It formed the basis of Shah's presentation on the first day of the 1997 NIH conference.)

Strickler, H. D., Rosenberg, P. S., Devesa, S. S., Hertel, J., Fraumeni, J. F., and Goedert, J. J. "Contamination of Poliovirus Vaccines with Simian Virus 40 (1955–1963) and Subsequent Cancer Rates." *JAMA* 279:292–295 (1998). Study presented by Strickler at 1997 NIH conference.

CHAPTER 16: THE PERFECT WAR MACHINE

Interviews. Maurizio Bocchetta, May 23, 2003; Janet Butel, Aug. 2, 1999, Mar. 15, 1999; Jul. 8, 2003; Michele Carbone, Nov. 17, 1997, Mar. 18, 1999, Aug. 8, 1999, Sep. 23, 2000, Nov. 22, 2000, Mar. 30, 2001, Nov. 24, 2001, Mar. 10, 2002, May 5, 2002, Jan. 25, 2003; Carlo Croce, Aug. 3, 1999; Joseph Fraumeni, Jul. 23, 1999; Adi Gazdar, Sep. 10, 1999, Apr. 21, 2001, Jul. 14, 2003; Bharat Jasani, Jul. 17, 1999, Aug. 16, 1999, Mar. 5, 2001, Mar. 15, 2001, Aug. 8, 2003; Arnold J. Levine, Sep. 8, 1999; Ronald Kennedy, chairman, Department of Microbiology and Immunology, Texas Tech University Health Sciences Center, Sep. 9, 2000; George Klein, Aug. 8, 1999; John Lednicky, Feb. 23, 2001,

Apr. 2, 2001, Apr. 21, 2001, May 17, 2002, Oct. 23, 2002, Oct. 25, 2002, Oct. 28, 2002, Jan. 25, 2003; Brooke Mossman, Aug. 6, 1999; Harvey Pass, Dec. 24, 1998, Apr. 4, 2002, Oct. 28, 2002; Joseph Pagano, director emeritus, Lineberger Comprehensive Cancer Center, University of North Carolina, May 23, 2003; Paola Rizzo, Jul. 17, 1999; Janet Rowley, Blum-Riese Distinguished Service Professor of Medicine and Molecular Genetics and Cell Biology, University of Chicago Medical Center, Jul. 8, 1999; David Schrump, Mar. 18, 1999, Jul. 23, 1999; Joseph Testa, Aug. 27, 1999, Jan. 10, 2000, Feb. 20, 2001; Mauro Tognon, Apr. 21, 2001.

General Background. Most of the background for this chapter was provided through interviews with the scientists who have investigated SV40, their published works and the authors' attendance at various scientific meetings where SV40 was discussed. We also visited the laboratories of several of the scientists to gain additional insight into their work. Other background materials included personal correspondence with George Klein of the Microbiology and Tumor Biology Center, Karolinska Institute, Stockholm. Klein, a former member of the Nobel Assembly of the Karolinska Institute (1957–1993), has published more than a thousand papers in the fields of experimental cell research and cancer research. Leonard Hayflick, *How and Why We Age* (New York: Ballentine Books, 1994), pp. 132–136, provided information concerning the Hayflick limit and the role of telomeres in determining cell life span. James D. Watson, Nancy H. Hopkins, Jeffrey W. Roberts, Joan Argetsinger Steitz, and Alan M. Weiner, *Molecular Biology of the Gene* (Menlo Park, Calif.: Benjamin/Cummings, 1987), particularly chapter 25, "The Control of Cell Proliferation," and chapter 26, "The Genetic Basis of Cancer," provided an overview of how viruses cause molecular changes leading to cancer. A series of reviews published in Michele Carbone, guest editor, "SV40: From Monkeys to Humans," *Seminars in Cancer Biology* 11 (1):1–85 (Feb. 2001) was an additional background source. Some of the background information concerning Adi Gazdar comes from a biographical sketch at the University of Texas Southwestern Medical Center at Dallas Web site. Statistics concerning the incidence and mortality of lymphoma and leukemia were obtained from the American Cancer Society, "Cancer Facts and Figures, 2002."

Public Chronology. Apoorva Mandavilli, "SV40, Polio Vaccine, and Cancer: Now Beyond Coincidence?" *BioMedNet News,* Apr. 9, 2002.

Scientific Articles. The following articles are specifically referenced in the text. (For a complete list of scientific articles concerning SV40 and human tumors, see Appendix A.)

Bocchetta, M., Di Resta, I., Powers, A., Fresco, R., Tosolini, A., Testa, J. R., et al. "Human Mesothelial Cells Are Unusually Susceptible to Simian Virus 40-Mediated Transformation and Asbestos Cocarcinogencity." *Proceedings of the National Academy of Sciences, USA 97* (18):10214–10219 (2000). Study showing that mesothelial cells are much more readily transformed by SV40 than are fibroblasts.

Bocchetta, M., Miele, L., Pass, H. I., and Carbone, M. "Notch-1 Induction, a Novel Activity of SV40 Required for Growth of SV40-Transformed Human Mesothelial Cells." *Oncogene* 22:81–89 (2003). SV40 stimulates Notch-1 gene.

Cacciotti, P., Libener, R., Betta, P., Martini, F., Porta, C., Procopio, A., et al. "SV40 Replication in Human Mesothelial Cells Induces Met Receptor Activation: A Model for Viral-Related Carcinogenesis of Human Malignant Mesothelioma." *Proceedings of the National Academy of Sciences* 98:12032–12037 (2001). Study showing SV40 activates Met oncogene and stimulates neighboring cells to activate Met.

Cacciotti, P., Strizzi, L., Vianale, G., Iaccheri, L., Libener, R., Porta, C., et al. "The Presence of Simian-Virus 40 Sequences in Mesothelioma and Mesothelial Cells Is Associated with High Levels of Vascular Endothelial Growth Factor." *American Journal of Respiratory Cell Molecular Biology* 26:189–193 (2002). Study demonstrating that SV40 stimulates VEGF and thus encourages blood vessel growth toward tumors.

Carbone, M., et al. "Simian Virus-40 Large-T Antigen Binds P53 in Human Mesotheliomas." *Nature Medicine* 3:908–912 (1997). First Carbone experiment to show that SV40 disables p53.

DeLuca, A., et al. "The Retinoblastoma Gene Family Prb/P105, P107, Prb2/P130 and Simian Virus-40 Large T-Antigen In Human Mesotheliomas." *Nature Medicine* 3:913–916 (1997). This study demonstrated that SV40 inhibits Rbs; a companion to the p53 study in Carbone et al. (1997).

De Rienzo, A., et al. "Detection of SV40 DNA Sequences in Malignant Mesothelioma Specimens from the United States, but Not from Turkey." *Journal of Cell Biochemistry* 84:455–459 (2002). Survey of Turkish mesotheliomas; no SV40 found.

Emri, S., Kocagoz, T., Olut, A., Gungen, Y., Mutti, L., and Baris, Y. I. "Simian Virus 40 Is Not a Cofactor in the Pathogenesis of Environmentally Induced Malignant Pleural Mesothelioma in Turkey." *Anticancer Research* 20:891–894 (2000). Survey of Turkish mesotheliomas; no SV40 found.

Foddis, R., et al. "SV40 Infection Induces Telomerase Activity in Human Mesothelial Cells." *Oncogene* 21:1434–1442 (2002). Study showing that normal SV40 will induce telomerase activity, but with small t-antigen deleted will not. Study also found that asbestos alone does not induce telomerase activity.

Hirvonen, A., et al. "Simian Virus 40 (SV40)-Like DNA Sequences Not Detectable in Finnish Mesothelioma Patients Not Exposed to SV40-Contaminated Polio Vaccines." *Molecular Carcinogenesis* 26:93–99(1999). Study of Finnish mesotheliomas; no SV40 found.

Procopio, A., Strizzi, L., Vianale, G., Betta, P., Puntoni, R., Fontana, V., et al.. "Simian Virus-40 Sequences Are a Negative Prognostic Cofactor in Patients with Malignant Pleural Mesothelioma." *Genes, Chromosomes and Cancer* 29:173–179 (2000). Study showing that patients with SV40-positive mesotheliomas have worse prognosis than those whose tumors are SV40-negative.

Salewski, H., et al. "Increased Oncogenicity of Subclones of SV40 Large T-Induced Neuroectodermal Tumor Cell Lines after Loss of Large T Expression and Concomitant Mutation in p53." *Cancer Research* 59:1980–1986 (1999). German study on rats demonstrating "hit and run" mechanism for SV40-induced tumors.

Shivapurkar, N., Wiethege, T., Wistubu, I. I., Salomon, E., Milchgrup, S., Muller, K. M., et al. "Presence of Simian Virus 40 Sequences in Malignant Mesotheliomas and Mesothelial Cell Proliferations." *Journal of Cellular Biochemistry* 76:181–188 (1999). Gazdar laser microdissection experiment which found SV40 in malignant mesothelial cells but not in adjacent normal ones.

Shivapurkar, N., Harada, K., Reddy, J., Scheuermann, R. H., Xu, Y., Mckenna, R. W., et al. "Presence of Simian Virus 40 DNA Sequences in Human Lymphomas." *Lancet* 359: 85–52 (2002). Gazdar study finding SV40 in lymphomas.

Vilchez, R. A., et al. "Association between Simian Virus 40 and Non-Hodgkin's Lymphoma." *Lancet* 359:817–23 (2002). Butel study finding SV40 in lymphomas.

Waheed, I., Guo, Z. S., Chen, A., Weiser, T. S., Nguyen, D. M., and Schrump, D. S. "Antisense to SV40 Early Gene Region Induces Growth Arrest and Apoptosis in T-Antigen-Positive Human Pleural Mesothelioma Cells." *Cancer Research* 59:6068–6073 (1999). Schrump experiment which showed that removal of SV40 from mesothelioma cell lines stopped their growth.

CHAPTER 17: A STUDY MARRED BY STRIFE

Interviews. Janet Butel, Mar. 15, 2002, Jul. 8, 2003; Michele Carbone, Aug. 8, 1999, Mar. 31, 2000, Nov. 15, 2000, Apr. 11, 2002; Joseph Fraumeni, Jul. 23, 1999, Jun. 4, 2003; Adi Gazdar, Mar. 31, 2000; Allen Gibbs, Mar. 5, 2001; James Goedert, Jul. 23, 1999; Bharat Jasani, Aug. 16, 1999, Mar. 30 and 31, 2000, Mar. 5, 2001, Mar. 15, 2001; Richard Klausner, Jul. 23, 1999; John Lednicky, Feb. 23, 2001, Dec. 12, 2002, Jan. 25, 2003; Luciano Mutti, Mar. 31, 2000; Harvey Pass, Jul. 15, 1999, Apr. 4, 2002, Oct. 8, 2002; Alan Rabson, Jul. 16, 1999, Apr. 2, 2001, Jun. 2, 2003; Paola Rizzo, Jul. 17, 1999; Keerti Shah, Feb. 20, 2001, Jul. 18, 2003; Howard Strickler, Jul. 21, 1999; Joseph Testa, Aug. 27, 1999, Jan. 10, 2000, Feb. 20, 2001.

General Background. The interviews listed above and the documents described in Appendix D, "Memos and Correspondence Relating to the Multilaboratory Study," were the primary sources for this chapter. On Mar. 31, 2000, at a scientific conference in Boston, "Multimodality Therapy of Chest Malignancies: Update 2000 New Tools for the Millennium"—attended by the authors—Strickler presented "Evidence against SV40 Virus" as part of a workshop on the role of SV40 in mesothelioma. His presentation included a discussion of the status of the multilaboratory study and provided additional background for the events portrayed in this chapter. We also interviewed two government officials who wish to remain anonymous, who provided additional information concerning the events described in this chapter.

Michele Carbone provided the authors with copies of his correspondence and the responses he received when he asked the FDA and vaccine manufacturers how he could obtain samples of early polio vaccine. Carbone also provided copies of the package inserts from the 1955 vaccine that Herbert Ratner gave to him to test. Further background concerning Ratner was obtained from a correspondence between the authors and one of his daughters, Helen Dietz, through a review of Ratner's scientific publications, and from sworn statements by Dietz and Ratner's other daughter, Mary Baggot, in February 1998. (Ratner died in December 1997.) The attestations of the daughters concerned his career, in general, and the specific circumstances that led him to give vials of 1955 polio vaccine to Carbone, including the fact that the samples had been unopened or undisturbed in any fashion since Ratner first received them.

Documents. Appendix D provides a complete list of all correspondence, memos, etc., concerning the multilaboratory study.

Scientific Articles. The following articles are specifically referenced in the text. (For a complete list of scientific articles concerning SV40 and human tumors, see Appendix A.)

Rizzo, P., Di Resta, I., Power, A., Ratner, H., and Carbone, M. "Unique Strains of SV40 in Commercial Poliovaccines from 1955 Not Readily Identifiable with Current Testing for SV40 Infection." *Cancer Research* 59:6103–6108 (1999). Carbone study isolating SV40 from vials of polio vaccine produced in 1955.

Testa, J. R., Carbone, M., Hirvonen, A., Khalili, K., Krynska, B., Linnainmaa, K., et al. "A Multi-Institutional Study Confirms the Presence and Expression of Simian Virus 40 in Human Malignant Mesotheliomas." *Cancer Research* 58:4505–4509 (1998). International Mesothelioma Interest Group study involving four labs exchanging twelve blinded tumor samples.

Vilchez, R. A., et al. "Association between Simian Virus 40 and Non-Hodgkin's Lymphoma." *Lancet* 359:817–23 (2002). Butel study finding SV40 in lymphomas. When she sequenced some of the recovered SV40, she found the strains were identical to the SV40 strains Carbone had recovered from the 1955 vials of polio vaccine.

CHAPTER 18: WASTED TIME, WASTED MONEY

Interviews. Janet Butel, Mar. 15, 2002, Jul. 8, 2003; Michele Carbone, Mar. 30 and 31, 2000, Aug. 23, 2000, Sep. 21, 2000, Oct. 2 and 22, 2000, Feb. 28, 2001, Jun. 5, 2001; Joseph Fraumeni, Jul. 23, 1999, Jun. 4, 2003; Adi Gazdar, Mar. 31, 2000; Allen Gibbs, Mar. 5, 2001; James Goedert, Jul. 23, 1999, Jan. 30, 2000; Bharat Jasani, Aug. 16, 1999, Mar. 30 and 31, 2000, Mar. 5 and 15, 2001; Richard Klausner, Jul. 23, 1999; John Lednicky, Feb. 23, 2001, Dec. 12, 2002, Jan. 25, 2003; Luciano Mutti, Mar. 31, 2000; Drew Pardoll, Nov. 12, 2003; Harvey Pass, Jul. 15, 1999, Apr. 4, 2002, Oct. 8, 2002; Alan Rabson, Jul. 16, 1999, Apr. 2, 2001, Jun. 2, 2003; Paola Rizzo, Jul. 17, 1999; Keerti Shah, Feb. 20, 2001, Jul. 18, 2003.

General Background. As with chapter 17, the interviews listed above and the documents contained in Appendix D on the multilaboratory study were the primary sources for this chapter. Other background sources included the Strickler Mar. 31, 2000, presentation (see notes, chapter 17) and interviews with two anonymous government sources (see notes, chapter 17). The curriculum vitae of Bharat Jasani and a visit by the authors to Jasani's lab in Cardiff, Wales, on Mar. 5, 2001, provided additional background material.

Documents. Appendix D provides a complete list of all correspondence, memos, etc., concerning the multilaboratory study and the Carbone-Pass NCI grant application. Additional documents referenced in this chapter include:

Deposition of Keerti Shah, Jun. 24, 2002, pp. 8–23 (Shah's consulting work for Merck and Pfizer on SV40), 295–308, and 319–321 (Shah was provided positive controls in advance of other participants by Strickler and told that the positive controls were positive; Shah adjusted the technique until he could detect SV40 in positive samples). From *Horwin v. American Home Products, Inc.*, Case No. CV-00-04523 WJR (Ex), United States District Court for the Central District of California, Western Division.

MacLachlan, D. S. "SV40 in Human Tumors: New Documents Shed Light on the Apparent Controversy." *Anticancer Research* 22:3495–3500 (2002). MacLachlan reported on the Shah deposition in this article. MacLachlan's article provoked a series of responses. Butel, Lednicky, Jasani, and Gibbs wrote to the editor of *Cancer Epidemiology, Biomarkers and Prevention* and publicly disavowed the published results of the VEB multilaboratory study once they learned that Shah and Strickler had compromised the study's protocol. The editor of the journal, however, refused to allow them to retract their authorship and said that unless all sixty of the study's coauthors (from all nine of the participating labs and from the two subcontracting laboratories hired by Strickler) also retracted, he would not withdraw their names from the study. Strickler and Shah wrote a lengthy response to MacLachlan, published by *Anticancer Research* in 2003. The letter did not contest MacLachlan's disclosures, including Shah's advance knowledge of the identity of the positive controls. Instead, Strickler and Shah countered that MacLachlan "never makes it clear how this could have, in any way, affected the results of the study." Indeed, much of the letter was a recapitulation of their belief that the multilaboratory study remained superior to others that had sought to explore whether human tumors contained SV40. In the same issue of *Anticancer Research,* the editors published seven other letters on the subject. Jasani, Gibbs, and Butel jointly signed a letter to express their "dismay" about the "irregularity" MacLachlan had discovered.

They also said that they now wondered if one of the reasons for the negative results during the multilaboratory study "may have been due to a biased set of tumor samples obtained from one source," and noted that Richard Sugarbaker's Brigham and Women's laboratory, which had provided the samples, had just reported that its mesothelioma specimens "generally lack SV40." Raphael Bueno, Associate Chief of Thoracic Surgery at Brigham and Women's Hospital, wrote in support of Strickler and Shah and, referring to the negative Sugarbaker study, said the results were "suggest[ive] of contamination rather than causality" concerning SV40's presence in tumors. Lednicky wrote a lengthy letter detailing the history of the multilaboratory study and flaws in the protocol. He noted that the most serious implication concerning Shah's improvement of his SV40 detection technique was that "these measures prevented us from learning whether SV40 was not detected in the original study of Drs. Strickler and Shah [1995 negative VEB-Shah mesothelioma study] because the technique they used was not sensitive." Antonio Giordano wrote and directly addressed the issue of a potential conflict of interest posed by Shah's consulting roles with the pharmaceutical companies: "Dr. Shah would be at the same time the expert witness of the pharmaceutical companies in the SV40 litigation, yet if he were to find SV40 in samples provided by the VEB, he would be providing data useful to the plaintiff's lawyers, who have sued the companies he is supposed to be defending. It is unclear why the NCI would choose a laboratory with such a clear conflict of interest to contract their SV40 studies. This issue was not addressed in the reply by Dr. Shah and Dr. Strickler." All the responses to the MacLachlan article appeared in *Anticancer Research* 23:3109–3118 (2003).

Scientific Articles. The following articles are specifically referenced in the text. (For a complete list of scientific articles concerning SV40 and human tumors, see Appendix A.)

Jasani, B. "Simian Virus 40 and Human Pleural Mesothelioma." *Thorax* 54:750–752 (1999).
Jasani, B., et al. "Simian Virus 40 Detection in Human Mesothelioma: Reliability and Significance of the Available Molecular Evidence." *Frontiers in BioScience* 6e:12–22 (Apr. 12, 2001).

CHAPTER 19: NO FUNDING, NO RESEARCH

Interviews. Janet Butel, Jul. 8, 2003; Bharat Jasani, Aug. 8, 2003; Michele Carbone, Aug. 8, 1999, Apr. 20 and 21, 2001, Jul. 19, 2002; Carlo Croce, Aug. 3, 1999; Joseph Fraumeni, Jun. 4, 2003; Adi Gazdar, Apr. 20, 2001, Jul. 14, 2003; Denise Galloway, Jul. 2, 2003; Arnold J. Levine, Sep. 9, 1999; Frederick Mayall, Apr. 20, 2001; Paola Rizzo, Apr. 20, 2001; Luciano Mutti, Apr. 21, 2001; Antonio Procopio, Apr. 21, 2001; Alan Rabson, Jul. 16, 1999, Apr. 2, 2001, Jun. 2, 2003; Paola Rizzo, Jul. 17, 1999; Keerti Shah, Jul. 18, 2003; Mauro Tognon, Apr. 21, 2001; Umberto Saffiotti, Apr. 21, 2001; May Wong, Jul. 2, 2003.

General Background. The authors attended the April 2001 conference described in this chapter. Information concerning HTLV-1 seropositivity is reported in *Science,* 240:643–646 (1998); the number of seropositive individuals who will develop disease is noted in various medical textbooks and scientific articles (for example, see F. Mortreux, A. S. Gabet, and E. Wattel, "Molecular and Cellular Aspects of HTLV-1 Associated Leukemogenesis in Vivo," *Leukemia* 17:25–38 [2003]). Information concerning the National Cancer Institute's Request for Applications process and the role of the NCI's Executive Committee in the process was obtained from some of the interviews listed above, as well as a review of actual RFAs, and the NCI publication, "Grants Process and Administration," NIH Publication No. 02-1222, revised April 2002. Information on the amount of funding by the NCI and NIH for extramural research on SV40, HPV, and HTLV-1 was obtained from a review of the NIH's CRISP databases on extramural funding, a review of the NCI's database on extramural funding, and information provided by the NCI press office. Information concerning NCI and NIH funding for Janet Butel was obtained from the same sources; additionally, Butel's published papers list the source of grants used to support each of her studies. In August 2003, the NCI press office provided the authors with estimates of the amount of federal funds used to support some of the negative Viral Epidemiology Branch studies on SV40. The cost for the nine listed (including the multilaboratory one) was approximately $595,000. The VEB declined to reveal the amounts budgeted for any studies currently under way (there were at least two). The National Cancer Institute's "Simian Virus 40 and Human Cancer," fact sheet posted Sep. 23, 2002, and updated Apr. 3, 2003, and referred to in the text, is available on the NCI's Web site at its "News Center." As of July 2003, the CDC's fact sheet on SV40 continued to rely on VEB epidemiological research to support its statement that "[t]he majority of evidence suggests there is no causal relationship between receipt of SV40-contaminated polio vaccine and cancer development. . . ."

Documents. K. Stratton, D. Almario, M. McCormick, eds., "Immunization Safety Review: SV40 Contamination of Polio Vaccine and Cancer" (Washington, D.C.: National Academies Press, 2002). Report from Institute of Medicine Immunization Safety Review Committee, released October 22, 2002, pp. 6–7, Executive Summary.

Scientific Articles. The following articles are specifically referenced in the text. (For a complete list of scientific articles concerning SV40 and human tumors, see Appendix A.)

Carbone, M., et al. "SV40 and Human Brain Tumors." *International Journal of Cancer.* Letter signed by Carbone and ten other scientists criticizing flaws in the Shah/Engels study failing to find SV40 in brain tumors from northern India. (Note: Letter was in press at the time of the preparation of this manuscript.)

de Sanjose, S., Shah, K., Domingo-Domenech, E., Engels, E. A., Fernandez de Sevilla, A., Alvaro, T., Garcia-Villanueva, M., Fomagosa, V., Vonzalez-Barca, E., Viscidi, R. P. "Lack of Serological Evidence for an Association between Simian Virus 40 and Lymphoma." *International Journal of Cancer* 104:522–524 (2003).

Engels, E. A., Sarkar, C., Daniel, R. W., Gravott, E., Verma, K., Quezado, M., Shah, K. V., "Absence of Simian Virus 40 in Human Brain Tumors from Northern India." *International Journal of Cancer* 101:348–352 (2002).

Engels, E. A., et al. "Cancer Incidence in Denmark Following Exposure to Poliovirus Vaccine Contaminated with Simian Virus 40." *Journal of the National Cancer Institute* 95:24 (2003).

Huang, H., et al. "Identification in Human Brain Tumors of DNA Sequences Specific for SV40 Large T-Antigen." *Brain Pathology* 9:33–44 (1999).

Klein, G., Powers, A., Croce, C. "Meeting Review: Association of SV40 with Human Tumors." *Oncogene* 21:1141–1149 (2002).

Li, R. M., Branton, M. H., Tanawattanacharoen, S., Falk, R. A., Jennette, J. C., Kopp, J. B. "Molecular Identification of SV40 in Infection in Human Subjects and Possible Association with Kidney Disease." *Journal of the American Society of Nephrology* 13(9):2320–2330 (2002).

Krynska, B., et al. "Detection of Human Neurotropic JC Virus DNA Sequences and Expression of the Viral Oncogenic Protein in Pediatric Human Medulloblastomas." *Proceedings of the National Academy of Sciences, USA* 96:11519–11524 (1999).

Puntoni, R., et al. "Re: Trends in U.S. Pleural Mesothelioma Incidence Rates Following

Simian Virus 40 Contamination of Early Poliovirus Vaccines." *Journal of the National Cancer Institute* 95(9):687–688 (2003). Letter to the editor criticizing Strickler study.

Strickler, H., et al. "Trends in U.S. Pleural Mesothelioma Incidence Rates Following Simian Virus 40 Contamination of Early Poliovirus Vaccines." *Journal of the National Cancer Institute* 95(1):38–45 (2003).

Vilchez, R. A., and Butel, J. S. "Re: Trends in U.S. Pleural Mesothelioma Incidence Rates Following Simian Virus 40 Contamination of Early Poliovirus Vaccines." *Journal of the National Cancer Institute* 95(9):687 (2003). Letter to the editor criticizing Strickler study.

Vilchez, R. A., Kozinetz, C. A., Butel, J. S. "Essay: Conventional Epidemiology and the Link between SV40 and Human Cancers." *Lancet Oncology* 4:188–190 (2003).

Vilchez, R. A., Kozinetz, C, A., Arrington, A. S., Madden, C. R., and Butel, J. S. "Simian Virus 40 in Human Cancers." *American Journal of Medicine* 114:675–684 (2003). Butel's meta-analysis of all studies that had looked for SV40 in human tumors.

Zhen, H. N., et al. "Expression of the Simian Virus 40 Large Tumor Antigen (Tag) and Formation of Tag-p53 and Tag-pRb complexes in Human Brain Tumors." *Cancer* 86: 2124–2132 (1999).

CHAPTER 20: ALEXANDER'S TUMOR

Interviews. Audrey Ashby, spokeswoman for Lederle Laboratories, May 10, 1996; Michele Carbone, Jan. 19, 2002, May 16, 2002, Oct. 18, 2002; William Egan, Center for Biologics Evaluation and Control, Food and Drug Administration, Jul. 23, 1999, Mar. 13, 2001, Mar. 5, 2003; Adi Gazdar, Jul. 14, 2003; Michael and Raphaele Horwin, Mar. 7, 2000, May 6, 2000, Feb. 26, 2001, Mar. 26, 2001, Dec. 6, 2001, Jul. 16, 2002, Jan. 23, 2003, Aug. 10, 2003; Stan Kops, Aug. 15, 2003; John Lednicky, Jul. 25, 2002, Dec. 12, 2002, Dec. 16, 2002, Feb. 7, 2003, Jun. 20, 2003; Don MacLachlan, Jun. 30, 2002, Sep. 16, 2002, Feb. 5, 2003, Apr. 29, 2003, Nov. 28, 2003; Frederick Mayall, M.D., Waikato Hospital, Hamilton, New Zealand, Apr. 20, 2001; Harvey Pass, Dec. 24, 1998.

General Background. The statistics concerning the occurrence of brain tumors in children are taken from the American Brain Tumor Association (ABTA), "Facts and Statistics," and "A Primer of Brain Tumors" (1997 statistics). The ABTA notes that brain tumors are the second leading cause of cancer death in children under age fifteen. The source for statistics in brain cancer incidence in children and adults in 2003 is the American Cancer Society. The rise in childhood central nervous system tumors during the latter part of the twentieth century is documented in several sources; one of them is a September 2, 1998, press release from the National Cancer Institute. A written personal communication from Michele Carbone, May 31, 2002, also provided background on his criticisms of the two studies that tested old samples of American and British polio vaccines.

Concerning some of the internal Lederle manufacturing processes, sources include a letter from R. J. Vallancourt, D.V.M, Manager, Biological Section, Lederle Laboratories, to Harry Meyer, M.D., Director of Bureau of Biologics, October 4, 1976 (explaining that Lederle will begin to use monkeys from the Caribbean for vaccine production); and a written personal communication from Audrey Ashby, Director of Public Relations, Wyeth-Lederle Ayerst, to the authors, May 24, 1996 (referring to the company's continued use of a special colony of African green monkeys, bred in the Caribbean specifically for oral polio vaccine production). The description of Lederle's manufacturing process from Sabin's master seed strain to working seed to final monopool was derived in part from "Declaration of Lynn Kelleher," filed August 12, 2003, in *Moreno v. American Home Products et al.*, Superior Court of New Jersey Law Division, Bergen County, Docket No. BER-L-577-02. Another source is a Lederle document, "Final Report, Orimune Seed Program" authored by J. Brandt, Product and Process Improvement, December 1978, which specifically references the SV40 neutralization of the Sabin strain material as the first step. A presentation by Lederle spokesperson, Bonnie Brock, at the 1997 NIH conference on SV40 is one source for the description of the company's SV40 testing procedures (B. Brock, L. Kelleher, and B. Zlotnik, "Product Quality Control Testing for Oral Polio Vaccine," *Developments in Biological Standards* 94: 217–219 [1998]).

David Brown, "Polio Vaccine Change Is Urged to Cut Risk of Contracting Disease," *Washington Post,* Oct. 19, 1995, p. A3; and Andrea Rock, "The Lethal Challengers of the Billion-Dollar Vaccine Business," *Money,* Dec. 1996, pp. 148–163, both note that the only cases of polio occurring in the United States since the 1970s are those caused by the vaccine itself. See also "Vaccine Controversies," *CQ Researcher* 10(28):641–672 (Aug. 25, 2000), which notes that the last case of wild polio in the entire Western Hemisphere occurred in Peru in August 1991. The Centers for Disease Control fact sheet "Polio Vaccine" (1997) also notes that oral polio vaccine causes one case of polio for every 2.4 million doses of vaccine. Problems with Sabin's Type III strain appeared almost as soon as his vaccine began to be widely used in the United States. In the summer of 1962, Sabin's Type III vaccine suffered its own mini-version of a Cutter incident when it was linked to paralysis in eleven vaccinees, at least according to official Public Health statistics. (See "Polio Shot Controversy," *Time,* Sep. 28, 1962, p. 72.) Klein, *Trial by Fury,* p. 149, says the number of paralysis cases probably caused by Sabin's Type III vaccine was closer to sixty; Carter, *Breakthrough,* p. 382, suggests the number may have been triple that. Whatever the actual number, there was sufficient reason for the Public Health Service to suspend use of Sabin's Type III vaccine during the second half of 1962. Vaccinations resumed with Type III vaccine in December 1962. ("All Sabin Shots Get U.S. Approval," *New York Times,* December 20, 1962, p. 8.) Internally, Lederle acknowledged the problems the Sabin Type III strain caused for vaccine it produced. For an example, see March 14, 1979, memo cited in Documents, notes for this chapter.

The FDA regulations concerning tests for screening for SV40 (and other viral contaminants) are found in the Code of Federal Regulations, 630.13 (b)(3), (4) and (7); and 630.18 (a)(5), (6) and (7). These explain the requirement to use two separate fourteen-day observation periods in tissue culture (primary culture and subculture, described in this chapter) as the mandated detection method for the presence of viral contaminants, including SV40, in polio vaccine. A review of the 1961 regulations when compared to updated versions published in 1973 and again in 1994 show that there has been no change in the detection method (light microscope) nor in the length of the tissue culture observation periods since the original 1961 regulations.

Additional cases that have been filed against Lederle alleging SV40-caused disease or death from contaminated vaccine include: *Moreno v. American Home Products et al.*, Superior Court of New Jersey Law Division, Bergen County, Docket No. BER–L–577–02 (Pfizer is listed as a codefendant in this suit); *Gannon v. American Home Products et al.*, Superior Court of New Jersey Law Division, Bergen County, Docket No. BER–L–8470–01; *Rivard v. American Home Products et al.*, Superior Court of New Jersey Law Division, Bergen County, Docket No. BER–L–3343–01.

Public Chronology. The quote by Wyeth spokesperson Natalie de Vane denying any SV40 contamination of Lederle vaccine appeared in Mark Benjamin, "Polio Vaccine Might Have Carried Virus," United Press International, Sep. 9, 2003.

Congressional Hearings and Scientific Meetings. The following are referenced in the text:.

Conference on Cell Cultures for Virus Vaccine Production, Nov. 6–7, 1967, National Institutes of Health, Bethesda, Maryland, *NCI Monographs,* No. 29, pp. 474–475. This is the source of Murray's statement that the Marburg scare has not resulted in a halt in vaccine production, but that, instead, there has been a switch back to rhesus monkey kidneys as substrate:

> A number of statements have been made at various times during the meeting which lead one to believe that there is an understanding that production of vaccines on monkey kidney has entirely come to a halt. This is not so. Vaccines are still being produced on rhesus and cynomolgus kidney cultures.

Submitted testimony of Stanley Kops, Esq., before the Subcommittee on Wellness and Human Rights, Committee on Government Reform, U.S. House of Representatives, Sep. 10, 2003. (Note: The transcript of this hearing had not been published at the time of the preparation of this manuscript.) Documents that Kops introduced during his testimony were attached to his submitted testimony as exhibits.

Testimony of William Egan, acting director, Office of Vaccine Research and Review, Center of Biologics Evaluation and Research, Food and Drug Administration before the Subcommittee on Wellness and Human Rights, Committee on Government Reform, U.S. House of Representatives, Nov. 13, 2003. (Note: The transcript of this hearing had not been published at the time of the preparation of this manuscript.)

Documents. The following were referenced or relied upon for the text of this chapter:

James L. Bittle, Lederle Laboratories, to Dr. I. S. Danielson, Lederle Laboratories, memo, Nov. 8, 1961. "Presence of SV40 in Vaccine Lots." This memo details that Murray has allowed three lots that were SV40-positive during tissue culture observations to pass. It also reports on SV40 contamination of African green monkey kidneys. A portion of the text follows:

> The following is a summary of the incidence of SV40 found at the PCB-2 level [subculture] of the fifteen lots released for clinical trial [3 lots listed: Lots 114, 216, and 317]. . . . The decision by Dr. Murray to allow SV40 to be present at the PCB-2 level was the basis for allowing these lots to pass. Would we be wise in asking the NIH to allow us to substitute three new lots in place of those mentioned above? . . . I believe we should also consider a new emphasis on cercopithecus monkey [African green monkey] kidney for production purposes. . . . Our results indicate that SV40 is found in about 10% of the cercopithecus monkey kidneys harvested at Lederle.

I. S. Danielson to S. Aiston (and other Lederle officials), memo, Nov. 21, 1961. This memo notes that DBS believes African green monkeys are contracting SV40 because of contact with rhesus monkeys during shipment.

Roderick Murray, Director of Division of Biological Standards to Frances Bingham, Department Head, Biological Testing, Lederle Laboratories, Jan. 8, 1962. Murray lists the Lederle oral polio vaccine lots that are being included in its application (later approved) for oral polio vaccine. The three SV40-positive lots (114, 216, and 317) are among the fifteen lots listed.

I. S. Danielson, Manager, Biological Production, Lederle Laboratories, to George Hottle,

Division of Biological Standards, letter with attached report, Feb. 12, 1962. Report notes that, "during this period we were troubled with SV40 laboratory contamination" (p. 3) It also lists three poliovirus harvests that appeared to evidence the presence of SV40. The harvests were either retested (and deemed to have passed) or the presence of SV40 was ascribed to laboratory contamination.

Albert Sabin to I. S. Danielson, Lederle Laboratories, Oct. 8, 1962, enclosed with five milliliters of Type III virus, used as seed for the large lots prepared for Sabin by Merck, Sharp and Dohme Research Laboratories in 1956. Relevant portion of letter:

> I should like to point out that this preparation was negative for SV40 in tests carried out by Dr. Hilleman and his associates, but he told me at the time the tests were made they were not observing the cultures for as long as they are now and he could not be certain that there may not be a trace of SV40 virus in this material.

Roderick Murray, Director of Division of Biologics Standards, to Manufacturers of Poliomyelitis and Adenovirus Vaccines, memo, Jun. 4, 1964. "The DBS views with considerable concern . . . [that manufacturers are] still submitting for release lots of vaccine . . . inactivated prior to March 1963."

R. J. Vallancourt, Lederle Laboratories, to Mr. G. P. Bywater, Dr. F. E. Fontane, Mr. H. Perlmutter, Dr. P. J. Vasington, memo, Jan. 31, 1972. Memo details the extent of problems the company was having with simian cytomegalovirus (SCMV) contamination during vaccine production with African green monkeys:

> Cytomegalo virus (CMV) is a recent example of an adventitious agent which, although it exists in cell cultures, is not being tested for at this time. For a manufacturer, and especially a regulatory agency, to accept this situation can only be judged a dichotomy. . . . Nevertheless, the DBS will soon be pressured into issuing a test for this agent. Since one hundred percent of the monkeys are serologically positive (antibody) for CMV, no screening of monkeys prior to production can take place. We will not know which monkeys are suitable for production until kidneys are processed. Our data show that fifty per cent of today's "clean" monkeys would be disqualified for production needs [if new DBS regulations were in effect].

R. J. Vallancourt, Lederle Laboratories, to Mr. D. Carroll, Mr. H. Perlmutter, Lederle Laboratories, memo, Aug. 4, 1972. Further details on SCMV contamination problems:

> The Lederle Laboratories-Bureau of Biologics [former DBS, renamed in April 1972] cooperative CMV study has been completed. All eleven monkeys demonstrated the presence of CMV-like agents. . . . After discussion of the results of the collaborative study, we would have to acknowledge the facts as we have them; i.e., prolonged investigation indicates 100 percent of the monkeys tested in the study to be contaminated with CMV. . . . [I]f this virus is as ubiquitous as the study seems to indicate, it is reasonable to assume that it has been present in our environment for at least as long as poliovirus vaccine has been produced. Therefore, all substrate used to this date conceivably has been "contaminated."

M. S. Cooper to Dr. Elkas, et al., Lederle Laboratories, memo, Dec. 27, 1977. Subject: Meeting at the Bureau of Biologics Held 12/21/77. "Dr. Meyer asked us to bear with them in their efforts to change regulations. . . ."

S. S. Aiston (technical superintendent, polio operations) to W. P. Cekleniak, memo, Mar.

14, 1979. Subject: Orimune, Request for additional information for registration in Australia. This memo discusses the so-called Sabin Original strains provided by Albert Sabin to Merck. Memo notes that Lederle used a small amount of these strains to produce its working seeds, which were then used to produce oral polio vaccine. Memo also notes that Lederle has had considerable difficulty with the Type III Sabin strain because of recurring neurovirulence. Portion of the memo referred to in the text, states:

> It should be made clear that Lederle did not test the original Sabin seeds for extraneous agents or neurovirulence since only 50 ml or less of each seed were provided by Dr. Sabin. It was presumed that if progeny of these seeds proved to be free of extraneous agents and have satisfactory neurovirulence the parent seeds were satisfactory.

"Detection of Adventitious Agents in Poliovirus Production Substrate, January 1970 through August 1983." Internal Lederle Laboratories report. "A history of the examination of the poliovirus production control bottles and tissue culture safety tests results from the 14 day fluids therefrom was tabulated between January 1970 and August 1983." Report states that kidney tissues from 2,239 African green monkeys were cultured for vaccine production during this time period and "962 monkeys or 43% were rejected during this period." Thirty-eight percent of the rejections (367) were for SCMV, 1% (10) were rejected because of SV40.

Deposition of Mary Ritchey, employee of American Cyanamid, parent company of Lederle, by Stanley Kops, April 13, 1998, in *Graham et al. v. American Cyanamid*, CV C2–94–423, United States District Court for the Southern District of Ohio, Eastern District. During deposition (pp. 12–16, 33–35, 38–42), Ritchey states there are no records of tests for SV40 for many of the original strains and working seeds used by Lederle during vaccine manufacture.

Documents from *Horwin v. American Home Products, Inc.*, Case No. CV-00-04523 WJR (Ex), United States District Court for the Central District of California, Western Division: Complaint; Letters from Michele Carbone, Oct. 27, 1999, and Dec. 3, 1999, to Raphaele and Michael Horwin (detailing results of tests on medulloblastoma and cord blood); Declaration of Dr. John Lednicky, Aug. 25, 2002, and including expert opinion letter attached thereto, Apr. 22, 2002; Declaration of Bharat Jasani, Aug. 26, 2002, and including expert opinion letter attached thereto, Aug. 25, 2002; Declaration of Adi F. Gazdar, M.D., Aug. 26, 2002, and including expert opinion letter attached thereto, Jul. 17, 2002; Supplemental Declaration of Dr. John Lednicky, Sep. 4, 2002; Transcript of Daubert Hearing, Feb. 11, 12, 14, 18, 19, 20, 21, 25, 27, 28, 2003; Tentative Ruling, May 8, 2003 ; Declaration of Stanley P. Kops, May 27, 2003; Plaintiffs' Reply in Support of Motion to Amend Judgment Pursuant to Federal Rule 59(e), Jun. 16, 2003; Plaintiffs' Memorandum of Points and Authorities in Support of Motion for Relief from Final Judgment under FRCP, Rule 60(b) 2 & 3, Nov. 25, 2003.

Exhibit 10, as attached to "Submitted testimony of Stanley P. Kops, Esquire: "Oral Presentation to the Subcommittee on Human Rights and Wellness of the Committee on Government Reform: 'The SV40 Virus: Has Tainted Polio Vaccine Caused an Increase in Cancer?' " Sep. 10, 2003. Fourteen pages of documents that Kops presented to subcommittee show seven working seeds of Type I and Type II poliovirus were produced on rhesus monkey kidney tissues.

Exhibit 11, as attached to "Submitted testimony of Stanley P. Kops, Esquire: "Oral Presentation to the Subcommittee on Human Rights and Wellness of the Committee on Government Reform: 'The SV40 Virus: Has Tainted Polio Vaccine Caused an Increase in

Cancer?' " Sep. 10, 2003. A forty-nine-page document, entitled "Release Protocol" for Type II bulk monopool 2-2825. Kops said the protocol shows that a Type II monopool was produced on rhesus monkey kidney tissues and was also released for use. Protocol shows that kidneys from six different rhesus monkeys were used to produce the almost 227 liters of Type II poliovirus that comprised this monopool.

Exhibit 13, as attached to "Submitted testimony of Stanley P. Kops, Esquire: "Oral Presentation to the Subcommittee on Human Rights and Wellness of the Committee on Government Reform: 'The SV40 Virus: Has Tainted Polio Vaccine Caused an Increase in Cancer?' " Sep. 10, 2003. Jan. 15, 1990 letter from the Lederle director of quality control to the FDA asking for permission to release three monopools produced on rhesus monkey kidneys and representing "several million doses of trivalent oral polio vaccine."

Scientific Articles. The following were referenced or relied upon for the text in this chapter:

Kops, S. "Oral Polio Vaccine and Human Cancer: A Reassessment of SV40 as a Contaminant Based upon Legal Documents." *Anticancer Research* 20:4745–4750 (2000).

Rizzo, P., Di Resta, I., Powers, A., Ratner, H., and Carbone, M. "Unique Strains of SV40 In Commercial Poliovaccines from 1955 Not Readily Identifiable with Current Testing for SV40 Infection." *Cancer Research* 59:6103–6108 (1999). Carbone's tests on Ratner's 1955 vials of vaccine showing SV40 in vials took nineteen days to grow out.

Sangar, D., et al. "Examination of Poliovirus Vaccine Preparations for SV40 Sequences." *Biologicals* 27(1):1–10 (March 1999). This is the British study on old samples of British oral polio vaccine. Carbone states that the conclusion by the authors that there were no SV40 sequences in the lots they tested is not supported by their results and that some of the samples appear to have contained SV40.

Sierra-Honigmann, A., and Krause, P. R. "Live Oral Poliovirus Vaccines Do Not Contain Detectable SV40 DNA." *Biologicals* 28(1):1–4 (March 2000). This is the FDA study that found no SV40 in old samples of oral polio vaccine released in the United States. Carbone criticizes the methodology of this study as inadequate to detect SV40 if it were present in the samples.

Sierra-Honigmann, A., and Krause, P. R. "Live Oral Poliovirus Vaccines and Simian Cytomegalovirus." *Biologicals* 30:167–174 (2002). PCR survey by FDA of old samples of oral polio vaccine finds SCMV DNA in three lots tested (one from 1972, two from 1976). All post-1980 lots tested were negative.

CONCLUSION

Interviews. Jonathan Allan, University of Texas Southwest, Foundation for Biomedical Research, Apr. 18, 1996; Ronald Kennedy, Sep. 9, 2000; Hilary Koprowski, Feb. 15, 2001; Barbara Loe Fisher, Sep. 9, 2000; Jan. 19, 2002.

General Background. Koprowski's work in developing plant-based vaccines was obtained from our interview with him, as well as the following: H. Koprowski, and V. Yusibov, "The Green Revolution: Plants as Heterologous Expression Vectors," *Vaccine* 19:2375–2741 (2001); "Breaking Ground for a Healthier Tomorrow: Using Plants to Make Safer, More Economical Vaccines and Therapeutic Products," publicity pamphlet of the BioTechnology Foundation, Inc., BioTechnology Laboratories at Thomas Jefferson University, Philadelphia, Pa.; and "Plant-Based Vaccines Show Promise Against Infections Diseases," American Medical Association media advisory, Oct. 4, 2001.

Sources for the discussion of the rise of the consumers choice movement in relation to vaccines and some of its concerns include the interviews with Barbara Loe Fisher, listed above, as well as the following: Harris L. Coulter and Barbara Loe Fisher, *A Shot in the Dark* (Orlando, Fla.: Harcourt Brace Jovanovich, 1985); and Barbara Loe Fisher, "Shots in the Dark," *The Next City* (summer 1999). Fisher is the president and cofounder of the National Vaccine Information Center, a Vienna, Va., consumer organization promoting vaccine safety. In both her book and the magazine story, Fisher reviews a number of vaccine safety issues. She also examines vaccination as a public policy question from the standpoint of the Nuremberg Code, which states that the advancement of science (in this case, disease eradication through vaccination) should never take precedence over individual inviolability (in this case, the right of the individual to determine what medical intervention he or she receives). Fisher is a former member of the FDA Vaccines and Related Biological Products Advisory Committee and of the National Academy of Science's Institute of Medicine Vaccine Safety Forum.

Information concerning the use of thimerosal in vaccines and the federal government's response to it was obtained from several sources, including "Thimerosal in Vaccines," fact sheet from the Center for Biologicals Evaluation and Research (CBER), Food and Drug Administration, as posted on CBER Web site. See also "Vaccine Controversies," *CQ Researcher*, Aug. 25, 2000, 10(28):641–672, which reports on this issue.

Concerning viral contamination of vaccine substrates, see Nicholas Wade, "Division of Biologics Standards: Scientific Management Questioned," *Science* 175:966–970 (Mar. 3, 1972) (virus-like particles in duck eggs used to produce rubella vaccine); Nicholas Wade, "Division of Biologics Standards: The Boat That Never Rocked," *Science* 175:1225–1229 (Mar. 17, 1972) (discovery of herpes virus in the dog kidney cell substrate that the DBS proposed to use for the production of rubella vaccine); Gina Kolata, "Phage in Live Virus Vaccines: Are They Harmful to People?" *Science* 187:522–523 (Feb. 14, 1975) (a report on FDA determination that "all live virus vaccines" grown in tissue culture "are grossly contaminated with phage [viruses that infect bacteria]." The viruses, Kolata reports, are a common contaminant of the fetal bovine growth serum used to provide "growth factors" for culture medium.). For more modern examples, see letter from Stuart L. Nightingale, M.D., Associate Commissioner for Health Affairs, Food and Drug Administration, Jan. 4, 1996: "Dear Colleague, The purpose of this letter is to alert you and members of your organization to the significance of a recent scientific development. . . . Investigators from several institutions have found extremely low levels of a reverse transcriptase (Rtase) activity in several viral vaccines, including measles and mumps vaccines, produced in chicken cells." Nightingale notes "articles about this finding have begun to appear in U.S. newspapers." (Note: Readers who wish to learn more about safety issues related to vaccines including additives and substrates used in the manufacture of vaccines may wish to refer to a "Consumers Guide to Vaccines" and other informational materials and resources produced by the National Vaccine Information Center (http://www.nvic.org).

Concerning the business aspects of vaccines and the special protections pharmaceutical companies have lobbied for in recent years, see "Vaccines Seen a $10 Billion Market by 2006," *Reuters*, Jan. 7, 2003; Bob Herbert, "Whose Hands Are Dirty?" (op-ed), *New York Times*, Nov. 25, 2002, which describes the inclusion of a provision in the bill creating the Department of Homeland Security that protected Eli Lilly and some other pharmaceuticals from lawsuits by parents who believe their children were harmed by thimerosal, the mercury-based preservative used in some vaccines; Sheryl Gay Stolberg, "Republicans Press for Bill to Shield Vaccine Makers from Suits" *New York Times*, Apr. 9, 2003, describes efforts to resurrect the legislation that protected Eli Lilly and other pharmaceuticals that manufacture vaccine additives, after it was repealed following its passage in the Department of Homeland Security bill.

Concerning allegations of conflicts of interests on the part of some scientists who have advisory roles on vaccine policy, see "FDA Advisors Tied to Industry," *USA Today*, Oct. 25, 2000, page 1. ("More than half of the experts hired to advise the government on the safety and effectiveness of medicine have financial relationships with the pharmaceutical companies that will be helped or hurt by their decisions, a *USA Today* study found.") In this regard, Mark Benjamin, "The Vaccine Conflict," United Press International, Jul. 20, 2003, focuses on the industry connections of some members and former members of the Centers for Disease Control Advisory Committee on Immunization Practices (ACIP), which decides which vaccines to recommend for universal use. The UPI article examines the committee's decision to recommend the vaccine Rotashield, developed to prevent infant diarrhea caused by the rotavirus. Four out of eight committee members who voted to approve guidelines for the rotavirus vaccine in June 1998 had financial ties to pharmaceutical companies that were developing different versions of the vaccine, according to a House Government Reform Committee August 2001 report. The vaccine was recalled after reports that it caused the intestines of some children to fold in on themselves; 8 children died and 232 were hospitalized, according to the CDC's public database. Members of the CDC advisory committee deny that their financial ties to vaccine manufacturers influence their decisions: "I am probably just the kind of person you are talking about," Paul Offit, chief of infectious diseases at the Children's Hospital of Philadelphia, and former committee member, told UPI. At the time he voted in favor of recommending the vaccine, he shared a patent for another rotavirus vaccine. Merck has funded Offit's research for thirteen years. "I am a co-holder of a patent for a [rotavirus] vaccine. If this vaccine were to become a routinely recommended vaccine, I would make money off of that," Offit said. "When I review safety data, am I biased? That answer is really easy: absolutely not. . . . Is there an unholy alliance between the people who make recommendations about vaccines and the vaccine manufacturers? The answer is no."

The UPI article also reports on other examples of possible conflicts of interest by ACIP members, including that of Sam Katz, who was chairman of the advisory committee in 1991 when it recommended that all infants receive the hepatitis B vaccine. Katz developed a measles vaccine now manufactured by Merck, which also manufactures a hepatitis B vaccine; he was a paid consultant for Merck, Wyeth, and "most major vaccine manufacturers," according to the article, but denies any conflict of interest. (Note: Katz was on the 1971 American Academy of Pediatrics committee lobbied by Lederle to not recommend Pfizer's Diplovax over the Lederle's oral polio vaccine, Orimune. According to a Nov. 29, 1971, Lederle internal memo, Katz agreed that that AAP would not recommend Pfizer vaccine, but instead would merely let doctors know an alternative to Lederle's was available. See notes to chapter 10.) In another example reported by UPI, Neal Halsey, director of the division of disease control at Johns Hopkins University, also advised the CDC committee during the 1990s. The UPI story reveals that Halsey was receiving money from vaccine manufacturers for other activities at the same time he was advising the CDC. The CDC says that in October 2002, it adopted new guidelines designed to preclude people with conflicts such as those described by the UPI from sitting on the advisory committee.

Appendix A

Association of SV40 with Human Disease

This appendix lists in chronological order studies related to SV40 and human disease published between 1972 and fall 2003. For reference purposes, it is divided into categories:

Studies Associating SV40 with Human Tumors and Human Disease
Studies That Failed to Associate SV40 with Human Tumors or Human Disease
The Multilaboratory Study Organized by Howard Strickler and James Goedert
Early Epidemiological Studies
Serological and Epidemiological Studies Produced by or under the Auspices of the Viral Epidemiology Branch Failing to Associate SV40 with Human Tumors or Human Disease
Other Related Studies and Reviews That Support Association of SV40 with Human Disease

STUDIES ASSOCIATING SV40 WITH HUMAN TUMORS AND HUMAN DISEASE (INCLUDES POSITIVE SEROLOGICAL STUDIES) (89)

Weiner, L. P., et al. "Isolation of Virus Related to SV40 from Patients with Progressive Multifocal Leukoencephalopathy." *New England Journal of Medicine* 286(8):385–389 (Feb. 24, 1972).

Weiner, L. P., et al. "Further Studies of a Simian Virus 40-Like Virus Isolated from Human Brain," *Journal of Virology* 10:147–149 (1972).

Sack, G. H. et al. "The Nucleic Acid of an SV40-Like Virus Isolated from a Patient with Progressive Multifocal Leukoencephalopathy." *Virology* 51:345–350 (1973).

Santoli, D., et al. "Establishment of Continuous Multiple Sclerosis Brain Cultures after Transformation with PML-SV40 Virus." *Journal of the Neurological Sciences*, 24:385–390 (1975).

Soriano, F., Shelburne, C. E., and Gokeen, M. "Simian Virus 40 in a Human Cancer." *Nature* 249:421–424 (1974).

Weiss, A. F., et al. "Simian Virus 40-Related Antigens in Three Human Meningiomas with

Defined Chromosome Loss." *Proceedings of the National Academy of Sciences, USA* 72(2): 609–613 (1975).

Brandner, G., et al. "Isolation of Simian Virus 40 from a Newborn Child." *Journal of Clinical Microbiology* 5(2):250–252 (1977).

Tabuchi, K., et al. "Screening of Human Brain Tumors for SV40-related T Antigen." *International Journal of Cancer* 21:12–17 (1978).

Meinke, W., Goldstein, D. A., and Smith, R. A. "Simian Virus 40-Related DNA Sequences in a Human Brain Tumor." *Neurology* 29:1590–4 (1979).

Scherneck, S., et al. "Isolation of a SV40-like Papovavirus from a Human Glioblastoma." *International Journal of Cancer* 24:523–531 (1979).

Krieg, P., et al. "Episomal Simian Virus 40 Genomes in Human Brain Tumors." *Proceedings of the National Academy of Sciences, USA* 78: 6446–6450 (1981).

Scherneck, S., et al. "Isolation of a SV-40-Like Virus from a Patient with Progressive Multifocal Leukoencephalopathy." *Acta Virologie* 25(4):191–198 (1981).

Ibelgaufts, H., and Jones, K. W. "Papovavirus-Related RNA Sequences in Human Neurogenic Tumors." *Acta Neuropathologica* 56:118–122 (1982).

Stoian, M., et al. "Investigations on the Presence of Papovavirus in Certain Forms of Human Cancer. Note 2. Brain Tumors." *Revue Roumaine de Médicine-Virologie* 35:127–132 (1984).

Krieg, P., and Scherer, G. "Cloning of SV40 Genomes from Human Brain Tumors." *Virology* 138:336–340 (1984).

de Fromentel, C., et al. "Epithelial HBL-100 Cell Line Derived from Milk of an Apparently Healthy Woman Harbours SV40 Genetic Information." *Experimental Cell Research* 160: 83–94 (1985).

Bravo, M. P., et al. "Antibodies to Simian Vacuolating Virus 40 in Bladder Cancer Patients." *Urologica Internationalis* 42(6):427–430 (1987).

Bravo, M. P., and Del Rey-Calero, J. "Association between the Occurrence of Antibodies to Simian Vacuolating Virus and Bladder Cancer in Male Smokers." *Neoplasma* 35(3): 285–288 (1988).

Martin, J. D. "Regulatory Sequence of SV40 Variants Isolated from Patients with Progressive Multifocal Leukoencephalopathy." *Virus Research* 14(1):85–94 (1989).

Geissler, E. "SV40 and Human Brain Tumors." Melnick JL (ed):*Progress in Medical Virology* (Basel, Karger), 37:211–222 (1990).

Bergsagel, D. J., Finegold, M. J., Butel, J. S., Kupsky, W. J., and Garcea, R. L. "DNA Sequences Similar to Those of Simian Virus 40 in Ependymomas and Choroid Plexus Tumors of Childhood." *New England Journal of Medicine* 326:988–993 (1992).

Carbone, M., Pass, H. I., Rizzo, P., Marinetti, M., Di Muzio, M., Mew, D. J. Y., Levine, A. S., and Procopio, A. "Simian Virus 40-Like DNA Sequences in Human Pleural Mesothelioma." *Oncogene* 9:1781–1790 (1994).

Lednicky, J. A., Garcea, R. L., Bergsagel, D. J., and Butel, J. S. "Natural Simian Virus 40 Strains Are Present in Human Choroid Plexus and Ependymoma Tumors." *Virology*. 212:710–717 (1995).

Pepper, C., Jasani, B., Navabi, H., Wynford-Thomas, D., and Gibbs, A. R. "Simian Virus 40 Large T Antigen (SV40LTAg) Primer Specific DNA Amplification in Human Pleural Mesothelioma Tissue." *Thorax* 51:1071–1076 (1996).

Carbone, M., Rizzo, P., Procopio, A., Giuliano, M., Pass, H. I., Gebhardt, M. C., Mangham, C., et al. "SV40-Like Sequences in Human Bone Tumors." *Oncogene* 13:527–535 (1996).

Martini, F., Iaccheri, L., Lazzarin, L., Carinci, P., Corallini, A., Gerosa, M., et al. "SV40 Early Region and Large T Antigen in Human Brain Tumors, Peripheral Blood Cells, and Sperm Fluids from Healthy Individuals." *Cancer Research* 56:4820–4825 (1996).

Carbone, M., Rizzo, P., Grimley, P. M., Procopio, A., Mew, D. J, Y., Shridhar, V., et al. "Simian Virus-40 Large-T Antigen Binds p53 in Human Mesotheliomas." *Nature Medicine* 3:908–912 (1997).

DeLuca, A., Baldi, A., Esposito, V., Howard, C. M., Bagella, L., Rizzo, P., et al. "The Retinoblastoma Gene Family pRb/p105, p107, pRb2/p130 and Simian Virus-40 Large T-Antigen in Human Mesotheliomas." *Nature Medicine* 3:913–916 (1997).

Lednicky, J. A., Stewart, A. R., Jenkins, J. J., Finegold, M. J., and Butel, J. S. "SV40 DNA in Human Osteosarcomas Shows Sequence Variation among T-Antigen Genes." *International Journal of Cancer* 72:791–800 (1997).

Suzuki, S. O., Mizoguchi, M., and Iwaki, T. "Detection of SV40 T Antigen Genome in Human Gliomas." *Brain Tumor Pathology* 14:125–129 (1997).

Stewart, A. R., Lednicky, J. A., and Butel, J. S. "Sequence Analyses of Human Tumor-Associated SV40 DNAs and SV40 Viral Isolates from Monkeys and Humans." *Journal of Neurovirology* 4:182–193 (1998).

Pass, H. I., Donington, J. S., Wu, P., Rizzo, P., Nishimura, M., Kennedy, R., and Carbone, M. "Human Mesotheliomas Contain the Simian Virus-40 Regulatory Region and Large Tumor Antigen DNA Sequences. *Journal of Thoracic Cardiovascular Surgery* 116:854–859 (1998).

Pacini, F., Vivaldi, A., Santoro, M., Fedele, M., Fusco, A., Romei, C., et al. "Simian Virus 40-Like DNA Sequences in Human Papillary Thyroid Carcinomas." *Oncogene* 16:665–669 (1998).

Mendoza, S. M., Konishi, T., and Miller, C. W. "Integration of SV40 in Human Osteosarcoma DNA." *Oncogene* 17:2457–2462 (1998).

Griffiths, D. J., Nicholson, A. G., and Weiss, R. A. "Detection of SV40 Sequences in Human Mesothelioma." *Developments in Biological Standards* 94:127–136 (1998).

Galateau-Salle, F., Bidet, P. H., Iwatsubo, Y., Gennetay, E., Renier, A., Letourneux, M., et al. "SV40-Like DNA Sequences in Pleural Mesothelioma, Bronchopulmonary Carcinoma, and Non-malignant Pulmonary Diseases." *Journal of Pathology* 184:252–257 (1998).

Procopio, A., Marinacci, R., Marinetti, M. R., Strizzi, L., Paludi, D., Iezzi, T., et al. "SV40 Expression in Human Neoplastic and Non-neoplastic Tissues: Perspectives on Diagnosis, Prognosis and Therapy of Human Malignant Mesothelioma." *Development in Biological Standards* 94:361–367 (1998).

Mutti, L., De Luca, A., Claudio, P. P., Convertino, G., Carbone, M., and Giordano, A. "Simian Virus 40-like DNA Sequences and Large-T Antigen-Retinoblastoma Family Protein pRb2/p130 Interaction in Human Mesothelioma." *Developments in Biological Standards* 94:47–53 (1998).

Testa, J. R., Carbone, M., Hirvonen, A., Khalili, K., Krynska, B., Linnainmaa, K., et al. "A Multi-institutional Study Confirms the Presence and Expression of Simian Virus 40 in Human Malignant Mesotheliomas." *Cancer Research* 58:4505–4509 (1998).

Martini, F., Dolcetti, R., Gloghini, A., Iaccheri, L., Carbone, A., Boiocchi, M., et al. "Simian-Virus-40 Footprints in Human Lymphoproliferative Disorders of HIV- and HIV+ patients." *International Journal of Cancer* 78:669–674 (1998).

Jafar, S., Rodriquez-Barradas, M., Graham, D. Y., and Butel, J. S. "Serological Evidence of SV40 Infections in HIV-Infected and HIV-Negative Adults." *Journal of Medical Virology* 54:276–284 (1998).

Pass, H. I., Donington, J. S., Wu, P., Rizzo, P., Nishimura, M., Kennedy, R., et al. "Human Mesotheliomas Contain the Simian Virus-40 (SV40) Regulatory Region and Large Tumor (T) Antigen DNA Sequences." *Journal of Cardiothoracic Surgery* 116:854–859 (1998).

Hirvonen, A., Mattson, K., Karjalainen, A., Ollikainen, T., Tammilehto, L., Hovi, T., et al. "Simian Virus 40 (SV40)-Like DNA Sequences Not Detectable in Finnish Mesothelioma Patients Not Exposed to SV40-Contaminated Polio Vaccines." *Molecular Carcinogenesis* 26:93–99 (1999).

Xu, L., Flynn, B. J., Ungar, S., Pass, H. I., Linnainmaa, K., Mattson, K., et al. "Asbestos Induction of Extended Lifespan in Normal Human Mesothelial Cells: Interindividual Susceptibility and SV40 T Antigen." *Carcinogenesis* 20:773–783 (1999).

Butel, J. S., Arrington, A. S., Wong, C., Lednicky, J. A., and Finegold, M. J. "Molecular Evidence of Simian Virus 40 Infections in Children." *Journal of Infectious Diseases* 180: 884–887 (1999).

Butel, J. S., Jafar, S., Wong, C., Arrington, A. S., Opekun, A. R., Finegold, M. J., et al. "Evidence of SV40 Infections in Hospitalized Children." *Human Pathology* 30:496 (1999).

Krynska, B., Del Valle, L., Croul, S., Gordon, J., Katsetos, C. D., Carbone, M., et al. "Detection of Human Neurotropic JC Virus DNA Sequences and Expression of the Viral Oncogenic Protein in Pediatric Medulloblastomas." *Proceedings of the National Academy of Sciences, USA* 96:11519–11524 (1999).

Rizzo, P., Carbone, M., Fisher, S. G., Matker, C., Swinnen, L., J., Powers, A., et al. "Simian Virus 40 Is Present in Most United States Human Mesotheliomas, but It Is Rarely Present in Non-Hodgkin's Lymphoma." *Chest* 116:470S–473S (1999).

Huang, H., Reis, R., Yonekawa, Y., Lopes, J. M., Kleihues, P., Ohgaki, H. "Identification in Human Brain Tumors of DNA Sequences Specific for SV40 Large T Antigen." *Brain Pathology* 9: 33–44 (1999).

Dhaene, K., Verhulst, A., and Van Marck, E. "SV40 Large T-Antigen and Human Pleural Mesothelioma." *Virchows Archiv A, Pathological Anatomy and Histopathology* 435:1–7 (1999).

Mayall, F. G., Jacobson, G., and Wilkins, R. "Mutations of p53 Ggene and SV40 Sequences in Asbestos Associated and Non-Asbestos-Associated Mesotheliomas." *Journal of Clinical Pathology* 52: 291–293 (1999).

Zhen, H. N., Zhang, X., Bu, X. Y., Zhang, Z. W., Huang, W. J., Zhang, P., et al. "Expression of the Simian Virus 40 Large Tumor Antigen (Tag) and Formation of Tag-p53 and Tag-pRb Complexes in Human Brain Tumors." *Cancer* 86:2124–2132 (1999).

Waheed, I., Guo, Z. S., Chen, A., Weiser, T. S., Nguyen, D. M,, and Schrump, D. S. "Antisense to SV40 Early Gene Region Induces Growth Arrest and Apoptosis in T-Antigen-Positive Human Pleural Mesothelioma Cells." *Cancer Research* 59:6068–6073 (1999).

Shivapurkar, N., Wiethege, T., Wistubu. I. I., Salomon, E., Milchgrup, S., Muller, K. M., et al. "Presence of Simian Virus 40 Sequences in Malignant Mesotheliomas and Mesothelial Cell Proliferations." *Journal of Cell Biochemistry* 76:181–188 (1999).

Orengo, A. M., Spoletini, L., Procopio, A., Favoni, R. E., De Cupis, A., Ardizzoni, A., et al. "Establishment of Four New Mesothelioma Cell Lines: Characterization by Ultrastructural and Immunophenotypic Analysis." *European Respiratory Journal* 13:527–534 (1999).

Ramael, M., Nagels, J., Heylen, H., De Schepper, S., Paulussen, J., De Maeyer, M., et a;/ "Detection of SV40-Like Viral DNA and Viral Antigens in Malignant Pleural Mesothelioma." *European Respiratory Journal* 14:1381–1386 (1999).

Shivapurkar, N., Wiethege, T., Wistubu, I. I., Milchgrub, S., Muller, K. M., and Gazdar, A. F. "Presence of Simian Virus 40 Sequences in Malignant Pleural, Peritoneal and Non-invasive Mesotheliomas." *International Journal of Cancer* 85:743–745 (2000).

Weggen, S., Bayer, T. A., von Deimling, A., Reifenberger, G., von Schweinitz, D., Wiestler, O. D., et al. "Low Frequency of SV40, JC and BK Polyomavirus Sequences in

Human Medulloblastomas, Meningiomas and Ependymomas." *Brain Pathology* 10:85–92 (2000).

Gamberi, G., Benassi, S., Pompetti, F., Ferrari, C., Ragazzini, P., Sollazzo, M. R., et al. "Presence and Expression of the Simian Virus-40 Genome in Human Giant Cell Tumors of Bone." *Genes, Chromosomes and Cancer* 28:23–30 (2000).

Strizzi, L., Vianale, G., Giuliano, M., Sacco, R., Tassi, F., Chiodera, P., et al. "SV40, JC and BK Expression in Tissue, Urine and Blood Samples from Patients with Malignant and Nonmalignant Pleural Disease." *Anticancer Research* 20:885–890 (2000).

Emri, S., Kocagoz, T., Olut, A., Gungen, Y., Mutti, L., and Baris, Y. I. "Simian Virus 40 Is Not a Cofactor in the Pathogenesis of Environmentally Induced Malignant Pleural Mesothelioma in Turkey." *Anticancer Research* 20:891–894 (2000).

Cristaudo, A., Powers, A., Vivaldi, A., Foddisv, R., Guglielmi, G., Gattini, V., et al. "SV40 Can Be Reproducibly Detected in Paraffin-Embedded Mesothelioma Samples." *Anticancer Research* 20:895–898 (2000).

Arrington, A. S., Lednicky, J. A., and Butel, J. S. "Molecular Characterization of SV40 DNA in Multiple Samples from a Human Mesothelioma." *Anticancer Research* 20:879–884 (2000).

Yamamoto, H., Nakayama, T., Murakami, H., Hosaka, T., Nakamata, T., Tsuboyama, T., et al. "High Incidence of SV40-Like Sequences Detection in Tumour and Peripheral Blood Cells of Japanese Osteosarcoma Patients." *British Journal of Cancer* 82:1677–1881 (2000).

McLaren, B. R., Haenel, T., Stevenson, S., Mukherjee, S., Robinson, B. W., and Lake, R. A. "Simian Virus (SV) 40-Like Sequences in Cell Lines and Tumour Biopsies from Australian Malignant Mesotheliomas." *Australian and New Zealand Journal of Medicine* 30:450–456 (2000).

David, H., Mendoza, S., Konishi, T., and Miller, C. W. "Simian Virus 40 Is Present in Human Lymphomas and Normal Blood." *Cancer Letters* 162:57–64 (2001).

Kouhata, T., Fukuyama, K., Hagihara, N., and Tabuchi, K. "Detection of Simian Virus 40 DNA Sequence in Human Primary Glioblastomas Multiforme." *Journal of Neurosurgery* 95:96–101 (2001).

Heinsohn, S., Scholz, R. B., Weber, B., Wittenstein, B., Werner, M., Delling, G., et al. "SV40 Sequences in Human Osteosarcoma of German Origin." *Anticancer Research* 20:4539–4546 (2000).

Procopio, A., Strizzi, L., Vianale, G., Betta, P., Puntoni, R., Fontana, V., et al. "Simian Virus-40 Sequences Are a Negative Prognostic Cofactor in Patients with Malignant Pleural Mesothelioma." *Genes, Chromosomes and Cancer* 29:173–179 (2000).

Tognon, M., Martini, F., Iaccheri, L., Cultrera, R., and Contini, C. "Investigation of the Simian Polyomavirus SV40 as a Potential Causative Agent of Human Neurological Disorders in AIDS Patients." *Journal of Medical Microbiology (Virology)* 50(2): 165–172 (2001).

Malkin, D., Chilton-MacNeill, S., Meister, L. A., Sexsmith, E., Diller, L., and Garcea, R. L. "Tissue-Specific Expression of SV40 in Tumors Associated with the Li-Fraumeni Syndrome." *Oncogene* 20:4441–4449 (2001).

Cacciotti, P., Libener, R., Betta, P., Martini, F., Porta, C., Procopio, A., et al. "SV40 Replication in Human Mesothelial Cells Induces HGF/Met Receptor Activation: A Model for Viral-Related Carcinogenesis of Human Malignant Mesothelioma." *Proceedings of the National Academy of Sciences, USA* 98:12032–12037 (2001).

Toyooka, S., Pass, H. I., Shivapurkar, N., Fukuyama, Y., Maruyama, R., Toyooka, K. O., et al. "Aberrant Methylation and Simian Virus 40 Tag Sequences in Malignant Mesothelioma." *Cancer Research* 61:5727–5730 (2001).

Kouhata, T., Fukuyama, K., Hagihara, N., and Tabuchi, K. "Detection of Simian Virus 40 DNA Sequence in Human Primary Glioblastomas Multiforme." *Journal of Neurosurgery* 95:96–101 (2001).

Cacciotti, P., Strizzi, L., Vianale, G., Iaccheri, L., Libener, R., Porta, C., et al. "The Presence of Simian-Virus 40 Sequences in Mesothelioma and Mesothelial Cells Is Associated with High Levels of Vascular Endothelial Growth Factor." *American Journal of Respiratory Cell Molecular Biology* 26:189–193 (2002).

Shivapurkar, N., Harada, K., Reddy, J., Scheuermann, R. H., Xu, Y., Mckenna, R. W., et al. "Presence of Simian Virus 40 DNA Sequences in Human Lymphomas." *Lancet* 359: 851–52 (2002).

Vilchez, R. A., Madden, C. R., Kozinetz, C. A., Halvorson, S. J., White, Z. S., Jorgensen, J. L., and Finch, C. J. "Association between Simian Virus 40 and Non-Hodgkin's Lymphoma." *Lancet* 359:817–23 (2002).

De Rienzo, A., Tor, M., Sterman, D. H., Aksoy, F., Albelda, S. M., and Testa, J. R. "Detection of SV40 DNA Sequences in Malignant Mesothelioma Specimens from the United States, but Not from Turkey." *Journal of Cell Biochemistry* 84:455–459 (2002).

Gordon, G. J., Chen, C.-J., Jaklitsch, M. T., Richards, W. G., Sugarbaker, D. J., and Bueno, R. "Detection and Quantification of SV40 Large T-Antigen DNA in Mesothelioma Tissues and Cells Lines." *Oncology Reports* 9:631–634 (2002).

Baldi, A., Groeger, A. M., Esposito, V., Cassandro, R., Tonini, G., Battista, T., et al. "Expression of p21 in SV40 Large T Antigen Positive Human Pleural Mesothelioma: Relationship with Survival." *Thorax* 57:353–356 (2002).

Priftakis, P., Bogdanovio, G., Hjerpe, A., and Dalianis, T. "Presence of Simian Virus 40 (SV40) Is Not Frequent in Swedish Malignant Mesotheliomas." *Anticancer Research* 22: 1357–1360 (2002).

Leithner, A., Weinhaeusel, A., Windhager, R., Schlegl, R., Waldner, P., Lang, S., et al. "Absence of SV40 in Austrian Tumors Correlates with Low Incidence of Mesothelioma." *Cancer Biology and Therapy* 1:4, 375–379 (2002).

Martinelli, M., Martini, F., Rinaldi, E., Caramanico, L., Magri, E., Grandi, E., et al. "Simian Virus 40 Sequences and Expression of the Viral Large T Antigen Oncoprotein in Human Pleomorphic Adenomas of Parotid Glands." *American Journal of Pathology* 161:1127–1133 (2002).

Kim, J. Y. H., Koralnik, I. J., Le Fave, M., Segal, R. A., Pfister, L.-A., and Pomeroy, S. L. "Medulloblastomas and Primitive Neuroectodermal Tumors Rarely Contain Polymavirus DNA Sequences." *Neuro-Oncology* 4:165–170 (2002).

Li, R.-M., Mannon, R. B., Kleiner, D., Tsokos, M., Bynum, M., Kirk, A. D., et al. "BK Virus and SV40 Co-infection in Polyomavirus Nephropathy." *Transplantation* 74:1497–1504 (2002).

Vivaldi, A., Pacini, F., Martini, F., Iaccheri. L., Pezzetti, F., Elisei, R., et al. "Simian Virus 40-Like Sequences from Early and Late Regions in Human Thyroid Tumors of Different Histotypes." *Journal of Clinical Endocrinology and Metabolism* 88(2):892–899 (2003).

Bocchetta, M., Miele, L., Pass, H. I., and Carbone, M. "Notch-1 Induction, a Novel Activity of SV40 Required for Growth of SV40-Transformed Human Mesothelial Cells." *Oncogene* 22:81–89 (2003).

Dolcetti, R., Martini, F., Quaiai, M., Gloghini, A., Vignochhi, B., Cariati, et al. "Simian Virus 40 Sequences in Human Lymphoblastoid B-Cell Lines." *Journal of Virology* 77: 1595–1597 (2003).

Butel, J. S., et al. "Detection of Antibodies to Polyomavirus SV40 in Two Central European Countries." *Central European Journal of Public Health* 11:3–8 (2003).

STUDIES THAT FAILED TO ASSOCIATE SV40 WITH HUMAN TUMORS OR HUMAN DISEASE (8)

Strickler, H. D., Goedert, J. J., Fleming, M., Travis, W. D., Williams, A. E., Rabkin, C. S., et al. "Simian Virus 40 and Pleural Mesothelioma in Humans." *Cancer Epidemiology Biomarkers and Prevention* 5:473–475 (1996).

Mulatero, C., Surentheran, T., Breuer, J., and Rudd, R. M. "Simian Virus 40 and Human Pleural Mesothelioma." *Thorax* 54:60–61 (1999).

Pilatte, Y., Vivo, C., Reiner, A., Kheuang, L., Greffard, A., and Jaurand, M. C. "Absence of SV40 Large T-Antigen Expression in Human Mesothelioma Cell Lines." *American Journal of Respiratory Cell Molecular Biology* 23: 788–793 (2000).

Engels, A. E., Sarkar, C., Daniel, R. W., Gravott, E., Verma, K., Quezado, M., et al. "Absence of Simian Virus 40 in Human Brain Tumors from Northern India." *International Journal of Cancer* 101:348–352 (2002).

Hubner, R., and Van Marck, E. "Reappraisal of the Strong Association between Simian Virus 40 and Human Malignant Mesothelioma of the Pleura (Belgium)." *Cancer Causes and Control* 13:121–129 (2002).

Gordon, G. J., Chen, C. J., Jaklitsch, M. T., Richards, W. G., Sugarbaker, D. J., and Bueno, R. "Detection and Quantification of SV40 Large T-Antigen DNA in Mesothelioma Tissues and Cell Lines." *Oncology Report* 9:631–634 (2002).

MacKenzie, J., et al. "Association between Simian Virus 40 and Lymphoma in the United Kingdom." *Journal of the National Cancer Institute* 95:1001–1003 (2003).

Capello, D., Rossi, D., Gaudino, G., Carbone, A., Gaidano, G. "Simian Virus 40 Infection in Lymphoproliferative Disorders." *Lancet* 361:88–89 (2003).

THE MULTILABORATORY STUDY ORGANIZED BY HOWARD STRICKLER AND JAMES GOEDERT

Goedert, J. J., and International SV40 Working Group. "A Multicenter Evaluation of Assays for Detection of SV40 DNA and Results in Masked Mesothelioma Specimens." *Cancer Epidemiology, Biomarkers and Prevention* 10:523–532 (2001).

EARLY EPIDEMIOLOGICAL STUDIES (9)

Fraumeni, J. F., Ederer, F., and Miller, R. "An Evaluation of the Carcinogencity of Simian Virus 40 in Man." *JAMA* 185(9):713–718 (1963).

Innis, M.D. "Oncogenesis and Poliomyelitis Vaccine," *Nature* 219.972–973 (1968).

Fraumeni, J. F., Stark, C. R, "Simian Virus 40 in Polio Vaccine: Follow-up of Newborn Recipients." *Science* 167:59–60 (1970).

Heinonen, O. P., Shapiro, S., Monson, R. R., Hartz, S. C., Rosenberg, L., and Slone, D. "Immunization during Pregnancy against Poliomyelitis and Influenza in Relation to Childhood Malignancy." *International Journal of Epidemiology* 2:229–235 (1973).

Shah, K., and Nathanson, N. "Human Exposure to SV40: Review and Comment." *American Journal of Epidemiology* 103(1):1–12 (1976).

Mortimer, E. A., Lepow, M. L., Gold, E., Robbins, F. C., Burton, G. J., and Fraumeni, J. F. "Long-term Follow-up of Persons Inadvertently Inoculated with SV40 as Neonates." *New England Journal of Medicine* 305(25): 1517–1518 (1981).

Farwell, J. R., Dohrmann, G. J., Marret, L. D., and Meigs, J. W. "Effect of SV40 Virus-Contaminated Polio Vaccine on the Incidence and Type of CNS Neoplasms in Children: A Population-Based Study." *TransAmerican Neurological Association* 104:261–264 (1979).

Farwell, J. R., et al. "Medulloblastoma in Childhood: An Epidemiological, Study. *Journal of Neurosurgery* 61:657–664 (1984).

Geissler, E. "SV40 and Human Brain Tumors." Melnick, J. L., ed., *Progress in Medical Virology* (Basel: Karger), 37:211–222 (1990).

SEROLOGICAL AND EPIDEMIOLOGICAL STUDIES PRODUCED BY OR UNDER THE AUSPICES OF THE VIRAL EPIDEMIOLOGY BRANCH FAILING TO ASSOCIATE SV40 WITH HUMAN TUMORS OR HUMAN DISEASE (9)

Shah, K. V., Daniel, R. W., Strickler, H. D., and Goedert, J. J. "Investigation of Human Urine for Genomic Sequences of the Primate Polyomaviruses Simian Virus 40, BK Virus and JC Virus." *Journal of Infectious Diseases* 176:1618–21 (1997).

Strickler, H. D., Rosenberg, P. S., Devesa, S. S., Hertel, J., Fraumeni, J. F., and Goedert, J. J. "Contamination of Poliovirus Vaccines with Simian Virus 40 (1955–1963) and Subsequent Cancer Rates." *JAMA* 279:292–295 (1998).

Strickler, H. D., Rosenberg, P. S., Devesa, S. S., Fraumeni, J. F., and Goedert, J. J. "Contamination of Poliovirus Vaccine with SV40 and the Incidence of Medulloblastoma." *Medical and Pediatric Oncology* 32:777–78 (1999).

Carroll-Pankhurst, C., Engels, E. A., Strickler, H. D., Goedert J. J., Wagner, J., and Mortimer, E. A., "Thirty-five Year Mortality Following Receipt of SV40-Contaminated Polio Vaccine during the Neonatal Period." *British Journal of Cancer* 86(9):1295–1297 (2001).

Strickler, H., et al. "Trends in U.S. Pleural Mesothelioma Incidence Rates Following Simian Virus 40 Contamination of Early Poliovirus Vaccines." *Journal of the National Cancer Institute* 95(1): 38–45 (2003).

Engels, E. A., et al. "Cancer Incidence in Denmark Following Exposure to Poliovirus Vaccine Contaminated with Simian Virus 40." *Journal of the National Cancer Institute* 95:24 (2003).

Engels, E. A., Rodman, L. H., Frisch, M., Goedert, J. J., and Biggar, R. J. "Childhood Exposure to Simian Virus 40-Contaminated Poliovirus Vaccine and Risk of AIDS-Associated Non-Hodgkin's Lymphoma." *International Journal of Cancer* 106(7):283–287 (2003).

de Sanjose, S., Shah, K., Domingo-Domenech, E., Engels, E. A., Fernandez de Sevilla, A., Alvaro, T., Garcia-Villanueva, M., Fomagosa, V., Vonzalez-Barca, E., Viscidi, R. P. "Lack of Serological Evidence for an Association between Simian Virus 40 and Lymphoma." *International Journal of Cancer* 104:522–524 (2003).

Brenner, A. V., et al. "Polio Vaccination and the Risk of Brain Tumors in Adults. No Apparent Association." *Cancer Epidemiology, Biomarkers and Prevention* 12:177–178 (2003) (Note: Study was directed by the Radiation Epidemiology Branch, a sister lab to the VEB within the NCI's Division of Cancer Epidemiology and Genetics.)

OTHER RELATED STUDIES AND REVIEWS THAT SUPPORT ASSOCIATION OF SV40 WITH HUMAN DISEASE (37)

Carbone, M., Rizzo, P., and Pass, H. I. "Simian Virus 40, Poliovaccines and Human Tumors: A Review of Recent Developments." *Oncogene* 15:1877–1888 (1997).

Wiman, K. G., and Klein, G. "An Old Acquaintance Resurfaces in Human Mesothelioma. *Nature Medicine* 3:839 (1997).

Barbanti-Brodano, G., Martini, F., De Mattei, M., Lazzarin, L., Corallini, A., and Tognon, M. "BK and JC Human Polyomaviruses and Simian Virus 40: Natural History of Infections in Humans, Experimental Oncogenicity, and Association with Human Tumors." *Advances in Virology Research* 50:69–99 (1998).

Butel, J. S., and Lednicky, J. A. "Cell and Molecular Biology of Simian Virus 40: Implications for Human Infections and Disease." *Journal of the National Cancer Institute* 91: 119–134 (1999).

Carbone, M. "Simian Virus 40 and Human Tumors: It Is Time to Study Mechanisms." *Journal of Cell Biochemistry* 76:189–193 (1999).

Carbone, M., Fisher, S., Powers, A., Pass, H. I., and Rizzo, P. "New Molecular and Epidemiological Issues in Mesothelioma: Role of SV40." *Journal of Cell Physiology* 180:167–172 (1999).

Jasani, B. "Simian Virus 40 and Human Pleural Mesothelioma." *Thorax* 54:750–752, 1999.

Rizzo, P., Di Resta, I., Powers, A., Ratner, H., and Carbone, M. "Unique Strains of SV40 in Commercial Poliovaccines from 1955 Not Readily Identifiable with Current Testing for SV40 Infection." *Cancer Research* 59:6103–6108 (1999).

Salewski, H., Bayer, T. A., Eidhoff, U., Preuss, U., Weggen, S., and Scheidtmann, K. H. "Increased Oncogenicity of Subclones of SV40 Large T-Induced Neuroectodermal Tumor Cell Lines after Loss of Large T Expression and Concomitant Mutation of p53." *Cancer Research* 59:1980–1986 (1999).

Xie, Y. C., Hwang, C., Overwijk, W., Zeng, Z., Eng, M. H., Mule, J. J., et al. "Induction of Tumor Antigen-Specific Immunity in Vivo by a Novel Vaccinia Vector Encoding Safety-Modified Simian Virus 40 T Antigen." *Journal of the National Cancer Institute* 91: 169–175 (1999).

Fisher, S. G., Weber, L., and Carbone, M. "Cancer Risk Associated with Simian Virus 40-Contaminated Polio Vaccine." *Anticancer Research* 19:2173–2180 (1999). Fisher's retrospective study that concludes there is a correlation between exposure to SV40-contaminated Salk vaccine and several types of cancer.

Carbone, M., Rizzo, P., and Pass, H. "Simian Virus 40: The Link with Human Malignant Mesothelioma Is Well Established." *Anticancer Research* 20:875–878 (2000).

Testa, J. R., Pass, H. I., and Carbone, M. "Molecular Biology of Mesothelioma." In *Principles and Practical Oncology*, 6th ed., DeVita, Hellman, Rosenberg (eds). (2000).

Jasani, B., Jones, C. J., Radu, C., Wynford-Thomas, D., Navabi, H., Mason, M., et al. "Simian Virus 40 Detection in Human Mesothelioma: Reliability and Significance of the Available Molecular Evidence." *Frontiers in Bioscience* 6e:12–22 (2001).

Testa, J. R., and Giordano, A. "SV40 and Cell Cycle Perturbations in Malignant Mesothelioma," *Seminars in Cancer Biology* 11:31–38 (2001).

Lednicky, J. A., and Butel, J. S. "Simian Virus 40 Regulatory Region Structural Diversity and the Association of Viral Archetypal Regulatory Regions with Human Brain Tumors." *Seminars in Cancer Biology* 11:39–47 (2001).

Jasani, B., Cristaudo, A., Emri, S. A., Gazdar, A. F., Gibbs, A., Krynska, B., et al. "Association of SV40 with Human Tumours." *Seminars in Cancer Biology* 11:49–61 (2001).

Rizzo, P., Bocchetta, M., Powers, A., Foddis, R., Stekala, E., Pass, H. I., et al. "SV40 and the Pathogenesis of Mesothelioma." *Seminars in Cancer Biology* 11:63–71 (2001).

Schrump, D. S., and Waheed, I. "Strategies to Circumvent SV40 Oncoprotein Expression in Malignant Pleural Mesotheliomas." *Seminars in Cancer Biology* 11:73–80 (2001).

Imperiale, M. J., Pass, H. I., and Sanda, M. G. "Prospects for an SV40 Vaccine." *Seminars in Cancer Biology* 11:81–85 (2001).

Carbone, M. "SV40." *In Encyclopedic Reference of Cancer*, ed. M. Schwab (Berlin: Springer-Verlag), pp. 861–865 (2002).

Malkin, D. "Commentary: Simian Virus 40 and Non-Hodgkin's Llymphoma." *Lancet* 359: 812–813 (2002).

Klein, G., Powers, A., Croce, C. "Association of SV40 with Human Tumors." *Oncogene* 21: 1141–1149 (2002).

Carbone, M., Kratzke, R. A., and Testa, J. R. "The Pathogenesis of Mesothelioma." *Seminars in Oncology* 29:2–17 (2002).

Powers, A., Carbone, M. "The Role of Environmental Carcinogens, Viruses, and Genetic Predisposition in the Pathogenesis of Mesothelioma." *Cancer Biology and Therapy* (In press, 2002).

Mossman, B. T., and Gruenert, D. C. "SV40, Growth Factors, and Mesothelioma: Another Piece of the Puzzle." *American Journal of Respiratory Cell Molecular Biology* 26:167–170 (2002).

Gazdar, A. F., Butel, J. S., and Carbone, M. "SV40 and Human Tumors: Myth, Association or Causality?" *Nature Reviews/Cancer* 2:957–964 (2002).

Wong, M., Pagano, J. S., Schiller, J. T., Tevethia, S. S., Raab-Traub, N., and Gruber, J. "New Associations of Human Papillomavirus, Simian Virus 40, and Epstein-Barr Virus with Human Cancer." *Journal of the National Cancer Institute* 94:1832–1836 (2002).

Garcea, R. L., and Imperiale, M. J. "Simian Virus 40 Infection of Humans." *Journal of Virology* 77(9):5039–5045 (2003).

Croul, S., Otte, J., and Khalili, K. "Brain Tumors and Polyomaviruses." *Journal of Neurovirology* 9:173–182 (2003).

Carbone, M., and Pass, H. I. "Debate on the Link between SV40 and Human Cancer Continues." *Journal of the National Cancer Institute* 94:229–230 (2002).

Foddis, R., De Rienzo, A., Broccoli, D., Bocchetta, M., Stekala, E., Rizzo, P., et al. "SV40 Infection Induces Telomerase Activity in Human Mesothelial Cells." *Oncogene* 21:1434–1442 (2002).

Toyooka, S., Carbone, M., Toyooka, K. O., Shivapurkar, N., Minna, J. D., and Gazdar, A. F. "Progressive Aberrant Methylation of the RASSF1A Gene in Simian Virus 40 Infected Human Mesothelial Cells." *Oncogene* 21(27):4340–4344 (2002).

Carbone, M., Bocchetta, M., Cristaudo, A., Emri, S., Gazdar, A., Jasani, B., et al. "SV40 and Human Brain Tumors." *International Journal of Cancer* 106:140–142 (2003).

Vilchez, R., and Butel, J. "SV40 in Human Cancer and Non-Hodgkin's Lymphoma." *Oncogene* 22:5164–5172 (2003).

Vilchez, R., and Butel, J. "Simian Virus 40 and Its Association with Human Lymphomas." *Current Oncology Reports* 5:372–379 (2003).

Vilchez, R., et al. "Simian Virus 40 in Human Cancers." *American Journal of Medicine* 114: 675–684 (2003).

Appendix B

Correspondence Between Bernice Eddy, Joseph Smadel, and Roderick Murray (Chapters 6 and 7)

As described in the text for these chapters, Bernice Eddy was a career government researcher at the Division of Biologics Standards who first discovered that some unknown substance in the rhesus monkey kidney substrates used to produce polio vaccine caused cancer when injected into hamsters. When she brought this finding to the attention of her immediate superior, Joseph Smadel, he dismissed her hamster tumors as "lumps" and refused to take her research seriously. When she decided to announce her findings to the broader scientific world outside of the NIH, Smadel, with the support of DBS director Roderick Murray squelched her research, refused to let her speak publicly and deprived her of her laboratory. In 1960, researchers at Merck (Ben Sweet and Maurice Hilleman) announced the discovery of SV40. A year later, Eddy confirmed that SV40 and her rhesus monkey kidney substance were, indeed, one and the same.

Following is a complete listing of the memos and correspondence between Bernice Eddy, Joseph Smadel, and Roderick Murray during 1960 and 1961, referred to in chapters 6 and 7, relating to these events. These documents are included in the exhibits accompanying the "Hearings before the Subcommittee on Executive Reorganization and Government Research of the Senate Committee on Government Operations, Consumer Safety Act of 1972." Apr. 20–21, May 3–4, 1972 (Washington, D.C.: GPO, 1972).

Eddy to Murray, memo, Apr. 7, 1960. Handwritten notes, dating from sometime after Jun. 14, 1961, state Eddy lost her laboratory after discovery of SV40.

Eddy to Smadel, memo, Jul. 6, 1960. First notice to Smadel of Eddy's discovery. In addition to informing Smadel of her hamster tumor experiments, Eddy states that she has heard about Hilleman and Sweet's discovery of SV40 and is interested in trying to prove that what she has found and they have found are the same.

Eddy to Smadel, memo, Aug 10, 1960. Eddy states she needs more laboratory space to conduct her vaccine control work.

Smadel to Eddy, memo, Aug. 17, 1960. Smadel announces he intends to reduce Eddy's laboratory space.

Eddy to Smadel, memo, Aug. 18, 1960. Eddy responds to Smadel's memo.

Smadel to Eddy, memo, Oct. 24, 1960. Smadel memorializes the conversation in which he berates Eddy for speaking in public about her hamster tumor research. Memo announces Smadel's restrictions on Eddy's travel, publication, and research.

Eddy to Smadel, memo, Oct. 31, 1960. Eddy asks for permission to appear at scientific meeting.

Smadel to Eddy, memo, Nov. 2, 1960. Smadel denies above request.

Gilbert Dalldorf to Eddy, Nov. 2, 1960. Dalldorf was an outside researcher Eddy approached for help with Smadel.

Abstract by Bernice Eddy of proposed scientific publication, submitted to Joseph Smadel, November 1960. Smadel's handwritten notes rejecting publication of same dated Nov. 21, 1960, appear on the abstract.

Eddy to Murray, Nov. 23, 1960. Eddy notes that Smadel is rejecting her manuscripts and causing delay in publication of her research.

Eddy to Dalldorf, Nov. 28, 1960. Eddy writes that Smadel "is opposed to any tumor virus work, even the study on the tumors induced in hamsters with monkey kidney cell extracts" and that approval for her papers continues to be delayed.

Eddy to Murray, memo, Dec. 1, 1960. Eddy says that the Medical Society of New York wishes to publish the lecture she gave before the New York Cancer Society on October 11, 1960. This was the lecture in which she publicly announced her hamster tumor experiments. The lecture was never published.

Murray to Eddy, memo, Dec. 8, 1960. Murray states that any delay in DBS approval of publication of Eddy's papers is "only [that which] is compatible with the preparation of papers of good quality."

Eddy to Smadel and Murray, memo, Jan. 7, 1961. "This is to let you know that Dr. Herald Cox has learned about this work [on cancer in hamsters after injections with monkey kidney tissue] . . ."

Eddy to Smadel, memo, Jan. 24, 1961. Request by Eddy for publication of her original SV40 paper; her handwritten notes on the memo state that Smadel rejected her submission in February 1961.

Eddy to Dalldorf, Jan. 30, 1961. Eddy writes that "Dr. Smadel is holding up my paper on the monkey kidney tumor agent," and that she has approached Murray about the matter and "he ask[ed] me to put up with the situation for a while. I do not know what he has in mind."

Murray to Eddy, memo, Feb. 16, 1961. Murray makes clear what he has in mind. He announces that Eddy is losing her lab and her current position as of Jul. 1, 1961.

Eddy to Smadel and Murray, memo, Feb. 18, 1961. In her response, Eddy suggests that Smadel and Murray are "dictators" and that she wishes to keep her present position.

Smadel to Eddy, memo, Feb. 28, 1961. Smadel reiterates that Eddy's position will change and offers further details on her new position.

Eddy to Smadel, memo, Mar. 3, 1961. Eddy expresses continued uninterest in new position.

Smadel to Eddy, memo, Mar. 8, 1961. Further exchange on the issue. Smadel states that he will choose Eddy's new lab assistants.

Eddy to Murray, memo, Mar. 8, 1961. Eddy protests that she is being "forced to vacate my present position."

Eddy to Luther Terry, May 2, 1961. Eddy asks for appointment to see Terry, the U.S. surgeon general. "For reasons I am unable to understand, beginning with the first of this fiscal year, July 1, 1960, I have encountered obstacles and restrictions that have interfered with my work and been most discouraging. Now more restrictions are in store for me beginning July 1, 1961 . . ."

Eddy to W. C. Workman, Smadel, and Murray, memo, May 16, 1961. "Since the vacuolating virus is known to be exceedingly stable . . ."

Terry to Eddy, memo, May 22, 1961. In his reply to Eddy's request for an appointment Terry says that she must first talk to NIH Director Dr. James Shannon.

Smadel to Eddy, Jun. 6, 1961. Smadel rejects another Eddy scientific paper.

Lawrence Kilham to Dr. Hundley, Surgeon General's Office, Jun. 13, 1961. Kilham, a DBS colleague of Eddy's, describes Smadel and Murray's treatment of Eddy as "a somewhat Prussian-like attempt to hinder an outstanding scientist . . ."

Smadel to Eddy, memo, Jun. 14, 1961. Smadel states that the director of the NIH has approved her reassignment and that she is relieved of her present duties as of Jun. 30, 1961. She is being assigned much smaller laboratory facilities.

Smadel to Eddy, Jun. 20, 1961. He repeats the message.

Additional Notes: While researching this book, the authors discovered that Eddy had sent a manuscript of her original hamster study to Jonas Salk in the spring of 1961. In the files of Salk's papers at the Mandeville Special Collections Library at the University of California San Diego, there is a response by Salk to Eddy, dated April 4, 1961:

Dear Dr. Eddy,

I am very pleased to have the pre-publication copy of your paper on "Tumors Induced In Hamsters by Injection of Rhesus Monkey Kidney Cell Extracts."

I donder [*sic*] if you have had any experiences with material that would correspond to formalinized vaccine and, also, how far you can dilute the kidney cell extract and still be able to induce the effects you have observed.

Sincerely,

Jonas E. Salk, M.D.

Other than this copy of a letter to Eddy, an examination of Salk's papers at the Mandeville Special Collections finds few references to the issue of extraneous viruses in his (or other) vaccines.

Appendix C

Documents and Articles Concerning the Discovery of SV40 in Salk's and Sabin's Vaccines (Chapters 8 and 9)

Following are documents and further notes related to the discovery of SV40 in Salk's and Sabin's vaccines in early 1961 and the reactions to those discoveries. They are divided into three subcategories: Congressional Hearings and Scientific Meetings, Documents from the Division of Biologics Standards, and Other Documents.

CONGRESSIONAL HEARINGS AND SCIENTIFIC MEETINGS

"Hearings before a Subcommittee of the Committee on Interstate and Foreign Commerce of the House of Representatives: Developments with respect to the manufacture of live polio virus vaccine and results of utilization of killed virus polio vaccine. March 16 and 17, 1961." (Washington, D.C: GPO, 1961), pp. 118–119 (Roderick Murray testimony); pp. 250–251 (Albert Sabin testimony); pp. 278–308 (Jonas Salk testimony). Murray testified on March 16, 1961, to the effect that any SV40 in Salk's vaccine was dead. The *Lancet* letter contradicting the scientific assumptions that underlay Murray's testimony appeared in the March 18, 1961, issue. Whether Murray knew of the content of the letter on March 16 is difficult to say; Sabin clearly did. (See his testimony before same House subcommittee the following day as noted in the text of the book and notes.) Given the tight-knit world of polio vaccinologists at the time, it would be surprising that Murray was not privy to the British findings, while Sabin was. (It would also be uncharacteristic of Sabin to have kept such an important piece of news in his favor a secret from the very regulatory agency he was trying to persuade to license his vaccine.) If Murray did, in fact, know that Salk's vaccine at times contained SV40 when he testified on March 16th, then he misled the House subcommittee when he reassured them that the vaccine currently in use in the United States was free of SV40.

As for Salk, his silence on the issue before the subcommittee is puzzling. Sabin, who had immediately preceded him before the subcommittee that day, had just skewered the biggest advantage Salk's vaccine supposedly had over Sabin's: viral contaminants, such as SV40, had always been presumed to be dead in Salk's inactivated vaccine, while they would

347

be very much alive in his rival's live vaccine. Sabin had just admitted to this shortcoming concerning his own vaccine during his testimony, but was insisting to the Subcommittee that live SV40 in Salk's vaccine was infectious to humans, while the same live SV40 in his oral vaccine would not multiply in humans—and was therefore of little consequence. Salk's refusal to rebut Sabin on this point suggests either he was poorly informed on this issue (even though SV40 had become a preoccupation for every Salk vaccine manufacturer and vaccine regulator) or he simply found the issue as inconsequential as some of his peers suggest.

"Hearings before a Subcommittee of the Committee on Interstate and Foreign Commerce of the House of Representatives: Developments with respect to the manufacture of live polio virus vaccine and results of utilization of killed virus polio vaccine. March 16 and 17, 1961." (Washington, D.C.: GPO, 1961), p. 311. Hilary Koprowski's unsolicited letter to the subcommittee concerning the dangers of using monkey kidneys as a vaccine substrate. Relevant portions follow:

> [T]he Division of Biologics Standards continues to insist that the production of live poliovirus vaccine be in monkey kidney tissue culture. As monkey kidney tissue culture is host to innumerable simian viruses, the number found varying in relation to the amount of work expended to find them, the problem presented to the manufacturer is considerable, if not almost insuperable. He is faced with the prospect of having to discard most of his manufacturing lots of vaccine. This will inevitably raise the cost of the vaccine, and as our technical methods improve, we may find fewer and fewer lots of vaccines which can be called free of simian viruses. We believe that it would be sounder scientifically to switch to human cell strains for the production of live poliovirus vaccine.

DOCUMENTS FROM THE DIVISION OF BIOLOGICS STANDARDS AND THE TECHNICAL COMMITTEE

Roderick Murray, Director of Biologics Standards to Manufacturers of Poliomyelitis Vaccine and of Adenovirus Vaccine, memo, Apr. 10, 1961. Notice to manufacturers of DBS concern about SV40 contamination of Salk vaccine. Partial text follows:

> In the March 18 issue of *The Lancet*, there appeared a letter . . . strongly suggesting that live vacuolating agent was probably present in inactivated poliomyelitis vaccine . . . Since vacuolating virus (SV40) does not ordinarily produce cytopathogenic changes in Macaca [rhesus monkey] kidney cell cultures, safety tests as now carried out . . . can not be considered adequate . . . for detecting small amounts of this virus if it were present in the vaccine . . . [T]his Division proposes that Cercopithecus [African green monkey] kidney cell cultures be added to the test system. . . . It is proposed that this procedure be initiated at the earliest possible date. . . . Appropriate revision of the Regulations is under consideration.

Roderick Murray to Manufacturers of Poliomyelitis Vaccine and of Adenovirus Vaccine, memo, May 5, 1961. Murray reports the results of Paul Gerber's tests on Salk vaccine samples and urges that "every effort should be made to institute a program of testing to insure that vaccine reaching the market is free of simian agents." He adds that the results of Gerber's tests "indicate that substantial amounts of SV40 were present in the [Salk vaccine] samples which were positive."

"Report of the Technical Committee on Poliomyelitis Vaccine: Presence of Vacuolating

Agent in Poliomyelitis Vaccine," May 18, 1961. This is the decision by the Technical Committee to not recall contaminated vaccine or change vaccination policy in response to the discovery of SV40 in Salk's vaccine. Of interest concerning this first report by the Technical Committee on SV40 was its assertion that "steps have been taken to insure that future vaccines will be free of this agent [SV40]." As of May 18, 1961, Murray and the DBS had done nothing more than urge manufacturers to test more thoroughly for the presence of SV40. There were still no changes to vaccine manufacturing regulations, nor had any been proposed by Murray.

Roderick Murray to Manufacturers of Poliomyelitis Vaccine and of Adenovirus Vaccine, memo May 20, 1961. To this memo, Murray attached the Technical Committee's report of May 18. He also makes it clear that there will be no recall of contaminated stocks of vaccine: "It will be noted that the report does not visualize the withdrawal of lots from the market, but it does recommend that poliomyelitis vaccine distributed in the future should be free of this agent. The orderly implementation of this latter recommendation can only be accomplished after information concerning the magnitude of the problem is available. We hope it will be possible to accomplish this within the next week or so."

"Report of the Technical Committee on Poliomyelitis Vaccine: Presence of Vacuolating Agent in Poliomyelitis Vaccine," Jun. 20, 1961. This is the meeting during which the Technical Committee rejected Hilleman's appeal to suspend vaccine production and withdraw contaminated vaccines. Five of the six members of the Technical Committee members present at this crucial meeting had a strong connection to Salk's vaccine: David Bodian's connection extended back to at least 1954 when he played a key scientific advisory role during the Salk field trials. The connection to the Salk vaccine of four Technical Committee members in attendance that day—Joseph Smadel, Roderick Murray, Thomas Francis. and Jonas Salk—is well documented both in this book and in the other sources cited herein. The sixth member present that day, Richard Shope, had authored an editorial the previous year ("Koch's Postulates and a Viral Cause of Human Cancer," *Cancer Research* 20(8): 1119–1120, 1960), in which he strongly suggested that those who were seeking to connect viruses to cancer had little or no basis to do so—indicating that he had little predisposition to believe any contaminating virus present in Salk's vaccine was dangerous.

Roderick Murray to Manufacturers of Poliomyelitis Vaccine and of Adenovirus Vaccine, memo, Jun. 30, 1961. Murray tells manufacturers that as of Aug. 1, 1961, they must report the results of tests for presence of SV40 on vaccine lots, but does not attach the Jun. 20, 1961 Technical Committee report or inform them of Hilleman's presentation to the committee concerning Anthony Girardi's hamster tumor experiments. "Statement on Monkey Viruses in Relation to Salk Vaccine," Division of Biologics Standards (DBS), Jul. 7, 1961, and "Attachment: Background Information on SV40," Jul. 7, 1961, appended to the statement of the same date. These are the DBS official public statements on SV40 and the Salk vaccine. Like the DBS statement, which failed to mention the Merck researchers (Anthony Girardi, Ben Sweet, and Maurice Hilleman) or their hamster tumor findings, the DBS's attached "backgrounder" contains curious omissions. The document, which has a self-congratulatory tone, attributes the increase in SV40 knowledge between the summer of 1960 and the summer of 1961 to "experience . . . principally contributed by investigators of the DBS" and fails to acknowledge the work of Sweet, Hilleman, Girardi, and Robert Hull. It also fails to credit Bernice Eddy, even though she made the initial discovery of the contaminant, or to recognize her efforts to get her superiors to take the SV40 threat seriously—something they had only done, finally, under duress. "The DBS," the attachment adds, "has been geared up to do safety work on SV40." Manufacturers, according to the DBS, now had to test for SV40 per the new DBS requirement to do so. But this was a change that Murray would not make binding until August 1, 1961. The attachment also states that manufacturers who, according to the DBS, had been slow to react to SV40 (certainly not the case at Hilleman's Merck and Co.), were now being prodded by the DBS to get involved: "Following a period in which interest in SV40 lagged in the biological houses, there has been a flurry of activity created by the findings of the DBS regarding the presence of SV40 virus in killed poliomyelitis vaccine and adenovirus vaccine. It is to be anticipated that this interest and activity will expand." Noticeably absent from the one-and-one-third-page recitation of DBS accomplishments with relation to SV40 was any mention that a major reason, perhaps the primary reason, for the manufacturers' dilatory response up to that point had been the DBS's own marked public complacency about the virus throughout 1960 and the first few months of 1961.

Murray to Manufacturers of Poliomyelitis Vaccine and of Adenovirus Vaccine, memo, Aug. 6, 1962. Murray informs vaccine manufacturers of the DBS proposal to test poliovirus pools and prove them to be free of SV40 *prior* to the formaldehyde inactivation process. (This was as opposed to then-current requirement that tests for SV40 need only be performed on the *final* vaccine. Under regulations then in effect, the poliovirus pools could contain live SV40.) The regulation change would not become effective until March 1963, but Murray "hoped that each manufacturer will agree that it is in the public interest to institute such testing immediately rather than wait until this becomes an official requirement." However, unless manufacturers had switched over to an SV40-free monkey, such as African greens, it would have been virtually impossible for their viral pools to be free of SV40 prior to inactivation in 1962.

OTHER DOCUMENTS

"Notes on Acceptance Criteria and Requirements for Live Poliovirus Vaccines," submitted by Hilary Koprowski and Stanley Plotkin to Study Group on Requirements for Vaccine (Live, Attenuated Poliovirus), World Health Organization, Nov. 1, 1960, pp. 7–9. This document indicates that Koprowski had come to view use of monkey kidney tissues for vaccine production with considerable suspicion. Relevant portions follow:

> Rhesus monkey kidney cultures employed for production of poliovirus have been found to contain a number of viruses grouped under the name of simian agents and to all probability, all vaccine lots fed to millions of people around the world contained at least one of these agents in addition to the attenuated strains of poliovirus.

Koprowski and Plotkin continue with a discussion that the ability of polyoma virus to cause tumors in animals other than its mouse host raises the possibility that a theoretical tumor virus like polyoma could contaminate monkey kidneys:

> The fact that fresh kidney cultures will be obtained from hundreds of thousands of monkeys increases the chance of including hypothetical tumor virus in the vaccine pool and makes the case even weaker for the use of such tissue.

Editorial (unsigned). "Efficacy of Killed Poliomyelitis Vaccine," *Lancet*, Mar. 11, 1961, pp. 545–546. The backdrop for this *Lancet* editorial was the increasingly public and bitter debate over whether the United States, Canada, the United Kingdom, and other western European nations should abandon Salk's vaccine now that Sabin's was available. As noted in chapter 7, Sabin supporters appeared to have had the upper hand in the dispute until the discovery of SV40, which, as this *Lancet* editorial assumed, contaminated Sabin's, but not Salk's vaccine. Relevant portion of the editorial follows:

The discovery of the vacuolating virus in many seed lots of the [Sabin] vaccine raises doubts about its long-term safety. Exclusion of known contaminating viruses from the vaccine is extremely difficult, and there is an ever-present fear that unknown viruses may be incorporated. What little we know about tumor viruses suggests that it is unwise to use a possibly virus-contaminated living vaccine when there is an inactivated alternative.

Letter to the editors, signed A. P. Goffe (Wellcome Research Laboratories, Beckenham, Kent), J. Hale, and P. S. Gardner (Public Health Laboratory, Newcastle upon Tyne), *Lancet*, Mar. 18, 1961, p. 612. This is the letter that rebutted the editorial that had appeared in the March 11 edition of the *Lancet*. Partial text of the letter follows:

> Sir—The annotation of March 11 mentioned the fact that the vacuolating virus had been found in many batches of attenuated [Sabin] vaccine. It failed to mention that no tests for the vacuolating virus were done on any batches of killed vaccine up to 1961 . . . [E]xperiments at one of these laboratories (W.R.L.) show that the virus is resistant to formaldehyde. . . . It was therefore not surprising that a proportion of individuals who had received Salk vaccine in this country have antibodies to vacuolating virus. . . . There is, therefore an accumulating body of evidence that killed poliomyelitis vaccine in the past has contained vacuolating virus, probably in the living state. . . . One is left with the suspicion that vacuolating virus will not be the last agent to be discovered lurking "hitherto undetected" in monkey-kidney preparations. In this respect the attenuated vaccine seems to have . . . advantages over the killed. . . . [T]he oral route uses the alimentary tract as a selective screen, as in the case of vacuolating virus, while subcutaneous injection carries the certainty of introducing directly into the tissue whatever is in the syringe. The last sentence of your annotation could in fact be rewritten. "What little we know about tumor viruses suggests that it is unwise to use a possibly virus-contaminated vaccine by injection when there is an oral alternative."

Interestingly, four months after the above letter was published in the *Lancet*, a study appeared in the *British Medical Journal*, which also found SV40 antibodies in the blood of children who had been injected with Salk vaccines. The authors (researchers at the British equivalent of the DBS), like the *Lancet* letter signers, could not detect antibodies to SV40 in Sabin vaccinees. (Magrath, D. I., Russel, K., Tobin, J.O'H., "Vacuolating Agent [Preliminary Communication]," *British Medical Journal* [July 29, 1961]: 287–288.) But this second British study was not the final word on whether SV40 in an oral vaccine could multiply in humans. In addition to Joseph Melnick's 1962 study (see notes, chapter 7), a study from the early 1960s proved that the virus did infect humans if taken orally. Hungarian researchers in 1964 published a study that followed 35 infants fed contaminated oral vaccine. Two weeks later, a third of the infants were excreting SV40 in their stools. (Horváth, B. L., and Fornosi, F, "Excretion of SV40 Virus after Oral Administration of Contaminated Vaccine," *Acta Microbiologica Academiae Scientarium Hungaricae* 11:271–275 [1964]). Russians exposed to SV40 in Sabin's vaccine also developed antibodies to the virus (see chapter 9 and notes), again suggesting the virus, when present in an oral vaccine, was quite infectious. And, in 1968, the *Lancet* published a letter from three Italian researchers from Turin University who said that they had examined thirty hospitalized children under age ten, all of whom had been vaccinated with live polio vaccine prior to age two. Sixteen of the children had antibodies to SV40. (Letter to the editors, signed N. Nigro, L. Benso, M. R. Brunet, "Anti-SV40 Complement-Fixing Antibodies in Children's Serum," *Lancet*, 917 [1968]).

Gerber, P., Hottle, G. A., and Grubbs, R. E. "Inactivation of Vacuolating Virus (SV40) by Formaldehyde." *Proceedings of the Society of Experimental Biology and Medicine* 108:205–209 (October 1961). This was the Gerber experiment that proved SV40 was not always inactivated by formaldehyde.

Girardi, A.J., et al. "Development of Tumors in Hamsters Inoculated in the Neonatal Period with Vacuolating Virus, SV40." *Proceedings of the Society of Experimental Biology and Medicine* 109:649–660 (March 1962). When Hilleman presented the results of this experiment to the Technical Committee, the committee rejected Hilleman's appeal to suspend production of Salk vaccine. One of the reasons the Technical Committee was not moved by Hilleman's appeals appears to have been doubt whether the "substance" Eddy described in her original May 1961 paper in hamsters was the same as SV40. Any committee member or DBS bureaucrat who wished to resolve this ambiguity could have easily done so. Eddy began her experiments to test whether her "substance" and SV40 were one and the same in January 1961. By the time of Technical Committee's second meeting on June 20, 1961, she had preliminary results available that, indeed, they were.

Appendix D

Memos and Correspondence Relating to Multi-Laboratory Study
and Carbone-Pass Rapid Access to Intervention Development
(RAID) Grant (Chapters 17 and 18)

This appendix presents a summary of the documents relating to the events portrayed in chapters 17 and 18. As described in the text, there was a serious disagreement between the National Cancer Institute's Viral Epidemiology Branch and two of the laboratories that participated in the multilaboratory study. The controversy stretched over three years and eventually encompassed a separate, but related incident concerning the denial of an NCI grant application by Pass and Carbone. These documents provide further background to those events.

In the interest of brevity, writers identified in the text are not further identified. Other participants are identified by their professional position at first appearance.

The authors collected these documents through requests under the Freedom of Information Act and from other sources.

Strickler and Goedert to Lewis and Levine, May 8, 1997. The draft protocol for multilaboratory study to measure reproducibility of Simian Virus 40 PCR assays.

Agenda for PCR Working Group meeting, Jul. 1, 1997.

Lewis to the SV40-PCR Working Group, Oct. 8, 1997. The final draft of the summary of the July 1 meeting.

Draft minutes of July 1, 1997 meeting, Jul. 10, 1997.

Strickler to Fraumeni, memo, Jul. 11, 1997. Copied to James Goedert. Subject: A Multicenter Study of SV40 DNA PCR Assay Reproducibility. Strickler describes "conflicting reports" of SV40 in human tumors, and the "adversarial atmosphere which now divides the SV40 research community into two camps: individuals who believe that the detection of SV40 in human tissues is no longer in doubt and skeptics such as ourselves." He summarizes FDA efforts to work with VEB. He notes the "very contentious meeting" held July 1, 1997.

Carbone to Lewis, Aug. 5, 1997. Carbone offers his analysis of the goals of the study and whether protocol under discussion will reach them. He notes that if the goal of the study is to determine whether PCR is a reliable technique for detecting SV40 in human tumors, then study must be redesigned and funding must be dramatically increased.

Butel and Lednicky to Lewis, Aug. 6, 1997. They express concern about the size and cost of the study and inadequate funding.

"Draft Number 2 of Summary of July 1, 1997, SV40-PCR Working Group Meeting," September 23, 1997.

Strickler to SV40 Working Group, memo, Oct. 2, 1997. He apologizes for delays in sending out the "final draft protocol" and states that decisions will be made about what specimens to use "shortly depending on the availability of specimens. We do not wish to delay this project any longer."

Carbone to Lewis, memo, Oct. 2, 1997. Copied to all members of Working Group, including Strickler. Carbone is critical of Strickler's unilateral decision about the selection of specimens for the study. ("I do not understand the tone of this fax since the only job of Dr. Strickler was to provide appropriate specimens. If decisions need to be made, all the members of the panel must be consulted. Furthermore, you [Lewis] are the person who is coordinating this panel. . . .")

Strickler to SV40 Working Group, memo, Oct. 2, 1997. He takes up the concerns mentioned in Carbone's Oct. 2 memo. ("No one individual laboratory should be allowed to hold this important topic hostage. . . . A final protocol will be adopted soon and everyone will need to make their own decisions regarding participation.")

Strickler to Egan, memo, Oct. 16, 1997, concerning VEB's control over the multilaboratory study. Strickler notes that "[a]s agreed last week with Dr. Kathryn Zoon, Director of OVRR-CBER at FDA, VEB remains in control of this investigation, with a clear mandate. . . .")

Lewis to SV40 Working Group, Nov. 3, 1997. Lewis attaches "Draft 3a: Protocol to Measure the Reproducibility of Simian Virus 40 (SV40) PCR Assays," 25 pages. Lewis explicitly notes that VEB (Strickler) has revised and drafted the final protocol and informs the group that VEB "is taking the lead in developing the study."

Carbone to Lewis, Nov. 9, 1997. Copied to Levine and Strickler. Of changes in the multilaboratory study, Carbone writes:

> The objects of the study have been changed without consulting the members of the panel. . . . The resources available are inadequate. . . . [T]he Viral Epidemiology Branch at the NCI is taking a leading role. This must be corrected because. . . . Dr. Strickler and collaborators are biased. This [has] emerged every time they have spoken about this issue. . . . Furthermore, before signatures of participation are required, it must be decided who is going to write the paper, and how many people will contribute to it. . . .

Butel and Lednicky to Strickler, Nov. 20, 1997. On potential problems with the DNA extraction kit that Strickler's commercial contractor has chosen, as well as other problems with the proposed protocol. Butel and Lednicky also assert that the proposed reimbursement for participants is inadequate:

> If the efficiency of low-molecular-weight recovery by the kit is poor, then episomal viral [SV40] DNA might be lost from many samples, damaging the study. . . . The study is still quite large. . . . Authorship issues are vague. . . . The proposed financial reimbursement ($15,000–$25,000 including indirect costs) is inadequate. We have calculated the actual cost of the study to us as $43,290. . . . Last, but not least, the opening paragraph of the protocol sets a distrustful and biased tone and should be rewritten. . . .

Strickler to Carbone, Dec. 10, 1997. Copied to Rabson, Goedert, Egan, Lewis, and Levine: "We were disappointed to find your correspondence indicates that you will not be able to participate in the study without sufficient time to train a new technician (about 6 months) and without funding for 2–3 years. . . ."

Strickler to Pass, Dec. 10, 1997. Copied to Rabson, Goedert, Egan, Lewis, and Levine: "We were disappointed to find your correspondence indicates that you will not be able to participate in the study without extending the project up to 1–2 years and without $60,000–$80,000. . . ."

Strickler to All Study Participants, memo, Dec. 10, 1997. Strickler outlines further changes in the protocol and the addition of three more laboratories. (Note: Reimbursement offered to participating laboratories was increased; however, Carbone and Pass were not informed of this change in policy.)

"A Protocol to Measure the Reproducibility of Simian Virus 40 (SV40) Polymerase Chain Reaction Assays, December 10, 1997," 28 pages, including tables. No changes had been made to the protocol in response to Carbone's, Butel's, and Lednicky's criticisms. Section entitled "Report Preparation and Submission for Publication," includes authorship protocol for multilaboratory study:

All principal laboratory and clinical collaborators, in addition to the study organizers will be considered part of the "Publication Committee" unless they wish to defer. Draft versions of the manuscript will be submitted to this committee in preparation for publication. *No data will be presented in any public forum or in written reports until the interpretation of the results is agreed to by all Committee members,* with the important caveat that no one may block publication of this investigation. (Emphasis added.)

Strickler to All Laboratory Collaborators and Study Coordinator, memo, Dec. 11, 1998. Subject: Results in the SV40 study.

To our surprise, the "negative control" samples also gave positive signals in eight of nine laboratories, indicative of contamination with SV40 DNA before distribution. . . . It was learned that the processing laboratory had aliquoted samples from this first batch [of negative controls] immediately after aliquoting SV40 DNA positive control samples. Although the biosafety hood used had been cleared and laboratory personnel reported changing gloves between samples, the hood was not re-sterilized with (ultraviolet) irradiation before aliquoting the negative control samples. . . .

Attached is a memo to Strickler from Mark Consentino, Biotech Research Laboratories, Dec. 10, 1998, on his company's contamination of the negative control samples.

Shah to Strickler, e-mail, Dec. 17, 1998, 4:30 p.m. Subject: "SV40 of course." Shah provides Strickler with advice on DNA extraction question. He states that the DNA extraction kit being used by the commercial contractor, which Butel and Lednicky have criticized, "is unlikely to cause problems."

Strickler to Shah, e-mail, Dec. 17, 1998, 4:40 p.m. Copied to Goedert. Subject: "SV40 of course." Strickler signals that he is willing to reexamine the sensitivity of the DNA extraction kit. "Thanks for looking into this. I will review with Jim [Goedert]. My own opinion is, why live with even the slightest uncertainty. Let's examine five or 10 samples and be done with it."

Strickler to the SV40 Working Group, memo, January 20, 1999. Subject: Comments Regarding the Draft SV40 Manuscript. Strickler provides his new address at Albert Einstein College of Medicine and requests detailed comments on draft manuscript by Jan. 29, 1999.

Strickler to All SV40 Working Group Collaborators, memo, Feb. 22, 1999. Subject: Responses to Comments Regarding the SV40 Manuscript. "The current manuscript was drafted with the intention of submitting it to *Cancer Research*." This memo includes specific comments made by participating laboratories in response to the draft manuscript circulated by Strickler and is followed by his response. One is the concern of Butel and Lednicky about Shah's sudden improvement in DNA detection. Strickler writes in response:

> Keerti explains that they were disappointed in the sensitivity of their results during pretrial testing . . . which was [less sensitive] than in previous testing and took steps to make improvements . . . before the investigation began. They conducted repeat testing of some of the specimens when it was necessary.

Egan to Strickler, Feb. 25, 1999. Egan critiques draft manuscript for implying "unintentionally" that the positive results that have been reported are due to laboratory contamination. (See text, chapter 18.) Egan outlines alternative hypotheses (to laboratory contamination) that could explain the presence of SV40 in human tumors and suggests that Strickler is not properly interpreting the epidemiological studies to date:

> These [epidemiological] studies do not demonstrate that SV40 is not causally linked to human cancers. We might well imagine that SV40 is linked to human cancers and that the vaccine recipients either (1) did not get a sufficiently large dose to cause an increase in tumor rate or (2) that they were "inadvertently vaccinated" against SV40 [by receiving dead SV40 in the vaccine] or (3) that there was a mixed effect wherein some of the cohorts were adversely affected by the SV40 (got a large dose or were immune compromised) some of the cohorts were protected (vaccinated) and some were completely unaffected (got no SV40, or only a tiny dose, in the polio vaccine). As with many cancers, there are co-factors (e.g. asbestos) . . . I personally think that the evidence for the presence of SV40 in these tumors is reasonably good; the role of SV40 in [causing them], however, is uncertain.

Egan states that the results of the study "point . . . to [a] need to look more carefully at DNA extraction methods and techniques."

Strickler to Egan, Mar. 8, 1999. He responds to Egan's critique of the SV40 manuscript. Strickler largely rejects Egan's critique. (See text, chapter 18.)

Jasani to Strickler, Mar. 16, 1999. Concerning the draft manuscript. Jasani, like Butel and Lednicky, does not believe the DNA extraction kit used was adequate and, therefore, SV40 DNA was not properly extracted from the mesothelioma samples.

Butel and Lednicky to Strickler, Mar. 24, 1999. They address Strickler's response to the study participants' comments on the manuscript. ("Our major disagreement with the draft manuscript . . ." See text, chapter 18). They note that they do not feel their concerns about the weaknesses in the study's protocol have been addressed. In their six-page letter, they discuss ten areas of concern about the study. Paramount are the SV40 DNA extraction problems and their concerns about Keerti Shah's positive controls as reported in Strickler's draft manuscript: "How would they [Shah] know which samples should be retested until a positive result was obtained? We think sensitivity, reproducibility and reliability cannot be measured from this laboratory's test results." Butel and Lednicky also dispute Strickler's assertion that the relationship between human papilloma virus and cervical carcinoma is the appropriate model for understanding how SV40 causes human tumors:

> [I]t is . . . like comparing apples and oranges. Because of the differing biologics of the two groups of viruses, there will usually be more viral DNA in HPV-associated cervical cancers than in (SV40) associated tumors. . . . In addition, numerous studies have documented that whereas SV40 T-antigen may be required for early events leading to tumor formation, tumor progression can evolve to the point that the T-

antigen gene may no longer be required for transformation and may be lost from some cells. Hence, an advanced tumor might contain less than one T-antigen gene copy per tumor cell.

(Note: The importance of this distinction is that in SV40-related tumors, much less virus may be present than in HPV-related ones. Therefore, if the DNA extraction kit was insensitive, it could have easily failed to extract SV40 DNA present in the tumors.) Butel and Lednicky also take exception to Strickler's attempt in his draft conclusions to suggest that one negative study disproves the association of SV40 with tumors.)

Strickler to All SV40 Working Group Collaborators, memo, Apr. 13, 1999. Subject: SV40 Manuscript. Strickler apologizes for his "paraphrasing" of Shah's technique and includes a letter from Shah explaining his positive control testing procedure (below). He also responds to concerns concerning DNA extraction. He promises to undertake an experiment to "demonstrate that the DNA extraction method does not somehow preferentially lose SV40 DNA. . . ." He proposes using Shah's lab and Sugarbaker's lab to conduct the experiment.

Shah to Strickler, Mar. 31, 1999. "Re: Comment 4 in Dr. Butel's letter to you on March 24, 1999." Shah responds to concerns by Butel and Lednicky that he tested positive control specimens in advance of the study and then readjusted his protocol when the positive controls tested negative in his laboratory. Shah indicates a reluctance to provide much detail on the matter:

> In our study design, each laboratory was to provide its final result in the way described in the protocol. All of us have done that. I am not sure that there is any point in any of us going into great details about the tests in the individual laboratories.

Butel and Lednicky, to Strickler, Apr. 21, 1999. They raise concerns about the experiment proposed by Strickler that will demonstrate the effectiveness of the DNA extraction kit. They point out that the experiment as proposed will not prove whether the kit can detect small amounts of SV40: "The experiment is meaningless, as it will be unable to provide any useful information about what happens to low copy numbers of episomal viral genomes during the DNA extraction process. . . ."

Jasani and Gibbs to Strickler, Apr. 28, 1999. They write about the SV40 manuscript. "We hasten to add that Janet Butel, John Lednicky and our group in Cardiff are all very puzzled and extremely disappointed by the continued inadequacy of your responses to the criticism offered by us regarding some of the fundamental flaws in the above study." Jasani and Gibbs criticize the organization of the study and state that despite representations that the FDA's Andrew Lewis would direct the study,

> this entire study has been directed by you on a "mail order" basis with you reserving to yourself the absolute final right to decide every aspect of this study. . . . Interestingly, the laboratories you unilaterally chose to replace Carbone and Pass have been most passive throughout the scientific commentary phase and have apparently, for the most part, decided to follow your lead without indicating any contrary thought process.

Jasani and Gibbs note that several of the laboratories that have successfully identified SV40 DNA in human tumors have used techniques other than PCR to do so. These techniques include: Southern blot hybridization from total cellular DNA, SV40 mRNa by in situ hybridization, SV40 T-antigen by immunocytochemistry, and western blotting.

These results obviously rule out any concern about PCR contamination. . . . If you really want to state, as you are trying to suggest in the manuscript, that SV40 is not present in mesotheliomas, and by inference in other human tumors . . . we must have much stronger scientific evidence than provided in this study.

Goedert to Jasani and Gibbs, May 26, 1999. Goedert responds to their letter to Howard Strickler, dated Apr. 28, 1999, copied to Strickler, Fraumeni, Alan Rabson, deputy director of the NCI, and Richard Klausner, director of the NCI. In this five-page response, Goedert denies any bias on his or Strickler's part and states that he and Strickler have separated themselves from the compilation of the data. Goedert also writes to Jasani and Gibbs that "I believe you should personally apologize to Dr. Strickler for your April 28 letter."

Strickler to Goedert and Shah, fax cover sheet, Jun. 1, 1999. Subject: SV40/FDA Letter. Strickler objects to an FDA request to retest the DNA extraction kit. "Please find attached the response from FDA. I strongly disagree with the tact [*sic*] they are suggesting . . ." (Note: The retest of the DNA extraction kit was never performed.)

Butel to Egan, Jun. 2, 1999:

I have mounting concerns about the SV40 multi-institutional study. . . . These include lack of confidence in the company (BBI) that prepared the study test samples . . . concerns about data analysis and interpretation and concerns about the preparation of the manuscript. . . . I believe the SV40 PCR Working Group needs to be reconvened to discuss all the relevant issues that have become apparent.

Butel and Lednicky to Strickler, Jun. 2, 1999:

We believe you missed the point we made about the differences between polyomavirus tumors and HPV-induced cancers. . . . We feel our comments about data interpretation are being dismissed and ignored. . . . Regrettably, we must agree with Dr. Jasani that the entire working group needs to be reconvened. . . . [T]he entire group [should] consider . . . how to interpret and present the study data and who should draft the next version of the manuscript.

Strickler to Goedert, e-mail, Jun. 3, 1999, 9:45 A.M. Subject: SV40. Strickler has drafted a letter in which he apparently intends to publicly denounce his critics:

I am proposing the following letter: Recent communications [from the two laboratories of Butel and Lednicky, and Jasani and Gibbs] have made it clear that it will not be possible to reach agreement with all individuals on the SV40 manuscript. We intend to move forward . . . The most recent letter by Dr. Butel (see attached) demands that we reconvene the group meeting in Washington, D.C., to discuss the implementation of those adjunct studies and to begin the drafting of the manuscript over again. We feel this is outrageous, and that the project is being held hostage by this partisan minority who are fixed on proving that SV40 DNA is present in human tumors, regardless of the data. Therefore, we plan to submit the manuscript without further testing or delay. . . .

(Note: It would be a fair to say that several of Strickler's critics felt he was equally "fixed" on proving that SV40 DNA was *not* present in human tumors "regardless of the data.")

Goedert to Strickler, e-mail, Jun. 3, 1999, 5:16 P.M. Goedert has reviewed Strickler's proposed letter:

Basically, this looks OK (although I'd probably tone it down by removing "outrageous" etc.) Al Rabson got back to me with three excellent pieces of advice: 1. He agrees we should no longer negotiate, but should send it [the Strickler draft manuscript] in. . . . 2. I'll check with Bob Lanman, the head of the NIH Office of the General Counsel, to assure that we/the Government is unlikely to be sued. I'll need your advice and probably your help in assembling the correspondence, which . . . he would need to provide an informed legal opinion. . . . Should we be concerned. . . . If there is legal action, how much can/will the OGC help as this is clearly official (NIH) duties and not personal (non-NIH)? Is there any reason to think we need coverage from claims of misconduct?

Goedert then notes that Rabson "very much liked" Goedert's and Strickler's suggestion for a journal for publication of the study. Goedert closes the e-mail with this note from Rabson: "Alan also said 'poor Howard!' but advised you hang in there."

Jasani and Gibbs to Strickler and Goedert, Jun. 17, 1999. The writers respond to Goedert's letter to Jasani and Gibbs dated May 26, 1999, copied to other members of the study group:

> Our letter to Dr. Strickler was written principally to express our growing frustration at the piecemeal and at times dismissive approach adopted by Dr. Strickler to various points raised by us and others including Dr. Butel and Dr. Egan, highlighting several fundamental flaws in the study. We were also surprised at Dr. Strickler's eagerness to publish the generally negative findings of the study without the necessary careful analysis of the basis of the negative results. If the tone of our letter was perceived to be beyond the bounds of protocol, we apologize but it was entirely due to these reasons. Please extend our sincere apologies to Dr. Strickler in case we have hurt his feelings. . . .

Goedert to Fraumeni and the associate director of the Division of Cancer Epidemiology and Genetics, memo, Jun. 17, 1999. Subject: Evaluation Panel for the SV40 Reproducibility Study. "As you know, Dr. Howard Strickler and I have been at an impasse with a few member of the 'SV40 Working Group' on the SV40 Reproducibility Study. To improve our chances of coming to a consensus resolution of this impasse, I outline below a series of steps and would welcome your feedback." In this two-page memo, Goedert tells Fraumeni that he and Strickler will ask the FDA to convene a panel of experts to evaluate the study.

Strickler to Goedert, e-mail, Jun. 25, 1999, 1:24 P.M. Subject: SV40. Strickler attaches a draft of a letter to Bharat Jasani for Goedert to review:

> Dear Dr. Jasani, Your frustration and anger are inappropriate, as is the tone of your letter. Despite our best efforts to respond to each and every one of your comments you have issued over the past several months, you persist in undermining any possibility of amicable or constructive discussion. It is hard to imagine what you hope to gain from this. The situation is quite simple. We faithfully executed, to the letter, the protocol agreed to in writing by each and every laboratory collaborator. . . .

Later in the draft letter Strickler writes:

> "Your only intention appears to be to obstruct release of the study findings and your tone is belligerent. You have received no direct response from me regarding your previous invective because it deserved none. It was an obvious attempt to rewrite history. . . . The response from NIH was Jim Goedert's doing, because he felt your threatening tone required an official response from the Institution. Similarly your tongue-in-cheek comment that you now "extend sincere apologies" if you hurt my feelings, is simply obnoxious and pointless. Your attempts to seem intimidating are ridiculous. . . .

Goedert to Strickler, e-mail, Jun. 25, 1999, 1:46 P.M. Goedert has reviewed Strickler's draft letter to Jasani and has a one-line comment: "Howard—Don't send him anything. Jim."

Goedert to Lewis, Keith Peden, Philip Krause, all at FDA, e-mail, Jun. 25, 1999, 3:19 P.M. Subject: Definition and formulation of SV40 Reproducibility Study review panel. "Dear Andy, Keith, and Phil, As mentioned and discussed a bit on our telephone conference call this morning with Howard Strickler, I see an inevitable need to assemble an advisory panel (not really an arbitration panel) of experts to evaluate the SV40 Reproducibility Study . . ."

Strickler to Jasani, Jun. 29, 1999. Copied to all SV40 study group collaborators. Strickler has greatly edited the draft that he had shown Goedert on June 25. Letter begins: "The situation is quite simple. We faithfully executed, to the letter, the protocol agreed to in writing by each and every laboratory collaborator. . . ." Letter concludes that "efforts" by Strickler to "minimize" disputes "have apparently failed. Nevertheless, we are moving forward to try and resolve the major issues separating the study participants. There will be more on this shortly."

Strickler to all SV40 Working Group Collaborators, memo, Aug. 10, 1999. Subject: SV40 Study. "With the help of FDA we have made some progress in finding agreement among collaborators. By making reasonable revisions to the Discussion section . . . it appears it may be possible to complete a manuscript acceptable for submission to all major collaborators. . . ."

Krause (FDA) to Jasani, Butel, and Strickler, e-mail, Sep. 20, 1999. Subject: SV40 paper discussion, copied to Andrew Lewis, Keith Peden. "Here is a first draft of a discussion that we at CBER [FDA] think captures the main points of the study. . . ."

Pass to James Drake, coordinator of Rapid Access to Intervention Development (RAID) program at NCI, Jan. 27, 2000. Enclosed with Carbone/Pass 26-page RAID application entitled, "Vaccination of T-Antigen Expressing Human Mesotheliomas with a Novel Vaccinia Vector Encoding Safety Modified Simian Virus 40 T-Antigen."

Edward Sausville to Pass. Feb. 11, 2000. Sausville, associate director, Division of Cancer Treatment and Diagnosis, Developmental Therapeutics Program, NCI, acknowledges receipt of Pass's application and its conformance to the appropriate format.

Strickler to Carlo Croce, Editor in Chief, *Cancer Research*, Feb. 28, 2000. Strickler transmits the multilaboratory study manuscript for consideration.

Sausville to Pass, May 1, 2000. He notifies Pass that his application has been rejected. "Your application [for RAID program assistance], received in February 2000, has been reviewed by a panel of expert advisors to the NCI and has been assigned a priority score of 3.46. Unfortunately, this priority score does not allow funding by NCI of the initiative described in the RAID application at this time. . . ." The letter enclosed reviewers' summaries. (See text, chapter 18.)

Drake to Pass, May 24, 2000, Drake states they will establish a second review of Pass's application. "In a telephone conversation with Dr. Sausville earlier this month you voiced a concern that there was a disparity between your two RAID reviewers. As a result we are establishing a second review of your application. . . ."

Pass and Carbone to Margaret Foti, managing editor of *Cancer Research*, May 31, 2000. The letter memorializes a May 25, 2000, telephone conversation in which Foti advised them that the multilaboratory study paper was not about to be published by *Cancer Research*. "During the May 25 telephone conversation, you advised us that the paper by Strickler, et al., is not in press at this time in *Cancer Research*. Moreover, you could not even claim that it [the manuscript] is under review at this time."

Strickler to Jasani, Krause, Lewis, fax, May 31, 2000. Subject: SV40. Strickler explains that *Cancer Research* has not yet responded to manuscript submission. "We have not received correspondence from *Cancer Research*. It is not quite three months, but if we do not hear something soon I will contact them, and I will advise everyone when I have information."

Sausville to a new anonymous reviewer regarding Harvey Pass's resubmission of his application, June 20, 2000:

> I am writing you following a chat with Al Rabson. . . . Your expertise in the area of virology and potential suitability of a virus to act as a vaccination vehicle is particularly pertinent to this matter. Your position in the intramural research program likewise places you in an administratively separate sphere with respect to any immediate interest in this specific arena. . . .

This memo was copied to NCI personnel, including Deputy Director Alan Rabson. A similar memo was sent to a second, anonymous intramural reviewer with expertise in immunology.

Strickler to Violet Devairakkam, study coordinator, for circulation to all SV40 collaborators, fax, Jul. 28, 2000. Subject: SV40 manuscript. Strickler announces the rejection of the manuscript.

> Disappointingly the manuscript was refused by *Cancer Research*. . . . [M]y suggestion is that we make revisions to the manuscript . . . and submit it to another journal. I would strongly like to submit to *Cancer Epidemiology Biomarkers and Prevention*, since it is a sister journal to *Cancer Research* and would very likely give us an expedited review. . . .

Attached to Strickler's fax is the rejection letter from Margaret Foti, Jul. 14, 2000: "We regret to inform you that it is not acceptable for publication. . . ." Also attached are two letters from the journal's peer-reviewers; both criticize the data concerning the DNA extraction methodology and the contamination of the negative controls.

Jasani to Krause, Aug. 1, 2000. Copied to Butel, Lednicky, Gibbs:

> The fact that the above manuscript has been rejected is not unexpected since the flaws pointed out by the reviewers are essentially the same which Professor Janet Butel, Dr. John Lednicky, Dr. Allen Gibbs and I had repeatedly pointed out to you during the preparation of the manuscript. . . .

Pass and Carbone to members of the SV40 multilaboratory study group, Aug. 15, 2000. The letter discusses the rejection of the RAID application:

> Statements contained within the negative review clearly demonstrate an undisclosed and vehement bias against acceptance of even well established research findings regarding SV40 and human mesotheliomas. . . . Disturbingly, the negative reviewer felt quite comfortable utilizing unpublished data from a yet unpublished paper. . . . We are calling upon this individual to identify him or herself to us and the co-authors of their paper so that this matter can continue to be evaluated. . . .

(Note: Almost all participants, including Strickler, wrote back to Carbone and Pass disavowing any knowledge of the negative review.)

Lednicky to Pass and Carbone, Aug. 17, 2000. Copied to Krause, Lewis, Butel, Jasani, and Gibbs. "I do not feel the interests of Public Health and Science are served by hastily submitting the flawed manuscript. . . ." (See text, chapter 18.)

Jasani to Krause, Aug. 20, 2000. Jasani is critical of plans to resubmit manuscript without making major changes:

> I would like to emphasise [*sic*] that not only is the study flawed but it is also now obsolete. The study was conceived in 1997 in response of [*sic*] suggestions from a meeting organized by the FDA and NIH. A parallel study—actually started a few

months after ours—was conducted by the International Mesothelioma Interest Group. [Testa/Carbone study, see text, chapter 17.] That study . . . was published October 15, 1998, as the leading article in *Cancer Research*. It is ironical that two years later our own article has been rejected by the same Journal. Furthermore, rather than carefully reflecting on the flaws identified by the reviewers of *Cancer Research*, we have been urged to take the easy path of submitting the paper without any revision to a friendly journal of lesser scientific relevance. I do not think that this is the best way to serve the interest of Science and the Public. . . .

Pass and Carbone to Robert Wittes, M.D. director, Division of Cancer Treatment and Diagnosis, NCI, Sep. 11, 2000. Pass and Carbone request an investigation into the circumstances surrounding the biased negative review of Pass's RAID grant application.

Strickler to Butel, Sep. 12, 2000. Strickler disavows any connection to the negative RAID review. He also notes that there he has secured invitations from three journals ready to accept the manuscript with "expedited review."

Wittes to Pass and Carbone (individually), Oct. 2, 2000. He responds to their request for an inquiry. In his successful effort to convince Pass and Carbone not to further pursue an ethical inquiry into the identity and conduct of the negative reviewer, Wittes promises them that the individual will be banned from future RAID application reviews.

Jasani, Lednicky, and Gibbs to Krause, fax, Sep. 14, 2000. Concerning the multilaboratory study manuscript:

We are greatly concerned by the fact that you and your colleagues appear to [be] inexplicably pressing us to submit the manuscript for peer review "as it is" without any consideration for many of its existing deficiencies. . . . We do not need to remind you that once a paper is rejected in the peer review, a normal course of action would be to address the technical and other problems posed by the paper and only then consider resubmission. . . . On reflection, we are greatly unsettled by your earlier telephonic statements indicating, you were "under a lot of pressure to submit the paper." Yet at the same time, it does not seem as though you are under any pressure to correct the flaws of the paper or address the criticisms of the reviewer. Rather, it appears as though you are under continuous pressure to maintain and publish the flawed manuscript "as it is." We thus have the impression that the pressure you are feeling comes from the executive level. We are willing to explain our position to the individuals exerting this pressure upon you if you are willing to identify them to us. . . . We are greatly unsettled by all the energy being expended to obtain a favorable and expedited review of the manuscript in advance of its actually being submitted to a journal. . . .

Krause to Jasani, Lednicky, and Gibbs, e-mail, Sep. 15, 2000, 2:44 P.M. Krause responds to the September 14 fax:

FDA's sole goal has been to facilitate the publication in a peer-review journal of a manuscript that all the participants can agree upon. . . . There is and has been no intent to "pressure" anybody into doing anything. Neither I nor anyone else at FDA has stated that "we were under a lot of pressure to submit the paper." . . . To my knowledge there are no efforts to bypass the peer-review process. . . . Based on all data of which I am aware, your direct and implied accusations of ethical misconduct by . . . [Dr.] Strickler and myself are unfounded and distasteful. . . .

Lednicky to Krause, e-mail, September 19, 2000. Lednicky responds to Krause, saying that it is not his intention to accuse him, Strickler, or anyone at FDA of misconduct or lack of integrity. He notes his concern about Strickler's desire for an expedited review for the manuscript. "As we all know, there is a major difference among invited papers and a regularly submitted manuscript [in terms of the peer-review process]." Lednicky also states that many SV40 researchers feel "that there is an unfair bias against our work, fueled by hostile press-releases that unfortunately do sometimes emanate from certain people associated with the NCI" and adds that he feels that such publicity may contribute to the inability of SV40 researchers to obtain funding. He also raises the concern that the multilaboratory study will be used to further discredit SV40 research.

Krause to SV40 Working Group Collaborators, Oct. 16, 2000. Krause writes, concerning publication of the manuscript, that despite the fact that "many of us are fatigued by the protracted course of the SV40 study . . . it is important that we make the effort necessary to get the paper considered by another journal." He suggests submission to the *British Journal of Cancer.* He encloses two versions of the manuscript, one with revisions and one without, for consideration by the group.

Jasani and Gibbs to Krause, Nov. 8, 2000. Copied to other members of the SV40 working group. "We must admit that in many respects we are completely mystified by your letter dated October 16, 2000." Jasani and Gibbs note that they were not provided with the revised manuscript and that the revisions fail to address the study's flaws identified by the *Cancer Research* reviewers. ("The proposed response . . . avoids the most critical questions and glosses over the fundamental flaws in the study.") They also charge that Krause appears to have "surrendered your responsibility as impartial arbiter to Drs. Goedert and Strickler," and state that they do not agree with the "ethical underpinnings" of the "pre-arranged acceptance" of the manuscript by one of the three journals "because it will constitute a gross misrepresentation to the scientific community that this fundamentally flawed data and manuscript has been fairly peer-reviewed and all questions resolved in a scientifically and ethically appropriate manner. This is not the case." They also note that the letter reveals a "*sub rosa* process" among parties unknown to many members of the working group.

Lednicky to Krause, Nov. 6, 2000. Copied to other members of the SV40 working group. "It is presumptuous to say that the problems with the paper have all been corrected. . . ." Lednicky reiterates his detailed concerns about flaws in the DNA extraction process and other outstanding problems with the study.

Note: Shortly after this last memo, Krause resigned as arbiter for the group. Butel was given principal responsibility for redrafting the final manuscript. It was accepted and published by *Cancer Epidemiology Biomarkers and Prevention.* As noted in chapter 18 and notes to that chapter, when it was learned that Shah and Strickler had compromised the blinded nature of the positive controls, Butel, Lednicky, Gibbs, and Jasani all renounced their association with the published study.

Acknowledgments

We first began research for this book in 1995 while writing a series of articles on SV40, in particular a feature story in *The Atlantic Monthly* that appeared in February 2000. During the course of our research and writing, many persons have provided invaluable expertise and advice. We are particularly indebted to the professors and doctors with whom we spoke and spent time. Almost all of the living scientists who appear in this book agreed to be interviewed, and we are thankful to all of them for taking time from their busy schedules to talk with us. Within this group, we wish to especially thank those who graciously consented to lengthy interviews and in some cases laboratory visits, often on multiple occasions, and sometimes even when they were desperately trying to complete grant applications on deadline. In many cases, they discussed not only their own research, but also general concepts in biology, virology, epidemiology, and public health, making our task that much easier. These scientists include John Bergsagel, Janet Butel, Michele Carbone, William Egan, Susan Fisher, Adi Gazdar, Anthony Girardi, Leonard Hayflick, Maurice Hilleman, Bharat Jasani, Hilary Koprowski, John Lednicky, Arnold J. Levine, Luciano Mutti, Harvey Pass, Stanley Plotkin, Antonio Procopio, Paola Rizzo, Robert Stevenson, Ben Sweet, Joseph Testa, and Mauro Tognon. For their enormous insight into their respective fields, and particularly into the mysterious and intricate world of molecular biology, we are grateful.

We were also aided by some scientists not mentioned in the book, or mentioned only in passing. Professor Brooke Mossman, chair of the Department of Environmental Pathology at the University of Vermont (UVM), offered her unequaled expertise on the subject of the molecular pathways of asbestos carcinogenesis in mesothelioma. Professor Charles Novotny, of UVM, discussed general concepts in microbiology and laboratory technique with us and loaned us books, as did UVM's Ziqiang Yuan. The authors alone, of course, assume full responsibility for the contents of this book.

We are profoundly indebted to the individuals who provided access to archival data and information that we might not otherwise have obtained. Darrell Salk kindly granted us access to the papers of his father, Jonas Salk, which are housed in the Mandeville Special Collections Library at the University of California, San Diego. Fred Hill, the interlibrary loan officer at the Fletcher Free Library in Burlington, Vermont, was of invaluable assistance in procuring hard-to-find books and documents. Not only did he effectively turn this small public library into a world-class research institution, he graciously offered his expertise as a photographer, capturing on film historic documents and artifacts. Reference librarians at the UVM Bailey-Howe Library provided us access to newspaper and magazine archives, while those at the Federal Repository library at UVM provided us access to transcripts of congressional hearings. We also appreciate the assistance of the many reference librarians at the UVM Dana Medical Library who genially retrieved numerous hard-to-obtain scientific journals and articles of historical importance.

U.S. Senator Patrick Leahy and his able staff, led by Luke Albee, ensured that we received Freedom of Information Act documents in a timely fashion. We are particularly grateful to Senate Judiciary Committee minority counsel Beryl Howell for her help in this regard. Librarians Carmen Chand and Irma Perez at the Pan American Health Organization secured archival documents for us, as did Kelly Repas, journal manager for *Cancer Research*. Historian John Parascandola, at the National Library of Medicine, and archivist Brooke Fox, at the National Institutes of Health, graciously fulfilled numerous requests for documents and data.

CBS News National Editor Bill Felling generously allowed us to view archival tapes of William R. Murrow's news program *See It Now*. William Egan of the U.S. Food and Drug Administration assisted us in obtaining public documents from his agency. Two attorneys, Walter Kyle and Stanley Kops, who, together and separately, have spent many years litigating on behalf of individuals afflicted with vaccine-induced polio paralysis, shared with us numerous internal government and manufacturer documents concerning polio vaccine production and regulation, which they obtained during the discovery and trial process. Attorney Don MacLachlan kindly made many volumes of legal transcripts available to us; his capable staff members, Susan Fill, Gloria Bello, and Lorraine Botto made sure we received them. Chris Carucio and Theresa Hermann in the office of Michele Carbone at the Cardinal Bernadin Cancer Center were similarly helpful in providing documents. Helen Dietz and Mary Tim Baggott kindly provided us use of the archives of their father, the late Herbert Ratner, M.D.

We deeply appreciate the individuals who shared their personal histories with us. Jonathan Leopold brought alive the experience of contracting polio as a child, while his wife, Roxanne Leopold, gave an intimate account of growing up with an afflicted father, the late Roger E. Joseph. Roxanne's mother, the late Roslyn Steinfeldt, gave us an unflinching account of what it meant to live with a husband suffering from all three types of polio and permanently paralyzed from the chest down.

Four individuals who spoke to us at length about their personal histories and viewpoints deserve special mention: Barbara Loe Fisher and Kathi Williams, of the National Vaccine Information Center, and Raphaele and Michael Horwin, of San Diego, California. All four are brave parents in addition to being astute observers of public health policy; we deeply appreciate the time they spent with us. We also thank Dr. Harvey Pass and a number of his patients and their family members at the Barbara Ann Karmanos Cancer Institute in Detroit. They showed incredible grace and courage in facing their disease, and we deeply appreciate their willingness to allow us into their examining rooms at a painful time in their lives. In Italy, Professor Carmine Carbone M.D., aided by his granddaughter Martina Carbone as translator, spent hours providing us with background on the Carbone family history and the early education of Michele Carbone. We also benefited greatly from the reflections of Italietta and Giacomo Carbone, Niccolo LoConte, Carlo Parentela, Pietro Falbo, and Giorgio Valentini, and from the wisdom of Marcella Salvatori and Beatrice Brutto. And we thank Beth Chambers Carbone, a profoundly gracious and insightful individual.

William Whitworth, the longtime editor of *The Atlantic Monthly*, believed in the significance of this story when others chose to pass it by. To him we are particularly grateful. We are also indebted to the many outstanding staff members at *The Atlantic*, in particular, Managing Editor Cullen Murphy for his insightful editing of our article, Avril Cornel, for continuously smoothing the way, and Sue Parilla, whose meticulous fact-checking of the *Atlantic* article served as a valuable model for this book. David Black performed the hard work of a literary agent admirably; he is truly a rock. We are grateful to our editor at St. Martin's, Jennifer Weis, for her support. We are similarly thankful to her dedicated assistant editors, Robin Carter and Stefanie Lindskog, and to attorney Surie Rudoff for her meticulous attention to all matters legal. Finally, a special note of thanks to our copy editor, the venerable and charming Donald J. Davidson. We feel particularly lucky to have had such a talented "old school" master copyedit this text.

A number of dear friends and family members offered support and critical advice, in particular: Gina Blumenfeld, John Van Hoesen, Charles Kaiser, Steve Fishman, Karl-Ludwig Schibel, Joe Bookchin, Pat Lamson, and Michael Corkery. We deeply appreciate their help and friendship. Tom Lamson, Derrick Pitts, and Sally Pollack graciously read the book in its entirety; their criticism and insights made it much better than it otherwise would have been. Jonathan Leopold, Hamilton Davis, and Erik Esckilsen went above and beyond the call of duty, not only reading the book with a close critical eye, but offering line-by-line editing suggestions. We thank them immensely. We are also particularly indebted to John Lednicky, who gave us the benefit of his vast knowledge of virology, and Adi Gazdar, who shared with us his extraordinary expertise on matters relating to molecular research and medicine.

Two parents in one household working on the same project over a period of years presents its own special challenges. We must acknowledge the kindness of some lovely friends who happen to be the parents of our daughter's friends, and who, when every hour counted, graciously hosted far more than their fair share of play dates. We thank particularly Kara and Gus Buchanan, Guilaine Daoust and David Grossnickle, Alison and Jonathan Lampert, and Sue and Trey Anastasio.

Finally, we are especially grateful to two members of our family. Our daughter, Katya, who knows more about viruses and cancer than any nine-year-old should, was patient beyond her years. Her grandmother, Bea Bookchin, inspired us with her passion for learning, and supported us with love, nurturing, and wisdom throughout.

Index